GW00818373

the site

Daily hits on God's Word

Edited by
Craig Borlase

Hodder & Stoughton
LONDON SYDNEY AUCKLAND

The Site
Copyright © 2001 Hodder & Stoughton

Non-Bible material copyright ©2001 Craig Borlase

Holy Bible, New International Version
Copyright © 1973, 1978, 1984 by International Bible Society
First published in Great Britain 1979

The NIV may be quoted for non-commercial use in any form (written, visual, electronic or audio), up to and inclusive of five hundred (500) verses without express written permission of the publisher, providing the verses quoted do not amount to a complete book of the Bible nor do the verses quoted account for 25 per cent or more of the total text of the work in which they are quoted.

Notice of copyright must appear on the title or copyright page of the work as follows:

Scripture quotations taken from the HOLY BIBLE,
NEW INTERNATIONAL VERSION
Copyright © 1973, 1978, 1984 by International Bible Society
Used by permission of Hodder & Stoughton,
a division of Hodder Headline Ltd.
All rights reserved.
"NIV" is a registered trademark of International Bible Society.
UK trademark number 1448790

When quotations from the NIV are used in non-saleable media, such as church bulletins, orders of service, posters, transparencies, or similar media, a complete copyright notice is not required but the initials (NIV) must appear at the end of each quotation.

Any commentary or other biblical reference work produced for commercial sale that uses the New International Version must obtain written permission for use of the NIV text.

Permission requests for commercial use within the UK, EEC and EFTA countries that exceed the above guidelines must be directed to, and approved in writing by, Hodder & Stoughton, a division of Hodder Headline Ltd, 338 Euston Road, London NW1 3BH.

Permission requests for commercial use within the US and Canada that exceed the above guidelines should be directed to, and approved in writing by, Zondervan Publishing House.

Permission requests for non-commercial use which exceed the above guidelines, must be directed to and approved in writing by the International Bible society, 1820 Jet Stream Drive, Colorado Springs, CO 80921.

ISBN 0 340 75706 X

This publication is not included under licences issued by the Copyright Licensing Agency.

Typeset by Kenneth Burnley, Wirral, Cheshire. Printed in Great Britain for Hodder & Stoughton, a division of Hodder Headline Ltd, 338 Euston Road, London NW1 3BH by Clays Ltd, Bungay, Suffolk

Contents

Notes by Craig Borlase unless otherwise indicated

Introduction

Welcome to *the site*. If you're after a quick read, something that's going to have you turning the pages long into the night you're going to be disappointed. Sorry. But that's not because you've picked up a dud, for *the site* is something different. If all books are like food, then the one in your hand is that large German sausage the exchange student left under the bed last summer. You wouldn't want to scoff it all down at once, but a nibble here and a nibble there will have you hooked long before it all goes mouldy.

It all started with an idea to produce a year's worth of Bible notes, something to guide you through, day by day. But keeping up with the daily readings can be tough, and according to my *Bible In One Year* I'm still stuck somewhere around 3 February 1987. So we ditched the dates and just gave you numbers instead.

the site is designed to get your juices flowing when it comes to the Bible. Not every verse is covered, and we've skipped a few books here and there, but with each page comes a fresh insight into the most inspiring book of all time. On a couple of occasions Bible passages are covered twice. This isn't 'cos we ran out of ideas, but due to the fact that they are so important. The more you get into the Bible the more you'll discover, and hopefully this book will help you move along another step.

Here's how it works: the Bible excerpt is printed, but where the writers got carried away and just couldn't pick one small enough, the verse numbers that they want you to read are printed. You'll have to look in your own Bible for these, but they're few and far between. Most of the time you'll just be able to open up, read the scripture, read the blurb and chew over the final thought. Job done. Half of the stuff is written by a panel of organically grown, sugar-free

experts, while the other half was written by me. You'll see their names on their stuff, so if you don't like it you know who to blame.

Actually the writers have done a top job, and I'd like to thank them for all their hard word and inspirational input. Thanks are also due to all the stars at Hodder, including the one and only Mr Moloney, and especially to Jessica Dixon for having the idea in the first place and being just the creative driving force it needed.

And that's about it. Remember to have fun and watch out for low-flying truths: the Bible's full of them and they have a funny habit of coming along and changing the way we see things. Make sure you're open to as many of them as possible.

Craig Borlase
July 2000

Myth, magic or plain and simple truth? The creation story has the power to get people hot under the collar whatever the weather. So just what is it all about?

As far as punchy beginnings go this one has to be the best. There's no waffle, no meandering, no lengthy introduction explaining some tedious detail that no one bothers about. Instead it's in there right away. And with what? 'In the beginning God . . .' Nice one. Before it all kicked off God was already there. Before the story started he was part of the plot. Before the writer sat down at Genesis 1, God had already done the whole chapter. These first amazing words introduce us to a God that stretches way beyond our concept of time and space. Yet this massive God, this God that is so much more than we could ever comprehend, chose to create 'the heavens and the earth'. There's no arm twisting, no boredom, no 'wouldn't it be funny if I created a world' thoughts while waiting for the post to arrive. All we are told for now, all we need to know is this: God is bigger than the whole of creation put together, yet he chose to create the world himself.

No messing

genesis 1:1

1In the beginning God created the heavens and the earth.

chew it over

This is the first miracle: that God should choose us.

Human behaviour

genesis 1:26–8

[26]Then God said, "Let us make man in our image, in our likeness, and let them rule over the fish of the sea and the birds of the air, over the livestock, over all the earth, and over all the creatures that move along the ground."

[27]So God created man
in his own image,
in the image of God
he created him;
male and female
he created them.

[28]God blessed them and said to them, "Be fruitful and increase in number; fill the earth and subdue it. Rule over the fish of the sea and the birds of the air and over every living creature that moves on the ground."

chew it over

We may feel like we don't have much in the way of purpose in our lives, but Genesis 1 tells us a different story. We all have a purpose, we all have a job, we all have a Maker.

Making humankind in his own image means that Genesis has a strong message for us about how God views humanity. We all carry part of his genetic code, we all carry traces of his blueprint, and this is a good foundation for our view of others. As the Bible unfolds we find out about how God chooses the Israelites to act as a shining light for the rest of the world, demonstrating a true relationship with him and being a channel through which he can work. But it's not only through them that God works. The truth still stands today; humankind may have become dirtied, broken, lost and confused, but the Maker's fingerprints can still be seen. Every human is worthy of honour and respect.

That's not all though. There's sex and gardening. After all, that seems to sum up the first job description, as humankind are sent out to populate the earth and take charge of the land. This gives us a glimpse into the nature of the way things should be between us and God: to carry out the work set out for us and to enjoy his blessing.

Principles

genesis 1:31–2:3

31God saw all that he had made, and it was very good. And there was evening, and there was morning—the sixth day.

1Thus the heavens and the earth were completed in all their vast array.

2By the seventh day God had finished the work he had been doing; so on the seventh day he rested from all his work.
3And God blessed the seventh day and made it holy, because on it he rested from all the work of creating that he had done.

So what, God made the earth in seven days flat? Or does it just represent seven chunks of time? Perhaps you go for the line that the fact that the number seven (a number often used to indicate godly perfection) simply reinforces the idea that it was God who was the ultimate force behind creation. Whatever. Getting hung up on details can only serve to take us away from the truth: that God holds the ultimate power that pulled things together.

But why did he rest? Was he tired, a bit knackered and in need of some time out? Had he perhaps been pushing himself a little too hard to get it done on time? The real reason behind God's rest comes in verse 31, where he kicks back and gives it the old holy thumbs up. He reckoned that 'it was good', that what he had created was complete. There was no tweaking to be done, no more final adjustments to make things even better. The result of God's shaping of the world was that he was entirely happy with it.

Many of us get tempted to believe that God is a bit squeamish when it comes to the world, as if we have to protect him from it, what with this and that he only likes to hang out in church these days. Rubbish. God rested to celebrate what he had done: the trees, animals, sea, air, land, humans, he was happy with them all.

chew it over

Later the story shows how sin crept in, but we'd do well to remember that God's stamp of approval and ownership is all over the world. And he was here first.

NOAH

Real event or engaging story? Historical fact or mere Sunday School material? The story of Noah has been a hot potato for years, but in sticking to the edges with our discussions we miss some vital facts and inspiring lessons.

Timeline

Genesis 5:1–5

1This is the written
account of Adam's line.

When God created
man, he made him in
the likeness of God. 2He
created them male and
female and blessed them.
And when they were cre-
ated, he called them
"man".
3When Adam had
lived 130 years, he had a
son in his own likeness,
in his own image; and
he named him Seth.
4After Seth was born,
Adam lived 800 years
and had other sons and
daughters. 5Altogether,
Adam lived 930 years,
and then he died.

We all have a choice when it comes to God: to turn towards him or to turn away.

SEARCH

A 150-year-old bloke becomes a dad and then lives a further 800 years? His son tops 912 years and his grandson is pushing 906 by the time he snuffs it? You've got to be joking. I mean, just think of how rough they must have looked – after all, there's only so much that anti-ageing cream can help you with.

The point? Some people like to take the numbers at face value, but the passage loses none of its power if we don't. How come? Because it's not so much about *who* came next as it is about *how*. Let me explain: God made Adam in his own image, right? (Go back to 1:26 for proof if you need it.) This passage tells us that Adam also made a son in his own image. But, let's not forget that by this time Adam's image was not exactly up there with God's. The imperfections had crept in and humankind's direction was well and truly confirmed. Later the same chapter mentions Enoch, singling him out as one that 'walked with God'. Where he pursued a relationship with his Maker, the writer leaves us to assume that the others mentioned in the family tree did not.

So that's it, you say. Might as well pack up and go home now, huh? If we're doomed from the start why bother trying at all? You wouldn't be the first to struggle with this, but it's vital that we keep this introduction in mind when we read Noah's story. In fact the writer doesn't bang on about exactly what it was that the descendants did wrong, but it shows the drift of the tide away from an active relationship with God.

A desperate picture

Genesis 6:1–8

1When men began to increase
in number on the earth and
daughters were born to them,
2the sons of God saw that the
daughters of men were beautiful, and they married any of
them they chose. 3Then the
Lord said, "My Spirit will not
contend with man for ever, for
he is mortal; his days will be a
hundred and twenty years."
4The Nephilim were on the
earth in those days—and also
afterwards—when the sons of
God went to the daughters of
men and had children by
them. They were the heroes of
old, men of renown.
5The Lord saw how great
man's wickedness on the earth
had become, and that every
inclination of the thoughts of
his heart was only evil all the
time. 6The Lord was grieved
that he had made man on the
earth, and his heart was filled
with pain. 7So the Lord said, "I
will wipe mankind, whom I
have created, from the face of
the earth—men and animals,
and creatures that move along
the ground, and birds of the
air—for I am grieved that I
have made them." 8But Noah
found favour in the eyes of
the Lord.

SEARCH

The sons of God marrying daughters of men? What's this all about – angels marrying ladies? Nope. It's far more likely that the writer is talking about marriage between two groups: either the descendants of Cain and Seth, or the kings of neighbouring lands. But what's the point? God's people are moving away, they are diluting, losing their identity and becoming weak. There's political corruption (4) and the relationship with their Maker has all but vanished, hidden beneath a mound of evil deeds and thoughts. How far away is this picture from the face-to-face harmony of Adam, Eve and God in the Garden of Eden?

As if anyone was unsure that this was not the way things were meant to be, we're hit square in the face by God's reaction to the scene of total depravity: he grieves. Surely there's something wrong here if it's humankind that does the sinning and God that does the repenting? A change is needed, boundaries need to be set. The laws of freedom that characterised Eden no longer seem to work. No wonder God wants to start again.

GO

We cannot escape the consequences of our actions, but as we see next, God's desire to be in relationship with his people is a mighty force.

An unlikely hero – Part 1

Genesis 6:9–15

9 This is the account of
Noah.

Noah was a righteous
man, blameless among
the people of his time,
and he walked with God.
10 Noah had three sons:
Shem, Ham and Japheth.
11 Now the earth was
corrupt in God's sight
and was full of violence.
12 God saw how corrupt
the earth had become,
for all the people on
earth had corrupted their
ways. 13 So God said to
Noah, "I am going to
put an end to all people,
for the earth is filled with
violence because of
them. I am surely going
to destroy both them and
the earth. 14 So make
yourself an ark of cypress
wood; make rooms in it
and coat it with pitch
inside and out. 15 This is
how you are to build it:
The ark is to be 450 feet
long, 75 feet wide and 45
feet high."

SEARCH

And here he comes, Mr Noah. His family line made plenty of mistakes, and he's surrounded
by corruption and evil, but the man is still going strong with the Lord. Throughout the story he always seems like a bit of a loner – there's no account of him trying to sneak on board a few of his mates inside an early pantomime horse – but it's his integrity that marks him out. Time and time again the Bible shows us examples of God using 'ordinary' people, the kind about whom their neighbours would probably shake their heads in disbelief when they heard the story.

But Noah's neighbours never got to hear the full story, as he and his family were the last ones standing.

And this is where we come across a few problems. How did one man manage to build a boat half the length of the *QEII* without a shipyard? How did one man manage to attract pairs (not herds, groups, flocks or packs) of every living creature under the sun? *And he was 600 years old!*

Why did God choose Noah? He was righteous, living a life that pleased God.

GO

There was something else about Noah too: he was responsible, rational, creative, logical. He was a distant son of Adam and he still bore the marks of the true original.

An unlikely hero – Part 2

Genesis 7:17–23

17 For forty days the flood
kept coming on the
earth, and as the waters
increased they lifted the
ark high above the
earth. 18 The waters rose
and increased greatly on
the earth, and the ark
floated on the surface of
the water. 19 They rose
greatly on the earth, and
all the high mountains
under the entire heavens
were covered. 20 The
waters rose and covered
the mountains to a
depth of more than
twenty feet. 21 Every living thing that moved on
the earth perished—
birds, livestock, wild animals, all the creatures
that swarm over the
earth, and all mankind.
22 Everything on dry land
that had the breath of
life in its nostrils died.
23 Every living thing on
the face of the earth was
wiped out; men and ani-
mals and the creatures
that move along the
ground and the birds of
the air were wiped from
the earth. Only Noah
was left, and those with
him in the ark.

SEARCH

Where were we? Oh yes . . . *And he was 600 years old!* And then there's the flood. People have worked long and hard on explanations – tectonic faults, geological weirdness and meteors have all got the blame – but in focusing our attention so narrowly we miss the point. Yeah, God has the power to wipe out all life except that which he chooses to save. Big deal. He is God, after all. Isn't that the sort of thing he should be able to do? What is far more exciting is the message that the writer is trying to get us to see. As with Adam and Eve we learn that life can be fun, but that there are responsibilities that go with it. Adam and Eve had to obey God's commands and Noah's contemporaries refused. The picture emerges: living away from God has consequences. But there's something else in there too, a characteristic of God that we see more and more of throughout history. It's called 'salvation', and it goes alongside his judgment.

GO

Noah was a man of faith. That faith in God saved him.

It all becomes clear

Genesis 9:1–7

[1]Then God blessed Noah
and his sons, saying to
them, "Be fruitful and
increase in number and
fill the earth. [2]The fear
and dread of you will fall
upon all the beasts of the
earth and all the birds of
the air, upon every crea-
ture that moves along the
ground, and upon all the
fish of the sea; they are
given into your hands.
[3]Everything that lives and
moves will be food for
you. Just as I gave you the
green plants, I now give
you everything.
[4]"But you must not eat
meat that has its lifeblood
still in it. [5]And for your
lifeblood I will surely
demand an accounting. I
will demand an account-
ing from every animal.
And from each man, too, I
will demand an account-
ing for the life of his fellow man.

[6]"Whoever sheds the
blood of man,
by man shall his blood
be shed;
for in the image of God
has God made man.

[7]As for you, be fruitful and
increase in number; multi-
ply on the earth and
increase upon it."

SEARCH

Tension builds up, an argument follows and then it's time to make up. But if we're smart we won't leave it there, allowing the things that caused the tension in the first place to be swept under the carpet. We'll address them head on and work out how things should be in the future. And this is where we're at: the story has shown the deterioration of society, followed by the inevitable godly judgment. He has saved Noah, his family and the animals, but now it's time to put a few new things in place. It's a new beginning and it's time to do things a little differently.

Meat is now on the menu, but there are rules that go alongside. No eating of meat that has not been drained of blood, no murder. As we see later, blood is symbolic – we know from our biology lessons that it carries that all-important oxygen around our bodies – it gives life and was a vital part of sacrifices that had to be made to God. And why should God be anti-murder? Because men and women are still in his image, and the killing of a human not only shows contempt for God's creation but for God himself.

But yet again we're missing the point if we focus too narrowly. The writer makes sure we catch his drift when he repeats the blessing that God gave to Adam and Eve – he tells Noah to be fruitful and increase in number, just as he did back in 1:28, and he reminds him that he has provided the food he needs just as he did in 1:29–30.

GO

It's a fresh start for God's creation, but this is no case of sloppy seconds. God's blessing is just as good, his provision just as mighty.

A promise

Genesis 9:8–16

8Then God said to Noah and to
his sons with him: 9"I now
establish my covenant with
you and with your descendants
after you 10and with every living creature that was with
you—the birds, the livestock
and all the wild animals, all
those that came out of the ark
with you—every living creature
on earth. 11I establish my
covenant with you: Never
again will all life be cut off by
the waters of a flood; never
again will there be a flood to
destroy the earth."
12God said, "This is the sign
of the covenant I am making
between me and you and every
living creature with you, a
covenant for all generations to
come: 13I have set my rainbow
in the clouds, and it will be the
sign of the covenant between
me and the earth. 14Whenever
I bring clouds over the earth
and the rainbow appears in the
clouds, 15I will remember my
covenant between me and you
and all living creatures of every
kind. Never again will the
waters become a flood to
destroy all life. 16Whenever the
rainbow appears in the clouds,
I will see it and remember the
everlasting covenant between
God and all living creatures of
every kind on the earth."

SEARCH

What follows is another biblical first. There are more to come, but this is the first covenant – contract, if you like – that God makes with his people through one of their own. It's a deal that still stands today: God promises never to wipe out all of human life again with a natural disaster. It does not revolve around a personal relationship, but instead is 'between me and the earth'. God's fresh start, his ultimate New Deal, offers us security and the promise of something special: God's presence.

Pretty mind-blowing stuff, huh? I mean, if you'd just been through what Noah had been through, the chances are you'd be walking around in a daze. Funnily enough, Noah was, but it wasn't a blissed-out spirit trip that he was on. As soon as his grapes were ready he went out and got well and truly wasted on home brew, stripped off his clothes and passed out in his tent.

But what did God think? Had he picked a dud? Did he wish for a time machine so that he could go back and start all over, this time without boozy Noah? That's not the point. You see, there's only ever been one person without sin. Through the Old Testament we read story after story of God using people *despite* their weaknesses. Good job too, otherwise we'd be in a right old state.

God's promise marked a new beginning for humankind. Noah's party gave a few hints about human nature.

Our lives can be a strange mix: touched by God one minute and overcome by our own desires the next.

Luke Pt. I

Mission impossible

Hold tight as we take a rollercoaster ride through the life and times of the most important man in the history of life itself.

Matt Bird

Luke 1:26–7, 30–2, 34–5, 37–8

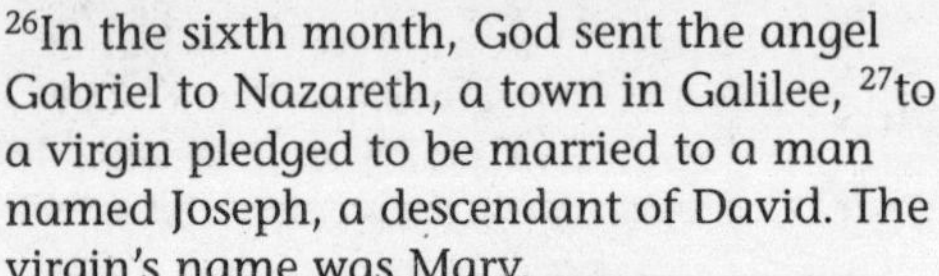

[26]In the sixth month, God sent the angel
Gabriel to Nazareth, a town in Galilee, [27]to
a virgin pledged to be married to a man
named Joseph, a descendant of David. The
virgin's name was Mary.
[30]But the angel said to her, "Do not be
afraid, Mary, you have found favour with
God. [31]You will be with child and give birth
to a son, and you are to give him the name
Jesus. [32]He will be great and will be called
the Son of the Most High. The Lord God will
give him the throne of his father David,"
[34]"How will this be," Mary asked the
angel, "since I am a virgin?"
[35]The angel answered, "The Holy Spirit
will come upon you, and the power of the
Most High will overshadow you. So the holy
one to be born will be called the Son of God.
[37]For nothing is impossible with God."
[38]"I am the Lord's servant," Mary
answered. "May it be to me as you have
said." Then the angel left her.

What are the impossibilities that we see in God's world? How can we allow God to do the impossible in our lives?

What a shocker! Talk about 'Mission Impossible': God chose to conceive a child in the womb of a teenager who was a virgin. God works in the natural processes of the conception of a new life, and in the supernatural of conception without human contribution. We had better believe it. God has, and always will, do the impossible; he can do no other because he is a God of the impossible.

Revival generation

Luke 1:46–53

46And Mary said:

"My soul glorifies the Lord
47 and my spirit rejoices in God my Saviour,
48for he has been mindful
of the humble state of his servant.
From now on all generations will call me blessed,
49 for the Mighty One has done great things for me—
holy is his name.
50His mercy extends to those who fear him,
from generation to generation.
51He has performed mighty deeds with his arm;
he has scattered those who are proud in their inmost thoughts.
52He has brought down rulers from their thrones
but has lifted up the humble.
53He has filled the hungry with good things
but has sent the rich away empty.

Where can you see God at work today? How close are you to being a part of what God is doing? What changes do you need to make in your life to be a part of this revival generation?

Well, here is the first worship song that Jesus ever inspired, and it is still sung and prayed in some churches today. From the womb he stirred his mum's heart to sing. The song celebrated that God works from generation to generation, not from second-hand faith but first-hand experience of who he was. His plan was one of mercy and restoration of a world living as he always intended them to live . . . revival.

In many ways Mary was singing of a revival generation. Our God is one who is alive and kicking, he cannot not be involved in each generation. It is impossible for God not to be active. In this generation God is looking for people who will bring about revival and a restoration of how he wants things done in his world.

History maker

Luke 2:1–7

1 In those days Caesar Augustus issued a
decree that a census should be taken of the
entire Roman world. 2 (This was the first census that took place while Quirinius was governor of Syria.) 3 And everyone went to his
own town to register.
4 So Joseph also went up from the town of
Nazareth in Galilee to Judea, to Bethlehem
the town of David, because he belonged to
the house and line of David. 5 He went there
to register with Mary, who was pledged to
be married to him and was expecting a
child. 6 While they were there, the time came
for the baby to be born, 7 and she gave birth
to her firstborn, a son. She wrapped him in
cloths and placed him in a manger, because
there was no room for them in the inn.

In what ways can you see God making history in the world through his people today? How can you begin to co-operate with Jesus in making history today?

The Christian God is not distant or far off from the realities of the world. At a specific point in history when 'Caesar Augustus issued a decree . . . while Quirinius was governor of Syria', God stepped into history. As *The Message* version of the Bible puts it, 'The word became flesh and blood, and moved into the neighborhood' (John 1:14) in the person of Jesus.

For millennia God has been understood as being completely otherworldly and existing in eternity. Around 3 BC God became worldly, human and a history maker in the life of his Son . . . Jesus. Since that time his story has become history. Christianity is not based upon a book, tradition, academia or authority, but revealed in a person. Jesus was a history maker and continues to make history people who follow him with their lives.

God on the margins

Luke 2:8–16

8 And there were shepherds living out in the
fields near by, keeping watch over their flocks at
night. 9 An angel of the Lord appeared to them,
and the glory of the Lord shone around them,
and they were terrified. 10 But the angel said to
them, "Do not be afraid. I bring you good news
of great joy that will be for all the people.
11 Today in the town of David a Saviour has
been born to you; he is Christ the Lord. 12 This
will be a sign to you: You will find a baby
wrapped in cloths and lying in a manger."
13 Suddenly a great company of the heavenly
host appeared with the angel, praising God and
saying,

14 "Glory to God in the highest,
and on earth peace to men on whom
his favour rests."

15 When the angels had left them and gone
into heaven, the shepherds said to one another,
"Let's go to Bethlehem and see this thing that
has happened, which the Lord has told us
about."
16 So they hurried off and found Mary and
Joseph, and the baby, who was lying in the
manger.

What sort of people do you think find themselves on the margins of your church? How can you and your church be like Jesus and help them know they are loved and included?

In the biography of Jesus' life written by Matthew the wise men who visited Jesus as a newborn baby represented those of privileged birth, education, wealth and position (Matthew 2:1–12). In Luke's edition, he records the birth being recognised by the shepherds – people who represented the poor, the lowly and those on the edges of society.

As we read through the Gospel of Luke we will see his emphasis to show Jesus' concern for those on the margins of society. We will see a Jesus who has a special interest and love for the poor, women, lepers, tax collectors, prostitutes, drunks and the outcasts of society. Today Jesus would be hanging out with people with HIV/AIDS, child molesters, terrorists, rapists, homosexuals and others who the religious find it easy to exclude. This is the miracle of inclusion.

He is the one

Luke 2:21, 25–6, 28–30, 36–8

21On the eighth day, when it was time to cir-
cumcise him, he was named Jesus, the name
the angel had given him before he had been
conceived.
25Now there was a man in Jerusalem called
Simeon, who was righteous and devout. He
was waiting for the consolation of Israel, and
the Holy Spirit was upon him. 26It had been
revealed to him by the Holy Spirit that he
would not die before he had seen the Lord's
Christ.
28Simeon took him in his arms and praised
God, saying:

29"Sovereign Lord, as you have promised,
you now dismiss your servant in peace.
30For my eyes have seen your salvation,"

What are you expecting Jesus to do in his world? How can you help others see 'He is the One'? Pray and ask that all people might see Jesus is the one they have been searching for.

36There was also a prophetess, Anna, the daughter of Phanuel,
of the tribe of Asher. She was very old; she had lived with her
husband seven years after her marriage, 37and then was a widow
until she was eighty-four. She never left the temple but worshipped night and day, fasting and praying. 38Coming up to
them at that very moment, she gave thanks to God and spoke
about the child to all who were looking forward to the redemption of Jerusalem.

The snip/circumcision was the Israelite practice of adjusting the manhood of their boys at eight days old in the temple. When Joseph and Mary took Jesus to the temple a righteous and devout man (Simeon) and a prophetess (Anna) recognised Jesus as the 'Christ'. In our Bibles at the bottom of the page is a footnote which explains that 'Christ' in Greek or 'Messiah' in Hebrew meant 'anointed one'. Jesus became known as Jesus Christ, the one sent by God.

The famous words of the mother of all futurist movies, *The Matrix*, sum it up: 'He is the one!' Jesus was 'the one' the Jewish people had been hoping would rescue them from the oppression of the Romans. It was prophesied that God's people would know the renewing of their hearts (Jeremiah 31:33–4, Ezekiel 11:19–20) and the pouring out of the Spirit on all people (Joel 2:28f).

Baptism

Luke 3:3–4, 7–9, 15–16, 21–2

If you haven't been baptised in water why not go for it? Whether you have been baptised or not, are there things about your life you would rather put behind you? Pray and ask God to fill you with his Holy Spirit today.

3He went into all the country around the Jordan,
preaching a baptism of repentance for the forgiveness of sins. 4As is written in the book of the
words of Isaiah the prophet:

"A voice of one calling in the desert,
'Prepare the way for the Lord,
make straight paths for him.'"

7John said to the crowds coming out to be baptised by him, "You brood of vipers! Who warned
you to flee from the coming wrath? 8Produce
fruit in keeping with repentance. And do not
begin to say to yourselves, 'We have Abraham
as our father.' For I tell you that out of these stones God can raise up
children for Abraham. 9The axe is already at the root of the trees,
and every tree that does not produce good fruit will be cut down and
thrown into the fire."

15The people were waiting expectantly and were all wondering in
their hearts if John might possibly be the Christ. 16John answered
them all, "I baptise you with water. But one more powerful than I
will come, the thongs of whose sandals I am not worthy to untie. He
will baptise you with the Holy Spirit and with fire."

21When all the people were being baptised, Jesus was baptised too.
And as he was praying, heaven was opened 22and the Holy Spirit
descended on him in bodily form like a dove. And a voice came from
heaven: "You are my Son, whom I love; with you I am well pleased."

John was known as the Baptist because he had a reputation for dunking and submerging people in water. He was the one Isaiah prophesied about (Isaiah 40:3–5) and he preached a message of the need to 'produce fruit in keeping with repentance'. Water baptism is a sign of repentance, of turning around from one way of living to another. This is a preparation for what God wants to do in a person's life. Spirit baptism is about the dynamic presence of God entering someone's life. For Jesus, water and Spirit baptism were experienced together (21–2). This was a turning point, an empowering marker in his life that showed him move from working as a carpenter to public preacher, carer and miracle worker.

You know you want to

Luke 4:1–5, 7–9, 12

[1]Jesus, full of the Holy Spirit, returned from
the Jordan and was led by the Spirit in the
desert, [2]where for forty days he was tempted
by the devil. He ate nothing during those
days, and at the end of them he was hungry.
[3]The devil said to him, "If you are the Son
of God, tell this stone to become bread."
[4]Jesus answered, "It is written: 'Man does
not live on bread alone.'"
[5]The devil led him up to a high place and
showed him in an instant all the kingdoms of
the world. "[7]So if you worship me, it will all
be yours."
[8]Jesus answered, "It is written: 'Worship the
Lord your God and serve him only.'"
[9]The devil led him to Jerusalem and had
him stand on the highest point of the temple.
"If you are the Son of God," he said, "throw
yourself down from here."
[12]Jesus answered, "It says: 'Do not put the
Lord your God to the test.'"

What are the temptations that you are most vulnerable to? What promises of God can you rely on when you are tempted in those ways? Pray and ask God to strengthen you to stand strong in him in times of temptation.

Straight after Jesus' intimate affirmation from the Father and his dynamic infilling with the Holy Spirit at his baptism, he was led by the same Spirit into a place of temptation. Jesus went through forty days of being tempted by the devil, and to assert his self-control he ate no food throughout.

We all know that little voice that says 'go on, you know you want to': whether it's buying something we can't afford, taking a lustful look or giving some verbal abuse. It is very often after we have had an intimate time with God that he leads us to a place where he can find out if we have really allowed him to make a difference in our lives.

A skyscraper built without steel girders, cranes or scaffolding? You've got to be joking. But the story of the Tower of Babel is less about bricks and mortar than it is about the basics of human nature. Stick around and you might just recognise a few.

The build up

genesis 10:1–5, 32

1This is the account of Shem, Ham and Japheth, Noah's sons, who themselves had sons after the flood.

2The sons of Japheth:
Gomer, Magog, Madai, Javan, Tubal, Meshech and Tiras.
3The sons of Gomer: Ashkenaz, Riphath and Togarmah.
4The sons of Javan: Elishah, Tarshish, the
Kittim and the Rodanim. 5(From these the
maritime peoples spread out into their territories by their clans within their nations, each with its own language.)

32These are the clans of Noah's sons, according to their lines of descent, within their nations. From these the nations spread out over the earth after the flood.

It's cruel using this section as a reading – it's not exactly Harry Potter, is it? But if you'll forgive this choice of slightly stodgy text, you'll see there's a point to it. Remember how God told Adam and Eve to 'be fruitful and increase in number' (1:28)? And remember how the same was repeated to Noah (9:7)? Well, chapter 10 shows that God's blessing was a good one. They certainly did increase in number, so that's all lovely.

But if we're not mistaken there was another thing that God mentioned to Adam and Eve. Remember that bit about them being banished from the garden (3:23) and how Cain went away, leaving behind God's presence (4:16)? Wasn't exactly a blessing, was it?

And so the story confronts us with two conflicting truths: God blessed them with multiplication, but their increase meant that they needed to move to find resources, following the lines of the punishment handed out long ago.

chew it over

We can love God and be loved by him, experiencing his blessing and fullness of life, yet we still have to live with the consequences of humankind's sinful behaviour.

No Fools

genesis 11:1–4

1 Now the whole world had one language
and a common speech. 2 As men moved
eastward, they found a plain in Shinar and
settled there.

3 They said to each other, "Come, let's
make bricks and bake them thoroughly."
They used brick instead of stone, and bitu-
men for mortar. 4 Then they said, "Come, let
us build ourselves a city, with a tower that
reaches to the heavens, so that we may
make a name for ourselves and not be scattered over the face of the whole earth."

Let's get it cleared up straight away, shall we? The writer here suggests that everyone chatted the same language, but it was only a handful of verses ago that he was banging on about Javan's descendants speaking their own unique languages. Other commentators go further to point out that instead of referring to all nations and tribes, this story refers to one particular group who settled on the plain in Shinar.

If we're suggesting that the issue of the people shouldn't be taken literally, then the same must be said for the building itself. As we mentioned in the introduction the idea of actually making a skyscraper with the available tools and materials does stretch the imagination, and yet again we find ourselves off the beaten track. The writer is keen to capture our imagination, to draw us in and make us think. In our dumbed-down minds we can often be in danger of missing the point, so it's good to take a step back and allow the drama of the story wash over you.

So what have we got? A bunch of people wanting to make a name for themselves, to do something impressive, to get a little WOW! into their lives. Take a closer look and it's clear that this is more than misguided energy, it's based on real arrogance, as their language explains: 'us . . . ourselves . . . we . . . ourselves . . .' Everything, it would seem, is related back to themselves. It's as if their only method of checking their self-worth and security is with the approval of others.

chew it over

Don't we all want to make a name for ourselves? Don't we all want to be liked? How much time do we spend building our own monuments and ignoring God?

The order of things

genesis 11:5–9

5But the Lord came down to see the city
and the tower that the men were building.
6The Lord said, "If as one people speaking
the same language they have begun to do
this, then nothing they plan to do will be
impossible for them. 7Come, let us go down
and confuse their language so they will not
understand each other."
8So the Lord scattered them from there
over all the earth, and they stopped building the city. 9That is why it was called
Babel—because there the Lord confused the
language of the whole world. From there
the Lord scattered them over the face of the
whole earth.

'But the Lord came down'. Do you get that? He came *down* – he had to stoop, to lower himself from greatness in order to get a glimpse of this group's pathetic monument to itself. This Tower of Babel was supposed to be something special, but in reality it was little to write home about.

But what of this chat from God? Doesn't he come off all paranoid, like the spoilt little rich kid who's worried that his friends will leave him as soon as they suss out just what he really is like? Well, not quite. God does have a point: if people did keep going together like this, convincing themselves that they had no need for God at all, then who knows where it might have all ended up? God was merely reinforcing the order of things, putting us back in our rightful place. Remember what the writer said at the beginning of the book? How humankind was created to partner God in the garden? The Tower of Babel was a long way off the mark.

Language changes naturally. As people move and cultures evolve, so too does their means of communication. There's nothing to suggest that the writer's putting this forward as the very first time that language evolved, but everything to suggest that what we're looking at is basic human nature: the desire to reach the glories for ourselves.

chew it over

Where are you at with God? Struggling to get by on your own or following his lead and living life for him?

EARTH MOTHER

Here we go with five mental chewings-over of the woman we call Mary. Remember her? She was Jesus' mother, the one whom God allowed to care for his son in his most stained and stinky state. She must have been something special . . .

Come on down

Luke 1:46–9

46 And Mary said:

"My soul glorifies the
Lord
47 and my spirit rejoices
in God my Saviour,
48 for he has been
mindful
of the humble state of
his servant.
From now on all
generations will call
me blessed,
49 for the Mighty One
has done great
things for me—
holy is his name."

SEARCH

You might be wondering what made Mary so special that she was given this 'unusual' task. It certainly wasn't to do with her bank balance, but what this passage shows is that while she might have been poor, Mary wasn't stupid. Check out her words above: she's one radical honey. Thirty years later Jesus would push out a similar message, turning society on its head as he challenged ungodly power structures. Mary's words here offer a powerful statement of God's love of the destruction of evil. Read through it carefully . . . it's pure dynamite.

We don't know much about Mary before all of this, and we can only wonder if this radical heart had been clearly beating for years or whether meeting the angel Gabriel was the spark to her flame? What we do know is that she had been making good plans with Joseph and that she was trying to be obedient to God. Those plans might have been decent, but God's were bigger and better: because she trusted him completely she got to be right at the heart of the action.

GO

Remember this: God is a God of transformation.

Does God prefer poultry?

Luke 2:22–4

[22]When the time of their
purification according to
the Law of Moses had
been completed, Joseph
and Mary took him to
Jerusalem to present him
to the Lord [23](as it is written in the Law of the
Lord, "Every firstborn
male is to be consecrated
to the Lord"), [24]and to
offer a sacrifice in keeping with what is said in
the Law of the Lord: "a
pair of doves or two
young pigeons".

SEARCH

OK, so we know Mary was young, poor and female, and that would have placed her distinctly in the 'Cannot Be Used By God' pile, according to the culture of the time. There's a clear picture of just how poor she and Joseph were here. Instead of sacrificing a lamb as part of the ritual purification process for their child, Mary and Joseph were forced to go for the bargain bins and offer instead a pair of pigeons. Leviticus 12:8 points out that this is an option for the poor.

So what do we learn from this? Does God prefer poultry? That's not the point; you see, no one is excluded from being part of God's plan. Different things can make us feel as if we are 'unusable' – our past, our failures, our doubts and fears, our age, wage, insecurities or pains – but God has a different measure by which he judges our suitability. As he reminded Samuel when he went to anoint the bloke who was to be King of Israel, 'The Lord does not look at the things man looks at. Man looks at the outward appearance, but the Lord looks at the heart' (1 Samuel 16:7).

Try this on for size: before anything else, God looks for a changed heart.

A good heart . . .

Luke 1: 49–55

49 for the Mighty One
has done great
things for me—
holy is his name.
50 His mercy extends to
those who fear him,
from generation to
generation.
51 He has performed
mighty deeds with
his arm;
he has scattered those
who are proud in
their inmost
thoughts.
52 He has brought down
rulers from their
thrones
but has lifted up the
humble.
53 He has filled the
hungry with good
things
but has sent the rich
away empty.
54 He has helped his
servant Israel,
remembering to be
merciful
55 to Abraham and his
descendants for
ever,
even as he said to our
fathers."

SEARCH

As if we weren't already sure of the fact that God had chosen well in Mary, here are a few extra reminders. As she gets the news from her celestial gynaecologist, her first thought is for Elizabeth and she hurries to meet her. When Elizabeth greets and praises her, Mary praises God. She also manages to find the balance between acknowledging what God has done for her and letting pride get in the way. As a true good friend, she stays with Elizabeth for three months and surely she would have been a great help to the elderly Elizabeth going through her first pregnancy.

How many times have we heard the 'God Can Use You' sermon? How many times have we concluded that God might use us in something **big**? We may have bought into a Size Matters view of God's gifts, but thankfully Mary was a little wiser. She knew that things were part of God's plan, despite the fact that what little social standing she had was headed for the sewers of social shame: not only was she appearing to be 'immoral', but she very nearly lost her fiancé, who planned on ditching her quietly as soon as he could (Matthew 1:18–24). For Mary, signing up for the greatest act of God in the history of time itself meant allowing God's agenda to pull rank over her own.

GO

When it comes to God's plans, they're best served solo.

The pain of God's calling

Luke 2:29–35

29"Sovereign Lord, as you
have promised,
you now dismiss your
servant in peace.
30For my eyes have seen
your salvation,
31 which you have
prepared in the
sight of all people,
32a light for revelation to
the Gentiles
and for glory to your
people Israel."

33The child's father and
mother marvelled at
what was said about
him. 34Then Simeon
blessed them and said to
Mary, his mother: "This
child is destined to cause
the falling and rising of
many in Israel, and to be
a sign that will be spo-
ken against, 35so that the
thoughts of many hearts
will be revealed. And a
sword will pierce your
own soul too."

SEARCH

Unmarried and pregnant, Mary realises that her public image could do with a little bit of touching up. So she does the decent thing: nothing. She carries on trusting in God. Having lost what social currency she may have had I wonder whether she ever wondered whether she might have to sacrifice her relationship with Joseph as well. However keen she was to do what God wanted, it must have been painful to break the news of her pregnancy to Joseph, watching him deal with all that disappointment and regret. But God dealt with that by speaking to Joseph direct. Later God also confirmed the promises he had given Mary about Jesus through the shepherds (considered by polite society to be thieves) and the wise men (even worse, they were *foreigners*).

But God's encouragements to the couple were hardly brimming with good news – check out what happened when they bumped into Simeon and Anna at the temple in the passage above. Although it must have been wonderful to hear God's words confirmed again, all that stuff about the sword that would pierce her heart must have stuck with Mary throughout her life as Jesus grew up and began his ministry. Not an easy thing to live with.

The pain of God's calling carried on: they were forced to live as a refugees (Matthew 2:13–23), only to return to realise how many friends and relatives had lost their baby boys during Herod's slaughter, all because of their son.

GO

Being 'used' by God can be difficult and painful. Then again, do we really want a nice, quiet life, free from godly adventure?

To smack or not to smack

John 2:1–8, 10

[1]On the third day a wedding took place at Cana
in Galilee. Jesus' mother
was there, [2]and Jesus and
his disciples had also
been invited to the wed-
ding. [3]When the wine was
gone, Jesus' mother said
to him, "They have no
more wine."
[4]"Dear woman, why do
you involve me?" Jesus
replied. "My time has not
yet come."
[5]His mother said to the
servants, "Do whatever he
tells you."
[6]Nearby stood six stone
water jars, the kind used
by the Jews for ceremoni-
al washing, each holding
from twenty to thirty gal-
lons.
[7]Jesus said to the ser-
vants, "Fill the jars with
water"; so they filled
them to the brim.
[8]Then he told them,
"Now draw some out and
take it to the master of
the banquet." They did
so,
[10]and said, "Everyone
brings out the choice wine
first and then the cheaper
wine after the guests have
had too much to drink;
but you have saved the
best till now."

SEARCH

Mary had to bring up God's son, but I can't help wondering what it was like to have Jesus in the family. After all, whose son was he? We know that he had brothers, and grew up as part of the family, initially going into the family carpentry business, but just how do you deal with a son or brother like Jesus? I don't imagine any parenting programme in the world has suggestions for bringing up a child 'without sin'. How did Mary balance Jesus' needs and the special promises she had about him with the needs of her other children? What did she think and feel during the three decades that led up to his public ministry?

Apart from the fact that he was a bit naughty as a nipper when he gave them the slip at the temple, the best evidence we have is Jesus' first miracle. Look at the passage here – do you see how they interact? Their exchange is marked more by what they don't say than by what they do: the trust and security of unspoken communication. God trusted Mary with his son and we have to conclude that she did a pretty good job, all things considered.

GO

What about you – what has God trusted you with?

The power of goodbye

Mark 3: 31–5

31Then Jesus' mother and
brothers arrived.
Standing outside, they
sent someone in to call
him. 32A crowd was sit-
ting around him, and
they told him, "Your
mother and brothers are
outside looking for you."
33"Who are my mother
and my brothers?" he
asked.
34Then he looked at
those seated in a circle
around him and said,
"Here are my mother
and my brothers!
35Whoever does God's
will is my brother and
sister and mother."

SEARCH

Can you imagine how it must have felt for Mary to hear Jesus say this? It must have hurt. But there was more to come, as Mary had to watch her son die a gruesome and shameful death (see John 19:25–7). Afterwards it must have been overwhelming as she gradually came to understand the significance of her son's life and death – for her and for the rest of the world.

Thinking about Mary encourages us to look at the idea of exactly what being used by God is all about. After all, are we supposed to find the right thing, the right 'ministry' so that we might get closer to God? Not quite – you see, God works the other way around. He's far more interested in the quality of our relationship with him.

We don't have to understand exactly what God's going to do with us – Mary didn't know the full story until after Jesus' resurrection. And we don't have to feel that we are up to the task; Mary asked Gabriel how on earth all of it was going to happen and he promised that the Holy Spirit would overshadow her. In the same way, God promises his Holy Spirit to help us do what we couldn't do alone.

The main thing seems to be our willingness to say, 'May it be to me as you have said' (Luke 1:38), and then a commitment of our will to stay close to God and stay faithful, whatever the journey holds.

GO

Remember the agendas – God's goes in front of ours.

Abraham

Over the next few days, we're going to take a little look at Abraham and see what he's got to tell us about God giving us **big** promises and dreams for the future. *J. Foster*

Promises, promises

genesis 15:1–6

1After this, the word of the Lord came to Abram in a vision:

"Do not be afraid, Abram.
I am your shield,
your very great reward."

2But Abram said, "O Sovereign Lord, what can
you give me since I remain childless and the
one who will inherit my estate is Eliezer of
Damascus?" 3And Abram said, "You have given
me no children; so a servant in my household
will be my heir."
4Then the word of the Lord came to him:
"This man will not be your heir, but a son coming from your own body will be your heir." 5He
took him outside and said, "Look up at the
heavens and count the stars—if indeed you can
count them." Then he said to him, "So shall
your offspring be."
6Abram believed the Lord, and he credited it
to him as righteousness.

Abram (soon to become Abraham) wants a son more than anything else. Even God promising to bless him in a big way is pointless to Abram unless he's got someone to pass it onto when he dies. So here we are with God promising Abram a family as numerous as the stars, and yet he's probably over eighty years old and hasn't managed even one kid with his wife Sarai yet. But Abram was a man of incredible faith. He would believe just about anything God said.

If you have hopes and dreams for the future, you need to start by being real with God. Abram told God what he desperately wanted, then God told Abram what his plan was. Often you'll find that in there somewhere amongst all your hopes for the future is something God's put in you that he wants to use. The key is to remember that God is more generous than you can imagine. He's got things for you that are beyond anything you would dare dream for. Ask God which dreams are from him. What are your hopes and dreams? What sort of thing gets you buzzing? (Writing, music, studying, sports, travelling . . .)

chew it over

Make a list of your hopes and dreams, put today's date on it and keep it in your Bible.

Jogging God's memory

genesis 16:1–6

1Now Sarai, Abram's wife, had borne him no
children. But she had an Egyptian maidservant named Hagar; 2so she said to Abram,
"The Lord has kept me from having children. Go, sleep with my maidservant; perhaps I can build a family through her."
Abram agreed to what Sarai said. 3So
after Abram had been living in Canaan ten
years, Sarai his wife took her Egyptian
maidservant Hagar and gave her to her husband to be his wife. 4He slept with Hagar,
and she conceived.
When she knew she was pregnant, she
began to despise her mistress. 5Then Sarai
said to Abram, "You are responsible for the
wrong I am suffering. I put my servant in
your arms, and now that she knows she is
pregnant, she despises me. May the Lord
judge between you and me."
6"Your servant is in your hands," Abram
said. "Do with her whatever you think best."
Then Sarai ill-treated Hagar; so she fled
from her.

Abram and Sarai still haven't had any kids. It's difficult to know for sure how long it is since the promise was made in chapter 15, but we're probably talking years. So they think, 'Well perhaps God's forgotten, or perhaps we need to give him a bit of a helping hand 'cos whatever he's doing doesn't seem to be working.' So this is the plan they come up with. Top plan guys – it does kinda work, Hagar does have a son (called Ishmael) but, boy, does it cause trouble in the Abram household!

They're trying to push God along, they're confused and disappointed 'cos they're still waiting. After all, God told them this was what was going to happen, didn't he? Here's the important bit. It's called God's timing, and it works something like this: God does things when he knows the time is right. The key point is that he knows more than us, so if he doesn't do things when we think the time looks right, don't be surprised, and don't worry. If you try to do God's bit for him, like Abram, it won't work out right.

chew it over

Have you ever been scared that he's forgotten about you? What did you do about it?

No way out

genesis 20:1–7, 21:2

1Now Abraham moved on from there into the
region of the Negev and lived between
Kadesh and Shur. For a while he stayed in
Gerar, 2and there Abraham said of his wife
Sarah, "She is my sister." Then Abimelech
king of Gerar sent for Sarah and took her.
3But God came to Abimelech in a dream
one night and said to him, "You are as good
as dead because of the woman you have
taken; she is a married woman."
4Now Abimelech had not gone near her,
so he said, "Lord, will you destroy an innocent nation? 5Did he not say to me, 'She is
my sister,' and didn't she also say, 'He is my
brother'? I have done this with a clear conscience and clean hands."
6Then God said to him in the dream, "Yes,
I know you did this with a clear conscience,
and so I have kept you from sinning against
me. That is why I did not let you touch her.
7Now return the man's wife, for he is a
prophet, and he will pray for you and you
will live. But if you do not return her, you
may be sure that you and all yours will die."

2Sarah became pregnant and bore a son to
Abraham in his old age, at the very time
God had promised him.

It's not the first time he's done this, and it nearly ended in tears last time as well (see chapter 12). If you read all of chapter 20 you hear Abraham coming up with lots of lame excuses, so many that he nearly caused God to wipe out an entire city! He's messed up big time. He thinks he's being smart, keeping one step ahead, but he got it badly wrong. We've all done it and it's encouraging to see people like Abraham do it too. So God obviously says, 'Sorry, Abe, but that's it, you've had several chances and you've blown it!' Well actually, no he doesn't, 'cos, as we see, the very next thing that happens is Sarah has the promised son at exactly the time God wanted it to happen. God's timing. Abraham sees clearly that it's not about him being perfect, but it's about God being unbelievably good to him.

That's how it works. We all mess up and cause trouble, big trouble sometimes. But God doesn't call everything off. That doesn't mean that there aren't consequences to what we do, but God cancelling all his plans for us isn't part of 'em.

chew it over

Do you feel like God won't give you your dreams 'cos you've done things wrong? Talk to him about it.

Sacrifice

genesis 22:1–2, 9–13

1 Some time later God tested Abraham. He
said to him, "Abraham!"
"Here I am," he replied.
2 Then God said, "Take your son, your
only son, Isaac, whom you love, and go to
the region of Moriah. Sacrifice him there as
a burnt offering on one of the mountains I
will tell you about."
9 When they reached the place God had
told him about, Abraham built an altar there
and arranged the wood on it. He bound his
son Isaac and laid him on the altar, on top
of the wood. 10 Then he reached out his hand
and took the knife to slay his son. 11 But the
angel of the Lord called out to him from
heaven, "Abraham! Abraham!"
"Here I am," he replied.
12 "Do not lay a hand on the boy," he
said. "Do not do anything to him. Now I
know that you fear God, because you have
not withheld from me your son, your only
son."
13 Abraham looked up and there in a thick-
et he saw a ram caught by its horns. He
went over and took the ram and sacrificed
it as a burnt offering instead of his son.

What is God playing at? He tells Abraham to take his son, the single most important thing to him in the world, the son he waited for so long to have, and sacrifice him. Abraham must have been gutted, confused and desperate for God to change his mind. But still he does it. Or at least was going to, until God had seen what he was hoping to see – Abraham's obedience.

You see, the dreams and opportunities he gives to us, he will ask for back. Why? God wants to see what's more important to you, God or the dream? Abraham didn't know God would stop him. You won't know if God will give those particular dreams back – he may have different dreams to give you – but the lesson is the same. When it comes to our relationship with God, and everything to do with it, including our dreams, everything begins with your heart. When that's right he'll give you dreams and opportunities, only then you'll see just how much more he has for you than you ever imagined.

chew it over

Get your list of dreams out (or actually write one this time!). Would you give these things up if God asked you to?

Dream on

genesis 25:1–4, 7–11

1Abraham took another wife, whose name
was Keturah. 2She bore him Zimran,
Jokshan, Medan, Midian, Ishbak and Shuah.
3Jokshan was the father of Sheba and
Dedan; the descendants of Dedan were the
Asshurites, the Letushites and the
Leummites. 4The sons of Midian were
Ephah, Epher, Hanoch, Abida and Eldaah.
All these were descendants of Keturah.
7Altogether, Abraham lived a hundred and
seventy-five years. 8Then Abraham breathed
his last and died at a good old age, an old
man and full of years; and he was gathered
to his people. 9His sons Isaac and Ishmael
buried him in the cave of Machpelah near
Mamre, in the field of Ephron son of Zohar
the Hittite, 10the field Abraham had bought
from the Hittites. There Abraham was buried
with his wife Sarah. 11After Abraham's death,
God blessed his son Isaac, who then lived
near Beer Lahai Roi.

Apart from telling us that Abraham had strange ideas about kids' names, what does this show? Well, let's have a look. First, in Abraham's culture (and early Old Testament culture in general) the signs of God's blessing were long life, children and prosperity. Abraham notched up a staggering 175 years! That list of dodgy names shows that his family line continued. He died a wealthy man. So all this points to the fact that God was very pleased with him. Second, Abraham was buried on land that he owned. That field was a part of the land that God promised Abraham's descendants (the Israelites), so it symbolises the fulfilment of that promise has begun. Also the number of descendants listed in that passage shows that the promise of Abraham's family being as 'numerous as the stars' is coming true.

Just as God has kept his promise to Abraham by giving him a son (Isaac), so he is starting to fulfil all the rest of his promises to Abraham. God is faithful. If he promises you something, he'll do it.

So you can trust God with all your dreams. If you keep being real with God, keep asking him which dreams of yours are from him, and keep God as the most important thing to you, and not the dream itself, then you'll see **big** things happen.

chew it over

Take your list of dreams out again, and spend some time dreaming and talking to God about it all!

ACTS

It's church, Jim, but not as we know it. The first three decades in the life of the early Church are put down in black and white here in the book of Acts. From mass rallies to communal living, personal triumph to public executions, the book really has got it all.

Nice start

Acts 2:42–7

42They devoted themselves to
the apostles' teaching and to
the fellowship, to the breaking of bread and to prayer.
43Everyone was filled with
awe, and many wonders and
miraculous signs were done
by the apostles. 44All the
believers were together and
had everything in common.
45Selling their possessions
and goods, they gave to anyone as he had need. 46Every
day they continued to meet
together in the temple
courts. They broke bread in
their homes and ate together
with glad and sincere hearts,
47praising God and enjoying
the favour of all the people.
And the Lord added to their
number daily those who
were being saved.

SEARCH

OK so this passage gets trotted out all the time whenever we look at Acts, so much so that the impact of the words can get slightly lost. Yeah, yeah, yeah, devotion, possessions, favour, big deal. But the truth is that it is a big deal: this is church as it's supposed to be.

All too often we think of church as something that happens to or for us. It's there on the Sunday and perhaps in the midweek meeting, well prepared, polished and ready for our attendance. And all we have to do is turn up, sing a few songs, say Amen and pop off home, a neat little tick placed in our Church box for that week.

But there's so much more to it than that. Look at what Luke describes here: it's a regular premium-grade mix of all the important stuff in the Christian life. It's even there in a nutshell in that first verse. There's the commitment to expanding their minds, the openness and commitment to one another and the importance placed on doing business with God. The following verses flesh it out even more, delivering the reader a clear image of what was involved for the early members. They were no idle passengers: they were active participants. Read it through again and imagine what it would have been like to have been part of it yourself.

GO

Church finds life in the lifestyles of the believers, not the colour of the pews. How much do you let church into the rest of your life?

Hard truth

Acts 4:32–7

32 All the believers were
one in heart and mind.
No-one claimed that any
of his possessions was his
own, but they shared
everything they had.
33 With great power the
apostles continued to testify to the resurrection of
the Lord Jesus, and much
grace was upon them all.
34 There were no needy
persons among them. For
from time to time those
who owned lands or
houses sold them,
brought the money from
the sales 35 and put it at
the apostles' feet, and it
was distributed to any-
one as he had need.
36 Joseph, a Levite from
Cyprus, whom the apos-
tles called Barnabas
(which means Son of
Encouragement), 37 sold a
field he owned and
brought the money and
put it at the apostles'
feet.

SEARCH

I hate bits like this. It would really be so much easier if the original scribes had somehow spilt the Tippex over passages like these. But try as we might, there's no getting away from the plain truth at the very heart of it.

Christian success is not shown by possessions or an easy life. The mark of a true Christian is to be found in how lightly they hold on to things rather than the amount of things they have to hold on to. Obedience, sacrifice and a relationship with God: those are the things that count. Here the believers, we are told, have made great progress, much greater than we have when it comes to getting their lifestyle to match up to their words. They preached about Jesus and told others about salvation, but their actions backed up all their fine words. Money and possessions were of little importance, and the level of commitment to both each other and equality meant that none of them were in need. Keep in mind that there were loads of them (3000 signed up at Pentecost alone – see Acts 2:41) and that's a pretty impressive claim.

We might talk about the importance of equality and community, we might bang on about how possessions don't matter to us, but do our lives back that up?

Even harder truth

Acts 5:1–10a

1 Now a man named Ananias, together with his wife Sapphira, also sold a
piece of property. 2 With his wife's full
knowledge he kept back part of the
money for himself, but brought the
rest and put it at the apostles' feet.
3 Then Peter said, "Ananias, how is
it that Satan has so filled your heart
that you have lied to the Holy Spirit
and have kept for yourself some of
the money you received for the land?
4 Didn't it belong to you before it was
sold? And after it was sold, wasn't the
money at your disposal? What made
you think of doing such a thing? You
have not lied to men but to God."
5 When Ananias heard this, he fell
down and died. And great fear seized
all who heard what had happened.
6 Then the young men came forward,
wrapped up his body, and carried him
out and buried him.
7 About three hours later his wife
came in, not knowing what had happened. 8 Peter asked her, "Tell me, is
this the price you and Ananias got for
the land?"
"Yes," she said, "that is the price."
9 Peter said to her, "How could you
agree to test the Spirit of the Lord?
Look! The feet of the men who buried
your husband are at the door, and
they will carry you out also."
10 At that moment she fell down at
his feet and died.

SEARCH

Say you win the lottery. Millions of pounds find their way into your Instant Saver and your bank manager is suddenly your best mate. You decide to give some to the church, pretty much all of it, but keeping just enough back for yourself. Fair enough, right? After all, you could just have easily decided to keep it all back.

Is that what this passage is about? I think not. Instead of being a warning to any who leave even the smallest coin in their pocket when the collection plate comes around, it's about the message that we give out when we give. Giving cash was purely voluntary, as Peter's question about 'Didn't it belong to you before it was sold?' makes clear. The problem comes when both Mr and Mrs pretend that the amount they're handing over is the full whack.

How often do we pretend that we're giving our all yet keeping just enough back for ourselves? We're not just talking money either, for so many of our prayers these days are along the lines of 'Use me, God, I want to live my life for you'. Are we really prepared for such a sacrifice? Are we really able to come up with the goods?

It might be easy to blag it with the people around us, but there's no fooling God. He doesn't need our money, and he certainly doesn't need our lies. What God demands is that our lives match up to our words.

Whose party?

Acts 8:1–8

1And Saul was there, giv-
ing approval to his
death.
On that day a great
persecution broke out
against the church at
Jerusalem, and all except
the apostles were scat-
tered throughout Judea
and Samaria. 2Godly
men buried Stephen and
mourned deeply for him.
3But Saul began to
destroy the church.
Going from house to
house, he dragged off
men and women and
put them in prison.
4Those who had been
scattered preached the
word wherever they
went. 5Philip went down
to a city in Samaria and
proclaimed the Christ
there. 6When the crowds
heard Philip and saw the
miraculous signs he did,
they all paid close attention to what he said.
7With shrieks, evil spirits
came out of many, and
many paralytics and
cripples were healed. 8So
there was great joy in
that city.

SEARCH

We touch down just after the first real low-point in the history of the early Church. Things had been going well until the religious authorities decided that enough was enough. These forces of conservatism were desperate to break up the party, and in murdering Stephen they certainly managed to put the wind up the early crew. They scarpered, and quick too, even quicker when bad boy Saul started putting the boot in. With the tears still fresh on their cheeks they scattered through the area. But instead of keeping their heads down, instead of admitting defeat and settling for a quiet life they kept up the preaching and praying wherever they went. This tale of Philip's arrival in a new Samaritan city shows the strength of his character. He's back to business and straight down to work. The result? The general chaos of godly activity and that all-important presence of 'great joy in that city'.

There are so many paradoxes in and around Christianity, and here's just one. With failure staring us in the face, with grief still weighing down our hearts, the good stuff can still go on. Does this mean that God doesn't care? Is Jesus a 'pull your socks up' kind of guy? No way. He comforts, understands and grieves along with us. But this is his gig, and you can't stop the joy coming when the Holy Spirit gets to work.

Let's be real with God. Instead of trying to pretend things are OK when we're hurting deep down, let's be honest about our feelings but still be open to seeing him work.

Who's in charge?

Acts 8:18–25

[18]When Simon saw that
the Spirit was given at
the laying on of the
apostles' hands, he
offered them money
[19]and said, "Give me also
this ability so that everyone on whom I lay my
hands may receive the
Holy Spirit."
[20]Peter answered: "May
your money perish with
you, because you
thought you could buy
the gift of God with
money! [21]You have no
part or share in this ministry, because your heart
is not right before God.
[22]Repent of this wickedness and pray to the
Lord. Perhaps he will forgive you for having such
a thought in your heart.
[23]For I see that you are
full of bitterness and cap-
tive to sin."
[24]Then Simon
answered, "Pray to the
Lord for me so that noth-
ing you have said may
happen to me."
[25]When they had testi-
fied and proclaimed the
word of the Lord, Peter
and John returned to
Jerusalem, preaching the
gospel in many
Samaritan villages.

SEARCH

This guy Simon was a regular strange one. Chances are that if he walked into a church today we'd have him straight out within seconds. He was into all kinds of weird stuff (sorcery mainly), and had been building up quite a following in non-Christian Samaria. He was trouble, even years later. Best off without him, if you ask me.

But thankfully I wasn't around to give advice at the time. It seems that Philip shared the good news with him and Simon made a commitment. It's obvious that he was fascinated by the stuff Philip was up to and wandered around lapping it all up.

But he made a mistake, asking Peter how much it would cost to get himself some of that good ol' Holy Spirit blessing for himself. Is Pete getting a little tired by this point? Isn't his reaction just a tad OTT? The plain fact is that Pete was tough with the man who knew plenty about 'spiritual' powers already. It can be easy for us to assume that evangelism is a matter of serving up the good news to a waiting public, believing that all who accept it do so out of pure motives. But Peter sussed that all was not quite as it seemed with Simon, and handled him wisely.

GO

But the truly amazing thing is this: they let him stay. Jesus is more than capable of putting up with those who are keen to use Christianity for their own devices. Salvation isn't just for the nice people out there . . .

The real hero

Acts 12:5–9

5So Peter was kept in
prison, but the church
was earnestly praying to
God for him.
6The night before
Herod was to bring him
to trial, Peter was sleeping between two soldiers,
bound with two chains,
and sentries stood guard
at the entrance.
7Suddenly an angel of
the Lord appeared and a
light shone in the cell.
He struck Peter on the
side and woke him up.
"Quick, get up!" he said,
and the chains fell off
Peter's wrists.
8Then the angel said to
him, "Put on your
clothes and sandals."
And Peter did so. "Wrap
your cloak around you
and follow me," the
angel told him. 9Peter
followed him out of the
prison, but he had no
idea that what the angel
was doing was really
happening; he thought
he was seeing a vision.

SEARCH

Peter, Paul, Barnabas, Stephen . . . all big names. Face facts, like the Gospels, Acts is a book that's crammed full of impressive people doing impressive things. These are the early church builders and it'd be pretty easy to get all carried away. You can just imagine it in those days, some twisted marketing campaign selling 'Paul's Crew Do It in the Temple' or 'Stephen's Lads Do It Stoned' bumper stickers for their donkeys. But that misses the point. There's only one hero out there today just as there was only one worth praising back then: God.

Who offers salvation? Who heals? Who gives life, knowledge and blessings? Just check out the tale here, as Peter manages to have got himself in a spot of bother. Death was on his mind, but God had other plans. There are more than a few jail-busts in the Bible, but this is one of the best. It's so amazing that Peter even thought it was a vision, a vivid dream that was playing out his desire to break free. But the light, the angel, the kick on the side to wake him up were as real as the prison they were leaving behind.

There's only one hero that we need to follow. The big name Christian speakers might be impressive enough from a distance but we all must never forget that it's God who's behind every miracle.

Joseph

Day dream believer

Arrogant squirt turned humble servant, the story of Joseph throws up more than its fair share of contradictions, lessons and inspirations.

Pete Greig

Genesis 37:5–11

5Joseph had a dream, and when he told it to
his brothers, they hated him all the more.
6He said to them, "Listen to this dream I had:
7We were binding sheaves of corn out in the
field when suddenly my sheaf rose and stood
upright, while your sheaves gathered round
mine and bowed down to it."
8His brothers said to him, "Do you intend
to reign over us? Will you actually rule us?"
And they hated him all the more because of
his dream and what he had said.
9Then he had another dream, and he told
it to his brothers. "Listen," he said, "I had
another dream, and this time the sun and
moon and eleven stars were bowing down to
me."
10When he told his father as well as his
brothers, his father rebuked him and said,
"What is this dream you had? Will your
mother and I and your brothers actually
come and bow down to the ground before
you?" 11His brothers were jealous of him, but
his father kept the matter in mind.

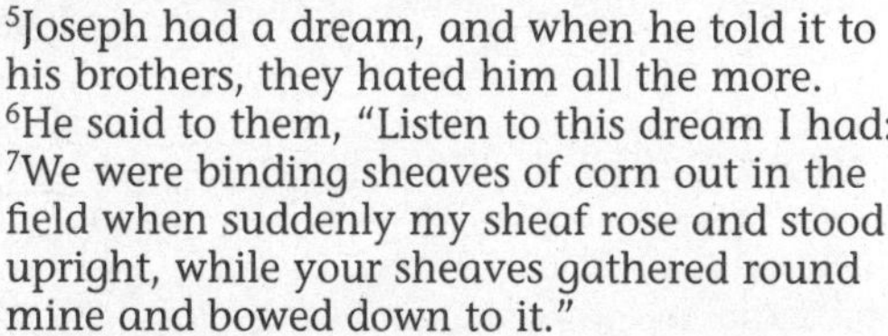

Take a few moments to dream. And dare to dream *big.* Thank God that he has amazing plans for your life. And then ask him to help you be humble, even when you feel like showing off.

Right from the word go Joseph knew he was different. He felt special. It wasn't because his family was particularly great (more like the Simpsons than the Waltons, I reckon). It wasn't that he had enough brothers to form a football team and provide the referee. It wasn't that Andrew Lloyd Webber would one day write a musical about him. He felt special because God's hand was on his young life. He had a 'calling' long before he knew what it was. God had dreams for Joseph's life long before Joseph had dreams himself. His life was ordinary, but he felt extraordinary.

And then at the age of seventeen Joseph has a couple of weirdo dreams about his family all bowing down to him. Now, if you had a dream like that one night, my guess is that you wouldn't bounce downstairs in the morning to share it across the breakfast table. But Joseph was a bit of a show-off and did just that. He'd always felt special, and suddenly he had divine confirmation. Although the dream was true (as we shall see), Joseph handled it badly, with terrible and bloody consequences.

What might God's dreams for your life be? Why has he given you the gifts and dreams you've got already?

Ouch!

Genesis 37:23–9

23So when Joseph came to his brothers, they
stripped him of his robe—the richly orna-
mented robe he was wearing—24and they
took him and threw him into the cistern. Now
the cistern was empty; there was no water in
it.
25As they sat down to eat their meal, they
looked up and saw a caravan of Ishmaelites
coming from Gilead. Their camels were
loaded with spices, balm and myrrh, and they
were on their way to take them down to
Egypt.
26Judah said to his brothers, "What will we
gain if we kill our brother and cover up his
blood? 27Come, let's sell him to the
Ishmaelites and not lay our hands on him;
after all, he is our brother, our own flesh and
blood." His brothers agreed.
28So when the Midianite merchants came
by, his brothers pulled Joseph up out of the
cistern and sold him for twenty shekels of silver to the Ishmaelites, who took him to Egypt.
29When Reuben returned to the cistern and
saw that Joseph was not there, he tore his
clothes.

God loves you too much to let you stay the same. Are you on a painful journey? Thank God that he is changing you day by day, preparing your character so that your dreams can come true.

Now this ain't exactly Happy Families. Joseph takes his brothers a packed lunch and they sell him into slavery. Why? For years Joseph had got away with murder because he was daddy's favourite. And Joseph had flaunted it. That flashy coat. Those arrogant dreams. The brothers were wrong to do what they did. But so was Joseph.

As Joseph set off in chains, betrayed by his brothers, helpless and hopeless, a journey was beginning. Not just a journey to Egypt. It was a journey of discipleship, a journey through the refiner's fire. A journey that would make Joseph the kind of person whose dreams could come true.

Cert. 18

Gen. 39:6b–8a, 9, 11–12, 16–17, 19–20a

Now Joseph was well-built and handsome,
[7]and after a while his master's wife took
notice of Joseph and said, "Come to bed with
me!"
[8]But he refused. [9]"No-one is greater in this
house than I am. My master has withheld
nothing from me except you, because you
are his wife. How then could I do such a
wicked thing and sin against God?"
[11]One day he went into the house to attend
to his duties, and none of the household servants was inside. [12]She caught him by his
cloak and said, "Come to bed with me!" But
he left his cloak in her hand and ran out of
the house.
[16]She kept his cloak beside her until his
master came home. [17]Then she told him this
story: "That Hebrew slave you brought us
came to me to make sport of me".
[19]When his master heard the story his wife
told him, saying, "This is how your slave
treated me," he burned with anger. [20]Joseph's
master took him and put him in prison, the
place where the king's prisoners were confined.

In what areas are you being tempted right now (be really honest with yourself). How can you avoid giving in? Are you playing with the temptation at all or are you saying a clear 'No'. Pray the Lord's Prayer.

Steamy stuff. Joseph has done well as a slave and turned into a bit of a looker too. His boss's wife takes a serious shine to him and day after day Joseph has to say 'No'. He doesn't flirt with her (even though flirting might have seemed harmless). He doesn't allow himself to be worn down by sexual temptation a day at a time. He probably tries to avoid being alone with her, and eventually he even has to peg it out of the room leaving her clutching his cardigan. And all this integrity lands him in jail.

The only way is up, baby!

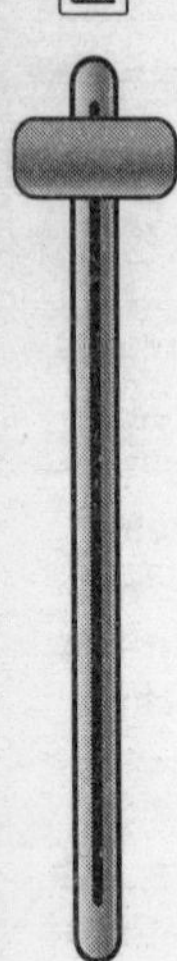

Genesis 39:20b–3

But while Joseph was there in the prison,
21the Lord was with him; he showed him
kindness and granted him favour in the
eyes of the prison warder. 22So the warder
put Joseph in charge of all those held in the
prison, and he was made responsible for all
that was done there. 23The warder paid no
attention to anything under Joseph's care,
because the Lord was with Joseph and gave
him success in whatever he did.

When Christians serve joyfully, it's like switching a light on that brightens up the lives of others. Think of something that you can do in your situation today to serve someone else regardless of the cost. And do it!

Every time Joseph gets thrown in the poo he seems to land on his feet, which if you think about it is much better than the alternative. He's one of twelve boys and God makes him kinda special. He's sold into slavery and ends up running his boss's whole business. He's thrown into jail and the prison warder puts him in charge. Why? What was Joseph's secret? The passage tells us that 'the Lord was with him'. It would have been easy for Joseph to have moaned. He could have disappeared up his own belly button questioning stuff or doubting God. He could have doubted his dreams and his call. But instead he sets about serving and working hard wherever he finds himself and however unfair life seems. He is a different Joseph from the guy who made his brothers want to kill him. Now everyone is able to see God's favour on him.

Are you serving as hard as you can wherever God has put you right now? Remember that Jesus is with you.

Becoming 'The One'

Genesis 41:39–43

39Then Pharaoh said to Joseph, "Since God
has made all this known to you, there is no-
one so discerning and wise as you. 40You
shall be in charge of my palace, and all my
people are to submit to your orders. Only
with respect to the throne will I be greater
than you."
41So Pharaoh said to Joseph, "I hereby put
you in charge of the whole land of Egypt."
42Then Pharaoh took his signet ring from
his finger and put it on Joseph's finger. He
dressed him in robes of fine linen and put a
gold chain around his neck. 43He had him
ride in a chariot as his second-in-command,
and men shouted before him, "Make way!"
Thus he put him in charge of the whole
land of Egypt.

Check out Hebrews 12:5–11 and thank God for loving you enough to walk you through tough times as well as the easy ones.

Over the years Joseph has learned a thing or two about dreams. He's learned how to understand them. He's learned that it's important what you say when to whom. And he's learned to find God in the strangest places – down wells, in business, in prison. Now comes the moment that God has been preparing him for all his life. He stands in front of the most important man in the entire world and interprets Pharaoh's dreams. Then he finds himself advising the biggest cheese in the known universe on his national, political strategy. Gulp. What would have happened if God had taken the seventeen-year-old Joseph straight to the courts of Pharaoh, bypassing all the character-shaping trials in between? How would he have coped? The bigger the call on your life, the tougher the training involved. Think of the training that Neo has to go through in *The Matrix* in order to become 'The One'.

JOHN PT. I

There's no getting away from the fact that Jesus was no ordinary man. What do you really believe about who he was, and what he did? Prepare to be challenged to the core . . . *Matt Stuart*

Beginnings

John 1:1–5

1In the beginning was
the Word, and the Word
was with God, and the
Word was God. 2He was
with God in the begin-
ning.
3Through him all
things were made; with-
out him nothing was
made that has been
made. 4In him was life,
and that life was the
light of men. 5The light
shines in the darkness,
but the darkness has not
understood it.

SEARCH

Deep stuff, huh? All this malarkey about 'the Word' this, and 'the Word' that. What the heck does it all mean? I find it easier here to substitute 'the Word' with the word 'Jesus'. Still with me? So it now reads: 'In the beginning was Jesus, and Jesus was with God, and Jesus was God. He was with God in the beginning.'

Starts to make a lot more sense, doesn't it? John goes on to tell us who Jesus is and what he came to earth to do. He made the universe, nothing was made without him. He's the meaning of life and we just have to believe in him. This makes us children of God. Just try and get your brain round that one. You are a child of the person who created everything you see. The biggest dude ever. With that kind of parent you can never be without the ultimate love, compassion, guidance and life that he alone can bring. That's a great place to worship him from.

Oh yeah. One last thing. God didn't stay away from us or hide himself like some Mystery Man. No, he got real and got stuck in showing us how to live it. He became flesh, or as *The Message* translation of the Bible puts it, 'moved into the neighbourhood'.

GO

Follow God, it's the way forward.

Superplonk

John 2:1–5

1On the third day a wed-
ding took place at Cana
in Galilee. Jesus' mother
was there, 2and Jesus
and his disciples had
also been invited to the
wedding. 3When the
wine was gone, Jesus'
mother said to him,
"They have no more
wine."
4"Dear woman, why do
you involve me?" Jesus
replied. "My time has
not yet come."
5His mother said to the
servants, "Do whatever
he tells you."

SEARCH

So Jesus is at a wedding with his mum. How embarrassing! Even worse his mates are there too. The plonk runs out and Mother Mary is right on the button. She's a sharp cookie. Jesus doesn't seem very impressed, does he? 'Lay off, Mum,' he says. 'I'm not ready yet.' How many times have I heard that before? Do you ever miss an opportunity because you're 'not ready'?

Mum sees the potential though. She gets sneaky, ignores Jesus' reluctance, and whispers some sly advice to the waiter. She's very confident in her son, don't you think? John tells us this is the first miracle Jesus ever does, yet Mary seems to know what he's capable of. Why? I reckon she remembers the promise of God that her son is a bit special and knows the boy has a trick or two up his sleeve.

Sure enough Jesus does the business and the party gets going again. I've always had a question in my head when I read about what happens here. Why'd he do the wine thing when there was loads of 'important stuff' he could have done? The clue's right there: it's a sign. Signs point to stuff. Jesus couldn't say it clearer if he had a microphone. So what's the message? 'It's party time!'

GO

Realise your potential and let's party with Jesus today.

Question time

John 3:4–12

4“How can a man be born
when he is old?” Nicodemus
asked. “Surely he cannot
enter a second time into his
mother’s womb to be born!”
5Jesus answered, “I tell you
the truth, no-one can enter
the kingdom of God unless
he is born of water and the
Spirit. 6Flesh gives birth to
flesh, but the Spirit gives
birth to spirit. 7You should
not be surprised at my saying, ‘You must be born
again.’ 8The wind blows
wherever it pleases. You hear
its sound, but you cannot
tell where it comes from or
where it is going. So it is
with everyone born of the
Spirit.”
9“How can this be?”
Nicodemus asked.
10“You are Israel’s
teacher,” said Jesus, “and do
you not understand these
things? 11I tell you the truth,
we speak of what we know,
and we testify to what we
have seen, but still you people do not accept our testimony. 12I have spoken to
you of earthly things and
you do not believe; how then
will you believe if I speak of
heavenly things?”

SEARCH

Nicodemus is an important chap. A lot of the guys on his team don’t like Jesus much, but Nic’s still to make up his mind, so he plays it cool. He’s confident Jesus is from God. A good place to start, I feel.

Jesus explains to him what it means to be born again. It’s not easy to get this sussed straight away. Even Big Nic, who is Israel’s teacher, takes a while to catch on. I see it like this: having a relationship with God was what we were born for. It’s the best thing we can do with our lives and it’s meant to be full-on twenty-four hours a day, 365 days a year, for the rest of our lives. We have to choose this though, it doesn’t happen automatically. When we say ‘yes’ to God’s offer of friendship our lives change. In many ways we start a new life – we are born again. You could say we are born into what we were born for.

God’s crazy about the world. He loves it. Jesus didn’t come to diss the world but to set it free. To save us. So when you hear someone slagging off the world be careful about what you believe.

Some people just love doom and gloom. It’s not that God likes all the bad stuff out there but he loves his creation and he loves his people.

Do you know that God loves you? He thinks you’re amazing and he wants to have an incredible friendship with you forever. I’m up for that. Your move.

Meeting point

John 4:9–11, 13–14

9 The Samaritan woman
said to him, "You are a
Jew and I am a
Samaritan woman. How
can you ask me for a
drink?" (For Jews do not
associate with
Samaritans.)
10 Jesus answered her,
"If you knew the gift of
God and who it is that
asks you for a drink, you
would have asked him
and he would have given
you living water."
11 "Sir," the woman
said, "you have nothing
to draw with and the
well is deep. Where can
you get this living
water?"
13 Jesus answered,
"Everyone who drinks
this water will be thirsty
again, 14 but whoever
drinks the water I give
him will never thirst.
Indeed, the water I give
him will become in him
a spring of water welling
up to eternal life."

SEARCH

Jesus is passing through Samaria (where the Good Samaritan was from) and is in need of refreshment, so he stops at a famous well that one of his ancestors had knocked up a while back. This foreign chick comes along and the banter begins. Jesus asks her for a drink.

Now you have to understand a bit of culture here to know why she goes all political on him. There are three reasons why Jesus shouldn't have spoken to this Samaritan woman.

1. She's a woman – men didn't speak to strange women in public in the first century AD.
2. She's a Samaritan – the Jews and the Samaritans weren't the best of friends (see Luke 10:30–5).
3. She's got a bit of a past – nuff said. Look what happens though. Jesus busts through all the cultural barriers and sees the woman as she is: a person that God loves. Totally.

The key bit here is Jesus' offer of living water, and this is just as relevant to us today. It doesn't matter what you are like: whether you're a 'success', what your parents are like, how many times you've stuffed it up – *God loves you!* The living water, the life, that Jesus offers this woman is for you, today, right here, right now. He knows everything there is to know about you and it doesn't put him off.

GO

So get drinkin'. It's God's round.

Best before . . .

John 6:27–35

27"Do not work for food that
spoils, but for food that endures
to eternal life, which the Son of
Man will give you. On him God
the Father has placed his seal of
approval."
28Then they asked him, "What
must we do to do the works God
requires?"
29Jesus answered, "The work of
God is this: to believe in the one
he has sent."
30So they asked him, "What
miraculous sign then will you
give that we may see it and
believe you? What will you do?
31Our forefathers ate the manna
in the desert; as it is written: 'He
gave them bread from heaven
to eat.'"
32Jesus said to them, "I tell
you the truth, it is not Moses
who has given you the bread
from heaven, but it is my Father
who gives you the true bread
from heaven. 33For the bread of
God is he who comes down from
heaven and gives life to the
world."
34"Sir," they said, "from now
on give us this bread."
35Then Jesus declared, "I am
the bread of life. He who comes
to me will never go hungry, and
he who believes in me will never
be thirsty."

SEARCH

I'm not good at eating old stuff (ask my mum). Anything in the fridge that's past its death date is out on its ear. It doesn't even have to be my house! So, I like this bit of John. It makes sense to me.

We're back to the belief thing again and it's worth asking yourself now and again what you believe. Our beliefs affect everything: who we are, how we treat people, and our relationship with the big man. Think about it for a second.

Jesus casually points out that anything other than him will not satisfy us. It will go off and start to pong a bit. It's an amazing claim, but he reckons that he can 'feed' us forever and that we'll never want anything else.

There's a challenge in there too. You see, the old geezers who asked him a lot of questions were living off some stuff that was at best a couple of thousand years old. Jesus had just rocked up with some fresh-from-the-oven goods and they didn't know how to handle it. Are we a bit like that? Do we try and rely on yesterday's rations when God offers us fresh bread for today?

Push into what Jesus has for you today and know that you will never go hungry with him helping you out.

Tough times

John 6:60–1, 63–9

60 On hearing it, many of his disciples said, "This is a hard
teaching. Who can accept it?"
61 Aware that his disciples were
grumbling about this, Jesus said
to them, "Does this offend you?
63 "The Spirit gives life; the
flesh counts for nothing. The
words I have spoken to you are
spirit and they are life. 64 Yet
there are some of you who do
not believe." For Jesus had
known from the beginning
which of them did not believe
and who would betray him.
65 He went on to say, "This is
why I told you that no-one can
come to me unless the Father
has enabled him."
66 From this time many of his
disciples turned back and no
longer followed him.
67 "You do not want to leave
too, do you?" Jesus asked the
Twelve.
68 Simon Peter answered him,
"Lord, to whom shall we go?
You have the words of eternal
life. 69 We believe and know that
you are the Holy One of God."

SEARCH

Sometimes it's really hard being a Christian. I don't just mean standing up for what you believe or talking to people who think you're a moron. Sometimes it just feels like there's nothing really there.

I've got a friend who preaches a lot. Sometimes after he's just led some big deal meeting where thousands of people have become Christians, and God has been working all over the shop, he'll be in his car and he'll think, 'I wonder if I'm making all this up? What if God doesn't exist?'

It happens to us all. That little voice in your head says, 'Don't be silly. How can you believe this stuff?' I'm very good at sitting in meetings where God is clearly present and doubting his reality. It doesn't help when a besandled bearded freak waving a flag like his life depends on it tries to convince me that dancing like a Russian bear is going to bring me closer to God.

The fact is we believe it 'cos it's true. God's spirit is life for us. It's all we have to live for. Peter knew it and here he gets it right.

Sometimes we need to say to Jesus, 'You have the words of eternal life. We believe and know that you are the Holy One of God.'

Holier than thou?

John 8:3–11

3The teachers of the law and the
Pharisees brought in a woman
caught in adultery. They made
her stand before the group 4and
said to Jesus, "Teacher, this
woman was caught in the act of
adultery. 5In the Law Moses commanded us to stone such women.
Now what do you say?" 6They
were using this question as a
trap, in order to have a basis for
accusing him.
But Jesus bent down and started to write on the ground with
his finger. 7When they kept on
questioning him, he straightened
up and said to them, "If any one
of you is without sin, let him be
the first to throw a stone at her."
8Again he stooped down and
wrote on the ground.
9At this, those who heard
began to go away one at a time,
the older ones first, until only
Jesus was left, with the woman
still standing there. 10Jesus
straightened up and asked her,
"Woman, where are they? Has
no-one condemned you?"
11"No-one, sir," she said.
"Then neither do I condemn
you," Jesus declared. "Go now
and leave your life of sin."

SEARCH

I hate bullies. I've never been bullied much but I've met a lot of people who have and it ain't nice. The Pharisees are the bullies of the Gospels: every time they pop up it means trouble.

Jesus came to live with us to bring a new order of things. To shake it all up, not just move the furniture around. The religious guys push this girl in front of him to try and set him up.

Jesus goes a bit weird at this point and starts to draw cartoons in the sand. But look at what he says: 'Is anyone perfect? No? Well, shut ya face then!' Some of us Christians really need to hear this: it's not good to moan and it's not good to want to point out other people's faults and make ourselves look good. None of us are perfect so let's work at becoming more like Jesus and encourage our mates to do the same.

Jesus didn't come to condemn the world but to save it (John 3:17), so all he does is tell the woman to leave her sin. I don't know what your life is like, but I guess, like mine, that there is still room for improvement. Hear these words: God loves us more than he hates our sin. That's why he forgives us when we stuff it up.

GO

Maybe now is a good time to let go of some of the rubbish that messes you up. Let's get praying.

Hard truths

John 10:14–21

14"I am the good shep-
herd; I know my sheep
and my sheep know
me— 15just as the Father
knows me and I know
the Father—and I lay
down my life for the
sheep. 16I have other
sheep that are not of this
sheep pen. I must bring
them also. They too will
listen to my voice, and
there shall be one flock
and one shepherd. 17The
reason my Father loves
me is that I lay down my
life—only to take it up
again. 18No-one takes it
from me, but I lay it
down of my own accord.
I have authority to lay it
down and authority to
take it up again. This
command I received
from my Father."
19At these words the
Jews were again divided.
20Many of them said,
"He is demon-possessed
and raving mad. Why
listen to him?"
21But others said,
"These are not the say-
ings of a man possessed
by a demon. Can a
demon open the eyes of
the blind?"

SEARCH

Jesus is talking to the Jews again. This time he says something that really upsets them. I love it when that happens. So what is it that gets them so mad? He claims to be God. You've got to admit that's pretty wild. He's very clear about it though. There's only one way to God and that's through Jesus. Some people reckon finding God is a bit like going up a mountain which has many paths to the top. Sorry, but that's cobblers. Jesus is the only option.

From that kind of position, Jesus can do pretty much whatever he likes. He chose to die for us and to offer us life. Now, your mates probably reckon that life as a Christian is boring. Come to that, you probably agree with them half the time. Well, it's not meant to be. Living as a Christian is to live life the Pepsi way: to the max, or 'to the full' as JC puts it.

It's funny but I find that the more I turn down the stuff that other people want to offer me (usually in exchange for money) and go for the God stuff, the more satisfied and fulfilled I am. Don't get me wrong, I'm not a hermit that lives in a cave and wears a sack.

GO

I just want to put God first and live life his way. After all, he designed me. I suggest you do the same.

Do you believe?

John 11:38–44

38 Jesus, once more deeply
moved, came to the tomb.
It was a cave with a stone
laid across the entrance.
39 "Take away the stone,"
he said.
"But, Lord," said Martha,
the sister of the dead man,
"by this time there is a bad
odour, for he has been
there four days."
40 Then Jesus said, "Did I
not tell you that if you
believed, you would see the
glory of God?"
41 So they took away the
stone. Then Jesus looked
up and said, "Father, I
thank you that you have
heard me. 42 I knew that
you always hear me, but I
said this for the benefit of
the people standing here,
that they may believe that
you sent me."
43 When he had said this,
Jesus called in a loud voice,
"Lazarus, come out!" 44 The
dead man came out, his
hands and feet wrapped
with strips of linen, and a
cloth around his face.
Jesus said to them, "Take
off the grave clothes and
let him go."

SEARCH

I sometimes ask people, 'Do you believe in God?' A silly question to ask a Christian, most people think. 'Of course I do,' they always say. 'No,' I say, 'do you believe in God?' Let me show you what I mean.

Martha's brother is dead. He is very, very dead. Just to prove it he's been in a hole for four days, smells like a dodgy kebab and is wrapped head to foot in Andrex. Martha, understandably, is not a happy bunny. Jesus, obviously wanting to make her feel much better, waltzes up to the tomb and tells her dead bro to take a walk on the wild side. Martha has a choice. Does she believe? She's known Jesus for a while and she knows he is a pretty capable dude. But even she thinks this is not going to happen.

Now we know that Jesus is pretty good at the 'rising from the dead trick' and we've probably heard this story before, but just think about how amazing this is! Sure enough Jesus prays (notice even he asks God for help) and yells at Lazarus to get up, and out he comes.

This guy Jesus can do anything. Just like Martha, we have to raise our expectations of what God can do and believe in him. So do you? Do you believe that Jesus can do anything? That he can be mates with all your friends and family? That he can heal people you pray for? That he can change the lives of every man, woman and child on the face of the planet?

GO

Get praying and ask God to raise your expectations of what you can see him do today.

From beginning to end Exodus plays out its story on an epic scale. If you're looking for an introduction to God, start right here. *Colin Brookes*

Rebel baby saved from watery grave

exodus 2:1–9

1Now a man of the house of Levi married a Levite
woman, 2and she became pregnant and gave birth
to a son. When she saw that he was a fine child,
she hid him for three months. 3But when she could
hide him no longer, she got a papyrus basket for
him and coated it with tar and pitch. Then she
placed the child in it and put it among the reeds
along the bank of the Nile. 4His sister stood at a
distance to see what would happen to him.

5Then Pharaoh's daughter went down to the Nile
to bathe, and her attendants were walking along
the river bank. She saw the basket among the
reeds and sent her slave girl to get it. 6She opened
it and saw the baby. He was crying, and she felt
sorry for him. "This is one of the Hebrew babies,"
she said.

7Then his sister asked Pharaoh's daughter, "Shall
I go and get one of the Hebrew women to nurse
the baby for you?"

8"Yes, go," she answered. And the girl went and
got the baby's mother. 9Pharaoh's daughter said to
her, "Take this baby and nurse him for me, and I
will pay you." So the woman took the baby and
nursed him.

The Hebrew people first moved to Egypt as welcome guests (Genesis 46:5–7). However, because they grew so quickly, the Egyptians started to oppress them – keep them weak so they don't take over. By the time Moses was born it was actually legal to murder male Hebrew babies at birth. They were drowned in the Nile to prevent any uprising . . . How ironic, then, that instead of being thrown *into* this river by the Egyptians, Moses, the ultimate upriser, was actually *brought out of it!* And not only was he rescued, but he was fed, educated, equipped and strengthened at the expense of the very man who'd tried to wipe him out. The phrase 'poetic justice' springs to mind.

But perhaps the best bit of this turn-around story is that the child's own mother, as poor as any of the Israelite slaves, ended up being paid by her oppressors to look after her baby! The Lord saw her pain, and acted.

If you are suffering, having to give up the precious things God has given you, hang in there. Remember, the Lord has a way of turning things around.

chew it over

God has an incredible way of bringing good out of the bad we do to each other.

Fired up for justice

exodus 3:1–2, 4–6, 9–12

1Now Moses was tending the flock of Jethro his
father-in-law, the priest of Midian, and he led
the flock to the far side of the desert and came
to Horeb, the mountain of God. 2There the angel
of the Lord appeared to him in flames of fire
from within a bush. Moses saw that though the
bush was on fire it did not burn up.
4When the Lord saw that he had gone over to
look, God called to him from within the bush,
"Moses! Moses!"
And Moses said, "Here I am."
5"Do not come any closer," God said. "Take
off your sandals, for the place where you are
standing is holy ground." 6Then he said, "I am
the God of your father, the God of Abraham, the
God of Isaac and the God of Jacob." At this,
Moses hid his face, because he was afraid to
look at God.
9"And now the cry of the Israelites has
reached me, and I have seen the way the
Egyptians are oppressing them. 10So now, go. I
am sending you to Pharaoh to bring my people
the Israelites out of Egypt."
11But Moses said to God, "Who am I, that I
should go to Pharaoh and bring the Israelites out
of Egypt?"
12And God said, "I will be with you. And this
will be the sign to you that it is I who have sent
you: When you have brought the people out of
Egypt, you will worship God on this mountain."

One day, when he had grown up, Moses killed an Egyptian slave driver. Fleeing for his life, he ended up in a place called Midian, where he married a lady called Zipporah. Moses began work for Zipporah's father as a shepherd, and settled down for a peaceful life in the hills, away from the pain and troubles of Egypt. God, however, remembered his people's suffering (see Exodus 2:24–5), and decided to jog Moses' memory. On the same mountain where he would later give Moses the Ten Commandments, God appears to him in a form that occurs again and again in Exodus – holy fire.

Whenever we begin to live in isolation from the world's suffering, God usually does something to remind us that we're supposed to get involved. We're called by God to fight for justice and speak out for the oppressed. But like Moses we can all too easily forget this, especially when we settle down into our comfortable lives. Typically, these are the times when God comes and lights his fire in our path.

chew it over

Our ability to forget is nearly as impressive as God's ability to remember.

Ball's in your court

exodus 11:1–9

1Now the Lord said to Moses, "I will bring one
more plague on Pharaoh and on Egypt. After
that, he will let you go from here, and when he
does, he will drive you out completely. 2Tell the
people that men and women alike are to ask
their neighbours for articles of silver and gold."
3(The Lord made the Egyptians favourably dis-
posed towards the people, and Moses himself
was highly regarded in Egypt by Pharaoh's officials and by the people.)

4So Moses said, "This is what the Lord says:
'About midnight I will go throughout Egypt.
5Every firstborn son in Egypt will die, from the
firstborn son of Pharaoh, who sits on the throne,
to the firstborn son of the slave girl, who is at
her hand mill, and all the firstborn of the cattle
as well. 6There will be loud wailing throughout
Egypt—worse than there has ever been or ever
will be again. 7But among the Israelites not a dog
will bark at any man or animal.' Then you will
know that the Lord makes a distinction between
Egypt and Israel. 8All these officials of yours will
come to me, bowing down before me and saying,
'Go, you and all the people who follow you!'
After that I will leave." Then Moses, hot with
anger, left Pharaoh.

9The Lord had said to Moses, "Pharaoh will
refuse to listen to you—so that my wonders may
be multiplied in Egypt."

Life is all about choices. If we make a habit of choosing honesty, faithfulness and kindness, our lives will begin to contain these qualities. If we choose unforgiveness, deceit and bitterness, our lives will fill up with these.

Moses went back to rescue his people. With a new Pharaoh on the throne, Moses pleaded for his people's release. Pharaoh refused. God did a pretty compelling miracle with Aaron's (Moses' brother) staff. Pharaoh refused. God sent plagues of blood, frogs, gnats, flies, livestock disease and hail which devastated Egypt. Pharaoh still refused.

If you've ever thought it was a bit unfair that God kept hardening Pharaoh's heart so the plagues could get worse and worse, look again. It's only with the later plagues of boils, locusts, darkness and death of the firstborn that God hardened Pharaoh's heart. Before that, Pharaoh's heart was already hard (e.g. Exodus 8:15 or 19). God was simply confirming what Pharaoh had already chosen for himself.

chew it over

To fear God or not. To honour God or not. To love God or not. What we choose today will determine the shape of tomorrow.

mint source

exodus 12:3, 5–8, 10–13

3"Tell the whole community of Israel that on the
tenth day of this month each man is to take a
lamb for his family, one for each household. 5The
animals you choose must be year-old males
without defect, and you may take them from the
sheep or the goats. 6Take care of them until the
fourteenth day of the month, when all the people
of the community of Israel must slaughter them
at twilight. 7Then they are to take some of the
blood and put it on the sides and tops of the
door-frames of the houses where they eat the
lambs. 8That same night they are to eat the meat
roasted over the fire, along with bitter herbs,
and bread made without yeast. 10Do not leave
any of it till morning; if some is left till morning,
you must burn it. 11This is how you are to eat it:
with your cloak tucked into your belt, your sandals on your feet and your staff in your hand.
Eat it in haste; it is the Lord's Passover.

12"On that same night I will pass through
Egypt and strike down every firstborn—both
men and animals—and I will bring judgment on
all the gods of Egypt. I am the Lord. 13The blood
will be a sign for you on the houses where you
are; and when I see the blood, I will pass over
you. No destructive plague will touch you when I
strike Egypt."

Have you ever wondered why we read the Old Testament? A fourteen-year-old scally from Manchester gives his life to Jesus, and we give him a massive, ancient text to read! Why bother, especially when it's full of details like making sure you've got your sandals on before you eat?

Our story picks up on the eve of the last plague. God, in his final sign to Pharaoh that he had chosen the wrong people to oppress, was to pass through Egypt and kill every firstborn, be they human or animal. The Israelites, however, were told how to avoid this. If they daubed the blood of a lamb on the doorframe of their house, the indiscriminate death sweeping across the whole land would 'pass over' them. So the blood of a lamb saved people from death . . . hmmm . . . now that rings a bell.

The fact is that without the Old Testament, the New doesn't really make sense. Images like the Passover lamb and, later, the goat killed in the Temple (Leviticus 16:1–10) set the scene for what Jesus did on the cross. The Bible is a whole. The gospel starts not with Matthew, but in Genesis. *That's* why we read the Old Testament.

chew it over

The fact is that, without the Old Testament, the New doesn't really make sense.

A fishy story

exodus 12:51, 14:5, 10, 15, 21-2

51And on that very day the Lord brought the Israelites out of Egypt by their divisions.

5When the king of Egypt was told that the people had fled, Pharaoh and his officials changed their minds about them and said, "What have we done? We have let the Israelites go and have lost their services!"

10As Pharaoh approached, the Israelites looked up, and there were the Egyptians, marching after them. They were terrified and cried out to the Lord.

15Then the Lord said to Moses, "Why are you crying out to me? Tell the Israelites to move on."

21Then Moses stretched out his hand over the sea, and all that night the Lord drove the sea back with a strong east wind and turned it into dry land. The waters were
divided, 22and the Israelites went through the sea on dry ground, with a wall of water on their right and on their left.

This is quite a scene! Have you ever wondered what the ground would have been like at the bottom of the Red Sea? Would there have been coral, rocks or even massive craters dropping down into the earth's crust? Would there have been sea creatures scuttling around or dead fish which didn't break in time to stay the other side of the sea wall? Some think if God could part the waters, surely he could flatten the sea bed as well. Others say it's a ridiculous legend. What do you think?

Whatever you choose to believe about the actual setting, the point the Bible is making is clear – when all seemed lost, God came through.

How many times have you been in an impossible situation and the Lord has miraculously created a way out? And how many times has he left it until the last minute? No one really knows why God sometimes waits until we're absolutely desperate before coming to the rescue. But wise people point out that it's usually not until we're desperate that we *really* pray . . . and that then we're willing to hope for the ridiculous.

chew it over

No matter how bad things get, trust God to come through.

Right here, right now

exodus 16:1–4a, 13–15, 19–20a, 31

1The whole Israelite community set out from Elim
and came to the Desert of Sin, which is between
Elim and Sinai, on the fifteenth day of the second month after they had come out of Egypt. 2In
the desert the whole community grumbled
against Moses and Aaron. 3The Israelites said to
them, "If only we had died by the Lord's hand in
Egypt! There we sat round pots of meat and ate
all the food we wanted, but you have brought us
out into this desert to starve this entire assembly
to death."
4Then the Lord said to Moses, "I will rain
down bread from heaven for you. The people are
to go out each day and gather enough for that
day."
13That evening quail came and covered the
camp, and in the morning there was a layer of
dew around the camp. 14When the dew was gone,
thin flakes like frost on the ground appeared on
the desert floor. 15When the Israelites saw it, they
said to each other, "What is it?" For they did not
know what it was.
Moses said to them, "It is the bread the Lord
has given you to eat."
19Then Moses said to them, "No-one is to keep
any of it until morning."
20However, some of them paid no attention to
Moses; they kept part of it until morning, but it
was full of maggots and began to smell.
31The people of Israel called the bread manna.
It was white like coriander seed and tasted like
wafers made with honey.

Have you ever wished that, as our provider, God would just stick £500,000 in our bank account and tell us to use it wisely for the rest of our lives? Or, when praying for guidance, that he would simply let us have a schedule for the next twenty years which we could just faithfully stick to?

One of the things we find hardest about the Lord is that he lives in the *present*, and calls us to do the same. We're experts at regretting what's been, or worrying about what will be, but not so good at simply taking each day as it comes. Like the Israelites who were either looking back to the 'good ol' days' in Egypt, or trying to gather enough manna to ensure their provision for the next day, we can spend our time living in the past or future, and not the present.

And yet God, who incidentally calls himself 'I *AM*' (Exodus 3:14), wants us to live in the present. To give him the things of yesterday and trust him for the things of tomorrow, so we can enjoy what he has for us today.

chew it over

God doesn't want us to have £500,000 or a twenty-year plan . . . he wants us to have *him*.

Looking is not seeing

exodus 17:1–7

1The whole Israelite community set out from
the Desert of Sin, travelling from place to
place as the Lord commanded. They camped
at Rephidim, but there was no water for the
people to drink. 2So they quarrelled with
Moses and said, "Give us water to drink."
Moses replied, "Why do you quarrel with
me? Why do you put the Lord to the test?"
3But the people were thirsty for water
there, and they grumbled against Moses. They
said, "Why did you bring us up out of Egypt
to make us and our children and livestock die
of thirst?"
4Then Moses cried out to the Lord, "What
am I to do with these people? They are almost
ready to stone me."
5The Lord answered Moses, "Walk on ahead
of the people. Take with you some of the
elders of Israel and take in your hand the staff
with which you struck the Nile, and go. 6I will
stand there before you by the rock at Horeb.
Strike the rock, and water will come out of it
for the people to drink." So Moses did this in
the sight of the elders of Israel. 7And he called
the place Massah and Meribah because the
Israelites quarrelled and because they tested
the Lord saying, "Is the Lord among us or
not?"

Ever been enjoying a really good adventure film and someone next to you says something like, 'He could *never* jump that far!'?

Some people have a tireless ability to miss the wonder of things. They get sidetracked by imperfections which keep them from seeing the big picture. So far, the Israelites seemed to display this ability in abundance.

All right, fair play – they were thirsty . . . but they'd recently seen ten plagues wipe out their oppressors, walked through the Red Sea and had food just drop out of the sky! You'd think that by now they'd have got the message that God was going to look after them. Where was their faith? We, of course, would have handled it completely differently – wouldn't we?

When our troubles or needs become so great that they obscure the big picture of God's goodness to us, we must stop, take a step back and consider again all that the Lord is and has done.

chew it over

Only by stepping back and looking at the big picture will we catch the wonder of the adventure God has called us on.

Argh - why all the rules?

exodus 19:1–3, 5, 16–19

[1]In the third month after the Israelites left
Egypt—on the very day—they came to the
Desert of Sinai. [2]After they set out from
Rephidim, they entered the Desert of Sinai, and
Israel camped there in the desert in front of the
mountain.
[3]Then Moses went up to God, and the Lord
called to him from the mountain and said, "This
is what you are to say to the house of Jacob and
what you are to tell the people of Israel:
[5]"'Now if you obey me fully and keep my
covenant, then out of all nations you will be my
treasured possession. Although the whole earth
is mine,'"
[16]On the morning of the third day there was
thunder and lightning, with a thick cloud over
the mountain, and a very loud trumpet blast.
Everyone in the camp trembled. [17]Then Moses led
the people out of the camp to meet with God,
and they stood at the foot of the mountain.
[18]Mount Sinai was covered with smoke, because
the Lord descended on it in fire. The smoke bil-
lowed up from it like smoke from a furnace, the
whole mountain trembled violently, [19]and the
sound of the trumpet grew louder and louder.
Then Moses spoke and the voice of God
answered him.

On the way to the land God promised them, the Israelites passed through Midian, the place where Moses had fled after he'd killed the Egyptian slave-driver. After spending some time with Moses' father-in-law, they came to the very mountain where, through a fiery bush, God had promised he would bring all the Israelites (Exodus 3:12). Standing once again on those remote grassy slopes, this time with the whole nation of Israel, must have been quite a monumental moment for Moses!

And it was there on Mount Sinai that God told the people of Israel that he wanted to mark them out from all the nations of the world as his treasure. What a privilege! How special did *they* feel?!

Yet with every position of privilege comes a need to behave in a way that's worthy of such honour. And so God, appearing again through fire, gave them ten life-enhancing commandments (Exodus 20:1–7).

chew it over

The Ten Commandments - *not* a list of finger-wagging dos and don'ts, but rather a formula - a pattern for the most wonderful, exciting and acclaimed life a group of people could ever have.

Tied up into freedom

exodus 22-3

"Do not allow a sorceress to live." (22:18)

"Do not take advantage of a widow or an orphan. If you do and they cry out to me, I will certainly hear their cry." (22:22–3)

"If you lend money to one of my people among you who is needy, do not be like a moneylender; charge him no interest." (22:25)

"If you come across your enemy's ox or donkey wandering off, be sure to take it back to him. If you see the donkey of someone who hates you fallen down under its load, do not leave it there; be sure you help him with it."(23:4–5)

"Do not deny justice to your poor people in their lawsuits." (23:6)

"For six years you are to sow your fields and harvest the crops, but during the seventh year let the land lie unploughed and unused. Then the poor among your people may get food from it, and the wild animals may eat what they leave. Do the same with your vineyard and your olive grove." (23:10–11)

The formula for privileged, abundant life continues on from the Ten Commandments . . . and then continues on . . . and on . . . and on . . .

It seems that God wants to give guidance on just about everything: from wiping out sorceresses to helping your enemy with his donkey! If something happened, God would have a law for it!

Now, at first glance you might think that with so many rules, the people's freedom would be constantly hampered. However, as *we ourselves* experience, it's actually rules that *bring* freedom. Without the rule about practising two hours a day, we'd never be able to play scorching guitar solos or somersault off parallel bars; without the rule about planting crops in spring, we'd have no food in autumn; without the rule about only driving on one side on the road, we'd all be killed in road accidents; and without the rule about not cheating on your boy or girlfriend, we'd never trust anyone and know the dizzying heights of love.

chew it over

When God *commands* something, it's always in order to bring freedom, unity and love. Good rules are there to enhance life, not limit it.

We did everything just as you like it

exodus 25:8–16

8“Then have them make a sanctuary for me,
and I will dwell among them. 9Make this
tabernacle and all its furnishings exactly
like the pattern I will show you.
10“Have them make a chest of acacia
wood—two and a half cubits long, a cubit
and a half wide, and a cubit and a half
high. 11Overlay it with pure gold, both inside
and out, and make a gold moulding around
it. 12Cast four gold rings for it and fasten
them to its four feet, with two rings on one
side and two rings on the other. 13Then
make poles of acacia wood and overlay
them with gold. 14Insert the poles into the
rings on the sides of the chest to carry it.
15The poles are to remain in the rings of this
ark; they are not to be removed. 16Then put
in the ark the Testimony, which I will give
you.”

After telling the Israelites God's laws, Moses was called back up Mount Sinai. This time he was away for ages. The Lord told Moses to make a large tent (the tabernacle) with five very special objects in it. The first, a wooden box overlaid with gold, was called the ark. Described down to the last detail, it would be an object that God himself would inhabit. It was a sacred thing which signified that the God of Heaven had chosen to dwell on earth . . . among the Israelites.

The other objects, a table, a lampstand, an incense altar and a bronze altar, were also described meticulously, as was the tent itself and what those working in it should wear. God even prescribes an exact recipe for the incense to be burned there.

Why all the details?

Imagine you wanted to honour your boss or teacher by inviting them to your house for a meal. As a sign of your respect and desire to please them, would you not clean your house until it was spotless and prepare every little thing to their liking, right down to their favourite side-salad dressing?!

God was not interested in the details of the tabernacle, so much as his people's willingness to attend to them.

chew it over

If ever you feel flippant about knowing God Almighty, go to the biggest cathedral you can find . . . and see if you can catch the sense of reverence and awe of the Lord dwelling among us.

Now let's see what you're made of

exodus 32:1–4

1When the people saw that Moses was so
long in coming down from the mountain,
they gathered round Aaron and said,
"Come, make us gods who will go before
us. As for this fellow Moses who brought us
up out of Egypt, we don't know what has
happened to him."
2Aaron answered them, "Take off the gold
ear-rings that your wives, your sons and
your daughters are wearing, and bring them
to me." 3So all the people took off their
ear-rings and brought them to Aaron. 4He
took what they handed him and made it
into an idol cast in the shape of a calf,
fashioning it with a tool. Then they said,
"These are your gods, O Israel, who
brought you up out of Egypt."

Moses, head buzzing with God's instructions for the ark and tabernacle, returned to the Israelites having been up Mount Sinai for a long time. He carried with him his two stone tablets on which God himself had written the Ten Commandments.

However, the so-called 'People of God' had got restless in his absence and decided to make their own god from a bunch of earrings! Predictably, Moses went ballistic! He smashed up the stone tablets, probably in a well-you've-cocked-this-lot-up-for-a-start kind of way. He then ordered thousands to be killed.

Can you *imagine* these people?! They'd seen the miraculous power of God rescue and bless them again and again . . . yet as soon as they were left on their own, they forgot all about God and started worshipping useless objects. They blew it.

And yet, *we* do this kind of thing all the time. How many of us, when God seems far away, try to find that much needed sense of security in worldly things? There's nothing wrong with TV, clothes, diets, cars, relationships or success – however, there *is* a problem when we use them to provide our sense of well-being. A lot of the Israelites met with a sticky end for their unfaithfulness. The question is, was this the end of the line for them?

chew it over

Only God can provide the sense of security which we all crave.

God with us

exodus 40:1–4, 34–8

1 Then the Lord said to Moses: 2 "Set up the
tabernacle, the Tent of Meeting, on the first
day of the first month. 3 Place the ark of the
Testimony in it and shield the ark with the
curtain. 4 Bring in the table and set out what
belongs on it. Then bring in the lampstand
and set up its lamps."
34 Then the cloud covered the Tent of
Meeting, and the glory of the Lord filled
the tabernacle. 35 Moses could not enter the
Tent of Meeting because the cloud had settled upon it, and the glory of the Lord filled
the tabernacle.
36 In all the travels of the Israelites, whenever the cloud lifted from above the tabernacle, they would set out; 37 but if the cloud
did not lift, they did not set out—until the
day it lifted. 38 So the cloud of the Lord was
over the tabernacle by day, and fire was in
the cloud by night, in the sight of all the
house of Israel during all their travels.

The Golden Calf thing caused a *major* hiccup in God's plan for his people – he told them he would no longer be with them on their journey (Exodus 33:3). This was the worst thing that could have happened to Israel. However, after much desperate pleading by Moses, the Lord relented (33:14). Moses pitched a tent outside their camp on which God would graciously descend and meet whoever had come to enquire of him. They called it the 'Tent of Meeting' (for obvious reasons).

Many other things happened: Moses hiked back up Mount Sinai, got another two tablets with the Ten Commandments, and returned with a face glowing more brightly than a sunburnt tourist. He had the tabernacle built (which for clarity's sake was *also* called the 'Tent of Meeting', even though it was a completely different tent), as he did the ark and the other bits and bobs God had commanded.

It was in the tabernacle, pitched *inside* the camp at the heart of Israel's community, where God chose to dwell. And so the Lord's presence remained with Israel.

As we leave the book of Exodus, let's remember that, as God rescues *us* from slavery and leads us into freedom, whatever we have or lack, the one thing that we need is his presence.

chew it over

We need God's presence. God leading us. God loving us. God with us.

Paul

BC

Apart, obviously, from Jesus there is one person who stands out as the major influence and shaper of Christianity – not St Cliff, but St Paul. He wrote more of the New Testament than anyone else, and we still don't know his second name. In the next few sessions we're going to look at some of the details of his life away from the glamour of all those shipwrecks and letters.

Chris Russell

Acts 7:54–60

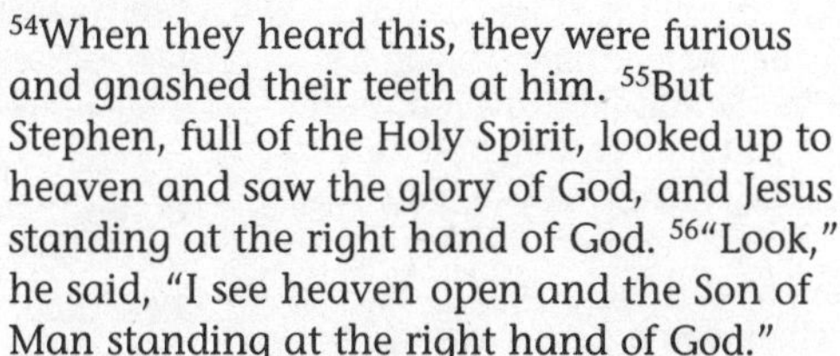

54 When they heard this, they were furious
and gnashed their teeth at him. 55 But
Stephen, full of the Holy Spirit, looked up to
heaven and saw the glory of God, and Jesus
standing at the right hand of God. 56 "Look,"
he said, "I see heaven open and the Son of
Man standing at the right hand of God."
57 At this they covered their ears and,
yelling at the top of their voices, they all
rushed at him, 58 dragged him out of the city
and began to stone him. Meanwhile, the
witnesses laid their clothes at the feet of a
young man named Saul.
59 While they were stoning him, Stephen
prayed, "Lord Jesus, receive my spirit."
60 Then he fell on his knees and cried out,
"Lord, do not hold this sin against them."
When he had said this, he fell asleep.

Saul is not going through a crisis of faith or searching for extra meaning. It's just that he meets Jesus. Think of those you know who think they are getting on fine without Jesus. Pray he'd meet them.

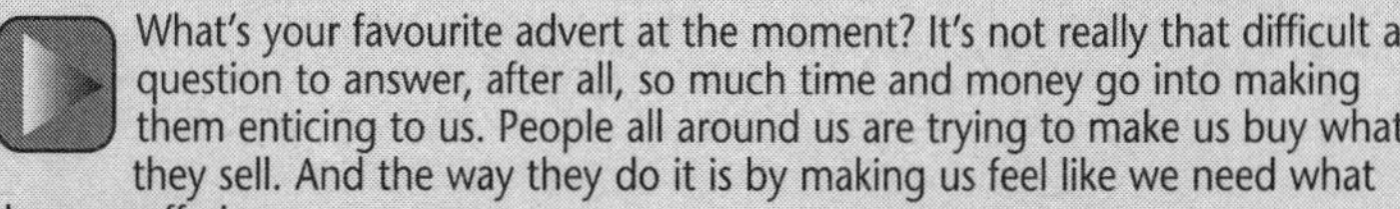

What's your favourite advert at the moment? It's not really that difficult a question to answer, after all, so much time and money go into making them enticing to us. People all around us are trying to make us buy what they sell. And the way they do it is by making us feel like we need what they are offering.

Living in such a world we often present Jesus like this – he can, we tell people, give them happiness, fulfil their lives, give them meaning, fill the emptiness inside, give them a family to belong to. And all this is wonderfully true.

But the danger is it gives the impression that people will only respond to Jesus when they see their need and turn to him for help.

Saul had no needs. He was getting on absolutely fine; in fact he was positively thriving. A Jewish leader, he was incredibly religious and very fulfilled. He was passionate about God and about defending the name of God. So when we first meet him he is holding the coats at the public execution of one of those perverters of the true religion. In fact he is so fulfilled in his own life he travels around towns arresting suspects and trying to wipe out Christianity.

Ch, Ch, Ch, Ch, Changes

Acts 9:1–6, 9, 17–18

1Meanwhile, Saul was still breathing out murder-
ous threats against the Lord's disciples. He went
to the high priest 2and asked him for letters to
the synagogues in Damascus, so that if he found
any there who belonged to the Way, whether
men or women, he might take them as prisoners
to Jerusalem. 3As he neared Damascus on his
journey, suddenly a light from heaven flashed
around him. 4He fell to the ground and heard a
voice say to him, "Saul, Saul, why do you persecute me?"

5"Who are you, Lord?" Saul asked.

"I am Jesus, whom you are persecuting," he
replied. 6"Now get up and go into the city, and
you will be told what you must do."

9For three days he was blind, and did not eat
or drink anything.

17Then Ananias went to the house and entered
it. Placing his hands on Saul, he said, "Brother
Saul, the Lord—Jesus, who appeared to you on
the road as you were coming here—has sent me
so that you may see again and be filled with the
Holy Spirit." 18Immediately, something like scales
fell from Saul's eyes, and he could see again. He
got up and was baptised,

The whole story is remarkable. It shows no one is ever an unlikely person to be called by God, no one is ever too far away. How does that encourage you in your life and your witness? Pray it.

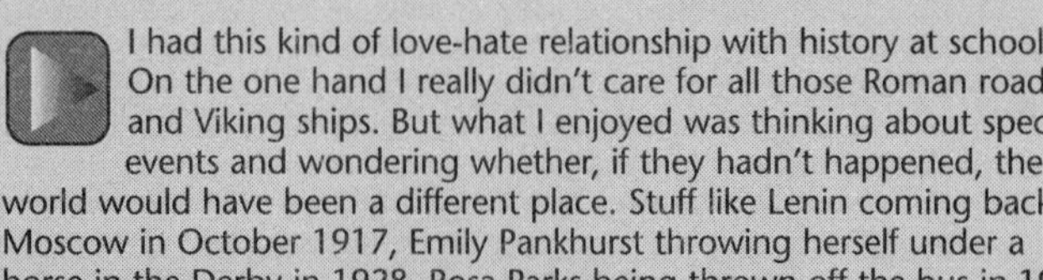

I had this kind of love-hate relationship with history at school. On the one hand I really didn't care for all those Roman roads and Viking ships. But what I enjoyed was thinking about specific events and wondering whether, if they hadn't happened, the world would have been a different place. Stuff like Lenin coming back to Moscow in October 1917, Emily Pankhurst throwing herself under a horse in the Derby in 1928, Rosa Parks being thrown off the bus in 1962 and Robbie leaving Take That in 1995.

This story is one of those pivots which history turns on. Saul is, as we saw last time, getting on just fine. He's off to round up a few more Christians (1–2) when his world and ours changes for ever. It changes not because he finds Jesus, but because Jesus finds him. There are a few special effects – lots of bright lights and voices (3–6) – but it seems that in more ways than one Saul is in the dark. But God wants him in the light and so sends a friend round, who, after a bit of protesting, goes to help.

First steps

Acts 9:19b–20, 23–5, 27a, 28–30

Saul spent several days with the disciples in
Damascus. 20At once he began to preach in the
synagogues that Jesus is the Son of God.
23After many days had gone by, the Jews con-
spired to kill him, 24but Saul learned of their
plan. Day and night they kept close watch on the
city gates in order to kill him. 25But his followers
took him by night and lowered him in a basket
through an opening in the wall.
27But Barnabas took him and brought him to
the apostles. 28So Saul stayed with them and
moved about freely in Jerusalem, speaking boldly
in the name of the Lord. 29He talked and debated
with the Grecian Jews, but they tried to kill him.
30When the brothers learned of this, they took
him down to Caesarea and sent him off to Tarsus.

You might have great dreams of what God will use you for. Fantastic. But how are you using the time of preparation?

What many of us love and hope for in the Christian world are famous Christians. Athletes, TV personalities, footballers, politicians and the trump card: pop stars. It seems we think it gives the faith an extra credibility, that people are more likely to be influenced by our message if recognisable and 'impressive' people endorse it. So what we do with famous Christians is get them opening events, endorsing books and joining speaking tours to give their glitzy side of the story. Best of all is when someone who is a bit of a celeb already actually becomes a Christian: we love seeing those testimonies in the press and wait for the book to hit the shops in six months.

So what does Paul do when he becomes a Christian, once he has got his calling from God to be a spreader of the good news of Jesus? Surely he should be straight out there on the circuit, preaching twice a week, giving his testimony. Um, actually nothing like that at all.

At first he gives his testimony and it rather causes a stir, so he has to leave. He goes to Jerusalem where the disciples are all too scared of him. So he leaves for Tarsus. Then it seems he goes into oblivion.

It's another couple of chapters till we hear of him again, and most New Testament boffins guestimate that a period of twelve years passes. Twelve years being inactive in his worldwide ministry. Why was he not straight out there?

He spends twelve years in the quiet of a local church in Tarsus because he is following the example of Jesus who, even though he had the highest calling on his life, spent thirty years in preparation. Should we allow our famous Christians time in oblivion rather than dragging them into the limelight?

Looking back

Philippians 3:4–8

4though I myself have reasons for such confidence.
If anyone else thinks he has reasons to
put confidence in the flesh, I have more:
5circumcised on the eighth day, of the people of Israel, of the tribe of Benjamin, a
Hebrew of Hebrews; in regard to the law, a
Pharisee; 6as for zeal, persecuting the
church; as for legalistic righteousness, fault-
less.
7But whatever was to my profit I now consider loss for the sake of Christ. 8What is
more, I consider everything a loss compared
to the surpassing greatness of knowing
Christ Jesus my Lord, for whose sake I have
lost all things. I consider them rubbish, that
I may gain Christ

Can you join in these words with Paul?

The other day I found a picture from my old youth group days. A massive group of us on a weekend away. Apart from having an embarrassing reminder of quite how ridiculous fashions were in the 1980s I got really sad when I thought how passionate we all were for God and when I counted up on one hand how many were still going for it with God.

Obviously there are as many reasons for that as there are people. But I can't help thinking why alternatives away from God are so attractive when I read these words that Paul wrote.

I mean he had everything: background, money and breeding, a great family, amazing education and wonderful prospects (5). But once he met Jesus he was able to look back on those things and call them 'rubbish', or more accurately in the original Greek (if you'll excuse my language, Mum) 'crap'. Everything he once had, all that was once going for him, is useless, a waste of time and space.

So why do we look at the other things that are going on around us and value them so highly? Might it be that we haven't really got hold of Jesus in quite the same way that Paul did? Could it be that everything else looks so attractive and enticing because we haven't looked closely enough at Jesus and all that he has for us?

The people's evangelist

Romans 16:1–8, 16

1I commend to you our sister Phoebe, a servant of the church in Cenchrea. 2I ask you to
receive her in the Lord in a way worthy of the
saints and to give her any help she may need
from you, for she has been a great help to
many people, including me.

3Greet Priscilla and Aquila, my fellow-workers
in Christ Jesus. 4They risked their lives for
me. Not only I but all the churches of the
Gentiles are grateful to them.
5Greet also the church that meets at their
house.
Greet my dear friend Epenetus, who was the
first convert to Christ in the province of
Asia.
6Greet Mary, who worked very hard for you.
7Greet Andronicus and Junias, my relatives
who have been in prison with me. They are
outstanding among the apostles, and they
were in Christ before I was.
8Greet Ampliatus, whom I love in the Lord.
16Greet one another with a holy kiss.
All the churches of Christ send greetings.

Life is about relationships. The reason Paul impacted the way he did was because of the way he loved. Who are the people God has given you to love? Are you making the most of these relationships?

Paul is remembered for being a top missionary. He lived a full life tripping from town to town to preach about Jesus, risking his life and limb to get his Saviour a hearing, taking on kings and emperors, rocking prisons and still having time to write most of the New Testament. He is an action-man Christian. Often if we look at his life we just focus on his achievements. And they are great.

But what we can miss when we look at his life are his relationships. If you turn to the end of most of his letters you get a list of names of people he wants to greet. All these are people Paul wants to give messages to. Often they are people he has stayed with for a number of years on his travels. People such as Priscilla and Aquila, whom he stayed with for over two years. Paul's life might seem to us to be a series of mission trips to different places but for him it was all about relationships. This is what caused him his tears and his laughter. His letters aren't written as inspirational texts to get into the Bible but in response to people he cares for who are going through it.

Best intentions

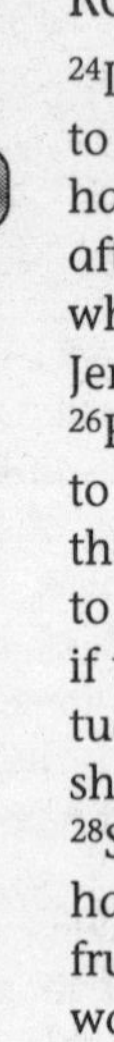

Romans 15:24–8

[24]I plan to do so when I go to Spain. I hope
to visit you while passing through and to
have you assist me on my journey there,
after I have enjoyed your company for a
while. [25]Now, however, I am on my way to
Jerusalem in the service of the saints there.
[26]For Macedonia and Achaia were pleased
to make a contribution for the poor among
the saints in Jerusalem. [27]They were pleased
to do it, and indeed they owe it to them. For
if the Gentiles have shared in the Jews' spiritual blessings, they owe it to the Jews to
share with them their material blessings.
[28]So after I have completed this task and
have made sure that they have received this
fruit, I will go to Spain and visit you on the
way.

We do things for God with specific intentions in mind, but we must allow him to achieve whatever he wants with them. Give all you do and intend to do for him over to him.

One of my most embarrassing moments was when I helped some boys on the estate I lived on take the wheel off their dad's car. It was embarrassing because it turned out not to be their dad's car. But amazingly it provided me with an opportunity to get to know the guy who ran out of his house shouting that his car only had three wheels. Over the next months we had great chats about God.

Often things we do with the best of intentions actually turn out to achieve something else completely different than what we intended. Romans is probably the best of all Paul's writing. It is the most inspiring, complex and wise of letters, and it has changed the lives of more people than any of the others. And it continues to do so.

But Paul wrote it because he wanted to go to Spain, and as they didn't have planes he needed a place to stop over. He wrote this letter to introduce himself personally to the Church in Rome so that he would have a comfy bed to stay in on his way to Benidorm. The thing is he probably never got to Spain. But in God's hand the book he wrote because he intended to get there achieved more than he could ever have imagined.

Freedom

Acts 28:16, 23–6, 28–31

16When we got to Rome, Paul was allowed to
live by himself, with a soldier to guard him.
23They arranged to meet Paul on a certain
day, and came in even larger numbers to the
place where he was staying. From morning till
evening he explained and declared to them the
kingdom of God and tried to convince them
about Jesus from the Law of Moses and from the
Prophets. 24Some were convinced by what he
said, but others would not believe. 25They dis-
agreed among themselves and began to leave
after Paul had made this final statement: "The Holy Spirit spoke the
truth to your forefathers when he said through Isaiah the prophet:

26"'Go to this people and say,
"You will be ever hearing but never understanding;
you will be ever seeing but never perceiving."

28"Therefore I want you to know that God's salvation has been
sent to the Gentiles, and they will listen!"
30For two whole years Paul stayed there in his own rented house
and welcomed all who came to see him. 31Boldly and without hindrance he preached the kingdom of God and taught about the Lord
Jesus Christ.

Whatever our circumstances are, if we are where God wants us, he will always be free to achieve all he wants. Even if it means being in chains, there is no more privileged place in the world.

In this day and age I'd guess we prize our freedom above anything else. Not only does Mrs Liberty stand over America but apparently more top twenty chart songs use the 'f' word than any other, apart from love and sex that is. And let's make no mistake, freedom is an extraordinarily wonderful thing to have.

But the thing about all these people in the Bible is that they had none of the liberties that we value, but they still seemed to have been wildly free, especially our old mate Paul. He had none of our so-called freedoms which we prize so highly. He didn't have our choice when it came to shopping, music or travel, and what's more he wasn't free to say whatever he wanted to say – he got into all sorts of trouble for it. And now at the end of his life he is under house arrest in Rome. His mouth has got him into trouble again, just because he has been using it to speak God's words of freedom.

So here in a small house guarded by soldiers in Rome, Paul is most definitely not free. But in a way he is, as he spends all day and night gossiping the gospel to anyone and everyone who will listen. Even though he can't get out, the news of God's love does. Paul might be imprisoned but God's work isn't: the last verse of the book tells us God's message of freedom goes out 'without hindrance'.

JOSHUA

Having wandered around the desert for forty years the Israelites needed a strong leader. Joshua had distinguished himself and was chosen as Moses' successor. This is the tale of what happened next, and it's a rip-roaring, blood and guts kind of a tale. Joshua is most definitely The Man, and he did a nice line in humble submission before God as well.

Preparation

Joshua 2:1–8

1 Then Joshua son of Nun secretly sent two
spies from Shittim. "Go, look over the
land," he said, "especially Jericho." So
they went and entered the house of a
prostitute named Rahab and stayed there.
2 The king of Jericho was told, "Look!
Some of the Israelites have come here
tonight to spy out the land." 3 So the king
of Jericho sent this message to Rahab:
"Bring out the men who came to you and
entered your house, because they have
come to spy out the whole land."
4 But the woman had taken the two
men and hidden them. She said, "Yes, the
men came to me, but I did not know
where they had come from. 5 At dusk,
when it was time to close the city gate,
the men left. I don't know which way they
went. Go after them quickly. You may
catch up with them." 6 (But she had taken
them up to the roof and hidden them
under the stalks of flax she had laid out
on the roof.) 7 So the men set out in pur-
suit of the spies on the road that leads to
the fords of the Jordan, and as soon as the
pursuers had gone out, the gate was shut.
8 Before the spies lay down for the
night, she went up on the roof

Whom do you respect? Whom do you expect to learn from? Does your list include any Rahabs?

SEARCH

With three days to go before leading his people into Canaan, Joshua does something sensible: he sends out spies. Espionage has played an important part in warfare both before and since, and God worked through this incident to great effect.

The spies meet Rahab, a prostitute. Bearing in mind her social position, the fact that she lives in the city wall paints a nice picture. She is on the fringes of society, pushed out by a structure that considers her to be of little worth.

It's a different story where God's concerned, and Rahab proves to be a valuable resource, enabling the spies to escape and make sure that Joshua is fully prepared for the attack on the city. Later, in return for her help, she is told to tie a scarlet cord in her window, as a sign that Joshua's army are not to hurt her. Remind you of anything? It's a replay of the Passover story, where the Israelites painted blood on their houses to show that their sacrifice had been made, so that God's judgment would pass them by.

Rahab, a prostitute on the edge of society, was treated like an Israelite. What's more, her courage and quick thinking was a huge favour and act of great kindness. As the spies return, the crew are ready to move out. Three wasted days? Not at all, as God underlined a massively important message: the Israelites may have been his people (he may even have been about to back them up as they fought for survival) but they were not to forget that there were unlikely people out there who could still teach them a thing or two.

Whose side?

Joshua 5:13–15

13Now when Joshua was
near Jericho, he looked
up and saw a man
standing in front of him
with a drawn sword in
his hand. Joshua went
up to him and asked,
"Are you for us or for our
enemies?"
14"Neither," he replied,
"but as commander of
the army of the Lord I
have now come." Then
Joshua fell face down to
the ground in reverence,
and asked him, "What
message does my Lord
have for his servant?"
15The commander of
the Lord's army replied,
"Take off your sandals,
for the place where you
are standing is holy."
And Joshua did so.

SEARCH

This heavenly figure is a bit out of the blue, to say the least. It's not assuming too much to suggest that Joshua might have been just a tad nervous at this point – what with the entire nation of Israelites behind him, waiting for him to lead them to victory – and the appearance of a single bloke waving a sword might not have come at the best time. There was no turning back as the Jordan had been crossed, and Joshua's question is both utterly wrong and completely understandable.

For Joshua this battle was about the Israelites against the Canaanites. Was God on his side? Not quite: this was about far more than two nations, one being backed by the Almighty. This was God's battle, and the real question was whether Joshua was on God's side. He is told to take off his shoes, a clear reminder that we fight on God's terms, not our own.

Knowing that we're just part of one large army might not do wonders for our ego, but it does introduce a fresh thought: if it's God's army with which we're fighting then the ultimate responsibility rests on his shoulders.

GO

I don't know about you, but judging by the state of my puny shoulders, that's very good news indeed.

The fight

Joshua 6:1–5

[1]Now Jericho was tightly
shut up because of the
Israelites. No-one went
out and no-one came in.
[2]Then the Lord said to
Joshua, "See, I have
delivered Jericho into
your hands, along with
its king and its fighting
men. [3]March around the
city once with all the
armed men. Do this for
six days. [4]Make seven
priests carry trumpets of
rams' horns in front of
the ark. On the seventh
day, march around the
city seven times, with the
priests blowing the trum-
pets. [5]When you hear
them sound a long blast
on the trumpets, make
all the people give a loud
shout; then the wall of
the city will collapse and
the people will go up,
every man straight in."

SEARCH

Forget the fact that this is the start of a new chapter, it reads better as a continuation of the scene we left last time. So there's Joshua, shoes off, chatting with someone who calls himself 'the commander of the army of the Lord'. Snappy title.

But in case we had forgotten that this was God's battle, the commands here are dripping with clues. Just take the number 'seven' for example. You've got seven priests, seven trumpets, seven days, seven circuits, the seventh day: perhaps someone is trying to say something. Seven was traditionally used as an indication of godly perfection and completion, and this battle certainly had the mark of God on it.

It all happened just as Joshua was commanded, and with the city out of the way the path was clear for them to deal with the kingdoms they had now split. Military campaigns followed to deal with the threats to the north and the south.

God's commander – whether you think that it was God in human form, or God speaking through another being – called the shots, not only in this battle but in future ones too. Joshua's bravery and military wisdom would have counted for little had he not been able to hear and had he not decided to obey his Lord.

GO

To have talent is one thing, but obedience is another league altogether.

Lessons learnt

Joshua 23:9–13

9"The Lord has driven
out before you great and
powerful nations; to this
day no-one has been
able to withstand you.
10One of you routs a
thousand, because the
Lord your God fights for
you, just as he promised.
11So be very careful to
love the Lord your God.
12"But if you turn away
and ally yourselves with
the survivors of these
nations that remain
among you and if you
intermarry with them
and associate with them,
13then you may be sure
that the Lord your God
will no longer drive out
these nations before you.
Instead, they will become
snares and traps for you,
whips on your backs and
thorns in your eyes, until
you perish from this
good land, which the
Lord your God has given
you."

SEARCH

After a long life crammed with bloodstained victory and divinely-assisted victory, Joshua wraps it up. He looks back at the victories and reminds the people of the part that God has played in them. But if all this has been God showing his generous side, then you could argue that the people could take things a little easier from then on. If the victories have just been gifts, then why bother with all those 'if you turn away' warnings?

Just as we saw at the start, it has been God's battle that they have been fighting all along. God has been the one who has saved them, he has been the one who has directed them, the one who has given them success way beyond their abilities. The job is not finished: God is still intent on building a nation that will give glory to him and be a light to all those that surround it.

It all goes back to the early stories: Adam and Eve giving in to the temptation to raise themselves up to be like God; Noah's contemporaries ignoring God and concentrating solely on themselves; the people at Shinar building a tower to boost their own reputation. Human nature has a definite kink in it, leading us towards self-obsession and an 'I'm-all-right-Jack' kind of attitude. Joshua's words fight against that, and God's actions try to keep us well on track, focused on him and reminded of just whose battle it is that we're fighting.

GO

We're not the sole players in a game constructed purely for our amusement. We're here to do business: to follow God.

Luke Pt. II

Jesus' manifesto

It's back to the book of Luke to pick up more of the Jesus story. We all know about the manger and the cross, but what did he actually *do* with the rest of his life?

Matt Bird

Luke 4:16–24

Find some space and reflect with God about what you value most in your life and what you sense God wants you to do for him.

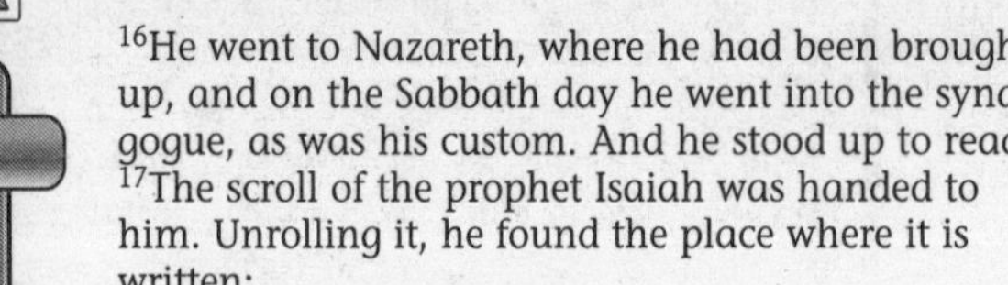

16 He went to Nazareth, where he had been brought
up, and on the Sabbath day he went into the synagogue, as was his custom. And he stood up to read.
17 The scroll of the prophet Isaiah was handed to
him. Unrolling it, he found the place where it is
written:

18 "The Spirit of the Lord is on me,
because he has anointed me
to preach good news to the poor.
He has sent me to proclaim freedom for the prisoners
and recovery of sight for the blind,
to release the oppressed,
19 to proclaim the year of the Lord's favour."

20 Then he rolled up the scroll, gave it back to the attendant and sat
down. The eyes of everyone in the synagogue were fastened on him,
21 and he began by saying to them, "Today this scripture is fulfilled in
your hearing."
22 All spoke well of him and were amazed at the gracious words that
came from his lips. "Isn't this Joseph's son?" they asked.
23 Jesus said to them, "Surely you will quote this proverb to me:
'Physician, heal yourself! Do here in your home town what we have
heard that you did in Capernaum.'"
24 "I tell you the truth," he continued, "no prophet is accepted in his
home town."

The first time you stand up publicly in your home church can be a bit scary. I'm sure it must have been the same for Jesus as he stood up in his local synagogue in Nazareth. The Spirit of God moved on him and he read Isaiah 61:1–2. People were amazed: it sounded very much like Jesus was claiming the words as his personal manifesto! This is where his public ministry of speaking, caring and miracles began.

Jesus' manifesto has a wonderful roundedness and completeness to it, containing promises of words of God (preaching and proclamation), works of God (good news for the poor and freedom for the prisoners) and wonders of God (sight for the blind). Just as in politics today there are pressure groups who want to emphasise one issue or policy above others, there have been groups within the Church that have wanted to emphasise preaching, social action or miracles more than the others. However, the heart of God wants meaningful words, actions and miracles which cannot be separated.

Healing and no healing

Luke 5:12–16

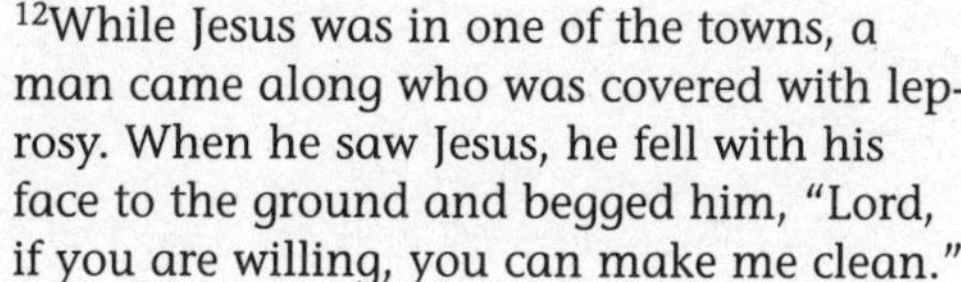

[12]While Jesus was in one of the towns, a
man came along who was covered with leprosy. When he saw Jesus, he fell with his
face to the ground and begged him, "Lord,
if you are willing, you can make me clean."
[13]Jesus reached out his hand and touched
the man. "I am willing," he said. "Be
clean!" And immediately the leprosy left
him.
[14]Then Jesus ordered him, "Don't tell anyone, but go, show yourself to the priest and
offer the sacrifices that Moses commanded
for your cleansing, as a testimony to them."
[15]Yet the news about him spread all the
more, so that crowds of people came to hear
him and to be healed of their sicknesses.
[16]But Jesus often withdrew to lonely places
and prayed.

Thank God for a healing you have heard of or seen. Reflect upon someone you know who has suffered despite prayers for healing. Ask God to show you someone today that you can pray for.

A man with a horrid skin disease came to Jesus, and bowed his face and pleaded with Jesus to heal him. This kind of act certainly gave Jesus public acclaim that he had never known in the carpentry trade, so he ordered the man to tell no one that he had been healed.

The greatest question about healing today is: why doesn't everyone who is prayed for get healed? My understanding is that at present we are caught in a world that is imperfect where sickness, injustice, hate and rebellion rule. However, God is in the business of building his perfect kingdom of health, justice, love and peace on earth. The reality is that we are caught between the now and not yet of this kingdom. In the meantime some people are miraculously healed and others are painfully not. So we need to pray in faith but also in sensitivity.

Authenticity

Luke 6:41–9

[41]"Why do you look at the speck of sawdust in your
brother's eye and pay no attention to the plank in
your own eye? [42]How can you say to your brother,
'Brother, let me take the speck out of your eye,' when
you yourself fail to see the plank in your own eye? You
hypocrite, first take the plank out of your eye, and
then you will see clearly to remove the speck from
your brother's eye.
[43]"No good tree bears bad fruit, nor does a bad tree
bear good fruit. [44]Each tree is recognised by its own
fruit. People do not pick figs from thorn-bushes, or
grapes from briers. [45]The good man brings good things
out of the good stored up in his heart, and the evil
man brings evil things out of the evil stored up in his
heart. For out of the overflow of his heart his mouth
speaks.
[46]"Why do you call me, 'Lord, Lord,' and do not do
what I say? [47]I will show you what he is like who
comes to me and hears my words and puts them into
practice. [48]He is like a man building a house, who dug
down deep and laid the foundation on rock. When the
flood came, the torrent struck that house but could not
shake it, because it was well built. [49]But the one who
hears my words and does not put them into practice is
like a man who built a house on the ground without a
foundation. The moment the torrent struck that house,
it collapsed and its destruction was complete."

What are the aspects of your life that you are not proud of? Being honest, are you ever two faced? Pray and ask God to change your heart that you might behave all of what you believe.

Well, we all know what it's like to have some self-righteous Christian point their finger at some aspect of our life and judge our behaviour. As Jesus subtly says, 'Don't point out the speck of sawdust in someone else's eye when you've a plank in your own.' What we are is what we do. If we are good people our lives display goodness, and the converse is true: if we are people of bad intent our lives will show us up. There are plenty of Christians around who use all the right language and yet who don't use the right behaviour. As Jesus puts it, it is as different as building on sand or building on rock.

The three challenges that Jesus makes here are all to do with our authenticity. Do we accuse people of one thing and do it ourselves? Are we people of goodness? Do we do what we claim to be? Christian discipleship is the process of behaving what we believe, of living genuinely transparent lives, shaking off hypocrisy and lies and pursuing integrity and authenticity.

Faith of the unchurched

Luke 7:2–10

2There a centurion's servant, whom his master
valued highly, was sick and about to die. 3The
centurion heard of Jesus and sent some elders
of the Jews to him, asking him to come and
heal his servant. 4When they came to Jesus,
they pleaded earnestly with him, "This man
deserves to have you do this, 5because he loves
our nation and has built our synagogue." 6So
Jesus went with them.

He was not far from the house when the
centurion sent friends to say to him: "Lord,
don't trouble yourself, for I do not deserve to
have you come under my roof. 7That is why I
did not even consider myself worthy to come
to you. But say the word, and my servant will
be healed. 8For I myself am a man under
authority, with soldiers under me. I tell this
one, 'Go', and he goes; and that one, 'Come',
and he comes. I say to my servant, 'Do this',
and he does it."

9When Jesus heard this, he was amazed at
him, and turning to the crowd following him,
he said, "I tell you, I have not found such
great faith even in Israel." 10Then the men
who had been sent returned to the house and
found the servant well.

In what ways have you seen faith amongst your friends? How can you encourage your church to exist to stir faith amongst the unchurched? In what ways can you help make your church a more inclusive place?

This account of a healing is more importantly a parable to the Jews that God is for the Gentiles (non-Jews), or for what we might call the unchurched. In the preceding centuries God had chosen the nation of Israel to make himself known to the nations. At the time of Jesus Israel had become self-indulgent and had lost any sense of God's mission to the nations. The Israelite faith had become an exclusive self-focused faith for 'insiders'. In many senses it was a little like the Church of today that has frequently lost sight of its mission to the unchurched.

The centurion in this story was commended for his massive faith, despite the fact that many might have been surprised to see any faith at all in a non-Jew. This 'faith of the unchurched' can still be found today, and the Church is often surprised to catch those who've never been a part of Christianity believing in Jesus.

How much do you love Jesus?

Luke 7:37–43, 48–9

37When a woman who had lived a sinful life
in that town learned that Jesus was eating at
the Pharisee's house, she brought an alabaster
jar of perfume, 38and as she stood behind him
at his feet weeping, she began to wet his feet
with her tears. Then she wiped them with her
hair, kissed them and poured perfume on
them.

39When the Pharisee who had invited him
saw this, he said to himself, "If this man were
a prophet, he would know who is touching
him and what kind of woman she is—that she
is a sinner."

40Jesus answered him, "Simon, I have something to tell you."

"Tell me, teacher," he said.

41"Two men owed money to a certain
money-lender. One owed him five hundred
denarii, and the other fifty. 42Neither of them
had the money to pay him back, so he cancelled the debts of both. Now which of them
will love him more?"

43Simon replied, "I suppose the one who had
the bigger debt cancelled."

"You have judged correctly," Jesus said.

48Then Jesus said to her, "Your sins are forgiven."

49The other guests began to say among
themselves, "Who is this who even forgives
sins?"

How much do you love Jesus? How big are your mistakes? How do the mistakes you make and the forgiveness you need change your love for Jesus? Pray and ask God to help you love him more today.

Here Luke tells a story within a story. Alongside the tale of a woman of questionable morals is another story of two men owing different amounts who were forgiven. Again we see Jesus' concern for people who are on the margins of society, those with questionable morals, those with debt and need of forgiveness. The point of both of these stories is that those who need and experience most forgiveness from Jesus will love him most.

Paying the cost

Luke 9:22–7

22 And he said, "The Son of Man must suffer
many things and be rejected by the elders,
chief priests and teachers of the law, and he
must be killed and on the third day be
raised to life."
23 Then he said to them all: "If anyone
would come after me, he must deny himself
and take up his cross daily and follow me.
24 For whoever wants to save his life will lose
it, but whoever loses his life for me will save
it. 25 What good is it for a man to gain the
whole world, and yet lose or forfeit his very
self? 26 If anyone is ashamed of me and my
words, the Son of Man will be ashamed of
him when he comes in his glory and in the
glory of the Father and of the holy angels.
27 I tell you the truth, some who are standing here will not taste death before they see
the kingdom of God."

Do you have any spoken or unspoken limits on what you would be willing to do, and where you would be willing to go for God? How do you react when you get laughed at because you are a Christian? Pray and offer your life in utter surrender to God even in the face of opposition.

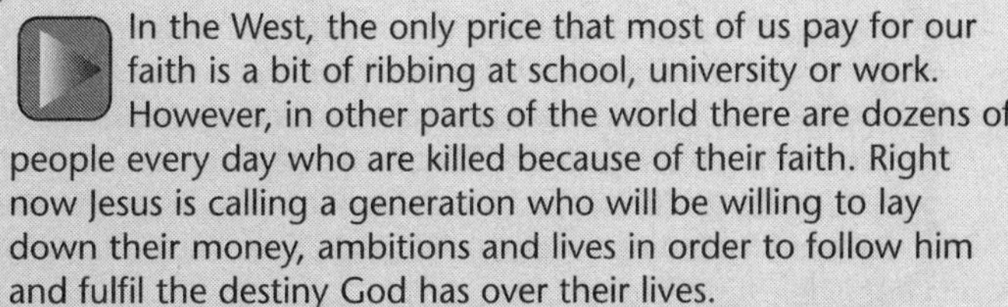

In the West, the only price that most of us pay for our faith is a bit of ribbing at school, university or work. However, in other parts of the world there are dozens of people every day who are killed because of their faith. Right now Jesus is calling a generation who will be willing to lay down their money, ambitions and lives in order to follow him and fulfil the destiny God has over their lives.

The Jesus prayer

Luke 11:1–4

[1]One day Jesus was praying in a certain
place. When he finished, one of his disciples
said to him, "Lord, teach us to pray, just as
John taught his disciples."
[2]He said to them, "When you pray, say:

"'Father,
hallowed be your name,
your kingdom come.
[3]Give us each day our daily bread.
[4]Forgive us our sins,
for we also forgive everyone who sins against us.
And lead us not into temptation.'"

Pray using the six Ps if you think that might be helpful to you. You might like to use the six Ps as a framework to write a prayer in your own words.

The way that Jesus lived his life is the definitive example of the way that we should live our lives.

This prayer that Jesus taught his disciples has often been used as a prayer in many churches, but it can also be used as a helpful shape for prayer. It can be summed up by the six Ps: Personally, Power, Purpose, Provision, Pardon, Protection.

God knows

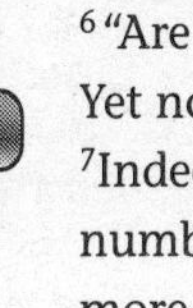

Luke 12:6–7

6 "Are not five sparrows sold for two pennies?
Yet not one of them is forgotten by God.
7 Indeed, the very hairs of your head are all
numbered. Don't be afraid; you are worth
more than many sparrows."

What difference does it make to remember that God knows your needs? How does it make you feel to realise that God knows your secrets? Pray and ask God to forgive you your history and to meet your needs today.

Jesus said that even something as seemingly insignificant as five sparrows sold for two pennies is known by God. You could say that a puppy isn't sold without God knowing, or an e-mail isn't sent without him knowing. How much more important are we than a puppy or an e-mail? Then how much more does God know everything there is to know about us? He simply knows.

There isn't anything that goes on in this world that God doesn't know about. The theologians call it 'omniscience' – 'omni' meaning all and 'science' meaning knowledge. God knows what we do at school or university, in our jobs, with our bank accounts, in our bedrooms and down the pub. God knows our needs, wants, thoughts, feelings and desires. God knows!

Everyone counts

Luke 15:1–9

1Now the tax collectors and "sinners" were
all gathering round to hear him. 2But the
Pharisees and the teachers of the law mut-
tered, "This man welcomes sinners, and eats
with them."
3Then Jesus told them this parable:
4"Suppose one of you has a hundred sheep
and loses one of them. Does he not leave
the ninety-nine in the open country and go
after the lost sheep until he finds it? 5And
when he finds it, he joyfully puts it on his
shoulders 6and goes home. Then he calls his
friends and neighbours together and says,
'Rejoice with me; I have found my lost
sheep.' 7I tell you that in the same way
there will be more rejoicing in heaven over
one sinner who repents than over ninety-
nine righteous persons who do not need to
repent.
8"Or suppose a woman has ten silver
coins and loses one. Does she not light a
lamp, sweep the house and search carefully
until she finds it? 9And when she finds it,
she calls her friends and neighbours together and says, 'Rejoice with me; I have found
my lost coin.'"

As one person how are you going to make your life count for others? What are you willing to risk so that the lost might be found? Pray and worship God for the fact that you were lost and now are found.

This isn't quite a *Stars Wars* trilogy but a 'Lost and Found' trilogy. The sheep, the coin, the son (15:11–32): all lost and found. To God every person counts. One in one hundred, one in ten, or one in two. When we are alone and isolated, desperate and distraught it matters to God. It matters so much that he is even willing to risk the found for the lost. When we are found there is great rejoicing, celebrating and partying in heaven.

Kingdom now

Luke 17:20–1

[20]Once, having been asked by the Pharisees
when the kingdom of God would come,
Jesus replied, "The kingdom of God does not
come with your careful observation, [21]nor
will people say, 'Here it is,' or 'There it is,'
because the kingdom of God is within you."

Where can you see the kingdom of God in your life? What is the kingdom of God causing to happen? Pray that God's kingdom might come on earth as it is in heaven.

The substance of Jesus' ministry was the kingdom of God. Jesus broke out of old religion and ushered in the dynamic presence and rule of God, namely the kingdom of God. Through Jesus' life the kingdom – which was far off and distant – became close and nearby. Wherever love, justice, peace, healing, forgiveness, righteousness are at work the kingdom of God is present.

Childlike faith

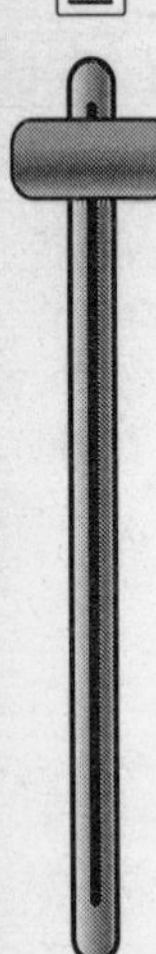

Luke 18:15–17

15People were also bringing babies to Jesus
to have him touch them. When the disciples
saw this, they rebuked them. 16But Jesus
called the children to him and said, "Let the
little children come to me, and do not hinder them, for the kingdom of God belongs
to such as these. 17I tell you the truth, anyone who will not receive the kingdom of
God like a little child will never enter it."

Are there hurtful experiences you have had that have numbed your childlike ability to trust? Reflect on the total reliability of God who loves and never fails. Pray and ask for God's healing.

The disciples are making mistakes and learning again, giving us a few lessons in the process.

The big question for us is: what is it about little children that we need to be like in order to receive the kingdom of God? In my limited experience of little children they can be many things ranging from adorable to detestable. What I think Jesus had in mind is that trusting thing that children are so good at. It is that childlike trust in God that we need in order to receive the kingdom of God.

Too busy is too busy

Luke 18:35–42

35As Jesus approached Jericho, a blind man
was sitting by the roadside begging. 36When
he heard the crowd going by, he asked what
was happening. 37They told him, "Jesus of
Nazareth is passing by."
38He called out, "Jesus, Son of David, have
mercy on me!"
39Those who led the way rebuked him and
told him to be quiet, but he shouted all the
more, "Son of David, have mercy on me!"
40Jesus stopped and ordered the man to be
brought to him. When he came near, Jesus
asked him, 41"What do you want me to do
for you?"
"Lord, I want to see," he replied.
42Jesus said to him, "Receive your sight;
your faith has healed you."

Pray by finding a very still place to quieten and still your mind and allow God to show you his priorities for the people you meet.

When you have read this sentence close your eyes and imagine you were the blind man in the story. Listen to all the noises you would have heard, the smells that might have been wafting around and replay the scene. Now reread the story of the blind man. Jesus was a man with a purpose and yet he was never too busy for what and who really mattered. It is easy for our lives and diaries to become so full that what and who really matters gets pushed out. If we are rushing so much that we have no love and compassion to show a person in need, then we are too busy. Quite simply if we are too busy we are too busy.

When was the last time you allowed your life to be interrupted to care for someone in need? Is your life too busy to be of use to what God might want you to do today?

Loadsamoney

Luke 19:2–10

2A man was there by the name of
Zacchaeus; he was a chief tax collector and
was wealthy. 3He wanted to see who Jesus
was, but being a short man he could not,
because of the crowd. 4So he ran ahead and
climbed a sycamore-fig tree to see him,
since Jesus was coming that way.
5When Jesus reached the spot, he looked
up and said to him, "Zacchaeus, come
down immediately. I must stay at your
house today." 6So he came down at once
and welcomed him gladly.
7All the people saw this and began to
mutter, "He has gone to be the guest of a
'sinner'."
8But Zacchaeus stood up and said to the
Lord, "Look, Lord! Here and now I give half
of my possessions to the poor, and if I have
cheated anybody out of anything, I will pay
back four times the amount."
9Jesus said to him, "Today salvation has
come to this house, because this man, too,
is a son of Abraham. 10For the Son of Man
came to seek and to save what was lost."

Pray and ask God to bring salvation to those who need to know his provision.

Well, here's Zacchaeus, your loadsamoney government official. Yet despite this he knew there was more to life, so when Jesus did a gig in his town he went to great lengths to see him. Jesus did the unexpected by not only taking a detour to Zac's house, but by offering the man salvation. When we think about how Zac experienced salvation we see how he reordered the priorities of his life, wealth and honesty. Then there were the 'poor' who were hanging around the area that day: getting Zac's payback was certainly the good news of salvation for them!

Could you allow God to reorder your money (whether pocket money, part-time job income, student grant or serious salary) so you give more away? What could you do to show God's provision to the poor?

Gideon

The usual suspects

No one expected Gideon to be used so mightily by God – least of all Gideon himself.

Judges 6:1–6

1Again the Israelites did evil in the eyes of
the Lord, and for seven years he gave them
into the hands of the Midianites. 2Because
the power of Midian was so oppressive, the
Israelites prepared shelters for themselves in
mountain clefts, caves and strongholds.
3Whenever the Israelites planted their crops,
the Midianites, Amalekites and other eastern peoples invaded the country. 4They
camped on the land and ruined the crops
all the way to Gaza and did not spare a living thing for Israel, neither sheep nor cattle
nor donkeys. 5They came up with their livestock and their tents like swarms of locusts.
It was impossible to count the men and
their camels; they invaded the land to rav-
age it. 6Midian so impoverished the
Israelites that they cried out to the Lord for
help.

Life with God isn't about getting away with as much selfishness as we can.

We join the story midway through another cycle: the Israelites had wandered away from God who would soon send someone to lead them back towards him and get them out of trouble with their pesky neighbours. We're told that it was the Midianites who were making life tough this time. There may not have been many of them, but these Midianites were sneaky, being perhaps the first to use their camels as part of their guerrilla warfare. What made it tougher was the fact that they were related: these desert nomads were descended from Abraham's second wife, Keturah.

God's response is becoming increasing familiar: 'I said I'd look after you if you stuck with me, but you went off and started worshipping other gods.' The fact is that it'll get said again and again as his people go through their seasons of worship and wandering, but for the moment they need help and God is not about to let them go under.

It can be tempting to assume that God will step in and save the day when our wandering hearts take us away from him, and the cycles shown through the book of Judges do show how fantastically gracious and loving God is.

Why Gideon?

Judges 6:11–16

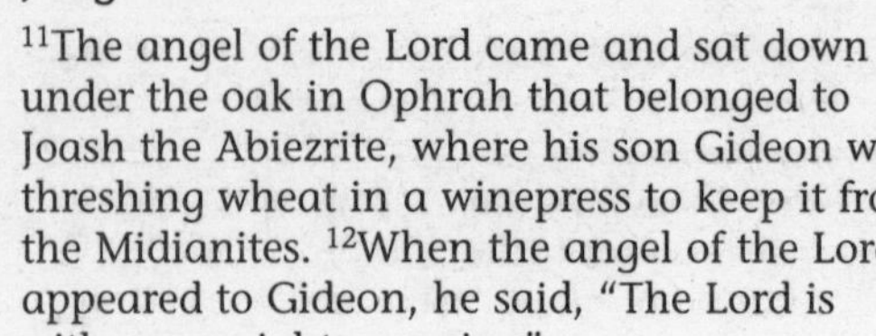

11 The angel of the Lord came and sat down
under the oak in Ophrah that belonged to
Joash the Abiezrite, where his son Gideon was
threshing wheat in a winepress to keep it from
the Midianites. 12 When the angel of the Lord
appeared to Gideon, he said, "The Lord is
with you, mighty warrior."
13 "But sir," Gideon replied, "if the Lord is
with us, why has all this happened to us?
Where are all his wonders that our fathers
told us about when they said, 'Did not the
Lord bring us up out of Egypt?' But now the
Lord has abandoned us and put us into the
hand of Midian."
14 The Lord turned to him and said, "Go in
the strength you have and save Israel out of
Midian's hand. Am I not sending you?"
15 "Lord," Gideon asked, "how can I save
Israel? My clan is the weakest in Manasseh,
and I am the least in my family."
16 The Lord answered, "I will be with you,
and you will strike down all the Midianites
together."

Don't try and force yourself into ambitions that don't fit your talents: God will use you in a way as unique as the combination of talents and abilities he has placed in you.

So why did God choose Gideon? After all, Gideon wasn't sure himself – was God getting desperate? In some ways Gideon's reaction to the Angel of the Lord gives a hint that he wasn't on top spiritual form. He failed to remember God's warning to Israel about following him and tried to get out of it by claiming that he was a nobody (not quite true as verse 27 mentions that he had a fair few servants).

So why Gideon? The key is in verse 14: 'go in the strength you have'. Gideon was unique. His experiences, outlook and knowledge all made him the right man for the job. Take the first mention of him in this passage. Instead of threshing his wheat out in the open where the wind could blow away the unwanted chaff, Gideon's working out of sight of the roving Midianites. Using a winepress – a sunken, confined pit – was a sneaky idea, and, as we see later on, sneaky ideas were just what God had in mind.

In the New Testament Paul writes about how our roles in life should be determined by the gifts that God has given us (1 Corinthians 12:1–11). Gideon may not have been a great spiritual leader, but he was a superb fighter, a real master of surprise.

Action

Judges 6:27–32

27So Gideon took ten of his servants and did as
the Lord told him. But because he was afraid of
his family and the men of the town, he did it at
night rather than in the daytime.
28In the morning when the men of the town got
up, there was Baal's altar, demolished, with the
Asherah pole beside it cut down and the second
bull sacrificed on the newly-built altar!
29They asked each other, "Who did this?"
When they carefully investigated, they were
told, "Gideon son of Joash did it."
30The men of the town demanded of Joash,
"Bring out your son. He must die, because he has
broken down Baal's altar and cut down the Asherah
pole beside it."
31But Joash replied to the hostile crowd around him,
"Are you going to plead Baal's cause? Are you trying
to save him? Whoever fights for him shall be put to
death by morning! If Baal really is a god, he can
defend himself when someone breaks down his altar."
32So that day they called Gideon "Jerub-Baal," saying,
"Let Baal contend with him," because he broke down
Baal's altar.

Even if Gideon's previous achievements hadn't been quite as grand, God was prepared to start afresh with his servant, encouraging him to do the right thing.

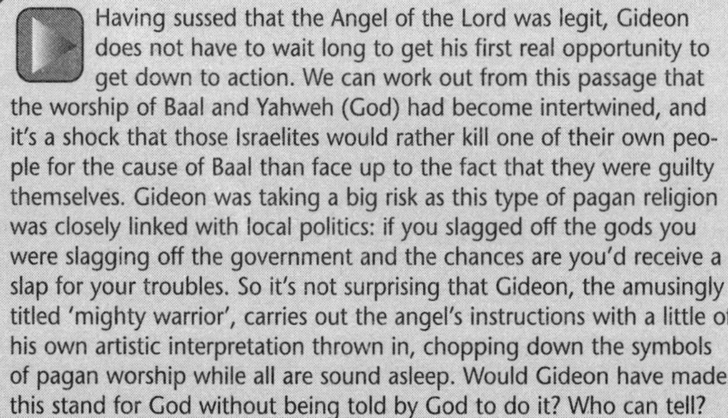

Having sussed that the Angel of the Lord was legit, Gideon does not have to wait long to get his first real opportunity to get down to action. We can work out from this passage that the worship of Baal and Yahweh (God) had become intertwined, and it's a shock that those Israelites would rather kill one of their own people for the cause of Baal than face up to the fact that they were guilty themselves. Gideon was taking a big risk as this type of pagan religion was closely linked with local politics: if you slagged off the gods you were slagging off the government and the chances are you'd receive a slap for your troubles. So it's not surprising that Gideon, the amusingly titled 'mighty warrior', carries out the angel's instructions with a little of his own artistic interpretation thrown in, chopping down the symbols of pagan worship while all are sound asleep. Would Gideon have made this stand for God without being told by God to do it? Who can tell?

Fleeced

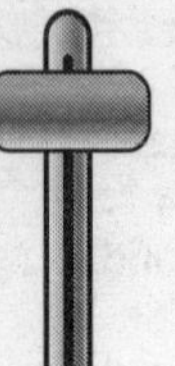

Judges 6:33–40

33Now all the Midianites, Amalekites and other eastern peoples joined forces and crossed over the Jordan and camped in the Valley of Jezreel. 34Then the Spirit of the Lord came upon Gideon, and he blew a trumpet, summoning the Abiezrites to follow him. 35He sent messengers throughout Manasseh, calling them to arms, and also into Asher, Zebulun and Naphtali, so that they too went up to meet them.

36Gideon said to God, "If you will save Israel by my hand as you have promised—37look, I will place a wool fleece on the threshing-floor. If there is dew only on the fleece and all the ground is dry, then I will know that you will save Israel by my hand, as you said." 38And that is what happened. Gideon rose early the next day; he squeezed the fleece and wrung out the dew—a bowlful of water.

39Then Gideon said to God, "Do not be angry with me. Let me make just one more request. Allow me one more test with the fleece. This time make the fleece dry and the ground covered with dew." 40That night God did so. Only the fleece was dry; all the ground was covered with dew.

Looking for God-inspired direction? Want to know the secret formula for getting God's view? Here you go: pray and study the Bible.

Ah yes, the fleece. Christians have developed a taste for mimicking Gideon's actions here by doing their own bit of 'laying fleeces' whenever they happen to be unsure about what course of action God might want them to take. 'God,' they may say, 'I'm not sure if this is the right job for me to take. If it is the right one, please make my cat speak in Spanish right now.'

While the writer of the story doesn't come out and say that Gideon's actions were wrong, there are more than a few hints that his deeds weren't exactly spot on. Gideon's motives were right: he wanted to defeat the Midianites, so that's good. But he didn't trust God. Gideon had already witnessed one miracle (the fire coming from the rock – see 6:21) which had accompanied the command (twice) to go and sort the Midianites out. Now he wanted even more confirmation. There's a hint that he knew God might not be best pleased with the whole deal, as he asks him not to be angry.

Gideon limited God by asking him to perform a couple of fairly unimpressive miracles – let's face it, a soggy or dry blanket doesn't even come close to burning bushes, parted seas or floating axe heads. Sure, decisions that we make need to be thought about, and we need God's perspective to open our eyes, but let's not try to make God into a performing monkey. One last thing: note that at first Gideon called all the people together when the Spirit of God was all over him. Why didn't the Spirit just stay on him all the time and bypass all this questioning? God wants our hearts to beat in time with his, to share his passions.

Who's boss?

Judges 7:1–8

[1]Early in the morning, Jerub-Baal (that is, Gideon)
and all his men camped at the spring of Harod. The
camp of Midian was north of them in the valley near
the hill of Moreh. [2]The Lord said to Gideon, "You
have too many men for me to deliver Midian into
their hands. In order that Israel may not boast
against me that her own strength has saved her,
[3]announce now to the people, 'Anyone who trembles
with fear may turn back and leave Mount Gilead.'"
So twenty-two thousand men left, while ten thousand
remained.
[4]But the Lord said to Gideon, "There are still too many men. Take them
down to the water, and I will sift them out for you there. If I say, 'This one
shall go with you,' he shall go; but if I say, 'This one shall not go with you,'
he shall not go."
[5]So Gideon took the men down to the water. There the Lord told him,
"Separate those who lap the water with their tongues like a dog from those
who kneel down to drink." [6]Three hundred men lapped with their hands to
their mouths. All the rest got down on their knees to drink.
[7]The Lord said to Gideon, "With the three hundred men that lapped I will
save you and give the Midianites into your hands. Let all the other men go,
each to his own place." [8]So Gideon sent the rest of the Israelites to their
tents but kept the three hundred, who took over the provisions and trumpets
of the others.
Now the camp of Midian lay below him in the valley.

God is as committed to us today as he was to Gideon and we still need to be reminded of the facts of life: we can trust God.

Perhaps this is stretching it a little, but there's a real sense that God is keen on making Gideon trust him. Sure there's all that bit about needing fewer men so that the Israelites would know that God had secured the victory, but I wonder whether there was one Israelite in particular that needed to learn the lesson.

Gideon's army first lost the ones who were scared. Then it lost the ones who drank without any thought for their own protection: exposing their backs to any sneak attack that might be coming their way.

With an army reduced from 32,000 to 300, Gideon was forced to conclude one thing: God was in charge. Throughout the Bible we see hundreds of examples of God telling his people to trust in him, to let him 'be God' and not try to fill his shoes themselves.

No prejudice

Judges 7:9–15

9During that night the Lord said to Gideon, "Get up,
go down against the camp, because I am going to
give it into your hands. 10If you are afraid to attack,
go down to the camp with your servant Purah 11and
listen to what they are saying. Afterwards, you will
be encouraged to attack the camp." So he and Purah
his servant went down to the outposts of the camp.
12The Midianites, the Amalekites and all the other
eastern peoples had settled in the valley, thick as
locusts. Their camels could no more be counted than
the sand on the seashore.
13Gideon arrived just as a man was telling a friend
his dream. "I had a dream," he was saying. "A
round loaf of barley bread came tumbling into the
Midianite camp. It struck the tent with such force
that the tent overturned and collapsed."
14His friend responded, "This can be nothing other
than the sword of Gideon son of Joash, the Israelite.
God has given the Midianites and the whole camp
into his hands."
15When Gideon heard the dream and its interpretation, he worshipped God. He returned to the camp
of Israel and called out, "Get up! The Lord has given
the Midianite camp into your hands."

Could God even choose to speak through people we consider to be on 'the other side'?

Now what's going on here? We know that dreams and their interpretations were important throughout the Old Testament, and that Jews and non-Jews alike thought of them as sources of wisdom and guidance. God used Joseph and Daniel to interpret dreams for non-believers, but this is something else: both the dreamer and the one interpreting it are non-Israelite. What's more, they were part of God's direct plans, and they were absolutely right. Their army was destroyed by a vastly inferior force, something picked up by the mention of the fact that the Terminator Loaf was made of barley – an inferior ingredient considered to be half as good as wheat.

God was working powerfully through Gideon, and the victory was one to remember. But let's not get carried away: God was keen that the Israelites didn't start believing that they had done it all in their own strength, and he was also keen to show that he would work through people that others may have considered unsuitable.

Gideon tried to tell God how to speak to him. God gave him a powerful lesson in just how he does speak to people. We may think we know whom God does and does not speak through, but are we really so sure that we've got it right?

Family resemblance might be something we either love or loathe, but we can't get away from it. Whether it's our nose, eyes, accent or temper we all give off clues about our heritage. But do we show the God family characteristics? The Sermon on the Mount holds God's measuring stick up against us. Let's see how we've grown. *Chris Russell*

Pay attention

matthew 5:1–2

1Now when he saw the crowds, he went up
on a mountainside and sat down. His disciples came to him, 2and he began to teach
them, saying:

Some actions mean more than others because of what they symbolise. So, if someone burns the national flag it's a powerful statement of protest and disdain against that country, much more than if someone happens to burn a dirty old curtain in their front garden. Symbolic actions are loaded with meaning.

On the face of it a thirty-year-old man going to sit on a high place to chat doesn't seem that symbolic. But when that chat is what follows, and when that man is who he is, you start to take a closer look.

Clue number one: he went up on a mountainside. Nothing unusual there you might think, but let's just freeze-frame it there. Remind you of anyone else who went up a mountain and gave instructions from God? Yup, old long-beard himself: Moses. Matthew wants us to see that what is about to happen is **huge.** Jesus – the new Moses – going up a mountain and teaching.

And his teaching isn't just the general 'Look both ways before you cross the road' type of thing. It's specific stuff just to the disciples.

chew it over

What follows are not lines for posters with pictures of cats wrapped in wool. They are life rules and principles for anyone who would count themselves a disciple. You up for it?

Revolution

matthew 5:3–7

3"Blessed are the poor in spirit,
for theirs is the kingdom of heaven.
4Blessed are those who mourn,
for they will be comforted.
5Blessed are the meek,
for they will inherit the earth.
6Blessed are those who hunger and thirst
for righteousness,
for they will be filled.
7Blessed are the merciful,
for they will be shown mercy."

Often when well-known people are interviewed and asked about their attitude to Christianity they'll say that the Sermon on the Mount means a lot to them even though they don't go to church. Fair game p'raps, but often if they're asked to name their favourite bit of the Sermon on the Mount they can't actually remember any of it!

But this idea that Jesus is just giving vague statements about who is blessed is really wide of the mark. Can you see that if these verses are interpreted just as general, fluffy remarks about life they could be accused of being rude and patronising: poor, mourning, hungry people being 'blessed'?

Jesus is not talking about people in general, he is talking to the disciples. He is telling them what to expect in life. When they do end up poor, mourning and hungry they're not to take it as a sign of punishment; they are to take it as blessing. It works the other way too: rather than riches, possessions and comfy living being a sign of blessing the opposite is the case.

And this, says Jesus, is the way life will be. It's part of the Jesus revolution.

chew it over

Has the Jesus revolution revolutionised you yet?

The right track

matthew 5:8–12

8"Blessed are the pure in heart,
for they will see God.
9Blessed are the peacemakers,
for they will be called sons of God.
10Blessed are those who are persecuted
because of righteousness,
for theirs is the kingdom of heaven.

11"Blessed are you when people insult
you, persecute you and falsely say all kinds
of evil against you because of me. 12Rejoice
and be glad, because great is your reward
in heaven, for in the same way they persecuted the prophets who were before you."

Think about what people get respected for in public life: money, talent, brains, influence, strength, looks, background. Now read these verses. If you are following Jesus expecting to get an easy life you may as well turn round and go now. Jesus spells out what is going to characterise the lives of the followers of God, pointing out the signs that will indicate that God is blessing them. First is the realisation that you're in dire need for God, that spiritually you have nothing (3 – look back at the last reading). Then there's a willingness to engage in the pain of the world around you and the sorrow at the state things are in (4). There's a degree of humility, a desire to put others before yourself and not think too much of yourself (5), along with a straining and striving for justice and right behaviour (6). Jesus goes on to mention forgiveness, kindness and compassion (7), purity of intentions and motives, a love for what is right and a determination to keep out of evil (8). Then we have the desire to work as a reconciler, not bringing conflict but unity (9) and finally the willingness not to be popular, not to be well thought of, but to face opposition because of Jesus (10).

chew it over

This is what will happen if you follow Jesus. And when it does, we're not meant to take it as a sign that everything's going wrong. It actually means we're blessed.

Salt and light

matthew 5:13–16

[13]"You are the salt of the earth. But if the
salt loses its saltiness, how can it be made
salty again? It is no longer good for anything, except to be thrown out and trampled by men.
[14]"You are the light of the world. A city
on a hill cannot be hidden. [15]Neither do
people light a lamp and put it under a
bowl. Instead they put it on its stand, and it
gives light to everyone in the house. [16]In the
same way, let your light shine before men,
that they may see your good deeds and
praise your Father in heaven."

Sometimes all we seem to hear about is the state this world's in and how bad it all is. Statistics, stories, pictures and opinions all paint such a negative picture of things. In the face of this, many Christians want to turn their back on everything around them. It's all just too frightening, too dangerous, too evil. But Jesus never gives his disciples that option. He gives us two pictures in these verses which encourage positive and long-term engagement with what is going on around us: salt and light.

Verse 13 mentions salt, the stuff that flavours and makes things taste better. Imagine the world being more tasteful for the presence of Christians! But much more than that, in Jesus' time salt was used as a preservative – no fridges or freezers then, just a healthy dose of salt was used to keep things from going off. Does this characterise the effect we have on what goes on around us, do we stop it going off? Might the reason why things are in the state they're in be because the Church has pulled out, or even lost its saltiness? Where are you called to give flavour? Where can you stop things going off?

Verse 14 tackles light, an essential element of all life, helping people to find their way and see clearly. Does this describe the effect we have on the world?

chew it over

Are the people around encouraged to grow through us? Are they living fuller lives because of our presence?

To the root

matthew 5:21–4

[21]"You have heard that it was said to the
people long ago, 'Do not murder, and anyone who murders will be subject to judgment.' [22]But I tell you that anyone who is
angry with his brother will be subject to
judgment. Again, anyone who says to his
brother, 'Raca,' is answerable to the
Sanhedrin. But anyone who says, 'You fool!'
will be in danger of the fire of hell.
[23]"Therefore, if you are offering your gift
at the altar and there remember that your
brother has something against you, [24]leave
your gift there in front of the altar. First go
and be reconciled to your brother; then
come and offer your gift."

Not being much of a gardener I didn't realise this lovely fast-growing plant with white flowers was a weed. It was apparently killing everything else in the garden. Imaginatively called 'bindweed', the only way to get rid of it is to ferret around and get the root. It's messy, time consuming and painful but if you want to solve the problem it's got to be done.

Often Jesus can be very uncomfortable to be around. He takes standards that most of us wouldn't have that much trouble keeping – like 'Do not murder' – and goes right to the root. Suddenly we find ourselves guilty of something we'd cleared ourselves of. It's messy and time consuming and painful.

It's not that we are told by Jesus not to get angry, have conflicts or speak strongly. Rather it's that in all these things we have got to watch out for hatred and animosity. It's not easy or natural and it's not a particularly human way to act. But in the light of Jesus we realise it's actually a godly way to act.

chew it over

Jesus gets to the root of murder - uncontrolled and vindictive anger. How's your temper? How's your language? Are you good at making peace?

Integrity

matthew 5:27–30

27"You have heard that it was said, 'Do not
commit adultery.' 28But I tell you that anyone who looks at a woman lustfully has
already committed adultery with her in his
heart. 29If your right eye causes you to sin,
gouge it out and throw it away. It is better
for you to lose one part of your body than
for your whole body to be thrown into hell.
30And if your right hand causes you to sin,
cut it off and throw it away. It is better for
you to lose one part of your body than for
your whole body to go into hell."

A married upstanding member of a church had an affair. 'I just don't know how it happened.'

'I do,' said his church leader. 'Have you ever thought about being unfaithful to your wife?'

The man confessed he had. 'Well, that's how it happened. It starts in your head and then your actions follow.'

Again Jesus gets to the heart of the matter: sexual immorality isn't just about what goes on physically. It's about what goes on mentally. In saying that we should not look at each other as objects that gratify our sexual desire Jesus is affirming the humanity of everybody. Women are not there for men's pleasure. As followers of Jesus, our eyes, mind and hearts have to be pure.

Jesus knows it's not easy. That's why he calls for the drastic action of verses 29–30. Don't play with fire, don't put yourself in places where you are going to be tempted.

chew it over

Take affirmative action. It's not a game. Whatever your past sexual experience choose today for purity – in public and in private.

Truth

matthew 5:33–7

33"Again, you have heard that it was said to
the people long ago, 'Do not break your
oath, but keep the oaths you have made to
the Lord.' 34But I tell you, Do not swear at
all: either by heaven, for it is God's throne;
35or by the earth, for it is his footstool; or
by Jerusalem, for it is the city of the Great
King. 36And do not swear by your head, for
you cannot make even one hair white or
black. 37Simply let your 'Yes' be 'Yes', and
your 'No', 'No'; anything beyond this comes
from the evil one."

Aesop, the famous teller of stories, was asked what the most powerful thing in the world was. 'The tongue,' he replied. 'And what is the most harmful thing in the world?' he was asked. 'The tongue,' he said again. Our tongues make up less than 0.045 per cent of our body weight, but they are our greatest asset and most destructive weapon.

Because God is a God of truth, because there is no lie in him, we who decide to follow him should aim to be the same. Do you find it easy to let your 'yes' be yes and your 'no' no? Many of us can find it really difficult to say no to things. Often it's because we don't want to let people down. But it can land us in hotter water than we would have got in had we the guts to say 'no' in the first place. Do you find it easy to tell the truth? Do you over commit yourself?

chew it over

When people hear our words and watch our lives, do they see a reflection of the true God?

Find the balance

matthew 6:1–4

1"Be careful not to do your 'acts of righteousness' before men, to be seen by them.
If you do, you will have no reward from
your Father in heaven.
2"So when you give to the needy, do not
announce it with trumpets, as the hypocrites do in the synagogues and on the
streets, to be honoured by men. I tell you
the truth, they have received their reward
in full. 3But when you give to the needy, do
not let your left hand know what your right
hand is doing, 4so that your giving may be
in secret. Then your Father, who sees what
is done in secret, will reward you."

There is a tragic story about a world-class yachtsman who sailed across the Atlantic in a boat called the *Cayote*. It was a brand new boat and he was a very experienced sailor. When the coastguard lost contact with him they thought nothing of it. But the silence grew and after six days a search party was sent out. They found the boat capsized with the sailor drowned. What had happened was the keel – the bit underneath the water – had snapped off, making the boat's weight above the surface heavier than the weight below. When this happens a boat capsizes.

The same is true for us: so much of the time we are obsessed with what is going on on the surface, with appearances and how we look. But if what is below the surface isn't heavier than what is seen, we will capsize.

Jesus encourages his followers to concentrate not on what people see, but on what is unseen. Character, humility, integrity are all watchwords for life with God.

Here Jesus doesn't suggest, he commands us to give in a secret way. To give for an audience of one. Why do you think this is so hard?

chew it over

Is there any person or any cause you can give secretly to in the near future? Think. Pray. Act.

A great show

matthew 6:5–9, 16–18

5“And when you pray, do not be like the
hypocrites, for they love to pray standing
in the synagogues and on the street corners
to be seen by men. I tell you the truth,
they have received their reward in full. 6But
when you pray, go into your room, close
the door and pray to your Father, who is
unseen. Then your Father, who sees what is
done in secret, will reward you. 7And when
you pray, do not keep on babbling like
pagans, for they think they will be heard
because of their many words. 8Do not be
like them, for your Father knows what you
need before you ask him.
9“This, then, is how you should pray:

“‘Our Father in heaven,
hallowed be your name,’

16“When you fast, do not look sombre as
the hypocrites do, for they disfigure their
faces to show men they are fasting. I tell
you the truth, they have received their
reward in full. 17But when you fast, put oil
on your head and wash your face, 18so that
it will not be obvious to men that you are
fasting, but only to your Father, who is
unseen; and your Father, who sees what is
done in secret, will reward you.”

chew it over

The God we worship sees through it all. It's the private, quiet, non-showy stuff he delights in. Let's delight in it too.

The secret life continues to be cultivated by Jesus. God is interested in a face to face, eyeball to eyeball relationship with us.

It seems anyone can do public acts of devotion for attention and respect. Fasting, praying – you can put on a great show for others and even for yourself if you try hard enough. But Jesus' rule is that we should go into a room and close the door and there, in the secrecy and privacy of that place, communicate with God. It's not that it is all just about me and God – what is fascinating is that Jesus says when you get on your own you pray *'our* Father'. Our faith is shared even when we're alone.

Have you ever prayed out loud for the benefit of others? Why do you think we do that?

It's not even about using long complicated words, or going on and on and on. Never be under the illusion that outward shows of religion count for much.

Jesus himself sets the example – going off again and again on his own to spend time with his Father. In public do we assume a different holy character than we actually practise in private?

Samson

History repeating

He was the first superman, and like our friend with the red pants and cape, there were two sides to Samson. He was one seriously anointed guy, but he had a taste for doing the wrong thing. That left him blind, ridiculed and ultimately dead . . . surprisingly, there's plenty we have in common.

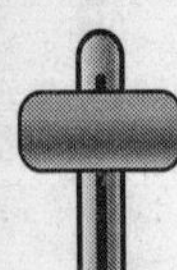

Judges 13:1

1 Again the Israelites did evil in the eyes of the Lord, so the Lord delivered them into the hands of the Philistines for forty years.

Let's not kid ourselves, Samson's story has plenty to teach us.

We need to kick off with a bit of history. You see, we join the story of the Israelites as something of a pattern seemed to be emerging. Here's how it went: God's people would wander away from him and start getting into worshipping idols (or other gods). God would then allow them to be taken control of by one of their enemies, and for a few years Israel would be an occupied nation. Eventually the people would put the pieces together and remember that what was called for was some serious repentance. So they'd get on their knees and God would send them a deliverer, someone to lead them out of oppression and back into his glorious freedom. This pattern gets repeated and becomes a familiar cycle that runs throughout the book of Judges. In chapter 13 we're in the seventh and last cycle of the book.

Mmm, repetitive sin, the ability to wander away from God and get sidetracked by other shining lights . . . remind you of anyone? Perhaps I'm on my own here, but it seems that my life is an almost constant tide of wandering and repentance followed by passion and wandering.

A good start

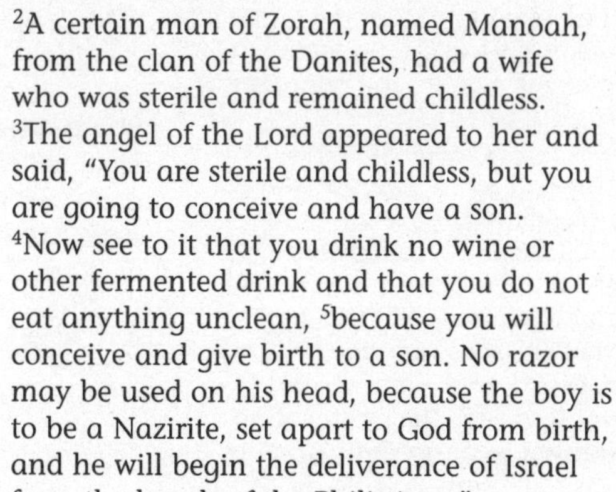

Judges 13:2–5

2A certain man of Zorah, named Manoah,
from the clan of the Danites, had a wife
who was sterile and remained childless.
3The angel of the Lord appeared to her and
said, "You are sterile and childless, but you
are going to conceive and have a son.
4Now see to it that you drink no wine or
other fermented drink and that you do not
eat anything unclean, 5because you will
conceive and give birth to a son. No razor
may be used on his head, because the boy is
to be a Nazirite, set apart to God from birth,
and he will begin the deliverance of Israel
from the hands of the Philistines."

A special call demanded special sacrifices, and the Nazirite vow took plenty of money as well as discipline. The result? Dependence on God. Let's face facts: God wants our hearts, not just our rituals.

So here we go: Israel is occupied by the Philistines (a particularly savage bunch from Egypt), and this couple are told that their son is going to be a key player in kicking the Philistines out of town. Nice one.

But there was a price to pay: he had to take a Nazirite vow from birth. We'll come on to look at what that meant in a minute, but for starters we need to understand just how unusual this was. Nazirite vows were usually taken by adults, not children, and then only for a short time. To dedicate a child from the beginning of his life was out of the ordinary, but as we see later, Sammy was no ordinary guy.

The Nazirite vow expressed the person's commitment to God in three ways: no touching of dead (or unclean) things, no cutting of the hair and no consumption of alcohol or even grapes, raisins or anything that grows on a vine. It was a serious undertaking, and showed that the person was keen to be pure (no dead things), dependent on God (no alcohol buzz) and prepared to look foolish in front of others (for a man to have longer hair than a woman was a definite cultural no-no).

The look of love

Judges 14:1–6
[1]Samson went down to Timnah and saw there
a young Philistine woman. [2]When he
returned, he said to his father and mother, "I
have seen a Philistine woman in Timnah; now
get her for me as my wife."
[3]His father and mother replied, "Isn't there
an acceptable woman among your relatives or
among all our people? Must you go to the
uncircumcised Philistines to get a wife?"
But Samson said to his father, "Get her for
me. She's the right one for me." [4](His parents
did not know that this was from the Lord, who
was seeking an occasion to confront the
Philistines; for at that time they were ruling
over Israel.) [5]Samson went down to Timnah
together with his father and mother. As they
approached the vineyards of Timnah, suddenly a young lion came roaring towards him.
[6]The Spirit of the Lord came upon him in
power so that he tore the lion apart with his
bare hands as he might have torn a young
goat. But he told neither his father nor his
mother what he had done.

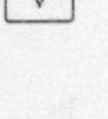

God's power goes hand in hand with grace: we don't get what we deserve.

The early years were promising. We are told that 'He grew and the Lord blessed him, and the Spirit of the Lord began to stir him . . .' (13:24–5). But things began to go wrong, especially when Samson started to think with his underpants. You see, Timnah was a small town about four miles away from Samson's home in Zorah, and his decision to marry a Philistine woman was a complete no-go. God had strict rules about the Israelites and whom they could and couldn't marry, and with violent enemies all around, it was important that the Israelites remained Israelites through and through.

But Samson had other ideas, and he got in a mood when his parents asked him whether he might prefer a nice Jewish girl instead. Living so close to Timnah and the territory of the Philistines is a tasty picture of how Samson lived on the edge spiritually as well as physically, but before we write him off as an idiot fool, we might need to swallow a bit of humble pie. You see, God's ways are not our ways, and when he was walking to Timnah through a vineyard with his parents, Samson saved them from an attack by a young lion. He was one seriously anointed chap, as the Bible makes clear: 'The Spirit of the Lord came upon him in power so that he tore the lion apart with his bare hands as he might have torn a young goat.'

Playing with fire

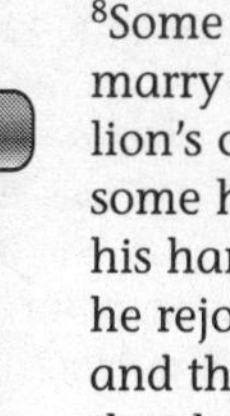

Judges 14:8–9

8Some time later, when he went back to
marry her, he turned aside to look at the
lion's carcass. In it was a swarm of bees and
some honey, 9 which he scooped out with
his hands and ate as he went along. When
he rejoined his parents, he gave them some,
and they too ate it. But he did not tell them
that he had taken the honey from the lion's
carcass.

God can turn our failings into his success stories. But we can turn those successes back into failings if we try hard enough.

For a man who had taken a vow not to touch grapes, doesn't it strike you as odd that he should be wandering around a vineyard? Samson is playing with fire, but he doesn't stop there. In eating the honey from the carcass he is breaking one of his Nazirite vows big time. Touching the dead lion would be bad enough, but eating something that has grown inside it? There's no doubt about him breaking that vow.

It's sad too as the killing of the lion in the first place was a tremendous act of God. Samson turned it around by his determination to pursue his own appetites. It wasn't even as if you could call it a momentary lapse, a quick slip up. He broke his vows carefully – the vineyard, the dead lion, the honey – in order to satisfy his hunger. He couldn't resist taking chances.

Playing with fire again

Judges 14:12–15, 17–18a, 19

12"Let me tell you a riddle," Samson said to them.
"If you can give me the answer within the seven
days of the feast, I will give you thirty linen garments and thirty sets of clothes. 13If you can't tell
me the answer, you must give me thirty linen garments and thirty sets of clothes."
"Tell us your riddle," they said. "Let's hear it."
14He replied,

"Out of the eater, something to eat;
out of the strong, something sweet."

For three days they could not give the answer.
15On the fourth day, they said to Samson's wife,
"Coax your husband into explaining the riddle for
us, or we will burn you and your father's household to death. Did you
invite us here to rob us?"
17She cried the whole seven days of the feast. So on the seventh day he
finally told her, because she continued to press him. She in turn explained
the riddle to her people.
18Before sunset on the seventh day the men of the town said to him,

"What is sweeter than honey?
What is stronger than a lion?"

19Then the Spirit of the Lord came upon him in power. He went down to
Ashkelon, struck down thirty of their men, stripped them of their belong-
ings and gave their clothes to those who had explained the riddle. Burning
with anger, he went up to his father's house.

Samson's life was scarred by sin and mistakes, but God still saw fit to use Samson to lead his people back to him.

So we're at the wedding of Samson and his Philistine chick from Timnah, when our man Sammy gets a little feisty and starts provoking the Philistines. (Remember, they're the occupying forces, right? And Samson probably knows that he's going to kick them out.) He sets them this riddle and allows them seven days to work it out. If they got it he would give them 'thirty linen garments and thirty sets of clothes'. If they failed, they'd give him these garments.

OK, so a few threads might not seem like much, but these were serious outfits, the sort that a man might only expect to own one of during his entire lifetime. The fact that their failure would mean them having to hand over two each was a pretty reasonable incentive to work the riddle out, and again Samson's playing with fire.

But what about the riddle, you ask. What's it all about? Well, it's all about the lion and the honey inside, isn't it? Samson's using God's miracle to line his own pockets, using God's gift to satisfy his own appetite.

What happens next is baffling. The Philistines wheedle the answer to the riddle out of Samson's wife, and queue up to collect their winnings. Facing bankruptcy because of his own stupidity, you'd imagine God would give Samson the cold shoulder. But no; Samson takes a thirty-mile hike to a coastal town called Ashkelon where he murders, loots and pillages until he has enough cash to pay back the Philistines. It's a horrific story, and it's made stranger by the fact that God helps him on his killing spree (19). But if you think this is a heavenly thumbs-up you're wrong.

. . . and again

Judges 16:2–3

2The people of Gaza were told, "Samson is
here!" So they surrounded the place and lay
in wait for him all night at the city gate.
They made no move during the night, saying, "At dawn we'll kill him."
3But Samson lay there only until the middle of the night. Then he got up and took
hold of the doors of the city gate, together
with the two posts, and tore them loose, bar
and all. He lifted them to his shoulders and
carried them to the top of the hill that faces
Hebron.

Sin and success . . . Samson's life was a real bitter-sweet symphony. Pray that God can help you succeed more than you sin in your own life.

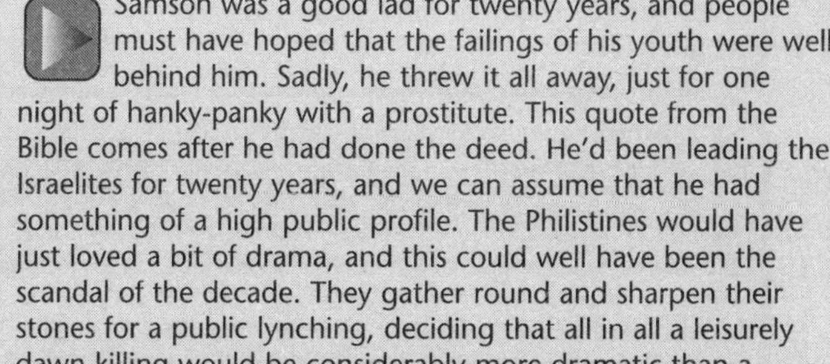

Samson was a good lad for twenty years, and people must have hoped that the failings of his youth were well behind him. Sadly, he threw it all away, just for one night of hanky-panky with a prostitute. This quote from the Bible comes after he had done the deed. He'd been leading the Israelites for twenty years, and we can assume that he had something of a high public profile. The Philistines would have just loved a bit of drama, and this could well have been the scandal of the decade. They gather round and sharpen their stones for a public lynching, deciding that all in all a leisurely dawn killing would be considerably more dramatic than a furtive one in the middle of the night.

But hey, guess what: God steps in and saves his booty one more time. Samson's God-given strength enables him to rip the city gates from their hinges and carry them back the thirty-eight miles to Hebron in Judah. I don't know about you, but this constant ping-ponging between Samson messing up and God stepping in is kind of confusing. But then again, Samson's life story is not unlike Israel's at the time: constantly wandering off in favour of not women, but Canaanite gods. Then again, that's not too dissimilar to us, is it?

Oops i did it again

Judges 16:15–19

[15]Then she said to him, "How can you say, 'I
love you,' when you won't confide in me? This
is the third time you have made a fool of me
and haven't told me the secret of your great
strength." [16]With such nagging she prodded
him day after day until he was tired to death.
[17]So he told her everything. "No razor has
ever been used on my head," he said, "because
I have been a Nazirite set apart to God since
birth. If my head were shaved, my strength
would leave me, and I would become as weak
as any other man."
[18]When Delilah saw that he had told her
everything, she sent word to the rulers of the
Philistines, "Come back once more; he has told
me everything." So the rulers of the Philistines
returned with the silver in their hands.
[19]Having put him to sleep on her lap, she
called a man to shave off the seven braids of
his hair, and so began to subdue him. And his
strength left him.

Samson's physical blindness mirrors the problem that has plagued him throughout his life: an inability to see where good behaviour ends and sin begins. How often do we share this problem?

Here we are, back in familiar territory as Samson kicks his Nazirite vows into touch for a bit of physical pleasure. This time he has hooked up with Delilah (whose name in Hebrew means weak), and she's busy doing the dirty work for the scheming Philistines. She stands to pocket 5500 pieces of silver if she finds out the secret of his strength, so the incentive is most definitely there.

What follows is a joke: Samson – the saviour of the Israelites – plays along with the pillow talk, telling Delilah a lie about what makes him so powerful. Each time Delilah tells the Philistines what Samson has told her, and they try it out: first binding him with fresh bowstrings, then with new ropes and finally by weaving seven locks of his hair into a web. I mean, Samson may have been a little partial to the ladies, but he wasn't stupid, so why did he not put a stop to it? He can hardly have thought that waking up to find seven strands of his hair woven together in a loom was a coincidence. But the man is strong and his heavenly anointing has stuck with him, through thick and thin.

Eventually, he gives in. Delilah's advances are too much and he tells all. He has finally given up the last of his vows, and is overcome by the Philistines who gouge out his eyes and set him to work pushing a great millstone around, a task usually carried out by an ox.

The final bow

Judges 16:28–30

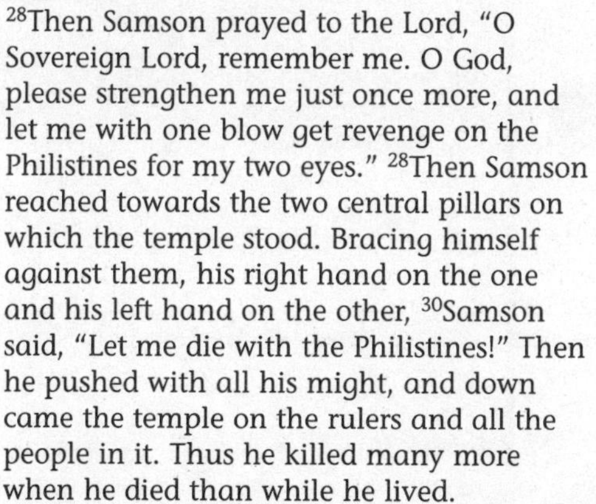

28Then Samson prayed to the Lord, “O
Sovereign Lord, remember me. O God,
please strengthen me just once more, and
let me with one blow get revenge on the
Philistines for my two eyes.” 28Then Samson
reached towards the two central pillars on
which the temple stood. Bracing himself
against them, his right hand on the one
and his left hand on the other, 30Samson
said, “Let me die with the Philistines!” Then
he pushed with all his might, and down
came the temple on the rulers and all the
people in it. Thus he killed many more
when he died than while he lived.

When God works through us it is for his own agenda, not ours.

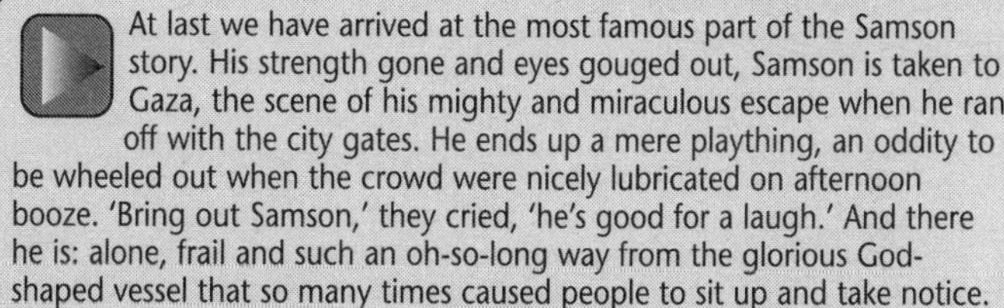

At last we have arrived at the most famous part of the Samson story. His strength gone and eyes gouged out, Samson is taken to Gaza, the scene of his mighty and miraculous escape when he ran off with the city gates. He ends up a mere plaything, an oddity to be wheeled out when the crowd were nicely lubricated on afternoon booze. ‘Bring out Samson,’ they cried, ‘he’s good for a laugh.’ And there he is: alone, frail and such an oh-so-long way from the glorious God-shaped vessel that so many times caused people to sit up and take notice.

Yet in the same way that Samson’s life was full of mess-ups followed by godly interventions, his death offers a few surprises too. We know the score – he pushes the pillars apart and kills a whole load of people, but there’s more to the story than that.

This passage offers us the Bible’s first and last record of Samson praying. That doesn’t mean he didn’t pray, but I suspect that the author could be trying to make a point: Samson – ever the man who followed his own agenda – is finally asking God for help. In asking God to strengthen him ‘just once more’, we get a clear indication that Samson recognised his strength came from God. Perhaps this is the truth he has waited his whole life to fathom, and the last line suggests a timely end as he kills more people in his death than he did throughout his life.

God can use us when we’re selfish and God can use us when we’re dependent on him, but quibbling about details misses the point. Did God really strengthen Samson that last time to avenge the loss of his two eyes? Perhaps not – perhaps God gave Samson strength to avenge the loss of his people’s hearts.

RESPECT

We're supposed to like people, even to love them, but there's one lesson Jesus taught that we seem to find the hardest: respecting people.

Status quo

Luke 10:25–9

25 On one occasion an
expert in the law stood
up to test Jesus.
"Teacher," he asked,
"what must I do to inher-
it eternal life?"
26 "What is written in
the Law?" he replied.
"How do you read it?"
27 He answered: "'Love
the Lord your God with
all your heart and with
all your soul and with all
your strength and with
all your mind'; and,
'Love your neighbour as
yourself.'"
28 "You have answered
correctly," Jesus replied.
"Do this and you will
live."
29 But he wanted to jus-
tify himself, so he asked
Jesus, "And who is my
neighbour?"

SEARCH

'Oh no,' you might be thinking to yourself, 'now they're going to get all Sunday School on us. First it's the parable of the Good Samaritan, then they'll be getting me doing finger painting and singing "Jesus' Love Is Very Wonderful".' But fear not. The parable of the Good Samaritan was not just put in the Bible to get six-year-olds to be nice to people: it's one of the most important stories Jesus told and it has plenty to say to us today.

Here's the scene: a bold and shiny religious toff fancies tripping up this cheeky chappy named Jesus, astounding the upstart with his knowledge of his favourite topic, the law. Jesus passes his test, something which more than likely left Mr Religious feeling a tad annoyed. So he tries again, this time asking Jesus one of those 'how long is a piece of string' questions in the form of 'Who is my neighbour?'

Instead of joining in this guy's game of intellectual ping-pong, Jesus gets to the heart of the matter: the toff was trying to trip Jesus up, trying to find out if he was familiar with the technicalities at the heart of his religion. The question about neighbours gave away the state of his heart. To him, people were there to be judged: either they made it into his exclusive 'friendship club' or they didn't. You get the impression that he was looking for Jesus to confirm his social structures, hoping that the Son of God would turn around and say, 'Who are your neighbours? Why, they're the ones who keep the Sabbath, observe all the laws and who generally keep their noses clean.' 'Oh, that's good,' you could imagine him replying. 'I'm glad I don't have to talk to those smelly cripples/Gentiles/women/children/prostitutes/shepherds . . . ' (you get the picture).

As we'll see next, God's club is not cosy.

The art of self-preservation

Luke 10:30–1

30In reply Jesus said: "A
man was going down
from Jerusalem to
Jericho, when he fell into
the hands of robbers.
They stripped him of his
clothes, beat him and
went away, leaving him
half-dead. 31A priest happened to be going down
the same road, and
when he saw the man,
he passed by on the
other side."

SEARCH

So here we go. Jesus sees through the toff's words and chooses not to get involved in some technical argument over the definition of 'neighbour'. Instead he goes straight for the heart, first with the introduction of the priest and a Levite, who both give the victim a miss. To a Jewish audience these two were not just decent people, they were Religious Success Stories, climbing the ladder and doing very nicely, thank you very much. Perhaps they were hurrying along to do something religious and important, something on a platform in front of the worshippers. After all, was it worth risking becoming ritually unclean just to help one man? Was it worth disrupting the schedule just for an ordinary bloke? They were doing God's work, and it seems clear that, in their minds, God's work did not involve helping the victim.

GO

What do you consider your greatest gift, your greatest possession and your greatest responsibility? Would you be prepared to sacrifice any of them to help a stranger?

It's a heart thing

Luke 10:33–5

33"But a Samaritan, as
he travelled, came where
the man was; and when
he saw him, he took pity
on him. 34He went to
him and bandaged his
wounds, pouring on oil
and wine. Then he put
the man on his own don-
key, brought him to an
inn and took care of
him. 35The next day he
took out two silver coins
and gave them to the
innkeeper. 'Look after
him,' he said, 'and when
I return, I will reimburse
you for any extra
expense you may have.'"

SEARCH

Along comes the Samaritan. Instead of blanking the victim, he helps out. What made him stop? Simple: he stopped because of his heart – he felt pity for him. In fact, the heart was the key for the others who blew the dying man out; they felt nothing at all.

The story carries on, and we find out that the Samaritan is much more than just a hit and run helper, he's seriously ready to go the distance. Even when the feelings of pity might have worn off, he took care of the man by putting up the cash to ensure his full recovery. It cost him twice: his pride and personal safety when he took care of him on the road – after all, there might have been more robbers waiting for a fresh victim. Later it cost him financially as he paid the bill at the inn.

It's all so beautifully simple: Jesus tells a suspense story, a real thriller, and as it probably got retold and re-used in the disciples' sermons, it would have had people eating out of the palm of their hand. There's the horror of the crime, the sadness as the victim goes un-helped. The audience never would have predicted the ending: a Samaritan doing a good turn? No chance. As the twist in the plot sunk in, the story leaves the audience to face up to a stark fact: their boys didn't do too well. The opposition won. But the maddening thing is this: according to Jesus they can't be the opposition any more.

Without the heart our actions lack the power.

He moves in mysterious ways

Luke 10:36–7

36"Which of these three do you think was a neighbour to the man who fell into the hands of robbers?"

37The expert in the law replied, "The one who had mercy on him."

Jesus told him, "Go and do likewise."

SEARCH

The raw power of this story is plain to see in the Religious Man's reaction to Jesus' question: he cannot even say 'the Samaritan'. I always imagine him screwing up his face as if he'd just drunk some sour milk, wincing as he said, 'The one who had mercy on him.'

It was a bitter pill for him to swallow. We're nice and cosy with the term Good Samaritan, using it to describe anyone who goes out of their way to do something for others. Back then, there was more likely a line like 'The only good Samaritan is a dead Samaritan'. You see, the Jews didn't like the Samaritans, and for Jesus to tell the story this way was something of a bold step.

The story of the Good Samaritan brings home some pretty basic truths; it doesn't matter how important we think we are, none of us is too important to help. It doesn't matter how unimportant you think you are, God can use you. It also answers the question that still puzzles us today: who is our neighbour? In the story it was the not the priest or the Levite who were the neighbour, but the Samaritan. Likewise we show that we are good neighbours by the way we treat others – with love and respect.

But the story isn't just about how we should be nice to people, stopping to help the injured instead of passing them by. It isn't even just a story about how we should be welcoming and loving to people from other nations. It's about something far more radical than that: it's about how God works through others.

To Mr Religious, there were two Religious Stars in the story (the priest and the Levite). To Jesus, I suspect there was only one (the Samaritan). God worked through the Samaritan while the spiritual ones remained caught up in their own little worlds.

GO

Are we the only people around whom God can work through?

R.E.S.P.E.C.T.

Mark 14:3–9

3While he was in Bethany,
reclining at the table in the
home of a man known as
Simon the Leper, a woman
came with an alabaster jar
of very expensive perfume,
made of pure nard. She
broke the jar and poured
the perfume on his head.
4Some of those present
were saying indignantly to
one another, "Why this
waste of perfume? 5It could
have been sold for more
than a year's wages and the
money given to the poor."
And they rebuked her
harshly.
6"Leave her alone," said
Jesus. "Why are you bother-
ing her? She has done a
beautiful thing to me. 7The
poor you will always have
with you, and you can help
them any time you want.
But you will not always
have me. 8She did what she
could. She poured perfume
on my body beforehand to
prepare for my burial. 9I tell
you the truth, wherever the
gospel is preached throughout the world, what she has
done will also be told, in
memory of her."

SEARCH

Too often we can believe the hype that we create about ourselves. We stand, chests swollen with pride, and tell others that we know the way and that all they need to do is to become more like us. Perhaps what we should be saying is that we know the way and that we all ought to be trying to become a little more like Jesus.

The woman in this story is thought by some to be the same one that Luke writes about in chapter 7. We can assume that, even if she was not a prostitute, she'd been with more than a few different men in her time. Whatever, one thing is crystal clear: she was not a good Jew. She was choosing to live her life contrary to the rules set down, and as such she was more than likely publicly humiliated for it.

But what does Jesus do? He sits there. Big deal, you may think, but the act of washing feet was an intimate and telling gesture – just look at the reaction Peter has when Jesus tries to wash his pinkies in John 13 (and I don't think it was just because Peter was embarrassed about his personal hygiene). It doesn't stop there, as she has a lesson to teach them, and us as well: relationship with Jesus is worth more than personal pride or selfish gain.

It's a good lesson, but in taking it in we can often overlook the fact that God can teach us things through people who don't fit our idea of 'teachers'.

The art of noise

Proverbs 22:17–18

17Pay attention and
listen to the sayings
of the wise;
apply your heart to
what I teach,
18for it is pleasing when
you keep them in
your heart
and have all of them
ready on your lips.

SEARCH

What does it mean to listen to someone? There's a bit of wisdom out there that suggests that to truly listen to someone, we have to be open to the possibility that they might have something to teach us. This certainly makes sense when we apply it to God: if we don't believe that the guy in the sky might have something to teach us, if we aren't prepared to act on what he might tell us, can we really be listening to him?

There's a problem with this: it doesn't suit our current way of thinking. We're OK with listening to God in this way, but what about when it comes to others? What about people who believe differently to us? How comfortable do we feel with the idea of chatting to a Muslim or a Buddhist, and learning from them?

This doesn't mean throwing it all away to the first person who seems nice and persuasive. Instead it means believing that someone is worth listening to. It means treating others with respect. Christianity is based on the rock of Jesus' life, death and resurrection, of our forgiveness and salvation. These are not up for debate, but are we really so sure that we've got everything else sussed? Do we really have the monopoly on doing the good works?

Sadly, this kind of goes against the grain. Like Mr Religious we like to think that we know whom we can and can't trust when it comes to teaching about God and stuff.

Jesus had other ideas for him, and perhaps he has other ideas for us.

Until the end of time

Proverbs 23:12

12 Apply your heart to
instruction
and your ears to words
of knowledge.

SEARCH

Jesus was the perfect example of how to treat others with respect, and we just have to look at the way he treated the disciples to find out more. He was a friend to Peter when his fishing was up the spout, when his enthusiasm made him into something of a buffoon and when his fear for his own safety prompted him to deny Jesus three times after he had been arrested. Yet Jesus stuck by him and, even more than that, he made it clear that he would be doing great things through him in the future. The fact is that Jesus was in it for the long haul. He had plenty of opportunities to give up on people like Peter, yet he stuck by him through thick and thin.

Too often it seems that we get frustrated when things don't go our way. Because we believe that we're doing something that God happens to be keen on, we consider any type of delay that may occur to be a sign that something is wrong. How many times have people who have struggled as they have come to know Jesus found themselves dropped by their Christian 'friends' who have swiftly moved on to a brighter prospect. I know I've been guilty of ditching people when I've got bored of waiting, and it's something I'm not proud of.

GO

Surely respecting someone doesn't have a Use By date?

Paul hadn't met the church in Rome, but here he gives a step by step guide covering more than just the basics of the Christian faith. It's different from many of his other, more personal letters, but manages to provide any reader with more than one doggy bag of take-homes.

Let's get things straight . . .

romans 1:16–17

16I am not ashamed of the gospel, because
it is the power of God for the salvation of
everyone who believes: first for the Jew,
then for the Gentile. 17For in the gospel a
righteousness from God is revealed, a righteousness that is by faith from first to last, just as it is written: "The righteous will live by faith."

He's not exactly big on suspense is our Paul, as this early paragraph sums up the entire letter. But that's no reason to leave it alone, as the two verses contain some real treats. 'I am not ashamed,' he says, giving a top-notch model to the fellow believers living right at the heart of the Roman empire. Nice one.

And for Paul it really was all about the power of salvation. Having met Jesus so powerfully on the way to Damascus, Paul's entire life from that point on was marked by an unshakeable belief that not only had Jesus risen from the dead, but that it was only through him that salvation was possible.

But there are some confusions in there too. Just look at that line about 'first for the Jew'. We know that there was a bit of grief going down among the Christians in Rome, mainly in the shape of friction between the backgrounds. The non-Jews felt that the Jews were unnecessarily attached to old Jewish laws about diet and sacred days. Is Paul just adding fuel to the fire here? Perhaps not. In truth things did all start with the Jews: the law, the covenants, the prophecies about the Messiah not to mention Jesus himself. But Paul understands that something has happened to cause a change, something that brings all the other people in too.

chew it over

Jesus' life, death and resurrection changed things for all of us, regardless of where we've come from.

Righteous = what?

romans 4:1–8

[1]What then shall we say that Abraham, our
forefather, discovered in this matter? [2]If, in
fact, Abraham was justified by works, he
had something to boast about—but not
before God. [3]What does the Scripture say?
"Abraham believed God, and it was credited
to him as righteousness."
[4]Now when a man works, his wages are
not credited to him as a gift, but as an
obligation. [5]However, to the man who does
not work but trusts God who justifies the
wicked, his faith is credited as righteousness. [6]David says the same thing when he
speaks of the blessedness of the man to
whom God credits righteousness apart from
works:

[7]"Blessed are they
whose transgressions are forgiven,
whose sins are covered.
[8]Blessed is the man
whose sin the Lord will never count
against him."

chew it over

God's standards are beyond ours. Our aim should be a relationship with God rather than working on a decent CV of accomplishments. We need the power of the Holy Spirit within us to live the life.

Righteous. Hmmmm. Not exactly an everyday word, is it? I mean, flick through the lonely hearts ads and they're hardly brimming with things like 'Man, 23, 6 ft, GSOH, extremely righteous, seeks female for fun and more'. Nope, as a word it leaves us with a large '?', so why does Paul go on about it so much?

The word 'righteousness' appears throughout Scripture, and it's a godly characteristic, a standard of good or right behaviour that is way beyond us. Paul picks up on this in Romans 3:10, quoting a whole bunch of Psalms which back him up. Great. But there's good news, as the word also describes something that God does: he sets his people 'in the right' with himself, a state which leads to salvation. Make sense? It's a gift, one that we can only really receive by faith, by living a life along God's lines. Finally, there's a third aspect to it: it becomes a standard that is expected of all believers. But didn't we say that living up to God's standards was impossible? Good point, but help is at hand in the form of the Holy Spirit. In Romans 8:2–4 Paul spells it out: the Spirit lives in us, helping us to do the right thing. OK?

As an example Paul suggests Abraham, a bit of a star for the Israelites. What made him righteous? His actions were good, but it was his faith, his belief in God, that served him so well.

Justification = what?

romans 6:15–23

[15]What then? Shall we sin because we are not
under law but under grace? By no means!
[16]Don't you know that when you offer yourselves to someone to obey him as slaves, you
are slaves to the one whom you obey—
whether you are slaves to sin, which leads to
death, or to obedience, which leads to righteousness? [17]But thanks be to God that, though
you used to be slaves to sin, you wholeheart-
edly obeyed the form of teaching to which
you were entrusted. [18]You have been set free
from sin and have become slaves to righteousness.

[19]I put this in human terms because you are
weak in your natural selves. Just as you used
to offer the parts of your body in slavery to
impurity and to ever-increasing wickedness, so
now offer them in slavery to righteousness
leading to holiness. [20]When you were slaves to
sin, you were free from the control of righteousness. [21]What benefit did you reap at that
time from the things you are now ashamed of?
Those things result in death! [22]But now that
you have been set free from sin and have
become slaves to God, the benefit you reap
leads to holiness, and the result is eternal life.
[23]For the wages of sin is death, but the gift of
God is eternal life in Christ Jesus our Lord.

chew it over

In God there is true freedom, not only in the relationship and full life we experience while on earth, but in the ultimate next chapter: eternal life.

And there's another word that buzzes around this letter, and although it doesn't appear directly in this passage, it's the key player behind the scenes. The issue of 'justification' was a bit of a hot potato, especially as it meant the act of God declaring us 'not guilty' for our sins. This had been something the Israelites had been trying to suss out (on and off) for centuries, but with Jesus came a new school of thought. Paul has already made clear that what counts in this arena is faith, as it's all bound in with righteousness. God's grace extends to all, and in return we need to live our lives for him.

But for some this made things confusing. If all that was needed was 'faith', wouldn't that mean some people would let their behaviour slip, that things would get a little immoral and hypocritical? Not at all, and this is where we get to see that 'faith' is not just about mouthing a few words like 'I believe in Jesus'. It's far more gutsy than that, and involves a way of life where instead of sin being the main man, righteousness (rightness before God, remember?) is our number one aim.

'I put this in human terms,' writes Paul, apologising for using an image of us as slaves in an effort to explain the deal. It's an imperfect picture: in reality we're a long way away from being slaves to God in the way we think of slaves: chained up, oppressed and unhappy. It's far from being the truth.

Free at last

romans 8:1–2

[1]Therefore, there is now no condemnation for those who are in Christ Jesus, [2]because through Christ Jesus the law of the Spirit of life set me free from the law of sin and death.

One of the worst things about sin is the temptation to keep on raking it over. You know the deal: you've messed up, confessed it to God and been forgiven, and are now perhaps living with the consequences. But still in the back of your mind goes the line, 'You're never going to be good enough. You did *that* and God will never be able to use you.' Slowly we get ground on down, reduced to the belief that our patterns of behaviour can never be broken, that we're locked into a cycle that will hold us forever. From there it's only a short step to another wrong belief: that there's no point trying to live a better life.

To different degrees we've all been there, and all go through it still. It can cause a dull staleness to infect our relationship with God, and as we turn our heads away from him we become increasingly focused on our own guilt, pain and frailty. Before we know it months have gone by and the pulsing colours that once described our faith have become toneless greys.

But it doesn't have to be that way. Why? Because Jesus breaks the cycle. The cross was stuck in the ground and declared that enough was enough: our sins are forgiven as we unite with Jesus, the one who paid the price.

chew it over

Remember, next time you feel as if your repeated failings take you off the team, 'There is no condemnation'. Try it, you might like it.

Past and present

romans 9:21, 32, 11:23

[21]Does not the potter have the right to make out of the same lump of clay some pottery for noble purposes and some for common use?

[32]Why not? Because they pursued it not by faith but as if it were by works. They stumbled over the "stumbling-stone".

[23]And if they do not persist in unbelief, they will be grafted in, for God is able to graft them in again.

Having laid down a tasty foundation so far in the letter, explaining all about how righteousness and justification are the new boys in town, Paul pauses before he goes on to explain how to actually live a right life before God. Here he picks up on an issue that had been a hot potato for the Christians in Rome: how did this affect the Jews? The new deal of faith leading to righteousness replaced the old lines about how following the law led to righteousness, and suddenly let in all manner of people – namely the Gentiles (non-Jews). For a bunch who had been known as God's chosen people, the ones whom he had saved again and again in such miraculous style, this was a bitter pill to swallow.

But there are three stages to Paul's argument. First, there's that bit about the potter and the clay. This doesn't mean that some people are worth more than others, but that God is in control. Just as a pot has no right to make demands on the maker, so too do we have no claim on God. He is in charge.

Then there was Israel's responsibility in the whole thing. God's rejection of Israel was not on a whim, but based on their rejection of Jesus, the Messiah who introduced this new way of gaining righteousness.

Finally, we can never forget God's compassionate heart. Those who have been cut off in the past because of their sin can be grafted back in.

chew it over

Rejection of God, denying who he is and living for self . . . sound familiar? Remember Paul's message to the people who had gone astray: God is able.

How to . . . part 1

romans 12:3–8

3For by the grace given me I say to every
one of you: Do not think of yourself more
highly than you ought, but rather think of
yourself with sober judgment, in accordance with the measure of faith God has
given you. 4Just as each of us has one body
with many members, and these members do
not all have the same function, 5so in Christ
we who are many form one body, and each
member belongs to all the others. 6We have
different gifts, according to the grace given
us. If a man's gift is prophesying, let him
use it in proportion to his faith. 7If it is
serving, let him serve; if it is teaching, let
him teach; 8if it is encouraging, let him
encourage; if it is contributing to the needs
of others, let him give generously; if it is
leadership, let him govern diligently; if it is
showing mercy, let him do it cheerfully.

So if we're looking for clues about how to live a righteous life, how to have that active, ongoing faith that makes the difference, then we've struck gold with this part of the letter. Here Paul looks at personal behaviour, and he makes himself beautifully clear.

There are many parts that go to make up the Church, the body of Christ. Each part is different and it just won't do to start banging on about how one bit is more important than another. But that line about the 'measure of faith' can be misleading. We need again to forget the idea of faith as that mysterious ability to believe, and remember that Paul is talking about the power within us to follow God. As each of us has been given different talents and abilities (if you like, different powers or measures) then each of us will have different things we can do for God.

chew it over

Don't get sucked into the belief that people who do 'Christian' things in public are better than you. Their gifts may be different, but yours are just as unique.

How to . . . part 2

romans 12:9–13, 17–20

9Love must be sincere. Hate what is evil;
cling to what is good. 10Be devoted to one
another in brotherly love. Honour one
another above yourselves. 11Never be lacking in zeal, but keep your spiritual fervour,
serving the Lord. 12Be joyful in hope, patient
in affliction, faithful in prayer. 13Share with
God's people who are in need. Practise hospitality.
17Do not repay anyone evil for evil. Be
careful to do what is right in the eyes of
everybody. 18If it is possible, as far as it
depends on you, live at peace with everyone. 19Do not take revenge, my friends, but
leave room for God's wrath, for it is written: "It is mine to avenge; I will repay,"
says the Lord. 20On the contrary:

"If your enemy is hungry, feed him;
if he is thirsty, give him something to drink.
In doing this, you will heap burning coals on his head."

It seems that in parts Paul is thinking about the way Christians should relate to those who don't share the same beliefs, especially the advice about people who persecute them. In general though it's a fully-fledged call to do the right thing in every aspect of our lives.

It's classic stuff really, and if ever anyone really thought that Christianity stopped the minute they left church, they obviously haven't taken this on board. It's impressive stuff, and the unity, selflessness, generosity, passion, humility and forgiveness all add up to make one tasty little cocktail. Can you imagine what life would be like if we all put this into action?

chew it over

Imagine yourself putting Paul's words into practice to a greater degree than you do already. How would life around you be affected? Pray and ask God to help you take a step closer to this goal.

How to . . . part 3

romans 13:1–7

[1]Everyone must submit himself to the governing authorities, for there is no authority
except that which God has established. The
authorities that exist have been established
by God. [2]Consequently, he who rebels
against the authority is rebelling against what
God has instituted, and those who do so will
bring judgment on themselves. [3]For rulers
hold no terror for those who do right, but
for those who do wrong. Do you want to be
free from fear of the one in authority? Then
do what is right and he will commend you.
[4]For he is God's servant to do you good. But
if you do wrong, be afraid, for he does not
bear the sword for nothing. He is God's servant, an agent of wrath to bring punishment
on the wrongdoer. [5]Therefore, it is necessary
to submit to the authorities, not only because
of possible punishment but also because of
conscience.

[6]This is also why you pay taxes, for the
authorities are God's servants, who give their
full time to governing. [7]Give everyone what
you owe him: If you owe taxes, pay taxes; if
revenue, then revenue; if respect, then
respect; if honour, then honour.

Here we go with a little bit of politics. Of course the relationship between the Christian and the State was kind of important for the original readers, and it remains vital for us too.

First, Paul makes clear that while there might be someone else on the throne, it is God who is the ultimate ruler of the nations. Christians should be obedient to the State so long as the laws don't conflict with God's authority. What's more, rebelling against them is rebelling against God.

Paul uses some interesting language, describing a ruler as 'God's servant', one who does the Lord's work. Many today would find that hard to swallow, that a non-Christian ruler could be used by God. But God's heart for justice and the fight against evil beats loud and strong, and he doesn't look for a fish on the back of the car before giving the thumbs up to a job well done.

chew it over

Being a Christian is not a free ticket to opt out. We are involved, joining in with the State powers to fight injustice and evil.

How to . . . part 4

romans 13:8–10

[8]Let no debt remain outstanding, except the
continuing debt to love one another, for he
who loves his fellow-man has fulfilled the
law. [9]The commandments, "Do not commit
adultery," "Do not murder," "Do not steal,"
"Do not covet," and whatever other commandment there may be, are summed up in
this one rule: "Love your neighbour as
yourself." [10]Love does no harm to its neighbour. Therefore love is the fulfilment
of the law.

And back we come to issues of personal morality, getting straight in with one of those 'oh no' verses. A debt that can never be repaid? That's how much love we should be giving out, again and again. There's not even a let-off clause that states we can get by with just loving the good-looking Christians we admire. Nope, we're supposed to be loving our fellow humans, non-Christians and believers alike. Get it? Good.

But does this mean we can ditch all those dusty old commandments given to that bloke with the beard up the mountain? Sorry but no. We're all locked in to a new phase, one that underlines the importance of love. Not only should we be loving in the sense of being nice to people, but loving in the broader sense: the way that would have us obey the commandments given to Moses. And so we see that this type of love underpins everything, from attitude to others to attitude to God. It's a radical, life-changing love, far more than just a squishy, mushy type of thing.

chew it over

It was precisely this love that caused Jesus to present himself as the sacrifice for our sins. That's some love.

And Finally . . .

romans 15:14–21

[14]I myself am convinced, my brothers, that you
yourselves are full of goodness, complete in
knowledge and competent to instruct one another. [15]I have written to you quite boldly on some
points, as if to remind you of them again,
because of the grace God gave me [16]to be a minister of Christ Jesus to the Gentiles with the
priestly duty of proclaiming the gospel of God,
so that the Gentiles might become an offering
acceptable to God, sanctified by the Holy Spirit.
[17]Therefore I glory in Christ Jesus in my service to God. [18]I will not venture to speak of anything except what Christ has accomplished
through me in leading the Gentiles to obey God
by what I have said and done—[19]by the power
of signs and miracles, through the power of the
Spirit. So from Jerusalem all the way round to
Illyricum, I have fully proclaimed the gospel of
Christ. [20]It has always been my ambition to
preach the gospel where Christ was not known,
so that I would not be building on someone
else's foundation. [21]Rather, as it is written:

"Those who were not told about him will
see,
and those who have not heard will
understand."

Quite boldly? Too right, Pablo. It's pretty hard to read Romans and not get the picture that Paul firmly believes in what he writes.

This letter was written with future trips in mind, and as such it's kind of an introduction. Perhaps Paul wanted to get a few things straight before he turned up, giving them a few areas to work on before he arrived and rolled up his sleeves live and direct, so to speak.

There's no chance of Paul coming over and dossing down on your floor before he pops off to Ibiza next summer, but why not try working back through the principles he's laid out: the issue of righteousness, the part that faith plays, the importance of lifestyle and the necessity of love? If he sounds a bit harsh at times remember this: he does it all with one thing in mind . . . that God might get all the glory.

chew it over

Whatever your circumstances and experience, you can serve God, love him and pursue him, finding out what he has in store for you and using the talents he has given. After all, that's just what Paul did.

RUTH

Ruth – one of just two women in the Bible with a book named after her. We'll see it was 'cos she was a bit special. But actually we come away from the book amazed not so much at Ruth and her commitment, but at the God who inspires her. Here is a story of great costly love and faithfulness. Let's pray he'll inspire us too. *Chris Russell*

Tough love

Ruth 1:1–5

1In the days when the
judges ruled, there was a
famine in the land, and
a man from Bethlehem
in Judah, together with
his wife and two sons,
went to live for a while
in the country of Moab.
2The man's name was
Elimelech, his wife's
name Naomi, and the
names of his two sons
were Mahlon and Kilion.
They were Ephrathites
from Bethlehem, Judah.
And they went to Moab
and lived there.
3Now Elimelech,
Naomi's husband, died,
and she was left with her
two sons. 4They married
Moabite women, one
named Orpah and the
other Ruth. After they
had lived there about ten
years, 5both Mahlon and
Kilion also died, and
Naomi was left without
her two sons and her
husband.

SEARCH

One of the biggest reasons people give for finding it difficult to believe in a loving God is because of the reality of suffering. It happens to us all, regardless of position, background, influence or wisdom. Take some time to think about someone (or a group of people) who is going through it at the moment.

The scene at the beginning of this little book is tragic. Naomi and her husband have to move because of famine to where the food is. Then her husband dies, leaving her two sons in charge of supporting her. They marry and then they die. Naomi is left in a foreign town, with no one to support her and her world in tatters.

In the middle of her suffering Naomi releases her daughters-in-law (Orpah and Ruth), giving them freedom to go back home.

GO

So many people suffer on their own. Pray for those who do.

Just do something

Ruth 1:16–18

[16]But Ruth replied,
"Don't urge me to leave
you or to turn back from
you. Where you go I will
go, and where you stay I
will stay. Your people will
be my people and your
God my God. [17]Where
you die I will die, and
there I will be buried.
May the Lord deal with
me, be it ever so severely,
if anything but death
separates you and me."
[18]When Naomi realised
that Ruth was deter-
mined to go with her, she
stopped urging her.

SEARCH

It's not just statistics that show that people suffer alone: many people's bitter experience tells the story. Naomi has got very little to look forward to: she has to return to her old town and, having freed her daughters-in-law from any obligation to go with her, faces the prospect of being truly alone. But Ruth has a different idea.

Ruth shows her commitment to Naomi. It's not that she has to, it's not required of her by law, it's that she chooses to be counted with Naomi.

Often we pray for those who suffer, we pray that God would do something about what they are going through. But often the answer to the prayer lies with our own willingness to do something.

You will know someone, old or young, a friend or relative, who is suffering. How can you take a leaf out of Ruth's book?

GO

We live in a world which encourages us to help ourselves rather than others, but we follow a God who says faith is never a private thing, it is all about how we live and treat others in the world around us.

Stranded

Ruth 2:2–9

[2]And Ruth the Moabitess said to Naomi, "Let me go to the fields and pick up the leftover grain behind anyone in whose eyes I find favour."

Naomi said to her, "Go ahead, my daughter." [3]So she went out and began to glean in the fields behind the harvesters. As it turned out, she found herself working in a field belonging to Boaz, who was from the clan of Elimelech.

[4]Just then Boaz arrived from Bethlehem and greeted the harvesters, "The Lord be with you!"

"The Lord bless you!" they called back.

[5]Boaz asked the foreman of his harvesters, "Whose young woman is that?"

[6]The foreman replied, "She is the Moabitess who came back from Moab with Naomi. [7]She said, 'Please let me glean and gather among the sheaves behind the harvesters.' She went into the field and has worked steadily from morning till now, except for a short rest in the shelter."

[8]So Boaz said to Ruth, "My daughter, listen to me. Don't go and glean in another field and don't go away from here. Stay here with my servant girls. [9]Watch the field where the men are harvesting, and follow along after the girls. I have told the men not to touch you. And whenever you are thirsty, go and get a drink from the water jars the men have filled."

SEARCH

I remember sitting in the middle of an airport in South America. It was my first day on the continent and I couldn't speak a word of Spanish. I didn't understand a word of what was going on around me and didn't have a clue how I was going to find the people I was meant to be meeting. I felt absolutely stranded, alone, powerless.

Have you ever felt completely helpless? What emotions did it bring to the surface?

Naomi and Ruth arrive back in Naomi's home town. Now they have to try to stay alive, finding food to feed themselves with.

Ruth is not going to take any of this lying down. She goes out to do all she can to provide for Naomi. She goes to the fields to pick up the scraps of wheat which are left over from the harvest. Boaz sees her and is generous to her. He is helping someone who needs it.

The Bible is clear that we have a responsibility to help not only the helpless people that we know but those we don't. Time and time again we are told to provide for the 'alien who comes to us' and to help the helpless. God cares for people through our care.

GO

Are you willing to pray that God would use you to help someone who is helpless? Be ready to get the answer to your prayer today.

Voyager

Ruth 4:11–12

11 Then the elders and all
those at the gate said,
“We are witnesses. May
the Lord make the
woman who is coming
into your home like
Rachel and Leah, who
together built up the
house of Israel. May you
have standing in
Ephrathah and be
famous in Bethlehem.
12 Through the offspring
the Lord gives you by
this young woman, may
your family be like that
of Perez, whom Tamar
bore to Judah.”

SEARCH

Ruth has character. Think of what she has done: she suffered the death of her young husband. Her best bet for security would have been to stay in her home country and remarry. She chose instead to accompany her – it has to be said – rather grumpy mother-in-law to a foreign country. There she goes out to find food in the fields and whilst she is doing that falls in love with the owner of the field. She then proceeds to ask him to marry her in the most unconventional manner (3:7–13).

Boaz sorts everything out and the marriage is announced. The onlookers celebrate and pray for blessing on them. They pray that Ruth would show many of the great qualities of the women of God in the past, Rachel, Leah and Perez.

Where the image of a woman of God as a shrinking violet comes from is a mystery to me. These women are feisty, strong and full of character.

Which characters in the Bible are the ones that really inspire you? Pray for some of their characteristics.

Following the example of this passage pray for someone else, asking that God would reproduce the characteristics of a figure from the Bible in them.

The next generation

Ruth 4:13–17

13So Boaz took Ruth and
she became his wife.
Then he went to her, and
the Lord enabled her to
conceive, and she gave
birth to a son. 14The
women said to Naomi:
"Praise be to the Lord,
who this day has not left
you without a kinsman-
redeemer. May he
become famous through-
out Israel! 15He will
renew your life and sus-
tain you in your old age.
For your daughter-in-law,
who loves you and who
is better to you than
seven sons, has given
him birth."
16Then Naomi took the
child, laid him in her lap
and cared for him. 17The
women living there said,
"Naomi has a son." And
they named him Obed.
He was the father of
Jesse, the father of David.

SEARCH

One of the things we never really see is the effect that our lives have on those who live after us.

The closing verse of this little book tells of Boaz and Ruth having a son called Obed. Then it tells us that Obed had a son and called him Jesse. Jesse had a son and called him David. Now stick with me on this one, but let's go forward around twenty-eight generations. In Matthew 1 we see listed the family tree, which tells us that Ruth and Boaz's great, great, great x 28 grandson was Jesus.

This was the sign of God's utter faithfulness to his people. Through circumstances which they would never have chosen God worked for the good. It's Romans 8:28 all the way – 'in all things God works for the good of those who love him'.

We might not, if given the choice, choose our circumstances, or the suffering we will go through. Life will not work out as we planned.

GO

We don't know what will come from what we do. But, in every single area, what we are called to be is faithful.

The original

Ruth 4:14

14 The women said to
Naomi: “Praise be to the
Lord, who this day has
not left you without a
kinsman-redeemer. May
he become famous
throughout Israel!”

SEARCH

The story of Ruth tells a far bigger story than simply God’s action and faithfulness to individuals. It tells of his faithfulness to all his people. It tells how he keeps his promise.

What marked out God’s people was that they had promised themselves to God, they had promised to be faithful to him and he had promised to be faithful to them. It’s really just like a marriage agreement. However, the history of the Old Testament is that the people are unfaithful, that they lie and cheat on him, that they run off with other gods and live for themselves rather than him. But before we get self-righteous it’s pretty obvious we are no different. We, like them, are the great covenant breakers.

God on the other hand is the great covenant keeper. His promise never fails or flinches. He is the great redeemer, the one who is committed to us no matter what, the one who remains faithful and true.

Ruth is a celebration not of a heroic woman, although she was one. It is really a testimony to God’s extraordinary capacity for faithfulness, goodness and commitment to people no matter what.

God’s commitment to us is worth staking your life on.

Mark

Success

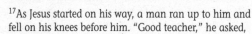

Relationship with God and action in the world – you can't separate the two. Mark digs deeper than the basics here, getting to the heart of following Jesus. *Pete Greig*

Mark 10:17–25

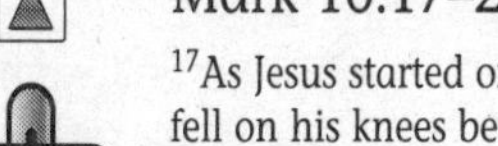

17As Jesus started on his way, a man ran up to him and
fell on his knees before him. "Good teacher," he asked,
"what must I do to inherit eternal life?"
18"Why do you call me good?" Jesus answered. "No-
one is good—except God alone. 19You know the commandments: 'Do not murder, do not commit adultery, do
not steal, do not give false testimony, do not defraud,
honour your father and mother.'"
20"Teacher," he declared, "all these I have kept since I
was a boy."
21Jesus looked at him and loved him. "One thing you
lack," he said. "Go, sell everything you have and give to
the poor, and you will have treasure in heaven. Then
come, follow me."
22At this the man's face fell. He went away sad,
because he had great wealth.
23Jesus looked around and said to his disciples, "How hard it is for the rich to
enter the kingdom of God!"
24The disciples were amazed at his words. But Jesus said again, "Children, how
hard it is to enter the kingdom of God! 25It is easier for a camel to go through the
eye of a needle than for a rich man to enter the kingdom of God."

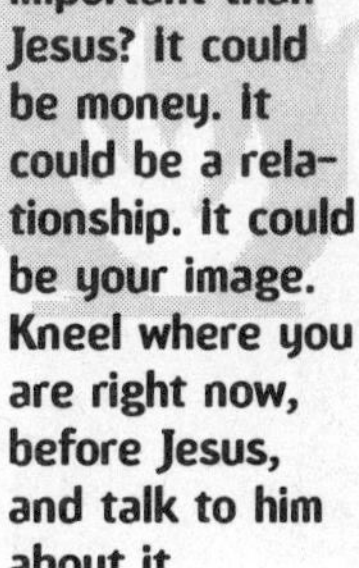

Is there anything in your life more important than Jesus? It could be money. It could be a relationship. It could be your image. Kneel where you are right now, before Jesus, and talk to him about it.

So this Porsche comes screeching to a halt in front of Jesus. Chart music blasting out of the stereo. A yuppy jumps out. Designer gear head to toe. The dot.com millionaire walks up to the scruffy guy covered in kids. Falls to his knees. Yes folks, it's just another weird moment in the life of Jesus Christ.

The rich young ruler was spiritually hungry like everyone else. He may have been receiving fan-mail from his bank manager, but he was insecure about his relationship with God. What should he do? Jesus blinks. He's just been cuddling kiddies and telling the crowd that children are the only ones who've got life sussed spiritually. And here's one of the kids a few years on, kneeling before him. A young guy who a few years earlier had been running around with other kids, not a care in the world, close with God without even having to worry about it. What's changed to make this guy so insecure? A few years. A bit of growing up. And most of all a whole lot of money.

In my church he'd be handed a collection plate and put in charge of the youth work before you could say 'spondoolies'. Jesus wasn't quite so desperate for cash. He looks at the guy, who's lived such a good life, and Mark says that he loved him. Perhaps he could still see the kid in his young eyes. But if this guy really wanted to kneel before Jesus he was gonna have to tear up his credit card, choose a simpler life, give to the poor.

No shame

Mark 10:46–52

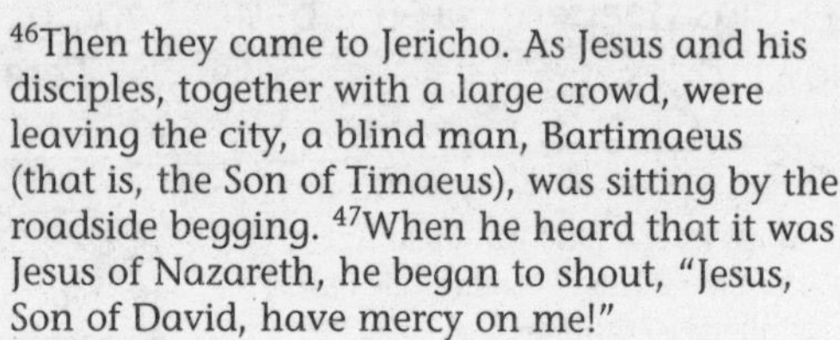

46 Then they came to Jericho. As Jesus and his
disciples, together with a large crowd, were
leaving the city, a blind man, Bartimaeus
(that is, the Son of Timaeus), was sitting by the
roadside begging. 47 When he heard that it was
Jesus of Nazareth, he began to shout, "Jesus,
Son of David, have mercy on me!"
48 Many rebuked him and told him to be
quiet, but he shouted all the more, "Son of
David, have mercy on me!"
49 Jesus stopped and said, "Call him."
So they called to the blind man, "Cheer up!
On your feet! He's calling you." 50 Throwing his
cloak aside, he jumped to his feet and came to
Jesus.
51 "What do you want me to do for you?"
Jesus asked him.
The blind man said, "Rabbi, I want to see."
52 "Go," said Jesus, "your faith has healed
you." Immediately he received his sight and
followed Jesus along the road.

What do you want Jesus to do for you? Make a decision that you're not gonna let self-pity or peer-pressure stop you getting hold of Jesus for yourself.

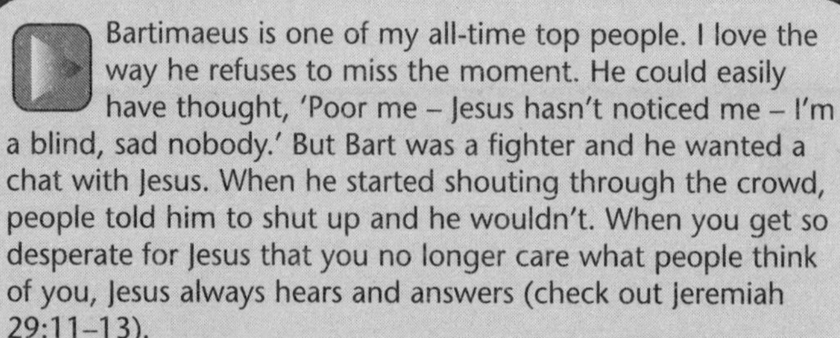

Bartimaeus is one of my all-time top people. I love the way he refuses to miss the moment. He could easily have thought, 'Poor me – Jesus hasn't noticed me – I'm a blind, sad nobody.' But Bart was a fighter and he wanted a chat with Jesus. When he started shouting through the crowd, people told him to shut up and he wouldn't. When you get so desperate for Jesus that you no longer care what people think of you, Jesus always hears and answers (check out Jeremiah 29:11–13).

Jesus calls Bart and he just casts his cloak aside. Big deal. His cloak was his most valuable possession. His blanket at night, his begging tool by day. And if he let go of it, he would never be able to find it again – unless he received his sight. Then Jesus asks him what he wants – I guess with a twinkle in his eye. Bart says he wants to be healed and blinks a couple of times before realising he can see. Wow!

Donkey Derby

Mark 11:1–9

[1]As they approached Jerusalem and came to
Bethphage and Bethany at the Mount of
Olives, Jesus sent two of his disciples, [2]saying
to them, "Go to the village ahead of you, and
just as you enter it, you will find a colt tied
there, which no-one has ever ridden. Untie it
and bring it here. [3]If anyone asks you, 'Why
are you doing this?' tell him, 'The Lord needs
it and will send it back here shortly.'"
[4]They went and found a colt outside in the
street, tied at a doorway. As they untied it,
[5]some people standing there asked, "What are
you doing, untying that colt?" [6]They answered
as Jesus had told them to, and the people let
them go. [7]When they brought the colt to Jesus
and threw their cloaks over it, he sat on it.
[8]Many people spread their cloaks on the road,
while others spread branches they had cut in
the fields. [9]Those who went ahead and those
who followed shouted,

"Hosanna!"

"Blessed is he who comes in the name of the Lord!"

Spend some time worshipping him for saving your life. While you worship him, remember that he's not there looking down on you. He's humble, sitting on a donkey, grinning back at you.

Most Christians would have said: 'I've got a picture of a donkey'! Jesus didn't. He just got on one and rode the stupid, smelly animal into town without so much as an explanation. (If you want to know why, check out Zechariah 9:9.) The people go crazy chucking their anoraks on the road for the bewildered donkey to – er – walk on. Red carpet treatment for the King. 'Hosanna!' they shout which literally just means 'Save!' It's like the spontaneous gasp that goes up from a football crowd when David Seaman pushes the German penalty wide of the posts in extra time. Sometimes when you get a glimpse of Jesus you can't help worshipping and laying stuff down.

One old hymn talks about being 'lost in wonder, love and praise'. Have you ever felt like that?

No more Mr Nice Guy!

Mark 11:12–18

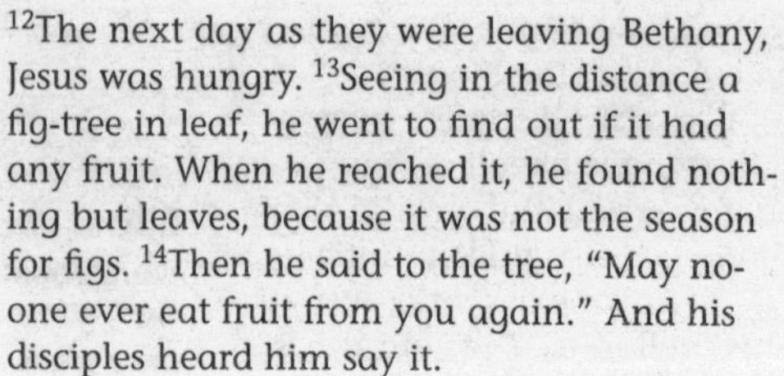

12 The next day as they were leaving Bethany,
Jesus was hungry. 13 Seeing in the distance a
fig-tree in leaf, he went to find out if it had
any fruit. When he reached it, he found nothing but leaves, because it was not the season
for figs. 14 Then he said to the tree, "May no-
one ever eat fruit from you again." And his
disciples heard him say it.
15 On reaching Jerusalem, Jesus entered the
temple area and began driving out those who
were buying and selling there. He overturned
the tables of the money-changers and the
benches of those selling doves, 16 and would
not allow anyone to carry merchandise
through the temple courts. 17 And as he taught
them, he said, "Is it not written:

"'My house will be called
a house of prayer for all nations'?

But you have made it 'a den of robbers'."
18 The chief priests and the teachers of the
law heard this and began looking for a way to
kill him, for they feared him, because the
whole crowd was amazed at his teaching.

What are the injustices that make Jesus angry today? You might find it helpful to read a newspaper. Take some time asking God to make you angry at injustice. Go buy the *Big Issue* and pay the seller double.

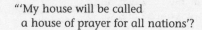

Some Christians are definitely nicer than Jesus. There's a time and a place for anger when you see injustice or hypocrisy. Jesus gets seriously angry in the temple courts. If it was today, he could have been arrested for vandalism. So what had naffed him off so much?

These traders were exploiting people who wanted to worship and meet with God. They were charging them loads of money for animals to sacrifice. A few days ago we read, in the story of the rich young man, that it is hard for rich people to follow Jesus. These traders were turning that round and making it too expensive for the poor to make their sacrifices while the rich could feel really great about their big, fat, impressive offerings.

Top tips

Mark 11:22–5

22"Have faith in God," Jesus answered. 23"I
tell you the truth, if anyone says to this
mountain, 'Go, throw yourself into the sea,'
and does not doubt in his heart but believes
that what he says will happen, it will be
done for him. 24Therefore I tell you, whatever you ask for in prayer, believe that you
have received it, and it will be yours. 25And
when you stand praying, if you hold anything against anyone, forgive him, so that
your Father in heaven may forgive you your
sins."

The second prayer-key Jesus gives us here is forgiveness. We need to get right with anyone we've got a problem with. Is there anyone you need to apologise to, or forgive, right now? What are you waiting for? Pick up the phone!

Some great tips from Jesus himself on prayer here. Especially if you fancy a bit of serious landscape gardening. It would be kinda fun to pop a mountain like Snowdon in the sea, just to get people's reactions – or how about moving the Isle of Wight into the North Sea for a couple of days?

First Jesus says that the key to miracles is faith. You've got to believe that it's possible when you pray. Now most of us would struggle with the Snowdon thing. But the mountain might be an illness you want God to heal, or a situation you need him to change. Faith is a bit like a muscle that gets stronger the more you use it. Not many of us have the faith to pray for the dead to be raised. But maybe we can imagine God healing a friend's headache. The more you exercise your faith on small things, the bigger your prayers will grow.

Wars, witches and the fight for life – 1 Samuel has it all. But throughout screams a message that still needs hearing today: God looks at the heart. Join Samuel, Saul and David to find out more.

False start?

1 samuel 1:1–5

1There was a certain man from Ramathaim, a
Zuphite from the hill country of Ephraim, whose
name was Elkanah son of Jeroham, the son of
Elihu, the son of Tohu, the son of Zuph, an
Ephraimite. 2He had two wives; one was called
Hannah and the other Peninnah. Peninnah had
children, but Hannah had none.
3Year after year this man went up from his
town to worship and sacrifice to the Lord
Almighty at Shiloh, where Hophni and Phinehas,
the two sons of Eli, were priests of the Lord.
4Whenever the day came for Elkanah to sacrifice,
he would give portions of the meat to his wife
Peninnah and to all her sons and daughters. 5But
to Hannah he gave a double portion because he
loved her, and the Lord had closed her womb.

You can't have a great football team without a great goalkeeper. They say the same about bands and drummers, and I guess it's true of stories: you can't have a good one without a great opening. Well, we know that the story of Samuel is pretty decent – I mean, it contains a massively important part in Israel's history, moving things on from the era when they were ruled by the judges to the time when they were ruled by kings – but is this really such a great opening? Why bother with this detail about Samuel's mum – especially when David's and Saul's birth stories get ignored? Couldn't it do with a rewrite? Something like . . .

'David let the cigarette fall to the ground, watching the small shower of sparks as it collided with the hardened earth. Picking up his saxophone he turned his thoughts to that magical week he'd spent in Tunisia last year. He put the sax to his lips and blew. It had been a special time for him, and as his fingers raced up and down, he remembered the lazy days and summer nights. But somehow he knew he'd never love again.'

Isn't that better? Perhaps not.

You see, the writer is making a point: David and Saul might be the big boys of the story, but God chose to kick off with some serious alternative focus. Samuel went on to anoint these two kings, carrying out God's wishes.

chew it over

The road to being used by God does not start with a privileged birth, it starts with commitment to him.

Consistently consistent

1 samuel 2:6–8

6"The Lord brings death and makes alive;
he brings down to the grave and raises up.
7The Lord sends poverty and wealth;
he humbles and he exalts.
8He raises the poor from the dust
and lifts the needy from the ash heap;
he seats them with princes
and has them inherit a throne of honour.

"For the foundations of the earth are the
Lord's;
upon them he has set the world."

OK, so Hannah's had a bit of an introduction, but the words of this prayer are the real insight into her character. The verses have sometimes been known as the Magnificat of the Old Testament because of their similarity to the words Mary spoke when she found herself in a similar situation (pregnant and surprised – see Luke 1:46–55). And just what is it that we find out? She is full of joy, but not solely because of her son, but because God has answered her prayer. She has been lifted up from a position of weakness to great strength by God. She has sussed that God often surprises his people, failing to do the predictable but always doing the good. Everything is in God's hands, from death to wealth, success to hardship. We cannot do it on our own; we need God's help.

These themes are not only true, they are consistent. It's not only Mary who comes out with similar lines and this certainly isn't just a prayer for the pregnant women amongst us. It's a state of mind, a realisation out of which great things can happen. And they did.

chew it over

The rhythm of God's message beats loud and clear: are we in time?

Have we lost the plot?

1 samuel 2:12–17

[12]Eli's sons were wicked men; they had no
regard for the Lord. [13]Now it was the practice
of the priests with the people that whenever
anyone offered a sacrifice and while the meat
was being boiled, the servant of the priest
would come with a three-pronged fork in his
hand. [14]He would plunge it into the pan or
kettle or cauldron or pot, and the priest would
take for himself whatever the fork brought up.
This is how they treated all the Israelites who
came to Shiloh. [15]But even before the fat was
burned, the servant of the priest would come
and say to the man who was sacrificing, "Give
the priest some meat to roast; he won't accept
boiled meat from you, but only raw."

[16]If the man said to him, "Let the fat be
burned up first, and then take whatever you
want," the servant would then answer, "No,
hand it over now; if you don't, I'll take it by
force."

[17]This sin of the young men was very great
in the Lord's sight, for they were treating the
Lord's offering with contempt.

I mean, I know the Bible's old and all that, but isn't this just a bit too bizarre? I mean, three-pronged forks and cauldrons of fat – why on earth does it matter? Eli's sons were wicked, right? Why? According to this it was because they were nicking meat from people. Hardly the crime of the century, is it? If blagging the odd quarter-pounder makes us wicked, then I'd rather not think about how God views the rest of my sins. But as ever, we need to engage our brains just a little to make some sense. Eli's sons were wicked, that's right, but it wasn't just their means of putting dinner on the table. They fell foul of God because in taking the meat they were stealing from God. And not just from his picnic either: they were stealing meat that was to be used specifically for worship.

This doesn't mean that God is some egotistical manic, obsessed with getting all the glory. It means that he loves nothing better than having his people get into relationship with him. When things get in the way of that, when people try to upset the correct order of things and steal for themselves what was meant for him, he is not best pleased.

chew it over

God is love, but he is also jealous. Are we making sure that he is getting all that is rightfully his?

What does God sound like?

1 samuel 3:2–10

2One night Eli, whose eyes were becoming
so weak that he could barely see, was lying
down in his usual place. 3The lamp of God
had not yet gone out, and Samuel was lying
down in the temple of the Lord, where the
ark of God was. 4Then the Lord called
Samuel.

Samuel answered, "Here I am." 5And he
ran to Eli and said, "Here I am; you called
me."

But Eli said, "I did not call; go back and
lie down." So he went and lay down.

6Again the Lord called, "Samuel!" And
Samuel got up and went to Eli and said,
"Here I am; you called me."

"My son," Eli said, "I did not call; go
back and lie down."

7Now Samuel did not yet know the Lord:
The word of the Lord had not yet been
revealed to him.

8The Lord called Samuel a third time, and
Samuel got up and went to Eli and said,
"Here I am; you called me."

Then Eli realised that the Lord was calling
the boy. 9So Eli told Samuel, "Go and lie
down, and if he calls you, say, 'Speak,
Lord, for your servant is listening.'" So
Samuel went and lay down in his place.

10The Lord came and stood there, calling
as at the other times, "Samuel! Samuel!"

Then Samuel said, "Speak, for your servant is listening."

Ah, you just can't beat a good old dose of slapstick, can you? There's more than a hint of Laurel and Hardy here, as old man Eli gets repeatedly woken up by a young (twelve-year-old) Samuel who mistakes the voice of God for his earthly master. But this obviously is more than light relief, especially as it raises a serious question: how do you hear God?

And the answer is . . . ? Unfortunately there are no rituals, riddles or tricks of the trade that can allow us to tune in to God's frequency, but if this passage holds a clue, it is in Samuel's last six words.

chew it over

Perhaps hearing God has less to do with our ears and more to do with our attitude.

Raiders of the lost . . .

1 samuel 4:5–11

5When the ark of the Lord's covenant came
into the camp, all Israel raised such a great
shout that the ground shook. 6Hearing the
uproar, the Philistines asked, "What's all
this shouting in the Hebrew camp?"
When they learned that the ark of the
Lord had come into the camp, 7the
Philistines were afraid. "A god has come
into the camp," they said. "We're in trouble!
Nothing like this has happened before.
8Woe to us! Who will deliver us from the
hand of these mighty gods? They are the
gods who struck the Egyptians with all
kinds of plagues in the desert. 9Be strong,
Philistines! Be men, or you will be subject
to the Hebrews, as they have been to you.
Be men, and fight!"
10So the Philistines fought, and the
Israelites were defeated and every man fled
to his tent. The slaughter was very great;
Israel lost thirty thousand foot soldiers.
11The ark of God was captured, and Eli's two
sons, Hophni and Phinehas, died.

It's been fought over between Harrison Ford and the Nazis, and it's all a bit spooky. The ark of the covenant – a chest that contained the stone tablets on which the Israelites' ancient laws had been written – had played a part in previous battles, and it seems fair to assume that the priests hoped that its presence after this particular defeat by the Philistines might just save their skins.

The Philistines certainly add to the sense of mystery, freaking out at the reaction the ark gets from the Israelites. But instead of a Spielberg moment where the ark spews spirits and knocks the baddies out for six, what follows is remarkably ordinary: the Philistines come out fighting, the Israelites go and hide and leave the ark to be carried off at their enemy's earliest convenience. No fuss. No magic. Bit disappointing really, isn't it?

Actually there's a point to all this: the priests were wrong to assume that getting God to save their hides was simply a case of bringing in the right objects, positioning the furniture in such a way that the auras and cosmic flow of energy ensured maximum success. God's not like that: Feng Shui just ain't his style. They lost because they had been disobedient to God, because they had been living for themselves for too long and needed to be taught once more to rely on him.

chew it over

Lifestyle counts for more than lucky charms.

Unpredictable

1 samuel 6:1–4, 7–10, 12

1When the ark of the Lord had been in
Philistine territory for seven months, 2the
Philistines called for the priests and the divin-
ers and said, "What shall we do with the ark
of the Lord? Tell us how we should send it
back to its place."
3They answered, "If you return the ark of
the god of Israel, do not send it away empty,
but by all means send a guilt offering to him.
Then you will be healed, and you will know
why his hand has not been lifted from you."
4The Philistines asked, "What guilt offering
should we send to him?"
They replied, "Five gold tumours and five
gold rats, according to the number of the
Philistine rulers, because the same plague has
struck both you and your rulers.
7"Now then, get a new cart ready, with two
cows that have calved and have never been
yoked. Hitch the cows to the cart, but take
their calves away and pen them up. 8Take the
ark of the Lord and put it on the cart, and in a
chest beside it put the gold objects you are
sending back to him as a guilt offering. Send it
on its way, 9but keep watching it. If it goes up
to its own territory, towards Beth Shemesh,
then the Lord has brought this great disaster
on us. But if it does not, then we shall know
that it was not his hand that struck us and that
it happened to us by chance."
10So they did this. They took two such cows
and hitched them to the cart and penned up
their calves.
12Then the cows went straight up towards
Beth Shemesh, keeping on the road and lowing all the way; they did not turn to the right
or to the left. The rulers of the Philistines followed them as far as the border of Beth
Shemesh.

But just when we were getting all cosy with this 'God doesn't do Feng Shui' line, we come across a passage like this. Some full-on freaky occurrences were taking place while the ark was in the enemy's hands, and they decide to off-load it sharpish. Now, forgive me for my ignorance, but I would have thought that the chances of a couple of cows pulling a cart the ten miles back to the homeland, mooing all the way without heading back towards their calves is pretty surprising. But not as surprising as God killing seventy of the blokes who sneaked a peek inside when it arrived.

So what do we learn? God didn't need any help from the Israelites to overrule.

chew it over

In the same way that God does not want his people to bind him up with superstition, he demands respect and honour.

Pleeeeease

1 samuel 8:6–9, 21–2

[6]But when they said, "Give us a king to lead
us," this displeased Samuel; so he prayed
to the Lord. [7]And the Lord told him: "Listen
to all that the people are saying to you; it
is not you they have rejected, but they
have rejected me as their king. [8]As they
have done from the day I brought them up
out of Egypt until this day, forsaking me
and serving other gods, so they are doing
to you. [9]Now listen to them; but warn them
solemnly and let them know what the king
who will reign over them will do."
[21]When Samuel heard all that the people
said, he repeated it before the Lord. [22]The
Lord answered, "Listen to them and give
them a king."

Then Samuel said to the men of Israel, "Everyone is to go back to his town."

Here's the deal: the Israelites are whingeing because they're unlike all the surrounding nations. They've all got kings, figureheads they can point to as symbols of their power and authority, while the Israelites have been ruled for ages by men known as judges. These people – appointed by God – had delivered the word of the Lord, but the Israelites were not happy. This was about as blatant a rejection of God as you could possibly imagine, yet despite his people saying an almighty NO to him, God stuck with them, eventually giving in to their desires.

So where does this leave us with God: are we now to think of him as a dribbling old fool, a pushover who'll give us as much pocket money as we like so long as we scream loud enough? Not at all. Sometimes God settles for less than the ideal for the sake of getting us to where he wants us to be.

chew it over

Given the choice between our imperfect and God's ideal, what would you choose?

Another low-key start

1 samuel 9:3–5, 18, 27, 10:1

3Now the donkeys belonging to Saul's father
Kish were lost, and Kish said to his son Saul,
"Take one of the servants with you and go
and look for the donkeys." 4So he passed
through the hill country of Ephraim and
through the area around Shalisha, but they
did not find them. They went on into the district of Shaalim, but the donkeys were not
there. Then he passed through the territory of
Benjamin, but they did not find them.
5When they reached the district of Zuph,
Saul said to the servant who was with him,
"Come, let's go back, or my father will stop
thinking about the donkeys and start worrying
about us."
18Saul approached Samuel in the gateway
and asked, "Would you please tell me where
the seer's house is?"
27As they were going down to the edge of
the town, Samuel said to Saul, "Tell the servant to go on ahead of us"—and the servant
did so—"but you stay here awhile, so that I
may give you a message from God."
1Then Samuel took a flask of oil and poured
it on Saul's head and kissed him, saying, "Has
not the Lord anointed you leader over his
inheritance?"

chew it over

Where do you think you're heading with God? Are you both going in the same direction?

Remember how the chapter kicked off? Well, here we go with another laid-back intro. Saul becomes Israel's first ever king, and is chosen specifically by God through Samuel, yet the very first glimpses that we get of him play along with the original idea that true greatness comes not from physical history but spiritual action.

OK, so Saul comes from an impressive family, but what is he doing when we meet him? Looking for lost donkeys, without a care in the world for political greatness or personal ambition. When he meets Samuel he fails to recognise him. Samuel, on the other hand, is locked into God's plan and knows all he needs to about this young future king. Again we get the message served up: it is God who is making the moves, God who is in charge. Our final selection shows the occasion when Samuel kicks off the ceremony anointing Saul as king. There is a public anointing later on, but this one is so private that even Saul's servant is not allowed to turn up. If you know the story of David this might be ringing bells already, but we'll come onto it later anyway. But the fact is clear: every aspect of God's choosing people to do his work – from the people he chooses, the way he tells them and the methods used to prepare them – plays by a different set of rules than those which we might expect.

Where did *that* come from?

1 samuel 15:22–3

22 But Samuel replied:

"Does the Lord delight in burnt offerings
and sacrifices
as much as in obeying the voice of the
Lord?
To obey is better than sacrifice,
and to heed is better than the fat of
rams.
23 For rebellion is like the sin of divination,
and arrogance like the evil of idolatry.
Because you have rejected the word of the
Lord,
he has rejected you as king."

A handful of chapters pass by and the story shows the end of Saul. He has failed to live up to expectations as king, and in the early days of his reign was guilty of impulsive and foolish action. Later, in the incident that leads up to this rejection by God Saul was guilty of something else: disobedience.

For us modern readers the story's a tough one. God tells Saul to 'totally destroy' the Amalekites and everything that belongs to them. That includes the whole lot: possessions, livestock, women, men and children. Saul holds back on a few – sparing the life of the king and keeping the best sheep and cattle – but slaughtering most of the others.

How do we read it? Had the old man freaked out? Was Saul acting as God's conscience? No. The Amalekites were ancient enemies of Israel, and the Hebrew phrase for 'total destruction' literally means 'to devote to Yahweh (God)'. Old Testament actions are often hard to understand, but we know at least that in failing to do as he was told, Saul left his enemies free to hassle God's people for years to come.

chew it over

The point is this: God's word is holy. Obedience rates higher than ceremony.

Never mind the height, feel the character

1 samuel 16:6–13

6 When they arrived, Samuel saw Eliab and
thought, "Surely the Lord's anointed stands
here before the Lord."
7 But the Lord said to Samuel, 'Do not
consider his appearance or his height, for I
have rejected him. The Lord does not look
at the things man looks at. Man looks at the
outward appearance, but the Lord looks at
the heart."
8 Then Jesse called Abinadab and made
him pass in front of Samuel. But Samuel
said, "The Lord has not chosen this one
either." 9 Jesse then made Shammah pass
by, but Samuel said, "Nor has the Lord
chosen this one." 10 Jesse made seven of his
sons pass before Samuel, but Samuel said
to him, "The Lord has not chosen these."
11 So he asked Jesse, "Are these all the sons
you have?"
"There is still the youngest," Jesse
answered, "but he is tending the sheep."
Samuel said, "Send for him; we will not
sit down until he arrives."
12 So he sent and had him brought in. He
was ruddy, with a fine appearance and
handsome features.
Then the Lord said, "Rise and anoint him;
he is the one."
13 So Samuel took the horn of oil and
anointed him in the presence of his brothers, and from that day on the Spirit of the
Lord came upon David in power. Samuel
then went to Ramah.

We're back, settling down with an old theme that we all still need to hear. With Saul rejected by God, Samuel's next mission is to go out and single out the new king of Israel. He follows the instructions (a wise move) and winds up here – in front of Jesse's sons – where he has been told he will find Saul's successor.

If you remember the deal with Saul, he was a good-looking chap (9:2, 10:23–4), and despite the fact that he was up to his elbows in lost donkeys, he had the look of someone who would be king. A little like Jesse's eldest, perhaps. But one of the Bible's favourite themes is being underlined here as God tells Samuel that outward appearance is not the measure by which he judges suitability. Instead he's told to look for the character of a king. It so happens that David – despite being young – was decent enough on the beauty scale (a nice hint that he was not inferior to Saul), but it's obvious why Samuel knew he was the one . . . 'There is still the youngest . . . but he is tending the sheep.'

chew it over

Character - you can't invest in anything better.

And as if we weren't sure . . .

1 samuel 17:45-51

45David said to the Philistine, "You come
against me with sword and spear and
javelin, but I come against you in the name
of the Lord Almighty, the God of the armies
of Israel, whom you have defied. 46This day
the Lord will hand you over to me, and I'll
strike you down and cut off your head.
Today I will give the carcasses of the
Philistine army to the birds of the air and
the beasts of the earth, and the whole
world will know that there is a God in
Israel. 47All those gathered here will know
that it is not by sword or spear that the
Lord saves; for the battle is the Lord's, and
he will give all of you into our hands."

48As the Philistine moved closer to attack
him, David ran quickly towards the battle
line to meet him. 49Reaching into his bag
and taking out a stone, he slung it and
struck the Philistine on the forehead. The
stone sank into his forehead, and he fell
face down on the ground.

50So David triumphed over the Philistine
with a sling and a stone; without a sword in
his hand he struck down the Philistine and
killed him.

51David ran and stood over him. He took
hold of the Philistine's sword and drew it
from the scabbard. After he killed him, he
cut off his head with the sword.

When the Philistines saw that their hero
was dead, they turned and ran.

It was common for the ancient Greeks (the Philistines were probably related to them) to settle the occasional war by pitching their prizefighter in a one-on-one with the enemy. This cut down on wastage and made for a nice day out. Goliath was their champion and Saul (Israel's own giant warrior – see 9:2 and 10:23) was scared.

Young and inexperienced as he was in physical battles, David had the real muscle to pull him through: he knew, loved and trusted God. His strength came from the fact that he was 100 per cent reliant on God. Think about that for a moment.

chew it over

It's easy to get lost in the story of David and Goliath, but at the heart of it is a perfect message: trust God. Trust God. Trust God.

You can't keep a good man down

1 samuel 19:9–12

9But an evil spirit from the Lord came upon
Saul as he was sitting in his house with his
spear in his hand. While David was playing
the harp, 10Saul tried to pin him to the wall
with his spear, but David eluded him as
Saul drove the spear into the wall. That
night David made good his escape.
11Saul sent men to David's house to watch
it and to kill him in the morning. But
Michal, David's wife, warned him, "If you
don't run for your life tonight, tomorrow
you'll be killed." 12So Michal let David down
through a window, and he fled and
escaped.

Saul is jealous of David (no surprises there), and here steps up his attempts to kill the young pretender. Having tried and failed to bump him off indirectly – by sending him into battle – Saul had to watch David's popularity rise as he became well known for his military successes. But even flesh and blood can't be relied on to do a bit of political spring cleaning, as Saul's son Jonathan has become top mates with David and warns him of his evil papa's intentions.

It can't have been easy for David. The rollercoaster ride that took him from the fields to the royal court gave him plenty of glimpses of death, plenty of reasons to bail out on all this Spiritual Destiny stuff and get back to basics.

chew it over

Whoever said God's calling came hand in hand with an easy life?

On the run

1 samuel 24:1–7

[1]After Saul returned from pursuing the
Philistines, he was told, "David is in the
Desert of En Gedi." [2]So Saul took three
thousand chosen men from all Israel and set
out to look for David and his men near the
Crags of the Wild Goats.
[3]He came to the sheep pens along the
way; a cave was there, and Saul went in to
relieve himself. David and his men were far
back in the cave. [4]The men said, "This is the
day the Lord spoke of when he said to you,
'I will give your enemy into your hands for
you to deal with as you wish.'" Then David
crept up unnoticed and cut off a corner of
Saul's robe.
[5]Afterwards, David was conscience-strick-
en for having cut off a corner of his robe.
[6]He said to his men, "The Lord forbid that I
should do such a thing to my master, the
Lord's anointed, or lift my hand against
him; for he is the anointed of the Lord."
[7]With these words David rebuked his men
and did not allow them to attack Saul. And
Saul left the cave and went his way.

With Saul continually on his tail, David enters a period as a fugitive that would test even the most dedicated character. He was on the run for years, and faced an almost continual threat from Saul. First he goes to Ramah, then Gibeath, Nob, the cave at Adullam, to the battle at Keilah, out to the Desert of Ziph, then to Horesh, the Desert of Maon and En Gedi . . . you get the picture. He was betrayed by those whom he thought he could trust and had to take help from those he thought he could not trust. It was enough to send the man insane, but look at the passage here and we see something remarkable. Saul was still the man anointed as king, and David was still his subject. Touching the king's clothing was almost like touching his person, and David's immediate regret shows his remarkable character: even after all the threats and hatred, he recognises the way of the world. Saul was chosen by God and it is up to God alone to remove him.

chew it over

Of course we all like to step in and give God a helping hand from time to time, but shouldn't we take things a little more seriously?

The same old story

1 samuel 28:3–8

3Now Samuel was dead, and all Israel had
mourned for him and buried him in his own
town of Ramah. Saul had expelled the
mediums and spiritists from the land.
4The Philistines assembled and came and
set up camp at Shunem, while Saul gathered all the Israelites and set up camp at
Gilboa. 5When Saul saw the Philistine army,
he was afraid; terror filled his heart. 6He
enquired of the Lord, but the Lord did not
answer him by dreams or Urim or prophets.
7Saul then said to his attendants, "Find me a
woman who is a medium, so that I may go
and enquire of her."
"There is one in Endor," they said.
8So Saul disguised himself, putting on
other clothes, and at night he and two men
went to the woman. "Consult a spirit for
me," he said, "and bring up for me the one
I name."

As if we needed a reason to put Saul's name in the list of Bad Kings, here's a reminder. He'd done a good job by getting rid of many of the mediums and spiritists from the land, but witchcraft was obviously so popular that totally eradicating it was impossible. Now Saul is desperate, and with Samuel out of the picture (perhaps put to death by the king) he has no means of hearing from God. And so he heads into enemy territory to chat with the Witch of Endor.

Just like the time when he failed to kill the Amalekites as God had instructed, Saul's actions fail to match up. In turning to the medium he enters the last phase of his life, rounding it off with a large dose of hypocrisy to add to all the other sins.

There's a huge difference between knowing what is wrong and doing what is right. Saul was good enough at condemning the mediums, but he still couldn't stop himself from sinning.

chew it over

Let's not be guilty of trying to pull a fast one on God.

Do the right thing

1 samuel 30:24–5

24"Who will listen to what you say? The
share of the man who stayed with the supplies is to be the same as that of him who
went down to the battle. All shall share
alike." 25David made this a statute and ordi-
nance for Israel from that day to this.

With the prospect of even his own men turning on him and threatening to kill him, David remains in the good books by turning to God, trusting him for advice on the right moves to make. He is able to distinguish between the victims and his true enemies, for as he comes across an Egyptian slave of the Amalekites, left by his master to die, he treats him with dignity and integrity. A wise move as the man leads David to where the Amalekites are camped. Within hours it's Game Over for the Amalekites and David's back on top.

But does he rest up here? No way – he swiftly moves in and makes his first legal decree: his soldiers are arguing about how much cash those that didn't fight should get. But David knows the way things should be, and declares that all should be treated equally.

This classic message reappears throughout the Bible, and Jesus made sure people heard it from him direct.

chew it over

Glamour, status and position count as nothing in the kingdom of God. We need to treat all people as equals.

A sad end

1 samuel 31:1–6

[1]Now the Philistines fought against Israel;
the Israelites fled before them, and many
fell slain on Mount Gilboa. [2]The Philistines
pressed hard after Saul and his sons, and
they killed his sons Jonathan, Abinadab and
Malki-Shua. [3]The fighting grew fierce around
Saul, and when the archers overtook him,
they wounded him critically.
[4]Saul said to his armour-bearer, "Draw
your sword and run me through, or these
uncircumcised fellows will come and run me
through and abuse me."
But the armour-bearer was terrified and
would not do it; so Saul took his own
sword and fell on it. [5]When the armour-
bearer saw that Saul was dead, he too fell
on his sword and died with him. [6]So Saul
and his three sons and his armour-bearer
and all his men died together that
same day.

David was right to trust God to deal with Saul. The king met his own end in suitable fashion: with his army fleeing from the pursuing Philistines, unable to get even his servant to carry out his final order. In the same way that David cut off the head of Goliath, the Philistines decapitated Saul. This was no way for a mighty king to die, but then again Saul's life was one long journey of self-destruction. Selfishness, fear, greed, ignorance – he had them all. How different things were at the end of his life than when we first met him.

It all goes back to Samuel: the man who was told by God not to look at the outward appearance but to ponder the character. Saul's character was crippled and ugly.

chew it over

Appearances are deceptive: what counts with God is character.

1 Corinthians

The wisdom of the wise

Corinth, what a tasty little town: plenty of trade and hundreds of 'sacred' prostitutes. Life was so saucy that the Greek verb 'to Corinthianise' came to mean 'to practise sexual immorality'. No wonder the church was up against it, and Paul's letters were aimed at sorting out many of their problems: divisions, instability, sexual immorality and the misuse of spiritual gifts. Nice one.

1 Corinthians 1:18–20

18For the message of the cross is foolishness
to those who are perishing, but to us who
are being saved it is the power of God. 19For
it is written:

"I will destroy the wisdom of the wise;
the intelligence of the intelligent I will
frustrate."

20Where is the wise man? Where is the
scholar? Where is the philosopher of this
age? Has not God made foolish the wisdom
of the world?

God may have chosen the foolish to shame the wise, but he still calls all us fools to find out more about him, getting to know him better.

This echoes a favourite theme that is doing the rounds in some parts of the Church today, especially when at first sight it appears that Paul is having a go at all those who like to use their brains. But can it really mean this? Is Paul really being so dumb?

Of course not, and a little study clears up the mess faster than a jug of bleach and a scrubbing brush. You see, the 'I will destroy . . . ' bit is a quotation from Isaiah (29:14 if you're keen). In it God is having a go at the so-called 'wise' men of Judah (among them Hezekiah) who chased after an alliance with Egypt when they were threatened by Assyria. It was a bad move which led to the Egyptians taking over. So much for wisdom. Apparently Corinth was full of such wise bods, always spouting off with their own solutions to the world's problems. According to Paul these men weren't truly wise: without acknowledging God as the ultimate boss, how could they be?

Back with us today, we seem to twist the passage and others like it. Some of us like to think that all wisdom comes a distant second to getting high with God, that the Lord pours scorn on all who study, that theology just gets in the way. But Paul is arguing against a culture that tried to win people over with clever argument and lengthy debate – a million miles away from the situation facing us today.

Paul is clear that Christianity draws its power from the most bizarre yet important event in history, as God drew a line in the sand: the death of Jesus on the cross. What happened there and in the days that followed changed the whole fabric of our lives: as God drew a line in the sand: do we accept the cross, the judgment and forgiveness, the sacrifice and pain?

Disorder

1 Corinthians 5:9–13

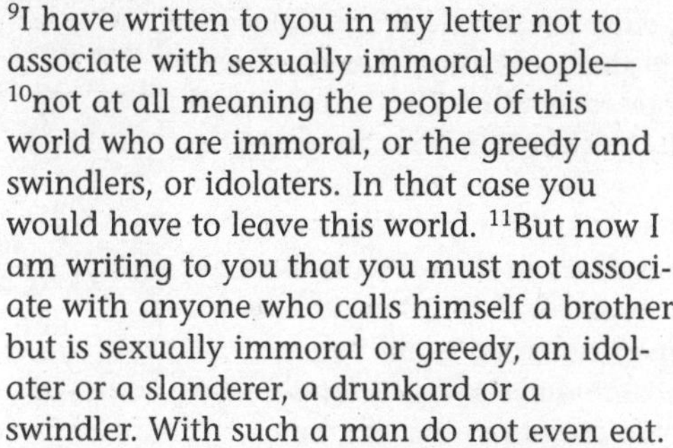

[9]I have written to you in my letter not to
associate with sexually immoral people—
[10]not at all meaning the people of this
world who are immoral, or the greedy and
swindlers, or idolaters. In that case you
would have to leave this world. [11]But now I
am writing to you that you must not associate with anyone who calls himself a brother
but is sexually immoral or greedy, an idolater or a slanderer, a drunkard or a
swindler. With such a man do not even eat.
[12]What business is it of mine to judge
those outside the church? Are you not to
judge those inside? [13]God will judge those
outside. "Expel the wicked man from
among you."

Sin, disorder, immorality: Paul brings it all back home with the message that the church should be radically different.

A letter – what letter? You see, somehow this other letter of Paul's to the Corinthians has got lost, so we're not sure what the whole deal was. One thing's for sure though: they'd got the wrong end of the stick. They'd taken it to mean that in an attempt to steer clear of sin, they should completely avoid any immoral person, non-Christians included. Instead, Paul here clears it up: don't tolerate immoral behaviour within the church – root out hypocrisy.

Paul said plenty of things to the church in Corinth, and he wasn't afraid to lay down the law. He doesn't do it for the power trip: in every situation he saw the whole picture. If we allow the Church to become corrupt, if we have double standards, then we do ourselves no favours. Likewise, if we cut ourselves off, if we wince at the sight of sin in others and have nothing to do with them, we miss the whole point of Jesus' message.

Finding God

1 Corinthians 7:17–24

17Nevertheless, each one should retain the
place in life that the Lord assigned to him and
to which God has called him. This is the rule I
lay down in all the churches. 18Was a man
already circumcised when he was called? He
should not become uncircumcised. Was a
man uncircumcised when he was called? He
should not be circumcised. 19Circumcision is
nothing and uncircumcision is nothing.
Keeping God's commands is what counts.
20Each one should remain in the situation
which he was in when God called him. 21Were
you a slave when you were called? Don't let it
trouble you—although if you can gain your
freedom, do so. 22For he who was a slave
when he was called by the Lord is the Lord's
freedman; similarly, he who was a free man
when he was called is Christ's slave. 23You
were bought at a price; do not become slaves
of men. 24Brothers, each man, as responsible
to God, should remain in the situation God
called him to.

Many people have tried, but the gospel of Jesus cannot be watered down: it is for everyone. Paul understood that God looks at the heart, not the history.

At the time, circumcision was a bit of a sore point (sorry, bad joke) in the church. Why? Because it was about who was allowed to become a Christian: was it just those who'd had the snip (the Jews) or was it open to those who hadn't (everyone else). Was there a league table, with the Jewish Christians coming out on top? Paul was keen to point out that Christ died for all, regardless of background.

But there's more. The bit about the circumcision issue is an example of how people should 'retain the place in life that the Lord assigned to him and to which God has called him' – or in other words, how people should try to live full-on lives for God whatever their background or current situation. Whether rich or poor, high society or down on luck, Jew or Gentile, Paul urged the members of the church in Corinth to find contentment with Jesus right where they were.

Where's the beef?

1 Corinthians 8:8–13

8But food does not bring us near to God; we
are no worse if we do not eat, and no better
if we do.
9Be careful, however, that the exercise of
your freedom does not become a stumbling-
block to the weak. 10For if anyone with a
weak conscience sees you who have this
knowledge eating in an idol's temple, won't
he be emboldened to eat what has been sacrificed to idols? 11So this weak brother, for
whom Christ died, is destroyed by your
knowledge. 12When you sin against your
brothers in this way and wound their weak
conscience, you sin against Christ.
13Therefore, if what I eat causes my brother
to fall into sin, I will never eat meat again,
so that I will not cause him to fall.

Paul understood what made the church tick: it's all about relationships.

Excuse me? 'Food does not bring us near to God'? I mean, what's going on here? Has Paul lost the plot? I mean, a double whopper and king fries is good, but it's not exactly paradise, is it? Of course food doesn't bring us closer to God, so why bother writing it?

The point is a simple one: the Corinthians were having a spot of bother over the issue of meat left over from pagan sacrifices. Some felt that the chance for a free meal after the temple service or some cheap cuts in the market was a good idea, and were unfussed about where the meat had come from. Others were convinced that if they ate it they were taking part in pagan worship. They'd written to Paul and asked for help.

His answer? 'Don't be so dumb . . . of course it doesn't contaminate you.' A sensible answer there, Paul. But just as the meat eaters might have been getting excited and stoking up the barbie, Paul adds something else in: 'But don't let it get in the way of the church's unity.' He didn't have a problem with it himself, but he was prepared to give up on the steaks out of respect for others. Paul valued unity above personal satisfaction, but that didn't make him a wimpish people-pleaser. It's good to note the way Paul refers to 'weak' and 'strong' Christians here. According to him our faith isn't about leaving others struggling to catch up; instead in the picture he paints unity is valued above personal freedom.

No passengers

1 Corinthians 12:14–20

14Now the body is not made up of one part
but of many. 15If the foot should say,
"Because I am not a hand, I do not belong
to the body," it would not for that reason
cease to be part of the body. 16And if the ear
should say, "Because I am not an eye, I do
not belong to the body," it would not for
that reason cease to be part of the body. 17If
the whole body were an eye, where would
the sense of hearing be? If the whole body
were an ear, where would the sense of smell
be? 18But in fact God has arranged the parts
in the body, every one of them, just as he
wanted them to be. 19If they were all one
part, where would the body be? 20As it is,
there are many parts, but one body.

Let's not leave spiritual 'success' to the people on the stage: let's find our own role and let God be the judge.

A popular passage this, especially as it carries on the theme that Paul has been so faithfully putting across: the need for unity within the Church. But it's particularly important for us today, especially as the Church has managed to create its own celebrity culture. You know the score: smiling speakers or brooding worship leaders who manage to stand on a stage and make it all look so easy. Let's face facts: there's nothing wrong with having people lead and teach the rest of us, but we should never forget the truth: we need to know our place.

This is no pop culture thing: we're not here to make the 'celebs' rich, nor are we here to have them as our heroes. OK, so it might sound a bit twee, but I'm convinced that there's only one hero we need in life. And Paul knows it too, which is why he takes the trouble he does here. In Corinth there was a sense of division between the spiritual success stories who had the gift of speaking in tongues and the lost Christian causes who didn't have it. According to Paul, those without had no reason either to feel bad or to place the tongue gabblers on some kind of pedestal. Why? Because it's the way God wants it. God happens to be bigger than the biggest Christian Celebrity, and he has 'arranged the parts of the body' as he pleases.

The spirit zone

1 Corinthians 13:1–8, 13

1If I speak in the tongues of men and of
angels, but have not love, I am only a
resounding gong or a clanging cymbal. 2If I
have the gift of prophecy and can fathom all
mysteries and all knowledge, and if I have a
faith that can move mountains, but have not
love, I am nothing. 3If I give all I possess to
the poor and surrender my body to the flames,
but have not love, I gain nothing.

4Love is patient, love is kind. It does not
envy, it does not boast, it is not proud. 5It is
not rude, it is not self-seeking, it is not easily
angered, it keeps no record of wrongs. 6Love
does not delight in evil but rejoices with the
truth. 7It always protects, always trusts, always
hopes, always perseveres.

8Love never fails. But where there are
prophecies, they will cease; where there are
tongues, they will be stilled; where there is
knowledge, it will pass away.

13And now these three remain: faith, hope
and love. But the greatest of these is love.

Why love? Because it's the one motivation that will stick it out till the bitter end.

The Holy Spirit is given to us much in the same way that he was given to Jesus. As the miracle maker, the Son of God perfectly demonstrated Paul's point: Jesus wasn't just about the deeds, he wasn't simply a guy with some fancy tricks up his sleeve. No, Jesus had something else – love. His compassion for a lost people led him to an agonising death on the cross. Ultimately, it was Jesus' love for his Father's creation that motivated him to take on the role of Most Sacrificial Human Ever.

So what's the story? We're signed up too. Like Jesus we are in line for the gifts of the Spirit – the tongues, prophecy, healing and so on. It's pre-packed and part of the deal, but there's something else in there too. In the same way that the Spirit led Jesus, so too can we expect to find ourselves being led along a similar path.

2 SAMUEL

The story continues as Israel's second ever king settles into the job. David's history marks him out as a unique man. His failings mark him out as perhaps a more normal one. But David's reign became a standard by which all later reigns were measured. Here's how.

Softly softly

2 Samuel 2:1–7

[1]In the course of time, David
enquired of the Lord. "Shall I go
up to one of the towns of Judah?"
he asked.
The Lord said, "Go up."
David asked, "Where shall I
go?"
"To Hebron," the Lord
answered.
[2]So David went up there with
his two wives, Ahinoam of Jezreel
and Abigail, the widow of Nabal
of Carmel. [3]David also took the
men who were with him, each
with his family, and they settled
in Hebron and its towns. [4]Then
the men of Judah came to Hebron
and there they anointed David
king over the house of Judah.
When David was told that it
was the men of Jabesh Gilead
who had buried Saul, [5]he sent
messengers to the men of Jabesh
Gilead to say to them, "The Lord
bless you for showing this kindness to Saul your master by bury-
ing him. [6]May the Lord now show
you kindness and faithfulness,
and I too will show you the same
favour because you have done
this. [7]Now then, be strong and
brave, for Saul your master is
dead, and the house of Judah has
anointed me king over them."

SEARCH

David knew that he was going to be king – Samuel, Jonathan and Saul had all confirmed this – and with Saul finally dead, you could be forgiven for expecting him to make a swift move for the throne. Instead he asks God if it is right for him to move back to Judah from Philistine territory. He'd seen what had happened when a king presumed too much without staying close to God. But the move back is a good one, not least because it prompts a public anointing from the people of Judah who declare David as king. It was all the way back in 1 Samuel 16 when he had been privately anointed by Samuel, and decades had passed between these two events.

GO

How are you at keeping hold of God's promises? Can you keep them fresh in your heart for weeks, months, even years?

Dancing in the street

2 Samuel 6:13–19

13 When those who were carrying the ark of the Lord had
taken six steps, he sacrificed
a bull and a fattened calf.
14 David, wearing a linen
ephod, danced before the
Lord with all his might,
15 while he and the entire
house of Israel brought up
the ark of the Lord with
shouts and the sound of
trumpets.
16 As the ark of the Lord
was entering the City of
David, Michal daughter of
Saul watched from a win-
dow. And when she saw King
David leaping and dancing
before the Lord, she despised
him in her heart.
17 They brought the ark of
the Lord and set it in its
place inside the tent that
David had pitched for it, and
David sacrificed burnt offerings and fellowship offerings
before the Lord. 18 After he
had finished sacrificing the
burnt offerings and fellowship offerings, he blessed the
people in the name of the
Lord Almighty. 19 Then he
gave a loaf of bread, a cake
of dates and a cake of raisins
to each person in the whole
crowd of Israelites, both men
and women. And all the
people went to their homes.

SEARCH

After all he'd been through you'd have thought that David deserved a break. But no, there's the small matter of Saul's remaining relatives to be dealt with. Well, he deals with them, and finally all the tribes of Israel (not just his original tribe of Judah) recognise him as king. He kicks the Jebusites out of this place, names it Jerusalem and declares it his capital city. The Philistines come looking for trouble, but get beaten, and all in all, I think we can conclude that he made a pretty decent start to his rule. But this is all a build-up, as the passage indicates. David knew that what really mattered was making a clear statement that he was ruling Israel under the authority of God. He brought the ark to Jerusalem, and was prepared to humiliate himself in order to express how important he felt the moment was.

Michal was famously unimpressed with her husband's performance, but perhaps that had something to do with what happened to her father, Saul. Back in 1 Samuel 19:24 Saul had an encounter with the Spirit of God that left him wandering around the streets dazed and half-naked. This became something of an in-joke among the people, and makes David's actions even more risky and impressive.

Given the choice, David opted for worship over massaging his own ego.

A house for a house

2 Samuel 7:1–2, 4–6, 8–9, 11b, 16

1After the king was settled in his
palace and the Lord had given
him rest from all his enemies
around him, 2he said to Nathan
the prophet, "Here I am, living in
a palace of cedar, while the ark of
God remains in a tent."
4That night the word of the Lord
came to Nathan, saying:

> 5"Go and tell my servant
> David, 'This is what the Lord
> says: Are you the one to build
> me a house to dwell in? 6I have
> not dwelt in a house from the
> day I brought the Israelites up
> out of Egypt to this day. I have
> been moving from place to place
> with a tent as my dwelling.
> 8"Now then, tell my servant
> David, 'This is what the Lord
> Almighty says: I took you from
> the pasture and from following
> the flock to be ruler over my peo-
> ple Israel. 9I have been with you
> wherever you have gone, and I
> have cut off all your enemies
> from before you. Now I will
> make your name great, like the
> names of the greatest men of the
> earth.
> 11b"'The Lord declares to you
> that the Lord himself will estab-
> lish a house for you: 16Your
> house and your kingdom shall
> endure for ever before me; your
> throne shall be established for
> ever.'"

SEARCH

This is perhaps the most important section of the books of Samuel. It shows the basis for the ancestral line that will produce Jesus, and it is a key landmark in the history of God's people. Note that it kicks off with David earning yet more gold stars by suggesting that he build a permanent home for the ark. Nice move, son, but God has even better plans. While the Lord was into the idea and saw the heart behind the suggestion, he rejects the pagan notion that he was like the other gods, interested only in having people maintain temples and follow rituals. Instead of having David build him a house for the ark, God offers to build the ex-shepherd a house. We're not talking bricks and mortar here, but a dynasty, a family line that 'shall endure for ever' (16). That's quite a promise, especially as it came out of the blue.

GO

Let's not forget that God said no to David's good intentions about building a home for the ark. At times our plans can seem good enough, yet still a 'no' comes back. Perhaps David's experience can give us a little encouragement.

The big picture

2 Samuel 7:25–9

25"And now, Lord God,
keep for ever the promise
you have made concern-
ing your servant and his
house. Do as you
promised, 26so that your
name will be great for
ever. Then men will say,
'The Lord Almighty is God
over Israel!' And the house
of your servant David will
be established before you.
27"O Lord Almighty, God
of Israel, you have
revealed this to your servant, saying, 'I will build a
house for you.' So your
servant has found courage
to offer you this prayer.
28O Sovereign Lord, you
are God! Your words are
trustworthy, and you have
promised these good
things to your servant.
29Now be pleased to bless
the house of your servant,
that it may continue for
ever in your sight; for you,
O Sovereign Lord, have
spoken, and with your
blessing the house of your
servant will be blessed for
ever."

SEARCH

So, being told that one of your descendants is going to be The Man must have been quite a trip for David, but like with Mary, the proof of the wisdom of God's blessing comes in the response. David gets straight down to prayer. Of course he's blown away by the whole thing and is extremely thankful, but David knows that there's more to it than that. The blessing is not just something cosy for himself, not just a pat on the back and a shot at early retirement with easy life in tow. He makes the connection between these fresh promises and those made to Moses for the nation years before. David knows that what God has promised is for the sake of Israel, so that his earlier promises might be fulfilled. And of course, the end result of that is glory and honour for God throughout the whole world.

GO

What's the big picture in your life? How are the gifts that God has given you able to fit in with his larger plans?

One giant leap?

2 Samuel 11:1–5

[1]In the spring, at the
time when kings go off to
war, David sent Joab out
with the king's men and
the whole Israelite army.
They destroyed the
Ammonites and besieged
Rabbah. But David
remained in Jerusalem.
[2]One evening David
got up from his bed and
walked around on the
roof of the palace. From
the roof he saw a woman
bathing. The woman was
very beautiful, [3]and
David sent someone to
find out about her. The
man said, "Isn't this
Bathsheba, the daughter
of Eliam and the wife of
Uriah the Hittite?" [4]Then
David sent messengers to
get her. She came to him,
and he slept with her.
(She had purified herself
from her uncleanness.)
Then she went back
home. [5]The woman con-
ceived and sent word to
David, saying, "I am
pregnant."

SEARCH

How quickly things can change. One minute David's got God handing out the ultimate fortune cookie, the next he's letting it all go for the sake of a little hanky-panky. The writer kicks off with a telling statement, mentioning that in staying back from the war David was failing to act like a true king. He manages to break four of the ten commandments – adultery, murder, false testimony and coveting – and there can be no doubt that the child is his, as the mention of Bathsheba's purification before sleeping with David makes it clear that she'd just completed a menstrual cycle. In the verses that follow we see David desperately trying to get out of trouble, but we know how it ends.

What caused his fall? Was it pride? Arrogance? Perhaps he was a victim of Bathsheba's cunning? Think about it for a minute: was this really the first time that David would have faced the temptation to sin? Maybe what caused it was nothing more complex than giving in, taking a second look at a beautiful body. This was no conspiracy, this was a failure to keep up his guard.

GO

It doesn't matter how good our pedigree, we must keep on our toes when it comes to facing temptation.

Revelation

2 Samuel 12:1–7a, 13a

1The Lord sent Nathan to David.
When he came to him, he said,
“There were two men in a certain
town, one rich and the other poor.
2The rich man had a very large
number of sheep and cattle, 3but the
poor man had nothing except one
little ewe lamb that he had bought.
He raised it, and it grew up with
him and his children. It shared his
food, drank from his cup and even
slept in his arms. It was like a
daughter to him.
4“Now a traveller came to the rich
man, but the rich man refrained
from taking one of his own sheep or
cattle to prepare a meal for the traveller who had come to him. Instead,
he took the ewe lamb that belonged
to the poor man and prepared it for
the one who had come to him.”
5David burned with anger against
the man and said to Nathan, “As
surely as the Lord lives, the man
who did this deserves to die! 6He
must pay for that lamb four times
over, because he did such a thing
and had no pity.”
7Then Nathan said to David, “You
are the man!”
13Then David said to Nathan, “I
have sinned against the Lord.”

SEARCH

Some months passed between Uriah’s death and the arrival of Nathan with this most powerful story. It works on two levels: not only does it invite David to condemn himself without realising it, but it appeals to him as king and the nation’s law-maker. David knows that the punishment for adultery and murder is death (Leviticus 20:10, 24:17), and his response is immediate and genuine: ‘I have sinned against the Lord’ (13). Too right he has. Not wanting to sound bad on Uriah’s family, but it was against God that David had committed the worst sin. Unlike Saul when he was confronted with his actions (1 Samuel 15:14), David accepts the truth and turns back to God.

Never just a bystander, God is involved in our lives and takes note of what we do. That includes celebrating at the good and feeling the wounds of the bad.

True worship

2 Samuel 12:15–20

15 After Nathan had gone home,
the Lord struck the child that
Uriah's wife had borne to David,
and he became ill. 16 David pleaded with God for the child. He fasted and went into his house and
spent the nights lying on the
ground. 17 The elders of his household stood beside him to get him
up from the ground, but he
refused, and he would not eat
any food with them.
18 On the seventh day the child
died. David's servants were afraid
to tell him that the child was
dead, for they thought, "While
the child was still living, we spoke
to David but he would not listen
to us. How can we tell him the
child is dead? He may do something desperate."
19 David noticed that his servants were whispering among
themselves and he realised that
the child was dead. "Is the child
dead?" he asked.
"Yes," they replied, "he is
dead."
20 Then David got up from the
ground. After he had washed, put
on lotions and changed his
clothes, he went into the house of
the Lord and worshipped. Then
he went to his own house, and at
his request they served him food,
and he ate.

SEARCH

There is always a consequence to sin, and we do ourselves no favours if we assume that God's forgiveness means that everything will be put back as it was. On finding out about the physical consequence of his actions – the death of his and Bathsheba's son – David heads off to the house of the Lord to worship. Perhaps he could have gone on a bender first, got mad with God and stayed out all night, but David had a true worshipper's heart. Turning to God and pouring himself out was not a means of escape but of communication with his Creator. He worshipped when things were going well, and he worshipped when things were going badly.

Can you still recognise God's grace even when you're living with the consequences?

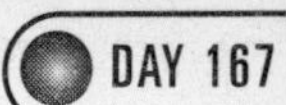

Here we find Paul in a kind of different mood to his first letter to the crew at Corinth, written earlier that year (AD 55). They'd been slagging him off rather viciously – calling him everything from a coward to an inferior speaker. There's just no pleasing some people.

You lookin' at me? [1]

2 corinthians 6:3–10

3We put no stumbling-block in anyone's path, so
that our ministry will not be discredited. 4Rather, as
servants of God we commend ourselves in every
way: in great endurance; in troubles, hardships and
distresses; 5in beatings, imprisonments and riots; in
hard work, sleepless nights and hunger; 6in purity,
understanding, patience and kindness; in the Holy
Spirit and in sincere love; 7in truthful speech and in
the power of God; with weapons of righteousness in
the right hand and in the left; 8through glory and
dishonour, bad report and good report; genuine,
yet regarded as impostors; 9known, yet regarded as
unknown; dying, and yet we live on; beaten, and
yet not killed; 10sorrowful, yet always rejoicing;
poor, yet making many rich; having nothing, and
yet possessing everything.

From shipwrecks to beatings, Paul went through it all. One thing's for sure, he knows that not all criticism comes from non-believers. This attack from the church must have hurt him, yet his response is fantastic. He picks up on the attacks aimed at him and sends them back with a beautiful double whammy. This excerpt is an example to us all of how to deal with criticism. He stands firm yet fails to get into a total mood about it all, choosing instead to keep the focus on God. Even though he may have nothing left, he never forgets that God is his everything. Paul has reached such a position of maturity and security in his relationship with God that it's as if he's ready to die even as he writes these words.

chew it over

Paul went on for a good few years after this incident. With this kind of attitude, it's easy to see how.

Aren't we forgetting something?

2 corinthians 9:8–9

8And God is able to make all grace abound
to you, so that in all things at all times,
having all that you need, you will abound
in every good work. 9As it is written:

"He has scattered abroad his gifts to the
poor;
his righteousness endures for ever."

There was a desperate need for financial support to help the Christians in Jerusalem, and Paul pauses midway through his dealings with the cheeky chaps in Corinth to bring a little perspective back into the proceedings. His words cut to the heart and are still ripe today. Too often we focus on the things that are affecting us – the annoyances, ambitions and anger – but we should never lose sight of what's truly important. Through God's grace he can give us all we need. But all we need for what? For cosy living and tasty luxury? Do God's people travel first class? Not quite. God gives us all we need for one thing: giving. We don't deserve his grace, his forgiveness or his attention to our lives, and we certainly don't deserve the gifts he gives.

By the way, this church in Jerusalem, they and Paul must have been pretty close, right? Wrong: Paul's fallings-out with the Jerusalem crew were legendary, yet he still chose to support and care for them, putting his neck on the line so that the church might be strengthened. That's quite some sacrifice.

chew it over

In every case - whether they're physical like health and wealth or 'spiritual' like teaching and prophecy - God's gifts are in us to be used, not sat on.

You lookin' at me [2]

2 corinthians 12:19–20

[19]Have you been thinking all along that we
have been defending ourselves to you? We
have been speaking in the sight of God as
those in Christ; and everything we do, dear
friends, is for your strengthening. [20]For I am
afraid that when I come I may not find you
as I want you to be, and you may not find
me as you want me to be. I fear that there
may be quarrelling, jealousy, outbursts of
anger, factions, slander, gossip, arrogance
and disorder.

The three chapters we have been looking at show Paul on fire. He lists all of his sufferings, loads up with sarcasm and goes on an all-out attack. Why? Does he do it for his own ego? Is he trying to ease the bruises to his over-inflated pride? No chance. Paul does it for God. The contents of his life – the sufferings, the humiliations, the threats, beatings and imprisonments – are all endured with one goal in mind: that Jesus might get all the glory.

chew it over

It's all about keeping focus - in the storm and in the calm.

Solomon

But was it worth it?

Art collector, writer, diplomat and all round Mr Wise Guy, Solomon had plenty going for him. But he had flaws that would give the people headaches for years to come. So while some things might be a tad confusing about him, what is for sure is that by the end of it all, Solomon knew that trying to find meaning in life without God is a pointless task.

1 Kings 6:11–14

11The word of the Lord came to Solomon:
12"As for this temple you are building, if
you follow my decrees, carry out my regula-
tions and keep all my commands and obey
them, I will fulfil through you the promise I
gave to David your father. 13And I will live
among the Israelites and will not abandon
my people Israel."
14So Solomon built the temple and completed it.

And still today God goes to great lengths for the objects of his affection, and the promise not to abandon the Israelites is one that, thanks to Jesus, we can claim for ourselves.

Solomon left his mark on Jerusalem in a rather special way: he built the temple that his father David had only dreamed of. It certainly was an impressive looking place – if you can wade through all the technical description – but was it worth it? God seems to have got by OK without it since AD 70 (when it was destroyed), but we can also assume that he was pretty happy with the whole thing at the time, signing up for the system of sacrifices that took place at the temple. It does seem strange though, all this money spent on a building, especially when Jesus went on to make such a big deal of the fact that not only would it be destroyed, but that true worship played by a different set of rules (John 4:21–4).

It's clear that God was prepared to stick to his word and continue the dynasty – started with David – through Solomon. Solomon's temple might seem out of place to us, but God's reaction remains the same: it was all about capturing the hearts of his chosen people.

Foreign policy

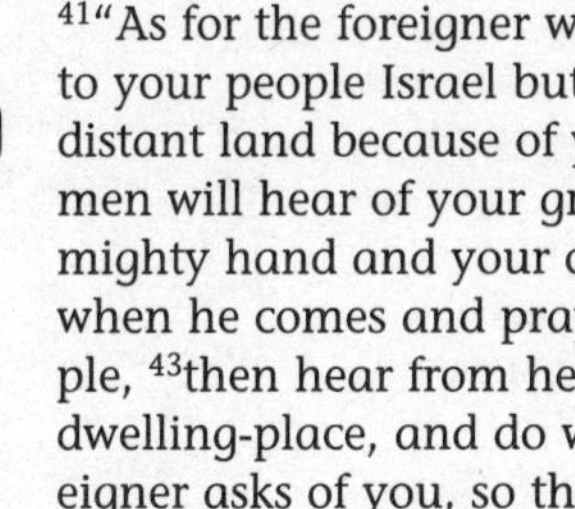

1 Kings 8:41–3

41 "As for the foreigner who does not belong
to your people Israel but has come from a
distant land because of your name—42 for
men will hear of your great name and your
mighty hand and your outstretched arm—
when he comes and prays towards this temple, 43 then hear from heaven, your
dwelling-place, and do whatever the foreigner asks of you, so that all the peoples of
the earth may know your name and fear
you, as do your own people Israel, and may
know that this house I have built bears your
Name."

Reaching out to the world is still on the agenda too, and being a light to others – regardless of nationality or history – is something we ignore at our own risk.

We catch Solomon mid-flow during his eloquent prayer of dedication. He covers the royal family, political problems, war, captivity and so on – all in all, quite a prayer. At the heart we find these verses, as Solomon turns his attention to non-Israelites who might come to worship God. It helps us join the dots between the Old and New Testaments, as it fits in nicely with the fact that Jesus came as the Saviour of all people, not just the Jews. When they first moved into the neighbourhood the Israelites weren't exactly cosy with some of the people they came across. But back then survival meant tough actions.

God hasn't softened up over the years. His heart has always been to bless others through his people, to reach the world through the Israelites. Their sin got in the way and Jesus came to finish the job.

Fatal flaw

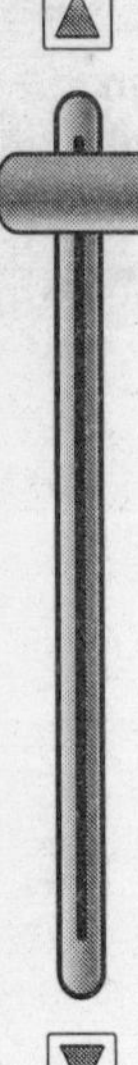

1 Kings 11:1–6

[1]King Solomon, however, loved many foreign
women besides Pharaoh's daughter—Moabites,
Ammonites, Edomites, Sidonians and Hittites.
[2]They were from nations about which the Lord
had told the Israelites, "You must not intermarry with them, because they will surely turn
your hearts after their gods." Nevertheless,
Solomon held fast to them in love. [3]He had
seven hundred wives of royal birth and three
hundred concubines, and his wives led him
astray. [4]As Solomon grew old, his wives turned
his heart after other gods, and his heart was
not fully devoted to the Lord his God, as the
heart of David his father had been. [5]He followed Ashtoreth the goddess of the Sidonians,
and Molech the detestable god of the
Ammonites. [6]So Solomon did evil in the eyes
of the Lord; he did not follow the Lord completely, as David his father had done.

We don't need to shack up in a cave, but we must keep an eye out for where our heart's treasure really does lie.

He might have been wise, but Solomon's habit of marrying at will brought him trouble. In having multiple wives from foreign countries he was probably sealing international links with their respective countries. Somehow I can't quite see this habit making a comeback into twenty-first-century politics.

God was not happy. Solomon had broken the rules: Deuteronomy 17:17 makes it clear that having 'many wives' was out of the question, but the real issue seems to be the fact that they were foreign. This isn't God in a right-wing mood, as we mention elsewhere in *the site*: foreign wives meant foreign habits and foreign gods. That meant that the Israelites became distracted, that their worship of God became diluted and their hearts began to wander.

Stacking up on marriage partners might not be quite our scene, but we can all be guilty of allowing our focus to wander from God, getting transfixed by the glitter of alternative interests.

Business is business

1 Kings 12:1–8

1Rehoboam went to Shechem, for all the Israelites
had gone there to make him king. 2When
Jeroboam son of Nebat heard this (he was still in
Egypt, where he had fled from King Solomon), he
returned from Egypt. 3So they sent for Jeroboam,
and he and the whole assembly of Israel went to
Rehoboam and said to him: 4"Your father put a
heavy yoke on us, but now lighten the harsh
labour and the heavy yoke he put on us, and we
will serve you."
5Rehoboam answered, "Go away for three days
and then come back to me." So the people went
away.
6Then King Rehoboam consulted the elders
who had served his father Solomon during his
lifetime. "How would you advise me to answer
these people?" he asked.
7They replied, "If today you will be a servant to
these people and serve them and give them a
favourable answer, they will always be your servants."
8But Rehoboam rejected the advice the elders
gave him and consulted the young men who had
grown up with him and were serving him.

It's never 'only business': it's always personal.

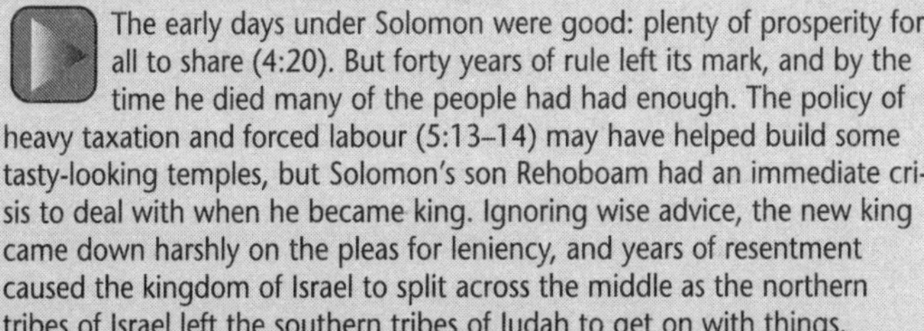

The early days under Solomon were good: plenty of prosperity for all to share (4:20). But forty years of rule left its mark, and by the time he died many of the people had had enough. The policy of heavy taxation and forced labour (5:13–14) may have helped build some tasty-looking temples, but Solomon's son Rehoboam had an immediate crisis to deal with when he became king. Ignoring wise advice, the new king came down harshly on the pleas for leniency, and years of resentment caused the kingdom of Israel to split across the middle as the northern tribes of Israel left the southern tribes of Judah to get on with things.

Perhaps Rehoboam got carried away with the foolish notion that great leaders need to be tough leaders. The idea's still around today with many people excusing all manner of heartless, harsh words and behaviour with the line 'It's only business'. The truth tells a different story: they might not fit neatly into our 'friends' category, but the people we spend time with at work or wherever have got to be treated right. We can't switch off our belief that each person is made and loved by God just because we'll get a better rate of return if we walk all over them.

SOLOMON AND THE TEMPLE

Solomon set himself the task of providing a suitable permanent home for the ark – holder of the two stone tablets from Moses' Ten Commandments lecture and symbol of God's presence on earth. It was a pretty important artefact and demanded a pretty special home. The story tells us loads about God, and is a perfect DIY manual for how to worship the Lord. *Mike Pilavachi*

The architect

1 Chronicles 28: 11–19

11 Then David gave his son
Solomon the plans for the por-
tico of the temple, its build-
ings, its storerooms, its upper
parts, its inner rooms and the
place of atonement. 12 He gave
him the plans of all that the
Spirit had put in his mind for
the courts of the temple of the
Lord and all the surrounding
rooms, for the treasuries of the
temple of God and for the
treasuries for the dedicated
things. 13 He gave him instruc-
tions for the divisions of the
priests and Levites, and for all
the work of serving in the tem-
ple of the Lord, as well as for
all the articles to be used in its
service. 14 He designated the
weight of gold for all the gold
articles to be used in various
kinds of service, and the
weight of silver for all the sil-
ver articles to be used in vari-
ous kinds of service: 15 the
weight of gold for the gold lampstands and their lamps, with the weight for each lampstand
and its lamps; and the weight of silver for each silver lampstand and its lamps, according to
the use of each lampstand; 16 the weight of gold for each table for consecrated bread; the
weight of silver for the silver tables; 17 the weight of pure gold for the forks, sprinkling bowls
and pitchers; the weight of gold for each gold dish; the weight of silver for each silver dish;
18 and the weight of the refined gold for the altar of incense. He also gave him the plan for the
chariot, that is, the cherubim of gold that spread their wings and shelter the ark of the
covenant of the Lord.
19 "All this," David said, "I have in writing from the hand of the Lord upon me, and he
gave me understanding in all the details of the plan."

SEARCH

Building the temple was a big deal, and it wasn't just any old shack they put together. It was an awe-inspiring building, designed by a pretty special architect: God. He had given the plans to David, who passed them down to his son Solomon. From the foundations to the furnishings, God directed their efforts and managed to send a message to them (and to us today) that worship is always on his terms, and not on ours. That's the truth about our worship: God likes it and he wants to make sure that we get it right.

But does that mean that all worship should look the same? Of course not, and it's wrong for us to try to make others worship on our terms, but that idea also extends to God: we don't have the last word in the direction of our own worship of God.

What we have to do is worship our Maker on his own terms.

Real worship

2 Chronicles 7:4–10

4Then the king and all the people
offered sacrifices before the Lord.
5And King Solomon offered a sacrifice
of twenty-two thousand head of cattle
and a hundred and twenty thousand
sheep and goats. So the king and all
the people dedicated the temple of
God. 6The priests took their positions,
as did the Levites with the Lord's
musical instruments, which King
David had made for praising the Lord
and which were used when he gave
thanks, saying, "His love endures for
ever." Opposite the Levites, the priests
blew their trumpets, and all the
Israelites were standing.
7Solomon consecrated the middle
part of the courtyard in front of the
temple of the Lord, and there he
offered burnt offerings and the fat of
the fellowship offerings, because the
bronze altar he had made could not
hold the burnt offerings, the grain
offerings and the fat portions.
8So Solomon observed the festival
at that time for seven days, and all
Israel with him—a vast assembly,
people from Lebo Hamath to the
Wadi of Egypt. 9On the eighth day
they held an assembly, for they had
celebrated the dedication of the altar
for seven days and the festival for
seven days more. 10On the twenty-
third day of the seventh month he
sent the people to their homes, joyful
and glad in heart for the good things
the Lord had done for David and
Solomon and for his people Israel.

SEARCH

This is some worship session. It tells us so much that a quick read often misses some of the juiciest bits. The whole temple project had been carried out on a huge scale: the labour force topped 153,600 men, there was enough gold inside to sink the *Titanic* and the dedication service lasted into a second week. The king offered a sacrifice of 22,000 cows and 120,000 sheep and goats. Can you imagine that? It wasn't even a barbecue thrown to say thank you to the workers: all this meat was, for want of a better word, wasted. They burnt it up and that was that, no nibbles, left-overs or packed lunches. The size of the sacrifice was so great that it would have had a drastic effect on the economy. According to Solomon's dad David, that was a good sign that the sacrifice was worthy – 'Shall I offer to God that which cost me nothing?' he once mused (2 Samuel 24:24). The answer is of course that David and Solomon didn't offer God the cheap stuff, and nor should we. Worship is meant to cost something. In Solomon's case, it was a significant dent in his treasury.

What's our currency when it comes to extravagant worship? A whole temple is out of our league, but in the same way that Jesus paid for our debt with his own life, we too can offer our lives as living sacrifices (see Romans 12:1).

We can pour out our hearts to God and waste our lives on extravagant worship.

Less is more

2 Chronicles 7:1–3

1 When Solomon finished
praying, fire came down
from heaven and con-
sumed the burnt offering
and the sacrifices, and
the glory of the Lord
filled the temple. 2 The
priests could not enter
the temple of the Lord
because the glory of the
Lord filled it. 3 When all
the Israelites saw the fire
coming down and the
glory of the Lord above
the temple, they knelt on
the pavement with their
faces to the ground, and
they worshipped and
gave thanks to the Lord,
saying,

"He is good;
his love endures for
ever."

SEARCH

Before we move on, let's rewind to these sneaky verses that appear before the description of the grand opening. After the months – even years – that had been spent building the temple, this ceremony was always going to be a special event and, as we saw in the last passage, it cost a fair few pennies, and you can be sure that it was all pretty well planned. But there is an important fact that is easily overlooked: as soon as Solomon had finished praying, God stepped in. Before the sacrifices got under way, God pressed pause. There was no question of the ceremony carrying on inside the temple – even the priests couldn't get in there, it was so full of God's presence, his 'Godness'.

Not only is God boss, calling for worship on his own terms, but he has a habit of stepping in, calling a halt to all our frantic activity and causing us to realise just how truly great he is.

Let's not forget

1 Chronicles 13:12–14

12David was afraid of
God that day and asked,
"How can I ever bring
the ark of God to me?"
13He did not take the ark
to be with him in the
City of David. Instead,
he took it aside to the
house of Obed-Edom the
Gittite. 14The ark of God
remained with the fami-
ly of Obed-Edom in his
house for three months,
and the Lord blessed his
household and every-
thing he had.

SEARCH

Just having the ark in his front room was enough to bring godly blessings on this man named Obed Edom. Strangely, opinion is divided about just who this man was: some say he was a Levite, others reckon he could have been a Philistine, but either way the story stands firm in its message: God's presence is a powerful thing. It can change lives, and not always in a good way: just look at what happened to the seventy blokes from Beth Shemesh in 1 Samuel 6:19. They paid the ultimate price for the sin of getting a little nosey and having a peek inside the ark.

The fact remains the same for us today: God's presence changes lives. Thankfully that presence is not confined to one artefact, and through the Holy Spirit God brings his power to our lives.

GO

Are we doing what Obed Edom did – living with the Holy Spirit every day?

Sacrifice

2 Samuel 6:12–15

12Now King David was
told, "The Lord has
blessed the household of
Obed-Edom and every-
thing he has, because of
the ark of God." So
David went down and
brought up the ark of
God from the house of
Obed-Edom to the City of
David with rejoicing.
13When those who were
carrying the ark of the
Lord had taken six steps,
he sacrificed a bull and a
fattened calf. 14David,
wearing a linen ephod,
danced before the Lord
with all his might,
15while he and the entire
house of Israel brought
up the ark of the Lord
with shouts and the
sound of trumpets.

SEARCH

Now we don't know how far away Obed Edom lived from Jerusalem but even if it was only a few miles, the journey would have been something of an epic. You see, it wasn't just a case of hitching up the old ark and trotting off down the road. The text suggests that the line about sacrificing the bull and the calf after six steps means that they performed this sacrifice *every* six steps. At the beginning it would probably have been a bit of a laugh, but the novelty was bound to have worn off. Killing bulls and calves isn't exactly speedy work, and doing it every six steps would have made for a serious drain on speed. It was also an issue of economics: those cattle had to come from somewhere, and coughing up came at a price.

Talking of prices, once the journey is over David makes the final sacrifice. Out goes his pride as he strips down to his linen ephod – a short garment worn by priests under their robes – and dances before his God. Don't get me wrong, this wasn't one big chore: it was a wild celebration of delight through sacrifice. Isn't that what love is like? Reckless, risky and totally un-sensible?

GO

Let's face facts: God's worth so much more than we give him.

What is God looking for? A decent CV of past achievements? Is he interested in how many conversion notches we've got on our Bible? Thankfully not, and Paul was keen to explain why.

Risky business

galatians 2:15–16

15"We who are Jews by birth and not 'Gentile sinners'
16know that a man is not justified by observing the law, but by faith in Jesus Christ. So we, too, have put our faith in Christ Jesus that we may be justified by faith in Christ and not by observing the law, because by observing the law no-one will be justified."

We find ourselves at the heart of Paul's letter to the church in the area of Galatia, combating a misinformed viewpoint that threatened to destabilise the entire church. Many Jewish Christians believed that various Old Testament practices still had to be on the menu for the New Testament Church.

But Paul is keen to point out this central truth of Christianity: no one is justified – no one is made pleasing to God – by observing the Law. If Christianity is a dance, then it is not a complex routine that needs to be learnt and performed. Instead it's passionate, wild and free, one that needs to come from the heart far more than it needs to be copied from a book. But hang on, you might be thinking, isn't this shooting yourself in the foot? After all, aren't these supposed to be Bible notes? Good point, and Paul was in no way suggesting that the church chuck out all laws, that people set about remaking Christianity in any way that suited them. Look at Romans 7:12 and you'll see that he respected the law fully. Instead Paul is pointing out that Jesus brought with him a new set of rules, one which replaced the old ones.

chew it over

We're in a new dance now, one in which we stand facing God.

A question of grammar

galatians 5:16

16So I say, live by the Spirit, and you will not gratify the desires of the sinful nature.

Paul tells us to live by the Spirit, and if you'll excuse the technicality, it's important to underline that word 'live'. Why? Because it's present tense in our translation, and it could equally have been written 'go on living'. Do you get the idea? We're not supposed to dip into the Holy Spirit every once in a while, to get one big fill-up at the start of the year and leave him alone the rest of the time. Here we find the key to Christian living: continuously looking to the Holy Spirit for guidance and promptings, inspiration and power.

chew it over

Christian living is all about being part of a bigger picture: a glorious painting with the Holy Spirit as the brush.

In the name of the law

galatians 6:12–16

12 Those who want to make a good impression outwardly are trying to compel you to
be circumcised. The only reason they do
this is to avoid being persecuted for the
cross of Christ. 13 Not even those who are
circumcised obey the law, yet they want
you to be circumcised that they may boast
about your flesh. 14 May I never boast except
in the cross of our Lord Jesus Christ,
through which the world has been crucified
to me, and I to the world. 15 Neither circumcision nor uncircumcision means anything;
what counts is a new creation. 16 Peace and
mercy to all who follow this rule, even to
the Israel of God.

Circumcision was a hot potato: the Jewish Christians said you had to have been done while those Christians from a non-Jewish background claimed that you didn't. 'Forget about it,' says Paul. 'There are more important things in life to worry about.' He's right, too: Christianity is about the heart, about a relationship with God and not a cynical display of religious technique.

But hang on just one minute. If we look back at Acts 16 we see something odd. Paul has Timothy (a non-Jewish Christian) circumcised. But why, if it was really no big deal? Had Paul lost his mind or are we to take everything he says with a pinch of salt? The truth is slightly more exciting. Paul was such a full-on evangelist, so keen to spread the gospel as thickly and as far as possible that he would do whatever he could to get the message further. When it came to Timothy Paul knew that the young lad would get a far better reception from the Jews if he'd been circumcised. If it meant that he'd be able to preach the gospel in the synagogues, Paul was all for doing whatever it took. With Titus Paul rejected the calls for circumcision as it was not essential for the preaching of the gospel.

chew it over

Being truly free from laws means being truly free to stick to them just as much as it does to ignore them.

ELIJAH

A life of extremes, Elijah's story takes in all the great themes: intimacy with God, a hunger for justice and the murder of many of his enemies. Bizarre it may be, but dull? Never. *Greg Valerio*

One man, one God – part 1

1 Kings 17:1–4

[1]Now Elijah the Tishbite, from Tishbe in Gilead, said to Ahab, "As the Lord, the God of Israel, lives, whom I serve, there will be neither dew nor rain in the next few years except at my word."

[2]Then the word of the Lord came to Elijah: [3]"Leave here, turn eastward and hide in the Kerith Ravine, east of the Jordan. [4]You will drink from the brook, and I have ordered the ravens to feed you there."

SEARCH

In classical mythology the raven is a sign of God's providence. That means a sign of God's intentions, his foresight, a sign of God's special care and wisdom at work in a situation or a person. Knowing this about ravens makes their appearance in the story of Elijah nicely significant. This prophet of God is generally considered to be one of the most important Old Testament figures alongside King David and the great leader of Israel, Moses. God introduces us to the man – the prophet – Elijah. As we discover his story we discover the true calling and nature of a prophet of God. We find out about the potential we all have to fall as we follow the story of a man who – like the rest of us – is capable of great things and in the same breath great atrocities.

Elijah explodes onto the scene of Israel's history with a dramatic statement. There will be no more rain in Israel until he says so. This man of God's authority is dramatic, and at the heart of this statement we find an essential element that must accompany any true prophet: authority. Prophets must be confident, secure and have an unfailing knowledge that God is in the words that they speak. For those who want to be prophetic this episode teaches us two things: we must have confidence and that confidence must flow from the knowledge that God has chosen us.

GO

Like Elijah we must rely on God. We must all be fed by the ravens.

One man, one God – part 2

1 Kings 17:4–7

4"You will drink from the
brook, and I have
ordered the ravens to
feed you there."
5So he did what the
Lord had told him. He
went to the Kerith
Ravine, east of the
Jordan, and stayed there.
6The ravens brought him
bread and meat in the
morning and bread and
meat in the evening, and
he drank from the brook.
7Some time later the
brook dried up because
there had been no rain
in the land.

SEARCH

When God calls people he does so for a reason. Elijah was called at a specific time in the history of Israel to be a light for people that had lost their way. But this light is more than just words, and Elijah had to do more than just talk: he had to be a living example, to *show* the people all the many facets of God's plan for them. He was called to challenge the false gods of his day, to act as a man of integrity in a society that had lost its moral centre. To offer and demonstrate a way of hope to a people that would struggle to understand his message. He was called, like all prophets, to challenge the structures of his day that perpetuated injustice; to challenge political corruption in the form of the power-hungry Ahab and to challenge the state-seducing religion of Baal worship through confrontation with Jezebel the queen.

We need to look beyond the story to the modern day. As followers of the same God of justice, what are the areas of our society that we should challenge? How about the ideology of materialism and capitalism that creates massive economic injustice in the rich and the poor? What do we have to say about the cult of sexual seduction that twists the image of God in people, that manipulates them through the media, leading them to chase after the so-called perfect body, the designer labels and the latest fashions? Or the lie of power and violence where humility is considered weakness, the mistaken belief that it is acceptable to spend billions of pounds on weapons designed to kill people that are then sold to us as necessary to keep the peace.

GO

Money, sex and power are the great enemies of the Christian who follows the peace-loving, non-violent, voluntarily poor Messiah called Jesus of Nazareth.

Not just words

1 Kings 17:12–16

12“As surely as the Lord
your God lives,” she replied,
“I don’t have any bread—
only a handful of flour in a
jar and a little oil in a jug. I
am gathering a few sticks to
take home and make a
meal for myself and my
son, that we may eat it—
and die.”
13Elijah said to her,
“Don’t be afraid. Go home
and do as you have said.
But first make a small cake
of bread for me from what
you have and bring it to
me, and then make some-
thing for yourself and your
son. 14For this is what the
Lord, the God of Israel, says:
‘The jar of flour will not be
used up and the jug of oil
will not run dry until the
day the Lord gives rain on
the land.’”
15She went away and did
as Elijah had told her. So
there was food every day for
Elijah and for the woman
and her family. 16For the jar
of flour was not used up
and the jug of oil did not
run dry, in keeping with the
word of the Lord spoken by
Elijah.

SEARCH

Very dramatic stuff this Elijah. ‘No rain in Israel until my word,’ he states. Of course this has big implications for the country: no rain means no crops, no crops mean no food, no food means hunger and starvation. This is exactly what happens next, and Elijah, like the rest of the people, struggles through this difficult time. But God has plans to use Elijah’s life to illustrate another central part of the life of the prophet: compassion for the poor and the meeting of very real needs. This is a story about the heart of God for the poor and the collision of the power of the Holy Spirit with social justice. The widow of Zarephath is dying. She, like many of the world’s poor is fatalistic, resigned to die alongside her young son. Elijah asks her for what she has – a little oil and a handful of flour. From this Elijah restores her fortunes by supernaturally causing these foods never to run out. God provides enough for the household and for the prophet.

It is justice for the poor that authenticates and confirms the work of the prophet, and in this story we get reminded of an important fact that seems to have got lost from the modern-day life of the western Church. The power of the Holy Spirit is bursting to impact the material world and bring about social transformation. Put another way, prophecy is not just about getting a word of encouragement from the platform speaker or predicting the future events of history.

Prophecy is about the holistic power of the Holy Spirit changing the social structures of the day and transforming lives forever. Anyone who tries to separate social transformation from the role of the prophet clearly is not one.

God trouble

1 Kings 18:7–10, 15–19

[7]As Obadiah was walking along,
Elijah met him. Obadiah recognised
him, bowed down to the ground, and
said, "Is it really you, my lord
Elijah?"
[8]"Yes," he replied. "Go tell your
master, 'Elijah is here.'"
[9]"What have I done wrong," asked
Obadiah, "that you are handing your
servant over to Ahab to be put to
death? [10]As surely as the Lord your
God lives, there is not a nation or
kingdom where my master has not
sent someone to look for you. And
whenever a nation or kingdom
claimed you were not there, he made
them swear they could not find you."
[15]Elijah said, "As the Lord
Almighty lives, whom I serve, I will
surely present myself to Ahab today."
[16]So Obadiah went to meet Ahab
and told him, and Ahab went to meet
Elijah. [17]When he saw Elijah, he said
to him, "Is that you, you troubler of
Israel?"
[18]"I have not made trouble for
Israel," Elijah replied. "But you and
your father's family have. You have
abandoned the Lord's commands and
have followed the Baals. [19]Now sum-
mon the people from all over Israel to
meet me on Mount Carmel. And
bring the four hundred and fifty
prophets of Baal and the four hundred prophets of Asherah, who eat at
Jezebel's table."

SEARCH

So far we have discovered that to be a prophet you need the providence of God, authority, the power of the Holy Spirit, compassion and the authenticating value of justice for the poor. In this episode with Obadiah we are introduced to the biggest problem facing all prophets: being a troublemaker. If you want to follow God you will always end up causing trouble. Trouble for politicians and kings as you challenge injustice, trouble for the religious people who think they have true faith but are self-deceiving and mostly trouble for yourself and your friends because you have to put yourself into difficult and dangerous situations.

Obadiah was a man of God who worked for the king. He was an insider at the royal court, a man who put his life on the line for the prophets of God, but a man who lacked the godly courage and authority that Elijah displayed. Elijah causes major trouble for Obadiah when he commands him to tell the angry vengeful King Ahab that Elijah is back in town ready for a showdown at Mount Carmel. He wants to take on the prophets of Baal, and it's a big fight, featuring the power of God against the deception of Baal worship, God's truth and ideology versus the dominant ideology of the day. Needless to say Obadiah was none too happy with the request but did as he was asked with the guarantee that Elijah would not disappear again. God's troublemaker is back in town.

GO

Long live the troublemakers!

Showtime

1 Kings 18:32–40

32 With the stones he built an altar in
the name of the Lord, and he dug a
trench round it large enough to hold
two seahs of seed. 33 He arranged the
wood, cut the bull into pieces and laid it
on the wood. Then he said to them, "Fill
four large jars with water and pour it
on the offering and on the wood."
34 "Do it again," he said, and they did
it again.
"Do it a third time," he ordered, and
they did it the third time. 35 The water
ran down around the altar and even
filled the trench.
36 At the time of sacrifice, the prophet
Elijah stepped forward and prayed: "O
Lord, God of Abraham, Isaac and Israel,
let it be known today that you are God
in Israel and that I am your servant
and have done all these things at your
command. 37 Answer me, O Lord,
answer me, so these people will know
that you, O Lord, are God, and that you
are turning their hearts back again."
38 Then the fire of the Lord fell and
burned up the sacrifice, the wood, the
stones and the soil, and also licked up
the water in the trench.
39 When all the people saw this, they
fell prostrate and cried, "The Lord—he is
God! The Lord—he is God!"
40 Then Elijah commanded them,
"Seize the prophets of Baal. Don't let
anyone get away!" They seized them,
and Elijah had them brought down to
the Kishon Valley and slaughtered
there.

SEARCH

Elijah is now a man on a mission. Once and for all he is going to prove to the people of Israel who God really is. He is going to challenge the Baal prophets: your god or my God, winner takes all. And just to up the anti, he wants all of Israel there to see what happens. It's a big deal as the nation has got into a terrible state and there's a lot at stake in this confrontation, but Elijah the trouble-maker is confident that God will prove himself given the opportunity. We are familiar with the outcome: God vindicates Elijah's faith and proves himself by barbecuing the sacrifice that has been drenched in water. God is God and all of Israel can see that now.

But there's a twist in the tail. Elijah, on a high from the most triumphant success of his life, seizes the opportunity to get his own back against the Baal prophets who for years have been the force behind the corruption and spiritual wanderings of the country. On a wave of emotion he incites the wholesale slaughter of all the prophets of Baal on the spot, thereby instigating an act of genocide that will catch up with him later.

Many of us think that when we see God working through someone it is a sign that God agrees with the person whom he chooses to use. Some believe that God makes people he likes rich. When they see him heal people they take it as a sign that their misguided philosophy is true. A far cry from the Jesus who was both humble and poor, and called on all rich people to engage in social transformation and economic justice.

Just because God uses us supernaturally does not mean that we have the truth or are right.

Communication

1 Kings 18:41–6

41 And Elijah said to
Ahab, "Go, eat and
drink, for there is the
sound of a heavy rain."
42 So Ahab went off to eat
and drink, but Elijah
climbed to the top of
Carmel, bent down to
the ground and put his
face between his knees.
43 "Go and look towards
the sea," he told his servant. And he went up
and looked.
"There is nothing
there," he said.
Seven times Elijah said,
"Go back."
44 The seventh time the
servant reported, "A
cloud as small as a
man's hand is rising
from the sea."
So Elijah said, "Go and
tell Ahab, 'Hitch up your
chariot and go down
before the rain stops
you.'"
45 Meanwhile, the sky
grew black with clouds,
the wind rose, a heavy
rain came on and Ahab
rode off to Jezreel. 46 The
power of the Lord came
upon Elijah and, tucking
his cloak into his belt, he
ran ahead of Ahab all
the way to Jezreel.

SEARCH

Another of those very obvious virtues in the lives of all the prophets is the fervour with which they prayed and the quality of godly intimacy which they experienced. This is one of the great paradoxes of Elijah: he was both a man who knew God through prayer and yet one who was capable of inciting murder. This intimacy that he had with God was one of the most profound aspects of his life. Like his forefathers King David and King Solomon he knew how to pray and it was from his prayer life that he derived all his authority and identity. It was this prayer life to which he would return when depression, remorse and self-doubt swept over him later on. His prayer life could command kings and they would respond; his prayer life could command the natural realm to do as he said and rain. His prayer life could overcome the physical limitations of the human body and he could outrun King Ahab on horseback.

There is no getting away from it: prayer is vital. Whether it's in a communal prayer meeting, contemplative meditation, a chat with God in the car, on the way to school or a walk in the countryside, in English or in tongues: however we pray we must pray. Only in prayer do we discover who we truly are and find the calling and authority to walk as Jesus walked. Only in prayer do we discover the courage to overcome our character faults and the forgiveness and grace of God that no matter what he loves us unconditionally.

GO

Pray.

From despair to where?

1 Kings 19:1–9a

1 Now Ahab told Jezebel everything
Elijah had done and how he had
killed all the prophets with the
sword. 2 So Jezebel sent a messenger
to Elijah to say, "May the gods deal
with me, be it ever so severely, if by
this time tomorrow I do not make
your life like that of one of them."
3 Elijah was afraid and ran for his
life. When he came to Beersheba in
Judah, he left his servant there,
4 while he himself went a day's journey into the desert. He came to a
broom tree, sat down under it and
prayed that he might die. "I have
had enough, Lord," he said. "Take
my life; I am no better than my
ancestors." 5 Then he lay down
under the tree and fell asleep.
All at once an angel touched him
and said, "Get up and eat." 6 He
looked around, and there by his
head was a cake of bread baked
over hot coals, and a jar of water.
He ate and drank and then lay
down again.
7 The angel of the Lord came back
a second time and touched him and
said, "Get up and eat, for the journey is too much for you." 8 So he got
up and ate and drank. Strengthened
by that food, he travelled for forty
days and forty nights until he
reached Horeb, the mountain of
God. 9 There he went into a cave
and spent the night.

SEARCH

God will always use adversity and our enemies to teach us a lesson or two. After his moment of popular triumph and success at Mount Carmel Elijah comes back down to earth with a bang. Jezebel is out to get him and the great man of God and national hero is running for his life. The reality of what he has done and the situation that he is in has finally caught up with him, leaving him wracked with fear for his life and remorse at the murder he is guilty of. Elijah is now at his lowest ebb and God is about to take him on a journey of self-discovery which is only possible for each of us when we reach rock bottom. He takes him back to total reliance on God – being fed by angels this time not ravens – reminding him of how he started in ministry. Elijah is learning that zeal alone will not get you to the finishing tape.

God teaches us in many different ways and with many different means, but always with the same goal in mind: a mature faith in Christ Jesus. The humiliation that Elijah suffers despite his great successes is always the forerunner of true humility. It is this virtue that God is looking for in all of us and it only comes through failure and facing up to our weaknesses.

For those of us with grand designs to see the gospel reach the furthest ends of the earth we need to heed the words of Jesus carefully. 'The meek will inherit the earth.' Interesting that Jesus does not say the successful!

Does size matter?

1 Kings 19:11–18

11The Lord said, "Go out and stand on
the mountain in the presence of the
Lord, for the Lord is about to pass by."
Then a great and powerful wind tore
the mountains apart and shattered the
rocks before the Lord, but the Lord was
not in the wind. After the wind there
was an earthquake, but the Lord was
not in the earthquake. 12After the
earthquake came a fire, but the Lord
was not in the fire. And after the fire
came a gentle whisper. 13When Elijah
heard it, he pulled his cloak over his
face and went out and stood at the
mouth of the cave.
Then a voice said to him, "What are
you doing here, Elijah?"
14He replied, "I have been very zeal-
ous for the Lord God Almighty. The
Israelites have rejected your covenant,
broken down your altars, and put your
prophets to death with the sword. I am
the only one left, and now they are trying to kill me too."
15The Lord said to him, "Go back the
way you came, and go to the Desert of
Damascus. When you get there, anoint
Hazael king over Aram. 16Also, anoint
Jehu son of Nimshi king over Israel,
and anoint Elisha son of Shaphat from
Abel Meholah to succeed you as
prophet. 17Jehu will put to death any
who escape the sword of Hazael, and
Elisha will put to death any who
escape the sword of Jehu. 18Yet I
reserve seven thousand in Israel—all
whose knees have not bowed down to
Baal and all whose mouths have not
kissed him."

SEARCH

Once again Elijah is set to meet God in a supernatural way. Already strengthened for the journey by angels and a heavenly supper, God is about to test whether Elijah has learnt the lesson of true maturity. Has he learnt that God resides in stillness, peace and humility or is Elijah still expectant of the dramatic miracle to restore his confidence? A wind cracks the mountain but Elijah sits firm; an earthquake shakes the mountain but Elijah sits firm. Even when the fire gets so close and rips through the mountain, Elijah is much wiser now and sits tight till it passes on. Only when the silence, the stillness, descends does Elijah move, responding to the voice of God. Elijah has learnt that peacefulness is the state that God wants him to live in. It is only then that God chooses to entrust Elijah with perhaps his greatest task, that of laying the seeds for the future generation and prosperity of the move of his Spirit.

For us who are impressed by the **big** – the **big** evangelist, the **big** Bible teacher, the **big** prophetic ministry, the **big** platform speaker – we should observe Elijah closely at this point. It is God's deeper desire for us that we should discover him in stillness and in peace.

The true centre of mature Christianity rests in peace with God and with oneself, with the ear that is tuned to stillness.

Wisdom v. fame

1 Kings 19:19–21

19So Elijah went from
there and found Elisha
son of Shaphat. He was
ploughing with twelve
yoke of oxen, and he
himself was driving the
twelfth pair. Elijah went
up to him and threw his
cloak around him.
20Elisha then left his
oxen and ran after
Elijah. "Let me kiss my
father and mother good-
bye," he said, "and then
I will come with you."
"Go back," Elijah
replied. "What have I
done to you?"
21So Elisha left him
and went back. He took
his yoke of oxen and
slaughtered them. He
burned the ploughing
equipment to cook the
meat and gave it to the
people, and they ate.
Then he set out to follow
Elijah and became his
attendant.

SEARCH

Elijah, having been instructed to anoint the three key figures of the next generation of Israel's history, seeks out Elisha and throws his mantle over him. In a fit of youthful enthusiasm Elisha rushes to follow Elijah, keen that he should be the next Prophet of Israel. Elijah, however, is distraught and looks to offer Elisha a way out. Elijah now understands in his age and experience what Elisha is blind to in his youth. Namely, the cost that Elisha will have to pay, the journey that he will have to walk, the mistakes that he will make and the loneliness he will have to endure.

This is true for many of us who are young in faith – the old head on young shoulders syndrome. To look for wisdom in early years and to learn from older people, although it might be highly unfashionable right now, will in the long term prove more valuable than many of the things we put our energies into these days. Our endless responses to appeals in meetings, our search for another prophetic word on which to get high or our desperate desire to climb the ministry ladder and be a successful Christian in the eyes of the Church take us away from the best path.

Look for wisdom, not glamour.

Elijah never dies

2 Kings 2:1–2, 7–12

1When the Lord was about to take Elijah
up to heaven in a whirlwind, Elijah and
Elisha were on their way from Gilgal. 2Elijah
said to Elisha, "Stay here; the Lord has sent
me to Bethel."

But Elisha said, "As surely as the Lord lives and as you live, I will not leave you." So they went down to Bethel.

7Fifty men of the company of the
prophets went and stood at a distance, facing the place where Elijah and Elisha had
stopped at the Jordan. 8Elijah took his cloak,
rolled it up and struck the water with it. The
water divided to the right and to the left,
and the two of them crossed over on dry
ground.

9When they had crossed, Elijah said to
Elisha, "Tell me, what can I do for you
before I am taken from you?"

"Let me inherit a double portion of your spirit," Elisha replied.

10"You have asked a difficult thing,"
Elijah said, "yet if you see me when I am
taken from you, it will be yours—otherwise
not."

11As they were walking along and talking
together, suddenly a chariot of fire and horses of fire appeared and separated the two of
them, and Elijah went up to heaven in a
whirlwind. 12Elisha saw this and cried out,
"My father! My father! The chariots and
horsemen of Israel!" And Elisha saw him no
more. Then he took hold of his own clothes
and tore them apart.

SEARCH

Great men and women of God are not created in an instant, but in a lifetime of faithfulness and hardship. This is true of Elijah. At the end of his life he has commanded kings, vanquished enemies, commanded the forces of nature, had compassion on the poor, seen fire fall from heaven, committed horrendous crimes, had a nervous breakdown, spoken with angels and come to live in peace with himself and with God. God's final reward for old man Elijah is a chariot ride to the side of God himself. The fact that Elijah never tastes death is difficult to grasp yet important to understand.

Elijah's life was about more than one man: he represented something of God in the prophet that lives on in the hearts of all people. His virtues showed this well: holiness, justice, compassion for the poor, strength and authority mixed with humility, wisdom and most of all a knowledge and relationship with our Maker.

GO

One man's story? No; these virtues that were very much a part of Elijah never die, and, like him, they lead us further on and further in, closer to God's heart.

Feelings

We're spending the next chunk thinking about how easy it can be to get caught up in our own feelings. Of course, no one ever said that having feelings was wrong, but there can be trouble when we allow them to colour in our picture of God.

Blank

psalm 42:1–5

1As the deer pants for streams of water,
so my soul pants for you, O God.
2My soul thirsts for God, for the living God.
When can I go and meet with God?
3My tears have been my food
day and night,
while men say to me all day long,
"Where is your God?"
4These things I remember
as I pour out my soul:
how I used to go with the multitude,
leading the procession to the house of God,
with shouts of joy and thanksgiving
among the festive throng.

5Why are you downcast, O my soul?
Why so disturbed within me?
Put your hope in God,
for I will yet praise him,
my Saviour and my God.

This psalm has always made me laugh: just the mention of 'deer pants' and I'm giggling about Bambi in Y fronts for hours. Thankfully I've managed to get over it long enough to get this down on paper. So what's going on? Mr Psalm Writer is upset. In fact, he's pretty much gutted: it feels like God's gone AWOL and he's nowhere to be found. What makes it even worse is that not long ago this guy was feeling like he was 100 per cent on fire: he was at the temple in Jerusalem – God's house – leading the crowd and generally having a good old spiritual feast. But now? Nothing. Not a drop. Sound familiar? The truth is that we've all been there; we've all tasted the highs of feeling like we're sitting on God's lap, only to feel totally alone and isolated at a later date. Is this our cue to give up? Not according to the psalmist: 'Put your hope in God'. Not bad advice . . .

chew it over

Think of a time when you really 'felt' God, a time when you knew that he was close. What made you think it was God? How long did it last? Did it change you?

Distant

psalm 42:6-11

6my God.

My soul is downcast within me;
therefore I will remember you
from the land of the Jordan,
the heights of Hermon—from Mount Mizar.
7Deep calls to deep
in the roar of your waterfalls;
all your waves and breakers
have swept over me.

8By day the Lord directs his love,
at night his song is with me—
a prayer to the God of my life.

9I say to God my Rock,
"Why have you forgotten me?
Why must I go about mourning,
oppressed by the enemy?"
10My bones suffer mortal agony
as my foes taunt me,
saying to me all day long,
"Where is your God?"

11Why are you downcast, O my soul?
Why so disturbed within me?
Put your hope in God,
for I will yet praise him,
my Saviour and my God.

This is the second part of the poem we started reading yesterday. It ends with the same 'Why are you downcast, O my soul?' and carries on the theme of how we can feel when God seems like a long way off. This time, though, we get a better picture of just how bad things are for him right now: 100 miles away from the scene of his spiritual high, he's now stuck up a mountain somewhere south of Jerusalem. What's worse, though, is the fact that other people are beginning to notice that God's just not around like he used to be, taunting the writer and rubbing it in. All in all, it doesn't sound like much fun, does it? But what does he decide to do? 'Put your hope in God . . . ' Seems to me like he's telling himself to do a bit of positive thinking, to focus in on the nature of God despite the fact that the feelings just aren't there to back it up.

chew it over

Think about a time when it felt as though God was a long way off. What was it that made you think he was absent? How long did it last? Did it change you?

Rollercoaster

psalm 43

1Vindicate me, O God,
and plead my cause against an ungodly nation;
rescue me from deceitful and wicked men.
2You are God my stronghold.
Why have you rejected me?
Why must I go about mourning,
oppressed by the enemy?
3Send forth your light and your truth,
let them guide me;
let them bring me to your holy mountain,
to the place where you dwell.
4Then will I go to the altar of God,
to God, my joy and my delight.
I will praise you with the harp,
O God, my God.

5Why are you downcast, O my soul?
Why so disturbed within me?
Put your hope in God,
for I will yet praise him,
my Saviour and my God.

Here we go with the last bit of the poem (in some original manuscripts of the Bible, Psalms 42 and 43 ran together as one psalm). Remember how we spent the last couple of days finding out about how and why the psalmist was feeling a little low? Today we start off with more of the same; he's surrounded by 'an ungodly nation' and yet he feels as though God has turned his back. The difference in today's reading, though, is this: there's a solution. Instead of going back – to Jerusalem, the temple and the spiritual highlife he was remembering earlier on – he needs to go forward. 'Show me where to find you now,' he asks God. 'Lead me on.'

This poem that we've been reading reminds me of a few things in my own life: what it feels like to go through a *low* after a spiritual *high*, what it feels like to be a Christian surrounded by people who don't believe the same, what it feels like to have people laugh at your faith and what it feels like to want to move on with God. Feelings are important – there's no denying that – but as we'll see over the next couple of sessions, sometimes we need to get back to trusting God. How do we do that? God's truth and light: the key to it all.

chew it over

What would you put in your Top Five Favourite things about God?

Blind

luke 24:15–24

15As they talked and discussed these things
with each other, Jesus himself came up and
walked along with them; 16but they were kept
from recognising him.
17He asked them, "What are you discussing
together as you walk along?"
They stood still, their faces downcast. 18One
of them, named Cleopas, asked him, "Are you
only a visitor to Jerusalem and do not know
the things that have happened there in these
days?"
19"What things?" he asked.
"About Jesus of Nazareth," they replied.
"He was a prophet, powerful in word and
deed before God and all the people. 20The
chief priests and our rulers handed him over
to be sentenced to death, and they crucified
him; 21but we had hoped that he was the one
who was going to redeem Israel. And what is
more, it is the third day since all this took
place. 22In addition, some of our women
amazed us. They went to the tomb early this
morning 23but didn't find his body. They came
and told us that they had seen a vision of
angels, who said he was alive. 24Then some of
our companions went to the tomb and found it
just as the women had said, but him they did
not see."

So here we are with a couple of Jesus' followers, feeling just a little shell-shocked and depressed after the most astounding three days in the history of the world. Everything seems to have gone wrong; the high of being around Jesus has vanished along with his body; Jesus himself appears to have been a fraud and everyone in Jerusalem knows that these followers had been barking up the wrong tree all along. Gutted.

Remember Psalms 42/43? It's the same deal here: spiritual high followed by spiritual low. The heart is sad and the situation is bleak. But is it really so bad? Were the followers reading the facts right? Were their feelings really so reliable? Tune in to the next reading to find out . . .

chew it over

Ask yourself what your life's like these days? Is everything going along nicely or are you feeling a little like the couple on the road to Emmaus – disappointed and confused?

Illumination

luke 24:25–33a

25He said to them, "How foolish you are,
and how slow of heart to believe all that
the prophets have spoken! 26Did not the
Christ have to suffer these things and then
enter his glory?" 27And beginning with
Moses and all the Prophets, he explained to
them what was said in all the Scriptures
concerning himself.

28As they approached the village to which
they were going, Jesus acted as if he were
going further. 29But they urged him strongly, "Stay with us, for it is nearly evening;
the day is almost over." So he went in to
stay with them.

30When he was at the table with them, he
took bread, gave thanks, broke it and began
to give it to them. 31Then their eyes were
opened and they recognised him, and he
disappeared from their sight. 32They asked
each other, "Were not our hearts burning
within us while he talked with us on the
road and opened the Scriptures to us?"

33They got up and returned at once to
Jerusalem.

chew it over

Do you need Jesus to show you what's really going on?

Having listened patiently to his travelling companions, Jesus switches on the light. They'd pieced together the facts – Jesus was supposed to be the Messiah yet now he was dead; people saying that his life was just a lot of fuss about nothing – and come up with a conclusion that was in line with their feelings: everything was wrong. Jesus, on the other hand, told them a different story, piecing together the facts and breaking bread with them. He opened their eyes and showed them the way things really were. Back in Psalms 42/43 we read how the writer was longing for 'light and truth' to help lead him out of his spiritual dry spell. This is just what the followers get: the truth about who Jesus was, the truth about what he did and the chance to know him, to feel him, living inside their hearts by breaking bread and sharing communion with him. The lesson today is simple: our feelings may tell us that life is going one way, but we all need more truth and light to find out what really is going on. How's life going for you? Do you need to gain a little heavenly perspective on things?

Ephesians

Choice

Paul wrote lots of letters! Let's have a look at what he wrote to the Ephesians and how we can learn from what Paul teaches them.

Chris Russell

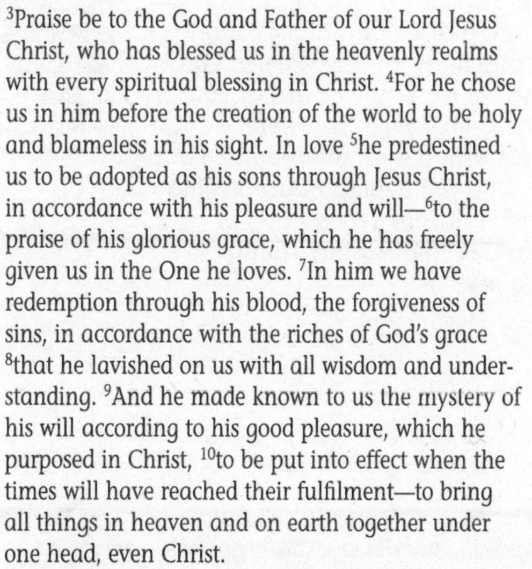

Ephesians 1:3–10

3Praise be to the God and Father of our Lord Jesus
Christ, who has blessed us in the heavenly realms
with every spiritual blessing in Christ. 4For he chose
us in him before the creation of the world to be holy
and blameless in his sight. In love 5he predestined
us to be adopted as his sons through Jesus Christ,
in accordance with his pleasure and will—6to the
praise of his glorious grace, which he has freely
given us in the One he loves. 7In him we have
redemption through his blood, the forgiveness of
sins, in accordance with the riches of God's grace
8that he lavished on us with all wisdom and understanding. 9And he made known to us the mystery of
his will according to his good pleasure, which he
purposed in Christ, 10to be put into effect when the
times will have reached their fulfilment—to bring
all things in heaven and on earth together under
one head, even Christ.

You and me, your neighbours, your friends and enemies – chosen as objects of God's love. No wonder Paul gets so carried away.

These days you just have to go into a supermarket to be overwhelmed: a simple search for a packet of crisps and a can might take ages as you walk up and down two aisles just to see everything on offer. We have more to choose from than any other generation of people anywhere on the globe.

Life seems to be made of choices, big and small, all affecting our lives for better or worse, and this passage turns our minds to the most important choice of all. The most vital choice to affect my life isn't one that I have made. It's one that God made before the foundation of the world (4–5; see also 1:11). From the beginning of the creation God chose to be God for us. He didn't have to – no one made him – but he freely chose to be the God for the world. And although we chose against him, his choice to be for us remains: constant, strong and unwavering.

Paul is saying that Jesus proves this: in him God has chosen to die for everyone's sin. God has chosen all people for all the blessing he outlines in verses 5–10.

The real deal

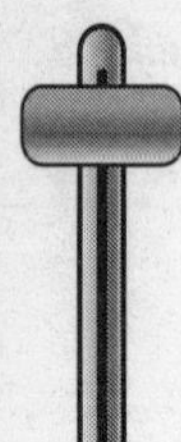

Ephesians 1:11–14

[11]In him we were also chosen, having been
predestined according to the plan of him
who works out everything in conformity
with the purpose of his will, [12]in order that
we, who were the first to hope in Christ,
might be for the praise of his glory. [13]And
you also were included in Christ when you
heard the word of truth, the gospel of your
salvation. Having believed, you were
marked in him with a seal, the promised
Holy Spirit, [14]who is a deposit guaranteeing
our inheritance until the redemption of
those who are God's possession—to the
praise of his glory.

Pray that your mates who don't know God has chosen them will hear the Spirit's voice and realise all that is theirs in Jesus.

Have you ever got one of those junk mail things through the door which begin 'Congratulations! Your name has been chosen to enter a prize draw for £50,000'? Then you read on and it turns out that no one actually has been chosen for anything more than a sales pitch on some encyclopaedias.

God's choice that we looked at yesterday isn't like that. Everybody has been chosen. In Jesus, God has chosen to pay for the sin of everyone in the world. We are chosen for life and not death. Chosen to be a child and not an enemy. Chosen for truth not lies. But his choice needs to become a reality for each one of us. And the mystery of how that happens is spelt out in verse 13 – it's something the Holy Spirit does in us. We only realise we are chosen with God's help. Everything in us cries out against us, but by the Spirit we hear God's shout for us above all the voices that shout against us. It's his voice that counts.

Free indeed

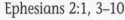

Ephesians 2:1, 3–10

1As for you, you were dead in your transgressions and sins,
3All of us also lived among them at one
time, gratifying the cravings of our sinful
nature and following its desires and thoughts.
Like the rest, we were by nature objects of
wrath. 4But because of his great love for us,
God, who is rich in mercy, 5made us alive with
Christ even when we were dead in transgressions—it is by grace you have been saved.
6And God raised us up with Christ and seated
us with him in the heavenly realms in Christ
Jesus, 7in order that in the coming ages he
might show the incomparable riches of his
grace, expressed in his kindness to us in Christ
Jesus. 8For it is by grace you have been saved,
through faith—and this not from yourselves, it
is the gift of God—9not by works, so that no-
one can boast. 10For we are God's workman-
ship, created in Christ Jesus to do good works,
which God prepared in advance for us to do.

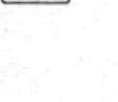

This is grace. Free. Pure and simple. You get not just some-thing, but every-thing for nothing with God. Have you grasped how amazing grace is?

There was a story in the papers a couple of years ago of a guy who went into a supermarket and saw an offer on bananas – it was one of those 'Double Your Reward Points' deals. He worked out that actually they were giving the bananas away. So he bought them all. Four trolleys full. Then he went out onto the high street and tried to give them away. Do you think people took them? No, they certainly did not. After all, you don't get something for nothing, do you?

One of the hardest things about Christianity is that it's too good to be true. Have a read of these verses. OK, so the first two aren't offering a very upbeat picture, but they are honest and realistic.

Then you have the gobsmacking news of verse 4: God has great love, he is rich in mercy. So he gives us, at great cost to himself, life. And life which he intends to keep showering on us in the ages to come (7). How is it ours? 'Cos we believe (8).

Why what did we do? Nothing. All we bring is our sin. He has done it all. He has chosen us, said yes to each of us.

Members only

Ephesians 2:11–18

[11]Therefore, remember that formerly you
who are Gentiles by birth and called "uncircumcised" by those who call themselves "the
circumcision" (that done in the body by the
hands of men)—[12]remember that at that time
you were separate from Christ, excluded from
citizenship in Israel and foreigners to the
covenants of the promise, without hope and
without God in the world. [13]But now in Christ
Jesus you who once were far away have been
brought near through the blood of Christ.

[14]For he himself is our peace, who has made
the two one and has destroyed the barrier, the
dividing wall of hostility, [15]by abolishing in his
flesh the law with its commandments and reg-
ulations. His purpose was to create in himself
one new man out of the two, thus making
peace, [16]and in this one body to reconcile both
of them to God through the cross, by which he
put to death their hostility. [17]He came and
preached peace to you who were far away and
peace to those who were near. [18]For through
him we both have access to the Father by one
Spirit.

Does our attitude to others reflect this inclusive God? Does our church reflect this? it's only when outsiders see the reality of it that they will start to believe what we say.

Sometimes the most important thing in life seems to be whether you are in or out. Papers and magazines are only interested in those who are in. Only the clever people get in in one place, the sporty people get in in another and the trendy people in others still. And on the surface it has been the same with God.

In the Old Testament God's people thought that was how God was with them. They were in with him and everyone else was out. That's what is being described in verses 11 and 12. They believed you were out with God by nature of your birth.

Paul is writing to people who were considered out by birth – they weren't Jews. But now (13–17) everyone can be in. Because in Jesus all that in and out stuff has been abolished. It's not about what race you were born into, or whether you are religious; it's not about whether you are clever, sporty or trendy. There's a new reality.

And that reality is in Jesus. Everyone can come in. Everyone can have access to God (18), everyone can now be a member of the household. Thank him.

Prayer club

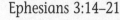

Ephesians 3:14–21

14 For this reason I kneel before the Father,
15 from whom his whole family in heaven
and on earth derives its name. 16 I pray that
out of his glorious riches he may strengthen
you with power through his Spirit in your
inner being, 17 so that Christ may dwell in
your hearts through faith. And I pray that
you, being rooted and established in love,
18 may have power, together with all the
saints, to grasp how wide and long and
high and deep is the love of Christ, 19 and to
know this love that surpasses knowledge—
that you may be filled to the measure of all
the fulness of God.
20 Now to him who is able to do immea-
surably more than all we ask or imagine,
according to his power that is at work within us, 21 to him be glory in the church and
in Christ Jesus throughout all generations,
for ever and ever! Amen.

Have we got the guts to pray like Paul ourselves? Will we pray this into being ourselves or simply leave it on the lips of Paul?

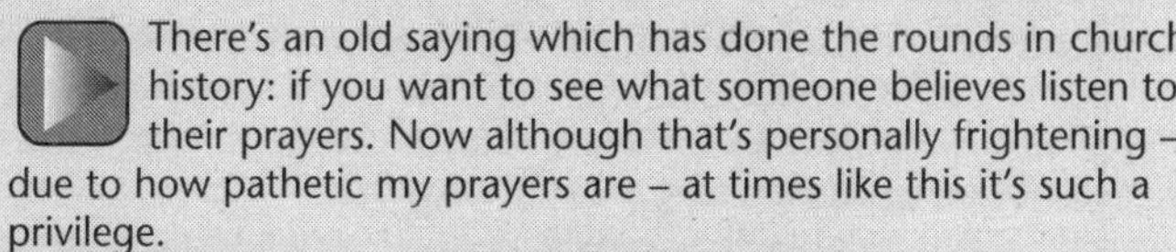

There's an old saying which has done the rounds in church history: if you want to see what someone believes listen to their prayers. Now although that's personally frightening – due to how pathetic my prayers are – at times like this it's such a privilege.

In these verses we have the privilege of listening in on one of the most inspiring and transforming prayers that has ever been written down. Take a deep breath and read it all in one go – out loud if you can.

The first thing to notice is that Paul acknowledges the God he addresses (14–15). Then look at what he prays for the Ephesians – not just a name check (16–19). Now list the things he specifically prays for them. Pray for this for yourself and then take time to pray it for two other Christians you know – replacing 'you' with their name. As always happens when Paul prays he gets carried away in praise (20–1). Imagine what the truth of this makes possible: the promise and hope that is held out.

Fight club

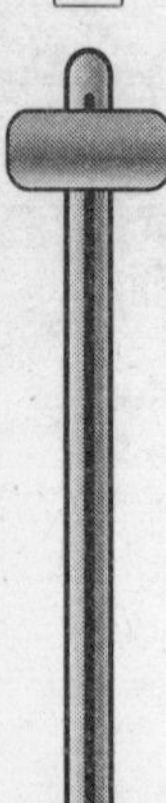

Ephesians 4:1–6

[1]As a prisoner for the Lord, then, I urge you
to live a life worthy of the calling you have
received. [2]Be completely humble and gentle;
be patient, bearing with one another in
love. [3]Make every effort to keep the unity of
the Spirit through the bond of peace. [4]There
is one body and one Spirit—just as you were
called to one hope when you were called—
[5]one Lord, one faith, one baptism; [6]one God
and Father of all, who is over all and
through all and in all.

The fighting inside the church is one of the biggest turn-offs and a contradiction of God. What can you do for unity? Pray it.

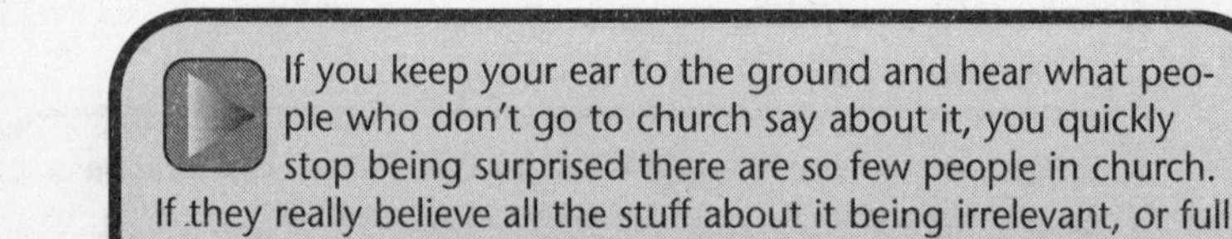

If you keep your ear to the ground and hear what people who don't go to church say about it, you quickly stop being surprised there are so few people in church. If they really believe all the stuff about it being irrelevant, or full of hypocrites, or different groups arguing with each other, it's not really surprising they stay away.

But if an outsider's view is warped, what actually are we about? In the first verse Paul encourages us to live lives worthy of God. Isn't that really it? Living lives that please and honour God. Do you think our life together as a church does that? If not, why not?

Verses 2–3 describe characteristics which, if you look at church history for longer than a second, you don't find much evidence of. Humility, gentleness, bearing with others, unity, peace. Which one of these are you worst at? Pray about it. Paul goes on to explain that the reason why division is so bad is because it contradicts who God is and what he has done (4–6). Count how many times he uses the word 'one'.

Imitate God

Ephesians 5:1–8, 10

[1]Be imitators of God, therefore, as dearly loved
children [2]and live a life of love, just as Christ
loved us and gave himself up for us as a fra-
grant offering and sacrifice to God.
[3]But among you there must not be even a
hint of sexual immorality, or of any kind of
impurity, or of greed, because these are
improper for God's holy people. [4]Nor should
there be obscenity, foolish talk or coarse joking, which are out of place, but rather thanksgiving. [5]For of this you can be sure: No
immoral, impure or greedy person—such a
man is an idolater—has any inheritance in
the kingdom of Christ and of God. [6]Let no-one
deceive you with empty words, for because of
such things God's wrath comes on those who
are disobedient. [7]Therefore do not be partners
with them.
[8]For you were once darkness, but now
you are light in the Lord. Live as children of
light . . .
[10]and find out what pleases the Lord.

Our aim should be to live to please him. For his eyes and pleasure only. How can life be the same?

Now this is really picking up speed. This is all about living a life worthy of God. It's not a list of stuff we've got to do to achieve love and salvation. It's because of love and salvation that we'll live this.

Grace might be free but it's not cheap: it's costly. And this is the way we should want to live if we've known the grace of God. Paul spells this out: a revolution has happened to you in Jesus (see 4:20–4). So live it. Because you have been made new in Jesus reflect his characteristics. God is truth. So we are to be full of truth. Where does it address your life? God is pure, encouraging, kind and forgiving (4:32). Do our lives reflect his character? Do we treat others like we have been treated by him? Imitate God, love like he loves, be pure as he is pure, generous as he is day after day, hour by hour.

Getting high

Ephesians 5:18–20

18 Do not get drunk on wine, which leads to
debauchery. Instead, be filled with the
Spirit. 19 Speak to one another with psalms,
hymns and spiritual songs. Sing and make
music in your heart to the Lord, 20 always
giving thanks to God the Father for everything, in the name of our Lord Jesus Christ.

A wise Christian told me once that the secret of them staying alive in Jesus was they sang everyday to him. Pick your favourite song and make some music in your heart.

Do you know that in the UK teenagers consume more alcohol per head of the population than any other country in Europe? The way I see it in the Bible there's nothing wrong with alcohol in itself. It's just when we start abusing it that problems arise and we fall. Have a think about why people drink too much? Escapism. Trying to numb the pain. Pleasure.

Sometimes people talk about getting off on God as if he were some kind of drug. It couldn't be further from the truth. God is about reality, quality, joy, helping you in situations rather than taking you out of them. And the after-effects are good for everyone. Think about the differences.

Paul encourages the young Christians not to get off on wine, but to be filled with God. To sing and praise not because they have lost their senses but because they have come to them. So he encourages us to sing.

The wardrobe

Ephesians 6:10–18

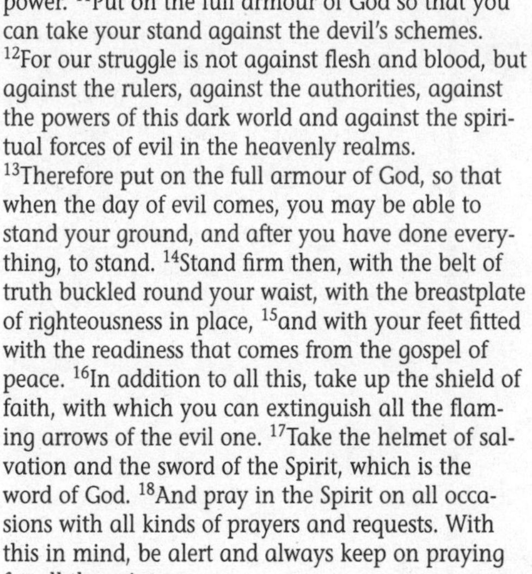

10 Finally, be strong in the Lord and in his mighty
power. 11 Put on the full armour of God so that you
can take your stand against the devil's schemes.
12 For our struggle is not against flesh and blood, but
against the rulers, against the authorities, against
the powers of this dark world and against the spiritual forces of evil in the heavenly realms.
13 Therefore put on the full armour of God, so that
when the day of evil comes, you may be able to
stand your ground, and after you have done everything, to stand. 14 Stand firm then, with the belt of
truth buckled round your waist, with the breastplate
of righteousness in place, 15 and with your feet fitted
with the readiness that comes from the gospel of
peace. 16 In addition to all this, take up the shield of
faith, with which you can extinguish all the flam-
ing arrows of the evil one. 17 Take the helmet of salvation and the sword of the Spirit, which is the
word of God. 18 And pray in the Spirit on all occasions with all kinds of prayers and requests. With
this in mind, be alert and always keep on praying
for all the saints.

Whose back are you covering? Pray for them.

If you are going to play in a football match what do you wear? If you are going to Buckingham Palace what do you wear? If you are a soldier going to fight a battle what do you wear? Of course you wear stuff that's appropriate to who you are and what you're going to do.

It seems from this that Paul is concerned some of the Christians in Ephesus might be trying to live life in a hostile world dressed only in their pyjamas. Without getting sensational about it and seeing devils under the bed and in the fridge, Paul is quite clear we are up against far more than we can handle on our own.

These are not God's fashion tips – they are essential for the task. And they are gifts for us from him. So read over them and think about what kind of equipment we need. Think about what the truth, the righteousness, the peace, the salvation and the word of God mean for you in practice. Pray them on.

There's one bit which is left uncovered. The back. Why? Could it be because we are all supposed to stand together and cover each other's?

ELISHA

Where his master Elijah was good with fire, Elisha was much more of a liquids man. The miraculous signs often used water or oil to show God's compassion for a needy and broken people, and throughout his story we understand more about the very nature of God.

Beginnings

1 Kings 19:19–21

[19]So Elijah went from there
and found Elisha son of
Shaphat. He was ploughing
with twelve yoke of oxen,
and he himself was driving
the twelfth pair. Elijah went
up to him and threw his
cloak around him. [20]Elisha
then left his oxen and ran
after Elijah. "Let me kiss my
father and mother good-
bye," he said, "and then I
will come with you."
"Go back," Elijah replied.
"What have I done to you?"
[21]So Elisha left him and
went back. He took his yoke
of oxen and slaughtered
them. He burned the
ploughing equipment to
cook the meat and gave it
to the people, and they ate.
Then he set out to follow
Elijah and became his
attendant.

Having heroes can be good, but God always demands that we keep the bigger picture in mind.

SEARCH

God has decided to give Elijah someone to carry on the business of rooting out the influences that had turned the Israelites' hearts away from him. This first encounter tells us a little of what to expect from Elisha's life.

Putting his cloak on the young man was symbolic of the relationship they would have: Elisha would carry on Elijah's work, and later all of his authority would be transferred over to his successor. Elisha, it would seem, is keen, sprinting off with delight to say a few farewells and settle into a life following this well-known prophet. But Elijah's reaction is key, telling him to take it easy. 'What have I done to you?' comes the question, and it all seems a bit odd. Has it gone sour? Is it like one of those blind dates where the good atmosphere can so easily get ruined by a line taken the wrong way?

But Elisha understands, and his actions speak volumes. He returns and serves a farewell dinner. He was clearly wealthy having all that equipment and assistance, and here he makes a clean break from his past job. What he is about to do, becoming Elijah's assistant, requires 100 per cent commitment. But as Elijah made kind of clear, it was not commitment to himself that he was after. Elisha had to do it for God. Burning his plough sent a message that he was in it for the long haul, even beyond the rest of Elijah's life.

God's call may have come through an enigmatic and inspiring leader, but Elijah was just another faithful servant.

Patience

2 Kings 2:1–2, 9–12

1When the Lord was about
to take Elijah up to heaven
in a whirlwind, Elijah and
Elisha were on their way
from Gilgal. 2Elijah said to
Elisha, "Stay here; the Lord
has sent me to Bethel."

But Elisha said, "As surely
as the Lord lives and as you
live, I will not leave you."
So they went down to
Bethel.

9When they had crossed,
Elijah said to Elisha, "Tell
me, what can I do for you
before I am taken from
you?"

"Let me inherit a double
portion of your spirit,"
Elisha replied.

10"You have asked a difficult thing," Elijah said, "yet
if you see me when I am
taken from you, it will be
yours—otherwise not."

11As they were walking
along and talking together,
suddenly a chariot of fire
and horses of fire appeared
and separated the two of
them, and Elijah went up to
heaven in a whirlwind.
12Elisha saw this and cried
out, "My father! My father!
The chariots and horsemen
of Israel!" And Elisha saw
him no more. Then he took
hold of his own clothes and
tore them apart.

SEARCH

A few chapters pass us by before we next catch word of Elisha. It's hard to put an actual date on things, but their initial meeting must have taken place some time around 857 BC. This section seems to come in after Jehoram has been King of Judah for a short time, and we know that he got the crown in 848 BC, which means that almost a decade has passed since Elisha was first taken on by Elijah.

Ten years with nothing happening that the writer considers worth putting down in the history books must have tested Elisha's character but, as we see here, he's fully committed to his master. But doesn't he look a bit greedy, asking for a double portion? Is this the result of ten years standing at the back thinking, 'I could do better than that'? Not at all, as it all ties up with the laws of inheritance. At the time the first-born son got twice as much of his father's remaining possessions as the others. Elisha wants the same, to be taken as Elijah's son, the one who inherits most and who carries on the family business.

GO

Elisha wasn't the only one in the Old Testament who had a long wait on his hands: just look at David. What are you in training for – admiration from people or relationship with God?

Oi! Baldie!

2 Kings 2:23–5

23 From there Elisha went
up to Bethel. As he was
walking along the road,
some youths came out of
the town and jeered at
him. "Go on up, you
baldhead!" they said.
"Go on up, you bald-
head!" 24 He turned
round, looked at them
and called down a curse
on them in the name of
the Lord. Then two bears
came out of the woods
and mauled forty-two of
the youths. 25 And he
went on to Mount
Carmel and from there
returned to Samaria.

SEARCH

Well, you've got to laugh, haven't you? Sometimes these prophets can all seem a little on the weird side, but at least we can recognise in Elisha something nice and normal. Kids slagging him off? Call down a curse and kill them. Nice one.

Like it or not this is a miracle and God seems to back up Elisha's curse. Just like with Samson murdering the thirty men in Ashkelon (Judges 14:19), it seems that our view of what is morally right and wrong doesn't always match up with God's.

It's unlikely that Elisha actually was bald – he lived for another fifty years and baldness wasn't much of a problem among the ancient Jews. But we know that Bethel was rammed with cults and other weird stuff, so this did at least have the advantage of showing that God meant business.

Perhaps it's helpful to look at the verses that come before this one, telling the story of how God uses Elisha to answer people's request for help with their contaminated water. Elisha does something with salt, but it's clear that all the praise is due to God. How different this is from the pesky kids.

For those looking for God's help and mercy it would be given, but those who had turned away could expect God's anger. Having said that, calling down curses on anyone who winds you up might not be the best advice.

Try getting some other hints from 1 Peter 2:23, 'when he suffered, he made no threats. Instead he entrusted himself to him who judges justly.'

The heart of God

2 Kings 4:1–7

1The wife of a man from the company of the prophets cried out to Elisha, "Your servant my husband is dead, and you know that he revered the Lord. But now his creditor is coming to take my two boys as his slaves."
2Elisha replied to her, "How can I help you? Tell me, what do you have in your house?"

"Your servant has nothing there at all," she said, "except a little oil."
3Elisha said, "Go round and ask all your neighbours for empty jars. Don't ask for just a few.
4Then go inside and shut the door behind you and your sons. Pour oil into all the jars, and as each is filled, put it to one side."
5She left him and afterwards shut the door behind her and her sons. They brought the jars to her and she kept pouring.
6When all the jars were full, she said to her son, "Bring me another one."

But he replied, "There is not a jar left." Then the oil stopped flowing.
7She went and told the man of God, and he said, "Go, sell the oil and pay your debts. You and your sons can live on what is left."

SEARCH

Elisha's actions show plenty about God's heart, and are clear evidence about what a true prophet is. As with Elijah the idea is plain for all to see: along with speaking God's word must come doing his work. That means helping the poor, spreading compassion and putting right the wrongs that humankind has done.

The widow's husband was one of the crew of prophets, a man who may have borrowed money to keep the prophets fed. The law stated that an unpaid debt could be paid by the work of a son (see Leviticus 25:39–41), but things weren't quite working out according to this ideal. People were being taken advantage of and the widow was understandably upset at the thought of losing her two sons. The situation is wrong and Elisha's act puts things back the right way, God's way.

It's funny that she could have as much oil as she wanted, depending on the number of jars she collected. That's a great picture of faith and ties in with the image of God as the ultimate in generosity.

So does God prefer us rich? Would we all be loaded if only we had enough faith? Should we be telling people to be more like the widow? Nope. Let's concentrate on getting ourselves compassionate and generous.

GO

Take the good news out in a way that gives the help that people need.

Simple

2 Kings 6:1–7

1The company of the
prophets said to Elisha,
"Look, the place where
we meet with you is too
small for us. 2Let us go to
the Jordan, where each
of us can get a pole; and
let us build a place there
for us to live."
And he said, "Go."
3Then one of them
said, "Won't you please
come with your ser-
vants?"
"I will," Elisha replied.
4And he went with them.
They went to the
Jordan and began to cut
down trees. 5As one of
them was cutting down a
tree, the iron axe-head
fell into the water. "Oh,
my lord," he cried out,
"it was borrowed!"
6The man of God
asked, "Where did it
fall?" When he showed
him the place, Elisha cut
a stick and threw it
there, and made the iron
float. 7"Lift it out," he
said. Then the man
reached out his hand
and took it.

SEARCH

The members of the group of prophets were poor. Elisha had helped them out during a famine by de-poisoning their stew, and now we see him pitch in again. Axe-heads were understandably expensive and for the prophet losing one that was borrowed would mean facing the prospect of working off the debt as a servant. These faithful people were already living on the edge and Elisha's miracle shows God's concern for their welfare.

Jesus did something similar in Matthew 17:27, and it really is that simple: God's heart is for the poor. So what, we stand by and wait for the miraculous cures, the bizarre bail-outs? Elisha did what he did because that's who he was: a man who expected to see God do unusual stuff. But what's more impressive: the fact that the axe-head floated or that God cared enough to help some people out of trouble?

Don't think that giving your time, money, energy or attention is any less of a good thing than Elisha's miracles. The true miracle is that our God cares.

Weird life, weird death

2 Kings 13:14–19

14Now Elisha was suffering
from the illness from which
he died. Jehoash king of
Israel went down to see him
and wept over him. "My
father! My father!" he cried.
"The chariots and horsemen
of Israel!"
15Elisha said, "Get a bow
and some arrows," and he
did so. 16"Take the bow in
your hands," he said to the
king of Israel. When he had
taken it, Elisha put his
hands on the king's hands.
17"Open the east win-
dow," he said, and he
opened it. "Shoot!" Elisha
said, and he shot. "The
Lord's arrow of victory, the
arrow of victory over
Aram!" Elisha declared.
"You will completely destroy
the Arameans at Aphek."
18Then he said, "Take the
arrows," and the king took
them. Elisha told him,
"Strike the ground." He
struck it three times and
stopped. 19The man of God
was angry with him and
said, "You should have
struck the ground five or six
times; then you would have
defeated Aram and com-
pletely destroyed it. But now
you will defeat it only three
times."

SEARCH

Just as Elisha's early ministry began with a period of silence, so there is a large gap between his mention in chapter 9 and this final appearance. All in all it's a 43-year break during which we know absolutely nothing of what he got up to. But just like before we see that he is still being used by God to speak to Israel. Jehoash is king and he lacks faith. He is unable to give a strong and godly lead to his people, although he does say that stuff about chariots when he sees the old man. Is Jehoash having a laugh? It would seem not, and that instead he's making a comment about just how much help Elisha has been to Israel (more than all its military hardware).

Jehoash might have recognised Elisha's godly influence, but it didn't seem to impact his life. His half-hearted response to Elisha's ground-slapping command shows his lack of passion for God. It would take his son Jeroboam II to beat the Arameans completely.

And with that Elisha has gone. No ceremony, no big death scene. Just like his beginning Elisha's end is low key. He may have been a big name, but God remains the real hero.

One last thing to mention: later someone was shoved into Elisha's tomb, and on contact with his bones the new addition to the grave came back to life. Just in case we were wondering who was in charge here, God sends a reminder: he doesn't even need us alive to perform miracles.

We love a good show, and mysterious people who seem to be able to have God's miracles on tap always get our attention.

GO

But let's never forget the miracle-worker's place, and let's never stop giving all the glory to its rightful recipient: God.

Philippians

Paul's letter to the church at Philippi is a bit of a classic, rammed with insights and great advice for a life lived to the full with Jesus. Unlike many of his others, this letter shows Paul giving advice as a friend first, rather than as a preacher. But he's no less on fire with good things that remain fresh today.

Update

philippians 1:19–26

19for I know that through your prayers and the
help given by the Spirit of Jesus Christ, what
has happened to me will turn out for my deliverance. 20I eagerly expect and hope that I will in
no way be ashamed, but will have sufficient
courage so that now as always Christ will be
exalted in my body, whether by life or by
death. 21For to me, to live is Christ and to die is
gain. 22If I am to go on living in the body, this
will mean fruitful labour for me. Yet what shall I
choose? I do not know! 23I am torn between the
two: I desire to depart and be with Christ,
which is better by far; 24but it is more necessary
for you that I remain in the body. 25Convinced
of this, I know that I will remain, and I will continue with all of you for your progress and joy
in the faith, 26so that through my being with
you again your joy in Christ Jesus will overflow
on account of me.

He's a good lad, is our Paul. He knows that they'll only be worrying about him back in Philippi, so one of the reasons for the letter is to let them all know that he's OK. Kind of. He's in prison, which they know already, and he's certainly managing to look on the bright side. In fact, Paul kicks off by saying just how great it is to be in chains. He's getting the chance to chat with everyone that he meets, telling them about Jesus.

But it's not just putting a brave face on it, as our Paul makes it clear that his faith really does have guts. There's a chance that he might wind up dead after this little caper, but he remains tipped up to the brim that the prayers of his mates will bring his 'deliverance'. Wow – believing that he was going to be set free from jail like that took guts. But it's not quite as simple: you see Paul uses 'deliverance' to mean either being set free from prison or death. Scary thought, but Paul's having none of it, and either way he's happy. The way Paul puts it, if he gets set free Christ gets the glory as he has more time to spread the good news, but if he dies he gets to be with Jesus, the ultimate result.

But there's no airy-fairy fantasy about it, as he knows there is work to be done. Death or freedom, he can't make the call about what God has planned, but either way he's happy.

chew it over

We all go through difficult times, but can you imagine facing them with Paul's attitude? How do you think he would have approached your last crisis?

A different view

philippians 1:27–30

27Whatever happens, conduct yourselves in
a manner worthy of the gospel of Christ.
Then, whether I come and see you or only
hear about you in my absence, I will know
that you stand firm in one spirit, contending
as one man for the faith of the gospel
28without being frightened in any way by
those who oppose you. This is a sign to
them that they will be destroyed, but that
you will be saved—and that by God. 29For
it has been granted to you on behalf of
Christ not only to believe on him, but also
to suffer for him, 30since you are going
through the same struggle you saw I had,
and now hear that I still have.

A bloke who's seen more trouble than Harry Potter tells you that you're now going through the same struggles as him. Gulp. That's the sort of news that's likely to see me packing my bags and heading for the nearest train to Snoozeville. Thanks, but no thanks, Uncle Paul. I'll leave the suffering up to you. Give me the quiet life any day.

But deep down I know that's not the way it's meant to be. If we believe that Jesus died and rose again, then we believe that death is not the final chapter. If we believe that Jesus offers eternal life, then we believe that suffering on earth is not . . . well, it's not the last straw.

So now we're all feeling totally miserable, let's get back to Paul. He's onto something here, talking about the need for unity. It seems that standing together 'in one spirit' is the sort of thing he's thinking of when he urges the Philippians to act 'in a manner worthy of the gospel of Christ'. And it isn't because he fancies himself as a drill sergeant either, for unity sends out a powerful signal that says God is at the centre, working through our lives.

But what do we know about suffering? We're free to express our beliefs unlike so many who have been persecuted over the years. We are, to borrow a phrase, rich Christians living in an age of hunger. What do we know about anything?

chew it over

Do you want to go further on with God? Do you want to make sacrifices for him? Be honest and talk to God about your feelings.

Keep humble and united

philippians 2:1–5

1 If you have any encouragement from being
united with Christ, if any comfort from his
love, if any fellowship with the Spirit, if any
tenderness and compassion, 2 then make my
joy complete by being like-minded, having
the same love, being one in spirit and purpose. 3 Do nothing out of selfish ambition or
vain conceit, but in humility consider others
better than yourselves. 4 Each of you should
look not only to your own interests, but
also to the interests of others.
5 Your attitude should be the same as that
of Christ Jesus:

And so we carry on with Paul from the previous session. We were left a little stranded, with Paul urging the readers to look forward to their sufferings, standing firm and in unity with each other, but we were wondering just how this works for us.

Thankfully Paul doesn't make us wait. He launches off with a hint tucked away in this first verse. What are we? 'United in Christ'. Get it? We're not like the Lone Ranger, taking it all alone. Paul bases his faith on the idea that salvation is all about some kind of personal relationship with Jesus. Being saved isn't about signing some one-off, cold-hearted contract. It's about discovering an intimate, living relationship with God. What's even more amazing is that out of that relationship comes all that we need in life: encouragement, tenderness, compassion.

Do you see where he's going? Signing up with Jesus is not about being sent off alone to soak up as much suffering as possible, it's about getting closer to him, receiving all that comes from God.

But why does it seem so fragile? Why is Paul so keen that people should stick together? The truth is simple: if we start to think that we're better than others, if we start to think more about our own needs than the needs of others, we become selfish. We turn our eyes in on ourselves and forget about others. We put 'me' first and push God out. Just like the Israelites we wander off and neglect God, although this time it's not other pagan gods we develop a fancy for, but our own wants.

chew it over

God's message is the same today: we are not the centre of the universe. The truth is even better than that: we are the sons and daughters of the Maker of heaven and earth. Remember, it's a team thing.

Check out Timothy

philippians 2:19–24

[19]I hope in the Lord Jesus to send Timothy
to you soon, that I also may be cheered
when I receive news about you. [20]I have no-
one else like him, who takes a genuine
interest in your welfare. [21]For everyone
looks out for his own interests, not those of
Jesus Christ. [22]But you know that Timothy
has proved himself, because as a son with
his father he has served with me in the
work of the gospel. [23]I hope, therefore, to
send him as soon as I see how things go
with me. [24]And I am confident in the Lord
that I myself will come soon.

The letter shifts from encouraging the believers at large to talking about a couple of specific members. First up is Timothy, the right-hand man who has served Paul like a son for many years. Losing him is hard, but again Paul knows the score: the aim in life is not to notch up as many happy points for himself, but to do the right thing, to push on and get the gospel spread and the Church strengthened, whatever the cost.

But giving Timothy this big-up is not just a neat way of teaching the church at Philippi without them feeling as though he's having a go at them. Paul also uses it to illustrate what he's spent the last few inches of parchment banging on about. Timothy does not put himself first, he is not afraid to walk the Jesus path, even though it often ends up considerably less comfortable than strolling along the Me First avenue.

chew it over

Where does this 'others first' attitude come from? How did Jesus show it?

Good lad

philippians 2:25–30

25But I think it is necessary to send back to
you Epaphroditus, my brother, fellow-work-
er and fellow-soldier, who is also your
messenger, whom you sent to take care of
my needs. 26For he longs for all of you and
is distressed because you heard he was ill.
27Indeed he was ill, and almost died. But
God had mercy on him, and not on him
only but also on me, to spare me sorrow
upon sorrow. 28Therefore I am all the more
eager to send him, so that when you see
him again you may be glad and I may have
less anxiety. 29Welcome him in the Lord
with great joy, and honour men like him,
30because he almost died for the work of
Christ, risking his life to make up for the
help you could not give me.

No sooner has he given Timothy a nice slap on the back than Paul is making another point about some other young man. The Philippians had scored many points when they heard that Paul was in jail by sending him to help out in any way that he could. Attending to his physical needs like that showed plenty of kindness as well as a good dose of common sense, but Paul is sending him back. He had become ill – critically ill – but had fought back with a little help from God. His brush with death made him eager to get home, and Paul is happy to send him on his way. Like Timothy, Epaphroditus travels with a gold star at the end of his name as Paul gives him maximum respect for his conduct. How come? Paul is wise as to the reaction old Epaphroditus' return might get: some may feel that he had failed to do his duty. It could have caused more than just a bit of aggro, and not only for Epaphroditus. Paul makes sure that the Philippians know that Epaphroditus was prepared to risk his life for serving Jesus, and his words are soaked with wisdom.

Think about it for a while. Epaphroditus was there to help in any way he could, and that meant doing menial tasks to help while Paul was under house arrest. Are you as confident that people serving quietly in the background get plenty of godly respect?

chew it over

Paul tells the readers to 'honour people like Epaphroditus'. Does that mean you?

Watch out

philippians 3:12–14

12Not that I have already obtained all this,
or have already been made perfect, but I
press on to take hold of that for which
Christ Jesus took hold of me. 13Brothers, I
do not consider myself yet to have taken
hold of it. But one thing I do: Forgetting
what is behind and straining towards what
is ahead, 14I press on towards the goal to
win the prize for which God has called me
heavenwards in Christ Jesus.

Ah! Pure dynamite here. This is another of those vintage passages that just seem to keep on getting better. Apparently some of the folks down at Philippi had begun to think that they had reached the goal, that they'd sussed what Christianity was all about and had got it all sewn up nicely, thank you very much. Ha!

Paul likes to use the metaphor of a race when talking about Christianity. Perhaps it's a chariot race or some other sporting occasion, but either way, he makes the point that it's a race that is still going on. It's not over, it's not a race that's been completed. No, this is an ultra-marathon, one that lasts as long as we have breath.

Don't get down about this: it doesn't mean that we can never finish it, just that the goal is a little harder to define. His goal is to grab onto what Jesus grabbed for him. Confused? It is a bit confusing, isn't it? But what Jesus grabbed for him, what he is now aiming at, was something special – salvation.

Of course, salvation is about what happens when we die, which kind of makes sense here. Keep going, says Paul, right up until death, right up until the very last. He's not going to take a year out, to sit back for a rest and let his relationship with Jesus get cold. He's in it till the very last breath has left his body.

But salvation is something else too. It means the forgiveness of sins, the sacrifice that Jesus made for us so that we can enjoy relationship with him. Salvation is about the moulding of our character, the changing of ourselves from within to become the person God made us to be.

chew it over

The race keeps going because God keeps going: changing, moulding and drawing us closer to him.

Thanks for the gift

philippians 4:10–14

10 I rejoice greatly in the Lord that at last
you have renewed your concern for me.
Indeed, you have been concerned, but you
had no opportunity to show it. 11 I am not
saying this because I am in need, for I have
learned to be content whatever the circumstances. 12 I know what it is to be in need,
and I know what it is to have plenty. I have learned the secret of being content in any and every situation, whether well fed or hungry, whether living in plenty or in want.
13 I can do everything through him who gives
me strength.

14 Yet it was good of you to share in my
troubles.

Paul has been saying 'and finally' for the last few pages, and it's as if he keeps on remembering things to say. He's on fire in this letter, chatting away and full up with things that he just can't wait to pass on. In returning Epaphroditus he wants to thank them once more for the kind gifts they sent, but even that can't be done without getting in a few wise words that seem to be burning on the tip of his tongue.

For a long time they 'had no opportunity' to send him stuff, and when they did it set off the old fireworks inside Paul. It showed that things were going well, that God was blessing them and he gave maximum glory to the original gift giver. But – and I don't think he's meaning to be rude here – he doesn't need physical things to be 'content' (or, as the original Greek puts it 'self-sufficient'). Come off it, mate, you're banged up! You've got no freedom. How can you be self-sufficient? But he can, and we all know how. There are no prizes for guessing what comes next, as Paul makes it clear that he has all he needs in Jesus.

Impressive stuff, this. But somehow I don't think Paul reckons he's learnt all there is. The race is still on and he's not letting the pace slow down.

chew it over

Read Paul's words over a few times. Not bad, are they? Fancy having a go at some new goals?

HEZEKIAH

If the Bible were a movie, then Hezekiah's part would appear pretty low down on the list of credits. But this is no bit part: Hezekiah was at the heart of the action.

Opening shot

2 Kings 17:18–19

18So the Lord was very angry with Israel and removed them from his presence. Only the tribe of Judah was left, 19and even Judah did not keep the commands of the Lord their God. They followed the practices Israel had introduced.

SEARCH

Solomon's concentration of most of the country's resources in the south had resulted in the splitting of God's people into regional groups, and things haven't been going too well. Up in the *Northern Kingdom* years of selfishness and backs turned to God have led to the arrival of God's judgment. Meanwhile Judah down in the south was following in the footsteps of Israel, its northern cousin. It, too, was becoming smitten with false gods.

So things were not looking good for Judah. In fact, things were looking bad, very bad. Going through a time of godly judgment was no picnic, and the people of Judah were facing a very serious situation. Many felt it would only be a matter of time before God, who judged Israel, would also bring judgment on Judah.

But, like in all good movies, there's an 'unless . . . '. God's judgment would certainly be poured out on Judah unless something amazing happened, unless somehow God's people turned back to him and began to serve him. Mmmm, now I wonder how that might happen . . .

GO

We live in a strange world: we may deserve to face the music, but God doesn't turn his back on us.

Enter Hezekiah

2 Chronicles 29: 1–3

[1]Hezekiah was twenty-five years old when he became king, and he reigned in Jerusalem for twenty-nine years. His mother's name was Abijah daughter of Zechariah. [2]He did what was right in the eyes of the Lord, just as his father David had done.

[3]In the first month of the first year of his reign, he opened the doors of the temple of the Lord and repaired them.

GO

You know that saying 'it takes two to tango'? Well, all Hezekiah's potential to reunite could only reach as far as the Israelites' humility would allow.

SEARCH

Here he comes: old enough to have the wisdom to know how to sort the problem out and young enough to have the energy. It was a gargantuan task, yet turning the people back towards God was one task that Hezekiah was determined to complete.

First up was the temple. OK, so taking over the throne isn't quite like moving into a student house, but the wisdom of Hezekiah's actions are confirmed by Student Folklore: while some foolish renters opt for setting up their hi-fis the minute they move into a new pad, the real wise ones will don the rubber gloves and set to with a bucket of bleach. You don't know who or what's been going on there before you, and King Hezekiah's decision to kick off his reign by cleansing the *temple* surely receives top marks.

The similarities kind of break down from here on in, as he then chooses to rededicate, and re-establish the worship of God within the temple. Still, this was one leader whose heart was 100 per cent committed to God, a man whose actions were followed by dramatic – and welcome – consequences. Soon after the reopening of the temple, he and the leaders invited everyone – not just the people of Judah but any remaining Israelites – to join in a massive worship session.

This was a bold move. The kingdoms of Judah and Israel had been divided for two hundred years, ever since Solomon's reign, and for many Israelites in the north the gesture may have seemed a further reminder of the South Is Best attitude that caused the split in the first place. Mainly the people were unreceptive to the invitation, apart from a few from Asher, Manasseh and Zebulun who 'humbled themselves and went to Jerusalem' (2 Chroncles 30:11).

The plot thickens

2 Chronicles 30: 23, 26–7

23The whole assembly
then agreed to celebrate
the festival seven more
days; so for another
seven days they celebrat-
ed joyfully.
26There was great joy
in Jerusalem, for since
the days of Solomon son
of David king of Israel
there had been nothing
like this in Jerusalem.
27The priests and the
Levites stood to bless the
people, and God heard
them, for their prayer
reached heaven, his holy
dwelling-place.

GO

God's in the restoration business.

SEARCH

So we've seen Hezekiah come forward and get things started by cleaning up the temple and restarting the worship sessions. The people of God took him up on the offer and some chose to come together. But here, we see something special happening: the session that's supposed to last for just one week turns out to be such a stormer that all agree to keep it rolling for another week. God's presence is so clearly there that the leaders are keen not to wrap things up too early.

So on one level we can all understand what's going on. After all, many of us have probably been in meetings that have failed to grab our attention, ones where we're desperate to get out the door as soon as possible. We may have experienced the other sort too, the type where things are going so nicely that it just seems a shame to end, even though the meeting should have finished long ago. So we can see that Hezekiah's reforms have been a success.

But there's another level to the story, one bound up in history. We've already mentioned how Solomon managed to cause friction, with Jeroboam (the king who followed him) splitting the kingdom, and it's not hard to see in 2 Chronicles 30 that similarities between him and Hezekiah are being drawn. Not only was this the first 'successful' meeting since Solomon's time (26), but Hezekiah's words (27) are supposed to remind us of the prayers spoken by Solomon when he dedicated the temple. It's clear that things are carrying on where Solomon left, two hundred years before.

The grand finale

2 Chronicles 31: 1–8

1 When all this had ended, the
Israelites who were there went out to
the towns of Judah, smashed the
sacred stones and cut down the
Asherah poles. They destroyed the
high places and the altars throughout
Judah and Benjamin and in Ephraim
and Manasseh. After they had
destroyed all of them, the Israelites
returned to their own towns and to
their own property.
2 Hezekiah assigned the priests and
Levites to divisions—each of them
according to their duties as priests or
Levites—to offer burnt offerings and
fellowship offerings, to minister, to
give thanks and to sing praises at the
gates of the Lord's dwelling. 3 The king
contributed from his own possessions
for the morning and evening burnt
offerings and for the burnt offerings
on the Sabbaths, New Moons and
appointed feasts as written in the Law
of the Lord. 4 He ordered the people living in Jerusalem to give the portion
due to the priests and Levites so that
they could devote themselves to the
Law of the Lord. 5 As soon as the order
went out, the Israelites generously
gave the firstfruits of their grain, new
wine, oil and honey and all that the
fields produced. They brought a great
amount, a tithe of everything. 6 The
men of Israel and Judah who lived in
the towns of Judah also brought a
tithe of their herds and flocks and a
tithe of the holy things dedicated to
the Lord their God, and they piled
them in heaps. 7 They began doing
this in the third month and finished in
the seventh month. 8 When Hezekiah
and his officials came and saw the
heaps, they praised the Lord and
blessed his people Israel.

SEARCH

There are three other direct references to the levels of joy among the people (2 Chronicles 30:21). But this was no spine-tingling bless up. This was real, and God was doing serious business among his people. Once they were there the freshly fired-up Israelites went out and destroyed all the tools associated with the worship of false gods. Not a bad result.

But there's more to come as verse 4 points out. Hezekiah is ordering the people to do their bit and support God's work financially. It goes down well and the people of Israel and Judah respond by giving a tenth of their herds and flocks and a pile of holy things dedicated to God (6). Again, not a bad result.

And still there's more to come. Chapter 32 tells us that the northern kingdom of Assyria has its eyes on the freshly polished Judah. Sennacherib threatens and intimidates, but Hezekiah returns to prayer and God sends an angel who annihilates the opposing army.

God was on Judah's side. Having turned back their hearts to him, the people were willing to make changes for the better and God stepped in with a miraculous save.

The closing shot

2 Kings 20:1–3

1 In those days Hezekiah
became ill and was at
the point of death. The
prophet Isaiah son of
Amoz went to him and
said, "This is what the
Lord says: Put your
house in order, because
you are going to die; you
will not recover."
2 Hezekiah turned his
face to the wall and
prayed to the Lord,
3 "Remember, O Lord,
how I have walked
before you faithfully and
with wholehearted devo-
tion and have done what
is good in your eyes."
And Hezekiah wept bit-
terly.

SEARCH

At the age of thirty-seven or thirty-eight Hezekiah is told that his life is about to end. His achievements have been impressive and he looks set to end on something of a high. But this is one closing shot that doesn't ease us gently down to a soft landing.

First up are the tears. OK, so no big deal really, but Hezekiah's pleading with God is worth noting. He doesn't say, 'I have done all this *stuff* for you': instead he understands that in God's currency what is valuable is a committed and faithful heart rather than 'impressive' tasks. In return God performs a miracle using a medicinal remedy and Hezekiah gets another fifteen years added on to the end of his life.

But there's room for a mistake. The golden boy slips up by entering into an unwise alliance with the Babylonians. This was foolish as after his death (about 115 years later) God's people would find themselves under the oppression of Nebuchadnezzar. According to Isaiah, the blame lay fairly and squarely at the feet of our man H. Oh dear.

There's chat about Hezekiah's pride, with some saying that he didn't care what happened after his death so long as it appeared on the surface that his reign was a success. That view's a little controversial, but at least we can see that Hezekiah was prepared to take God's judgment when necessary.

More than the achievements, it's the heart that matters.

Colossians

24-hour party people

False teachers get everywhere and they don't just wash off with bleach. Paul gets to grips with a culture that saw God as distant and Jesus as simply ordinary.

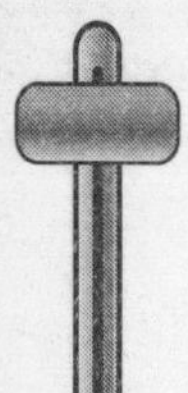

Colossians 2:16–19

16 Therefore do not let anyone judge you by
what you eat or drink, or with regard to a
religious festival, a New Moon celebration
or a Sabbath day. 17 These are a shadow of
the things that were to come; the reality,
however, is found in Christ. 18 Do not let
anyone who delights in false humility and
the worship of angels disqualify you for the
prize. Such a person goes into great detail
about what he has seen, and his unspiritual
mind puffs him up with idle notions. 19 He
has lost connection with the Head, from
whom the whole body, supported and held
together by its ligaments and sinews, grows
as God causes it to grow.

What about us: are we guilty of judging others? Do we accuse people of not matching up to a bunch of irrelevant standards?

We need a little background to work this one out. It seems that the people of Colosse had been holding on to some strict laws about festivals and the like. Nothing wrong with festivals, you may think, but it appears that these rules were getting in the way of people's personal relationship with Jesus. Nowhere in the New Testament does it suggest that we ought to punctuate our calendar with festivals and ceremonies. That's right: no instructions to have Christmas Day (it was originally a pagan festival anyway) and no directives about Easter Sunday. The Colossians were still practising a whole bundle of Old Testament rituals, and Paul was making a point when he called them 'a shadow of the things that were to come'. In the Old Testament these festivals and ceremonies existed as part of the run up to Jesus' arrival. With his life and death a new order of things was established: relationship with God. The church at Colosse needed to hear this, and needed to be reminded of the fact that Jesus was exactly who he said he was: God himself.

The chosen ones

Colossians 3:12–14

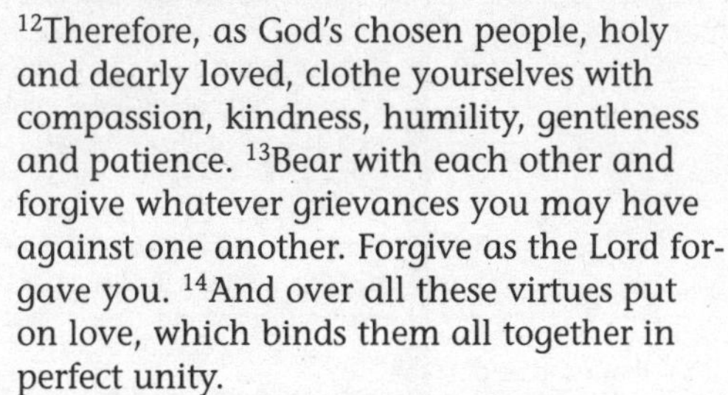

12 Therefore, as God's chosen people, holy
and dearly loved, clothe yourselves with
compassion, kindness, humility, gentleness
and patience. 13 Bear with each other and
forgive whatever grievances you may have
against one another. Forgive as the Lord forgave you. 14 And over all these virtues put
on love, which binds them all together in
perfect unity.

God's invitation of relationship with him is open to all, but there's an expectation placed upon us when we sign up.

So the audience are God's chosen people, huh? Not bad for a ragtag bunch of cultural mismatches. In the Old Testament it was the Israelites who received the honour of that 'chosen people' title, so does that mean that God has seasonal favourites? Does he change his mind with his socks?

Paul happens to be picking up on one of his favourite themes here: the Christian community is chosen by God. Nice. Does that mean we can take it easy? After all, with God on our side there are bound to be some pretty major perks, right? Not quite. The call for human responsibility is even louder for God's people. Paul spells it out: we need to be compassionate, kind, humble and so on.

Nehemiah

You knew where you were with a wall back then. So when Jerusalem's got squashed by Nebuchadnezzar it was important that the city walls were rebuilt ASAP. Enter Nehemiah.

The job

nehemiah 1:4–11

4When I heard these things, I sat down and wept.
For some days I mourned and fasted and prayed
before the God of heaven. 5Then I said:

"O Lord, God of heaven, the great and awesome God, who keeps his covenant of love
with those who love him and obey his commands, 6let your ear be attentive and your
eyes open to hear the prayer your servant is
praying before you day and night for your
servants, the people of Israel. I confess the
sins we Israelites, including myself and my
father's house, have committed against you.
7We have acted very wickedly towards you.
We have not obeyed the commands, decrees
and laws you gave your servant Moses.
8"Remember the instruction you gave your
servant Moses, saying, 'If you are unfaithful, I
will scatter you among the nations, 9but if you
return to me and obey my commands, then
even if your exiled people are at the farthest
horizon, I will gather them from there and
bring them to the place I have chosen as a
dwelling for my Name.'
10"They are your servants and your people,
whom you redeemed by your great strength
and your mighty hand. 11O Lord, let your ear
be attentive to the prayer of this your servant
and to the prayer of your servants who
delight in revering your name. Give your servant success today by granting him favour in
the presence of this man."

I was cupbearer to the king.

Having heard that Jerusalem happened to be in a bad state, Nehemiah gets down to business. First up are the tears. Tears seemed to be in fashion at the time, and this last of the historical books of the Old Testament is heavy on the tissues. But Nehemiah's tears are not for himself, they are for God's people. Nehemiah, it would seem, is in tune with God's heart.

But there's more to the story than that. He lived in Persia, serving King Artaxerxes. Nehemiah was one of the King's cupbearers, a position of immense responsibility and trust. He was the one who tasted the wine in the presence of the King to make sure that it was not poisoned. He was probably a eunuch – most cupbearers were – and it soon becomes clear that he was a man not only of great talent, but of great spiritual strength: he was able to sacrifice (quite literally), to live with the threat of death and be apart from his people, yet still his belief in God was rock solid. As we will see later, he was a brilliant man, and it seems that his time in Persia had taught him many lessons.

One last thing, Nehemiah would face a considerable risk if he went through with his plans to ask for the King's permission to help rebuild the walls. Why? Because it was Artaxerxes who had issued a decree just years before that no building work should be carried out on Jerusalem's walls. According to the King the Jews were a threat, and Nehemiah was about to walk a very fine line.

chew it over

You can't fake a relationship with God. Nehemiah's reaction showed that he knew his law and he knew his God. I wonder how . . .

The materials

nehemiah 2:1–6

1In the month of Nisan in the twentieth year of
King Artaxerxes, when wine was brought for
him, I took the wine and gave it to the king. I
had not been sad in his presence before; 2so
the king asked me, "Why does your face look
so sad when you are not ill? This can be nothing but sadness of heart."

I was very much afraid, 3but I said to the
king, "May the king live for ever! Why should my face not look sad when the city where my fathers are buried lies in ruins, and its gates have been destroyed by fire?"

4The king said to me, "What is it you
want?"

Then I prayed to the God of heaven, 5and I
answered the king, "If it pleases the king and if your servant has found favour in his sight, let him send me to the city in Judah where my fathers are buried so that I can rebuild it."

6Then the king, with the queen sitting
beside him, asked me, "How long will your journey take, and when will you get back?" It pleased the king to send me; so I set a time.

Nehemiah first heard about the plight of his people back in the month of Kislev, and it was not until the month of Nisan that he managed to bring the issue up with the King. In case you were wondering, that's a gap of about four months, during which we can assume that Nehemiah was praying the issue over. It might have been that the King was away or that Nehemiah's shift patterns didn't work out right, but either way Nehemiah's wait doesn't seem to have taken the edge off his relationship with God. It can be easy for us to get frustrated by long waits, especially when we are bursting to do something important, but Nehemiah's actions and the King's reactions show that prayer is far more than a handy way of filling time.

It seems that he was taking a risk right from the start, walking in with a face like a wet weekend. He'd never looked stroppy before, and there are hints that kings weren't that keen on miserable-looking servants – after all, you never knew what they might be up to.

chew it over

Heroes come in all shapes and sizes, but the qualities of godly ones never change: trust, prayer and a commitment to doing the right thing. How's it going with you?

The plan

nehemiah 2:12–16

12I set out during the night with a few men. I
had not told anyone what my God had put
in my heart to do for Jerusalem. There were
no mounts with me except the one I was
riding on.
13By night I went out through the Valley
Gate towards the Jackal Well and the Dung
Gate, examining the walls of Jerusalem,
which had been broken down, and its gates,
which had been destroyed by fire. 14Then I
moved on towards the Fountain Gate and
the King's Pool, but there was not enough
room for my mount to get through; 15so I
went up the valley by night, examining the
wall. Finally, I turned back and re-entered
through the Valley Gate. 16The officials did
not know where I had gone or what I was
doing, because as yet I had said nothing to
the Jews or the priests or nobles or officials
or any others who would be doing the
work.

We catch our man doing a spot of sneaky, late-night reconnaissance. How come? Because he's a clever wee chap and he knows the value of good planning, as we saw back in the previous chapter (1:7). When the King asked him how long his trip would take, Nehemiah had not only worked out the answer in advance, but had prepared a detailed list of requirements, from materials to official backing and protection. This late-night mission was more of the same, allowing Nehemiah to approach the job with a full picture of what needed to be done.

'But what,' you may be thinking, 'is he on about?' Surely as a trusting worshipper of Yahweh Nehemiah would have been able to ease back on the preparation and allow God to speak to him? Wasn't Nehemiah in some way doubting God, relying on his own strength and resources to rebuild the walls? 'Where,' you may ask, 'was his faith?'

Nehemiah was the man for the job precisely because of his ability to plan. He thought logically, carefully and with a good deal of informed opinion. He didn't leave it to chance, wing it or hope that God would magic down the blueprints in the morning. Does that mean he was a faith-failure? Not at all. Nehemiah was used wonderfully by God because he used something wonderful that God had given him: his brain.

Trusting God does not mean unplugging our brains and hoping it will all come good in the end. As St Francis of Assisi once wrote, when wanting God to do something in and through our lives we should pray as if the entire outcome depended on him and work as if it depended on us. Sums Nehemiah up pretty well, don't you think?

chew it over

God doesn't want a bunch of puppets. He wants us to interact with him and use the gifts he has given us.

The opposition

nehemiah 4:1–6

1When Sanballat heard that we were rebuilding
the wall, he became angry and was greatly
incensed. He ridiculed the Jews, 2and in the
presence of his associates and the army of
Samaria, he said, "What are those feeble Jews
doing? Will they restore their wall? Will they
offer sacrifices? Will they finish in a day? Can
they bring the stones back to life from those
heaps of rubble—burned as they are?"
3Tobiah the Ammonite, who was at his side,
said, "What they are building—if even a fox
climbed up on it, he would break down their
wall of stones!"

4Hear us, O our God, for we are despised.
Turn their insults back on their own heads.
Give them over as plunder in a land of captivity. 5Do not cover up their guilt or blot out
their sins from your sight, for they have
thrown insults in the face of the builders.

6So we rebuilt the wall till all of it reached
half its height, for the people worked with all
their heart.

It wasn't all plain sailing. Nehemiah and his crew faced plenty of opposition, mainly from a couple of splendid chaps: Sanballat the Horonite, governor of Samaria, and Tobiah the Ammonite, probably governor of Trans-Jordan. Their opposition came not from religious grounds – they were both likely to have been worshippers of Yahweh – but from political ambition. Nehemiah got in their way and they wanted him out. Here we see the first attempt at throwing the rebuilding into chaos: blatant ridicule, but in time the crew of two would resort to all sorts of desperate tricks to oppose the wall, from threat of violence to blackmail, from assassination to a smear campaign.

This first instance shows Nehemiah reacting well. He prays. Take a look at what he says – a good prayer, perhaps not the longest ever prayed, but nice enough. Then, in verse 6, he mentions that they simply carried on. There's a sense of assurance surrounding this account, as if Nehemiah knew that his prayers would be answered and that they needed to keep on working.

It's fascinating to look at the way Nehemiah prays, and the whole book is full of examples: we've already seen him on his knees at the start (1:4–11) as well as shooting up a quick word when facing the King (2:4). Take a look at 4:9; 5:19; 6:9 and 14; 13:14, 22, 29 and 31 for more examples.

chew it over

Opposition is to be expected. Like Nehemiah we need to remember the roles: pray that God will be God and move dramatically, while we keep our head down and carry on with the job in hand.

God's Foreman

nehemiah 5:1–8

[1]Now the men and their wives raised a great outcry against their Jewish brothers. [2]Some were
saying, "We and our sons and daughters are
numerous; in order for us to eat and stay alive,
we must get grain."

[3]Others were saying, "We are mortgaging our
fields, our vineyards and our homes to get grain
during the famine."

[4]Still others were saying, "We have had to
borrow money to pay the king's tax on our fields
and vineyards. [5]Although we are of the same
flesh and blood as our countrymen and though
our sons are as good as theirs, yet we have to
subject our sons and daughters to slavery. Some
of our daughters have already been enslaved,
but we are powerless, because our fields and our
vineyards belong to others."

[6]When I heard their outcry and these charges,
I was very angry. [7]I pondered them in my mind
and then accused the nobles and officials. I told
them, "You are exacting usury from your own
countrymen!" So I called together a large meeting to deal with them [8]and said: "As far as possible, we have bought back our Jewish brothers
who were sold to the Gentiles. Now you are selling your brothers, only for them to be sold back
to us!" They kept quiet, because they could find
nothing to say.

He wasn't only good with a trowel, this Nehemiah bloke. As we've already sussed out, he was well in tune with God's heartbeat, and he knew when things weren't right. Here we see the people complaining about the hardship they had been going through: some had no land and therefore no food, others had been forced to mortgage their properties and others still were being crippled by exorbitantly high interest rates on loans.

His claim that he got angry at this news reminds us of Jesus' reaction to the injustice he found in the temple (Mark 11:15–18), and it's important to remember that God's temper runs high when the poor are abused. Nehemiah knew this, and he had been working hard towards a more inclusive society, encouraging everyone from priests, rulers and Levites to merchants, perfumers and even women to work together on the wall. We also find out that he rejected the usual 'privileges' open to the governor, refusing to tax the people in order to pay for his own lavish lifestyle.

The longer we spend with Nehemiah, the more detailed the picture of his success becomes: not only was he smart, brave and dedicated to God, but he refused to compromise and refused to let success go to his head.

chew it over

Nehemiah may not have shown the miraculous sparkle of Samson or the pizzazz of Solomon, but he was bang in line with the message Jesus preached: he was fully in line with God's ways.

JOHN PT. II

He's not shy, this Jesus. Somehow he seemed to know that his days on Earth were numbered, but did that stop him having his say?

Matt Stuart

First things first

John 12:1–8

1 Six days before the Passover,
Jesus arrived at Bethany, where
Lazarus lived, whom Jesus had
raised from the dead. 2 Here a
dinner was given in Jesus' honour. Martha served, while
Lazarus was among those reclining at the table with him. 3 Then
Mary took about a pint of pure
nard, an expensive perfume; she
poured it on Jesus' feet and
wiped his feet with her hair. And
the house was filled with the fra-
grance of the perfume.

4 But one of his disciples, Judas
Iscariot, who was later to betray
him, objected, 5 "Why wasn't this
perfume sold and the money
given to the poor? It was worth a
year's wages." 6 He did not say
this because he cared about the
poor but because he was a thief;
as keeper of the money bag, he
used to help himself to what was
put into it.

7 "Leave her alone," Jesus
replied. "[It was intended] that
she should save this perfume for
the day of my burial. 8 You will
always have the poor among
you, but you will not always
have me."

SEARCH

Mary and Martha are as pleased as punch. In fact they're as happy as Larry – who just happens to be their once dead, now very much alive, bro. They all think Jesus is a top banana. So they decide to throw a little party for the big man.

They have different ways of serving the Lord. Martha keeps herself busy, doing stuff to please him, like cooking some top nosh. Mary loves to worship him, and blesses him by tipping a bottle of smelly stuff over his feet. Lazarus is just happy to be there and enjoy life alongside his friend. They all know and love Jesus and they all want to please him.

And then there's Judas, ever the party pooper. Poor Judas is in a mess. I understand his question but his motives are all wrong. He cares more about money than anything else. That's what leads him to do the dirty on Jesus later on. It's so easy for us to be like this in the society we live in. How often do we push Jesus aside to get all we can for ourselves first?

Have a think about your friendship with Jesus. Maybe you need to ask him to help you put him first again.

The meaning of life

John 12:23–8

23Jesus replied, "The hour
has come for the Son of
Man to be glorified. 24I
tell you the truth, unless
a grain of wheat falls to
the ground and dies, it
remains only a single
seed. But if it dies, it pro-
duces many seeds. 25The
man who loves his life
will lose it, while the
man who hates his life in
this world will keep it for
eternal life. 26Whoever
serves me must follow
me; and where I am, my
servant also will be. My
Father will honour the
one who serves me.
27"Now my heart is
troubled, and what shall
I say? 'Father, save me
from this hour'? No, it
was for this very reason I
came to this hour.
28Father, glorify your
name!"
Then a voice came
from heaven, "I have
glorified it, and will glorify it again."

SEARCH

We know the meaning of life. I know that sounds cocky but there's something about this guy Jesus . . . He was always having to explain things to people. It's not surprising really. This stuff is pretty hard to get. Understanding why Jesus had to die and rise again is tricky . . . but it is the meaning of life. Jesus came to die. He did a lot of stuff along the way, like show us how to live, but he came to die. This is God's amazing salvation plan for the people he loves so much. He made himself nothing, becoming a man, like us in every way. He lived a perfect life and then, obedient to Father God, gave himself to death on a cross. Why? Because he loves us and because we have done so much stuff that is not part of his plan for our lives. He knew that if he did not take our place in death we could never be with him in eternity.

GO

He rose again so that death is beaten for ever and so that when we die the grave will not hold us. We will be in heaven with him forever and a day. That's why we worship him.

Foot spa

John 13:6–11

6He came to Simon Peter,
who said to him, "Lord,
are you going to wash
my feet?"
7Jesus replied, "You do
not realise now what I
am doing, but later you
will understand."
8"No," said Peter, "you
shall never wash my
feet."
Jesus answered,
"Unless I wash you, you
have no part with me."
9"Then, Lord," Simon
Peter replied, "not just
my feet but my hands
and my head as well!"
10Jesus answered, "A
person who has had a
bath needs only to wash
his feet; his whole body
is clean. And you are
clean, though not every
one of you." 11For he
knew who was going to
betray him, and that was
why he said not every
one was clean.

SEARCH

My feet smell. So do yours I reckon, but probably not as bad as mine. Washing someone else's feet is not nice, but it says a lot. Let's watch Jesus and Peter here.

I don't know if you've noticed this, but Jesus isn't very religious. He does things differently. He loves to challenge the status quo. Most of the time Peter just doesn't get it. I guess that's why we identify with him so much.

Jesus washing his disciples' feet is outrageous. Peter wants so desperately to honour Jesus that he almost stops Jesus from blessing him. When he twigs, he goes typically OTT, grabs the Radox, and asks Jesus to scrub his back. Jesus gently explains that we only need to wash the bit of us that is dirty.

It's an amazing thought that God wants to serve us but it's true. Time and again God offers to wash us clean of the dirt we pick up as we walk through life. Just let him.

This is also the place we find our model for leadership. 'Wash each other's feet,' says Jesus. You may not think of yourself as a leader but the chances are other people are looking to you in some way. Is this how you will serve them?

From time to time the team I am a part of wash each other's feet to remind ourselves of all of this.

GO

Maybe there is someone whose feet you can wash today? If you're brave enough do it for real with a bowl and towel. I dare you.

Look out

John 13:31–5

[31]When he was gone,
Jesus said, "Now is the
Son of Man glorified and
God is glorified in him.
[32]If God is glorified in
him, God will glorify the
Son in himself, and will
glorify him at once.
[33]"My children, I will
be with you only a little
longer. You will look for
me, and just as I told the
Jews, so I tell you now:
Where I am going, you
cannot come.
[34]"A new command I
give you: Love one
another. As I have loved
you, so you must love
one another. [35]By this all
men will know that you
are my disciples, if you
love one another."

SEARCH

An encounter with Jesus often doesn't make much sense. It seems like everything changes when he turns up. That's good because so much of us and the world we live in is a mess and needs sorting out. It's also a challenge 'cos change is painful.

Jesus' mates are getting pretty used to him being around. They've just about got their heads round him being the Creator of the Universe, the Son of God, and their Lord and Master. Then, just to really freak them out, he starts talking about doing a bunk when they need him most. Sound familiar?

And what does he tell them to do? He says they have to love each other. Now, we really have a problem. I find it hard enough loving people I like, never mind those I don't. The solution is, I think, to see every individual as a person with real feelings and a unique personality. See, it's this that will point people to Jesus; they'll know we're in his posse because we love them.

Go with me on this one . . . I want you to think about someone you find it hard to like. OK? Think about how God sees them. They have feelings, they get lonely, they need love, they make mistakes. Just like you, aren't they?

GO

Pray for a person whom you find it hard to like for ten minutes asking God to bless their life and thanking him for his love for them.

Tough words

John 14:15–23

15"If you love me, you will
obey what I command. 16And
I will ask the Father, and he
will give you another
Counsellor to be with you for
ever—17the Spirit of truth.
The world cannot accept him,
because it neither sees him
nor knows him. But you
know him, for he lives with
you and will be in you. 18I
will not leave you as
orphans; I will come to you.
19Before long, the world will
not see me any more, but you
will see me. Because I live,
you also will live. 20On that
day you will realise that I am
in my Father, and you are in
me, and I am in you.
21Whoever has my com-
mands and obeys them, he is
the one who loves me. He
who loves me will be loved by
my Father, and I too will love
him and show myself to
him."
22Then Judas (not Judas
Iscariot) said, "But, Lord, why
do you intend to show yourself to us and not to the
world?"
23Jesus replied, "If anyone
loves me, he will obey my
teaching. My Father will love
him, and we will come to
him and make our home
with him."

SEARCH

'If you love me . . . ': these are hard words to hear. If my girlfriend started a sentence like that I wouldn't be very happy. Love isn't about demanding, is it? Let's dig a bit deeper here.

Jesus is talking about cause and effect. If one thing is true then it must result in another thing. If you love him you will obey him. It's not an order like an army chief might give. It's a fact. If you love him you will care for the sick. You will. You just will. You'll want to. In fact you won't be able to stop yourself. Get it?

The thing is we can't do what he asks on our own. Why? Because it doesn't come naturally to us. We need a bit of help. So he promises to send the Holy Spirit to help us out.

He also says that if we love him and obey him, he'll show himself to us. We'll know him. That'll help us love him more. And then we'll do what he asks us more. And then we'll get to know him more. Guess what? Then we'll love him more. You get the idea?

GO

Go deeper today. Ask for the Holy Spirit and expect to love, serve and know Jesus more.

Fruit tree

John 15:5–8

5“I am the vine; you are
the branches. If a man
remains in me and I in
him, he will bear much
fruit; apart from me you
can do nothing. 6If any-
one does not remain in
me, he is like a branch
that is thrown away and
withers; such branches
are picked up, thrown
into the fire and burned.
7If you remain in me and
my words remain in you,
ask whatever you wish,
and it will be given you.
8This is to my Father’s
glory, that you bear
much fruit, showing
yourselves to be my
disciples.”

SEARCH

Fruit is one of my favourite foods. It’s juicy, sweet and very good for you. I can’t get enough of the stuff. But there is a but . . . fruit goes off. Sometimes me and the lads I live with leave fruit around for a while. It goes a bit brown, then black with a few white bits, and eventually it’s just a mush of rank, rather pongy mould. You see, once you take it off the tree it’s all downhill to mouldsville.

We’re a bit like that. It’s pretty easy for us to go mouldy if we don’t stay on the tree. Jesus is our tree; he provides all we need. Once the fruit leaves the tree it can’t get food or water and it won’t grow anymore. Life away from Jesus means no food (‘I am the bread of life’, John 6:35), no water (‘whoever drinks the water I give him will never thirst’, John 4:14), and we won’t grow. Just like the fruit, we don’t go mouldy on day one, but bit by bit, day by day, we start to pong a bit and gradually turn sour.

We’re different from fruit in one way though. Even if we are apart from the tree for a while we can be re-attached. Jesus always takes us back. You can’t do that with fruit . . .

Maybe you need to check that you’re still on the tree?

Holy facts

John 16:7–15

7“But I tell you the truth: It
is for your good that I am
going away. Unless I go
away, the Counsellor will
not come to you; but if I go,
I will send him to you.
8When he comes, he will
convict the world of guilt in
regard to sin and righteousness and judgment: 9in
regard to sin, because men
do not believe in me; 10in
regard to righteousness,
because I am going to the
Father, where you can see
me no longer; 11and in
regard to judgment, because
the prince of this world now
stands condemned.
12“I have much more to
say to you, more than you
can now bear. 13But when
he, the Spirit of truth,
comes, he will guide you
into all truth. He will not
speak on his own; he will
speak only what he hears,
and he will tell you what is
yet to come. 14He will bring
glory to me by taking from
what is mine and making it
known to you. 15All that
belongs to the Father is
mine. That is why I said the
Spirit will take from what
is mine and make it known
to you.”

SEARCH

The Holy Spirit is essential to life as a Christian. It’s a common misconception that when you become a Christian, Jesus comes to live in you. Not true. Jesus is at the right hand of the Father. Paul tells us it’s the Holy Spirit that lives inside us and cries out to God ‘Abba, Father’ (Galatians 4:6). He makes it possible for us to have a relationship with Jesus, to resist from doing wrong things, by helping us to pray and worship.

It’s also the Holy Spirit who empowers us to do stuff for God. He boosts our natural gifts and helps us to do some stuff that is way beyond normal human capabilities. He helps us to know what to do and when. Perhaps the whole idea of the Holy Spirit freaks you out a bit? I don’t always understand it all but I know that life with the Holy Spirit in me is a lot easier than trying to go my own way. Without him I’m stuffed – it’s as simple as that.

GO

If you want the Holy Spirit to do more in your life, just ask him.

Esther

Queen for a day?

At one of the lowest points of the Jewish story God makes a dramatic move to save, inspire and draw the people closer to him. *Emma Borlase*

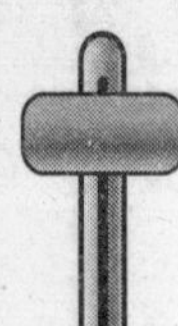

Esther 1:17–18

17"For the queen's conduct will become
known to all the women, and so they will
despise their husbands and say, 'King
Xerxes commanded Queen Vashti to be
brought before him, but she would not
come.' 18This very day the Persian and
Median women of the nobility who have
heard about the queen's conduct will
respond to all the king's nobles in the same
way. There will be no end of disrespect and
discord."

Insecure, frightened, unsure of God's plans . . . Sound familiar?

We join Esther as she finds her feet as the new Queen of Persia. Xerxes, her husband, had banished his previous Queen (Vashti) for insolence when she refused to come out and be admired by the drunken guests at the end of his 180-day party. Once he recovered from the hangover, he realised that he missed his wife. His attendants decided that the best thing was distraction and suggested a nationwide search to find the most beautiful young women in the realm. These women would have been forcibly removed from their homes and families and brought to the citadel of Susa. Twelve months of beauty treatments sounds glam but the girls would have become little more than slaves – taken to the King for sex and then returned to the harem to be called if he ever decided he wanted to see them again.

Her cousin Mordecai instructed Esther to keep quiet about her Jewish roots, which was a wise move designed to make her life in the harem a little more bearable. Mordecai's plan worked and the King chose Esther to take Vashti's place.

Uprooted, insecure, frightened and suddenly made Queen, probably the last thing Esther would have wanted was another challenge from God.

Feel the fear and do it anyway

Esther 4:12–16

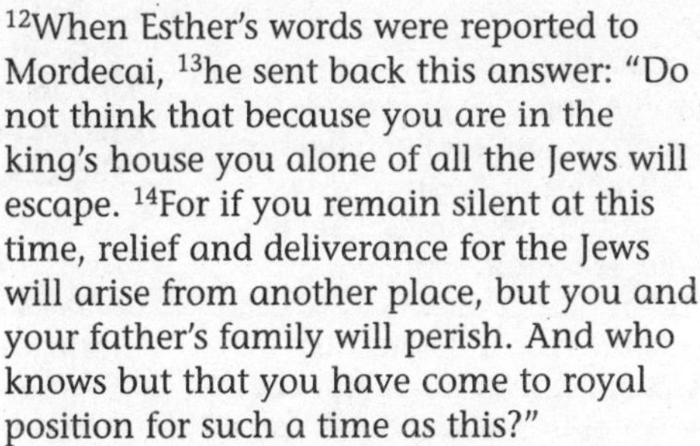

12When Esther's words were reported to
Mordecai, 13he sent back this answer: "Do
not think that because you are in the
king's house you alone of all the Jews will
escape. 14For if you remain silent at this
time, relief and deliverance for the Jews
will arise from another place, but you and
your father's family will perish. And who
knows but that you have come to royal
position for such a time as this?"
15Then Esther sent this reply to
Mordecai: 16"Go, gather together all the
Jews who are in Susa, and fast for me. Do
not eat or drink for three days, night or
day. I and my maids will fast as you do.
When this is done, I will go to the king,
even though it is against the law. And if I
perish, I perish."

God doesn't expect us to feel like spiritual warriors when he asks us to do something difficult. He simply asks us to do it – to be obedient. Esther knew what was right and she chose obedience despite her feelings.

God had plenty of plans for Esther. Mordecai discovers Haman's plot to destroy the Jews and sends word to Esther, urging her to beg the King for mercy. Here we see Esther's humanity – she was scared. Being the King's wife in those days wasn't anything like being married in the twenty-first century. She would only be expected to enter the King's presence if he summoned her and this hadn't happened for thirty days (Xerxes had a whole palace of concubines if you remember, so he could keep himself busy without her for a while). Esther reminds Mordecai that she is likely to be put to death if she enters the King's presence without permission. Mordecai reminds her that they are all going to die anyway, and she shouldn't think that she will be overlooked just because of her position. Esther's response is one of reluctant resignation. You can almost see her shrugging as she says, 'And if I perish, I perish.'

Esther 3:7–11

[7]In the twelfth year of King Xerxes, in the first
month, the month of Nisan, they cast the pur
(that is, the lot) in the presence of Haman to
select a day and month. And the lot fell on the
twelfth month, the month of Adar.
[8]Then Haman said to King Xerxes, "There is
a certain people dispersed and scattered
among the peoples in all the provinces of your
kingdom whose customs are different from
those of all other people and who do not obey
the king's laws; it is not in the king's best interest to tolerate them. [9]If it pleases the king, let
a decree be issued to destroy them, and I will
put ten thousand talents of silver into the
royal treasury for the men who carry out this
business."
[10]So the king took his signet ring from his
finger and gave it to Haman son of
Hammedatha, the Agagite, the enemy of the
Jews. [11]"Keep the money," the king said to
Haman, "and do with the people as you
please."

God is far bigger than human ambitions and superstitions. A plot to destroy the Israelites became the basis of a celebration of their deliverance.

As well as reminding Esther that her presence at the palace wouldn't save her from Haman's plot to kill the Jews, Mordecai comments that she may have been purposefully placed there 'for such a time as this' (4:14). Mordecai knew that God was in charge and could be trusted.

Haman, on the other hand, trusted a throw of the dice to tell him how and when to act. As it happened he never lived to see his 'lucky day', which tells us something about the worthlessness of superstition.

Many people have wondered just how much the book of Esther has to teach us as there is no direct mention of God in it. What we see clearly, however, is that God is at work throughout the story even though his name is not spoken. He rules sovereignly and refuses to allow mucky little humans like Haman to thwart his purposes. The Jewish people recognised God's hand in saving them and still celebrate the feast of Purim today.

The real hero

Esther 3:1–6

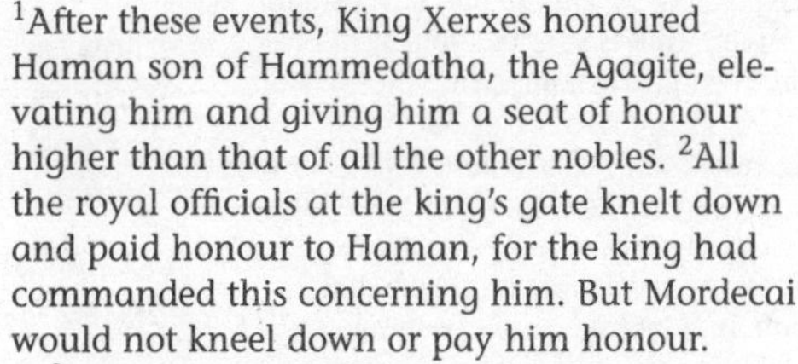

1 After these events, King Xerxes honoured
Haman son of Hammedatha, the Agagite, ele-
vating him and giving him a seat of honour
higher than that of all the other nobles. 2 All
the royal officials at the king's gate knelt down
and paid honour to Haman, for the king had
commanded this concerning him. But Mordecai
would not kneel down or pay him honour.
3 Then the royal officials at the king's gate
asked Mordecai, "Why do you disobey the
king's command?" 4 Day after day they spoke to
him but he refused to comply. Therefore they
told Haman about it to see whether Mordecai's
behaviour would be tolerated, for he had told
them he was a Jew.
5 When Haman saw that Mordecai would not
kneel down or pay him honour, he was
enraged. 6 Yet having learned who Mordecai's
people were, he scorned the idea of killing only
Mordecai. Instead Haman looked for a way to
destroy all Mordecai's people, the Jews,
throughout the whole kingdom of Xerxes.

Racial hatred, arrogance and self-promotion . . . these have no place on God's agenda. When we feel offended perhaps that's when we need to remember who the real hero is.

The book of Esther plays out against a background of arrogance and hatred. With the key players fighting to make a name for themselves the story underlines a vital message that unites it with the rest of the Bible: we are not the stars of the show, God is.

Haman's plan to kill the Jews was not something that came to him out of thin air. Instead he had a misguided role model in King Xerxes. The King was a complete egomaniac, one whose inflated sense of self is seen clearly through this inscription found in the ruins of ancient Persia: 'I am Xerxes, the great King, the only King, the King of all countries which speak all kinds of languages, the King of this big and far-reaching earth . . .'

Xerxes liked Haman and ordered all the royal officials to bow down and pay their respect to this splendid chap. The instruction bordered on a command to worship Haman but Mordecai remained faithful to the first commandment (Exodus 20:3) and refused to do so. Haman, like Xerxes, was so taken up with his own importance that his lust for revenge could only be satisfied by genocide.

Life in the grey

Esther 7:2–10

[2]and as they were drinking wine on that second day, the king
again asked, "Queen Esther, what is your petition? It will be
given you. What is your request? Even up to half the kingdom,
it will be granted."
[3]Then Queen Esther answered, "If I have found favour with
you, O king, and if it pleases your majesty, grant me my life—
this is my petition. And spare my people—this is my request.
[4]For I and my people have been sold for destruction and
slaughter and annihilation. If we had merely been sold as
male and female slaves, I would have kept quiet, because no
such distress would justify disturbing the king."
[5]King Xerxes asked Queen Esther, "Who is he? Where is the
man who has dared to do such a thing?"
[6]Esther said, "The adversary and enemy is this vile Haman."
Then Haman was terrified before the king and queen. [7]The
king got up in a rage, left his wine and went out into the
palace garden. But Haman, realising that the king had already
decided his fate, stayed behind to beg Queen Esther for his life.
[8]Just as the king returned from the palace garden to the
banquet hall, Haman was falling on the couch where Esther
was reclining.

The king exclaimed, "Will he even molest the queen while
she is with me in the house?"
As soon as the word left the king's mouth, they covered
Haman's face. [9]Then Harbona, one of the eunuchs attending
the king, said, "A gallows seventy-five feet high stands by
Haman's house. He had it made for Mordecai, who spoke up to
help the king."
The king said, "Hang him on it!" [10]So they hanged Haman
on the gallows he had prepared for Mordecai. Then the king's
fury subsided.

Just as Esther needed the prayers and support of the Jewish people as she lived life in the grey, we need people to support and pray for us as we take these things to God and search for answers.

Esther had to live in an alien culture, married to a cruel, self-important man who didn't share her beliefs, eating food that was forbidden to her by Jewish law. She obeyed Mordecai by refusing to reveal her Jewish identity until the time was right, but in doing so probably felt that to some extent she had to live a lie. There are no easy answers to the issues she faced. Elsewhere in the Bible we read how Daniel refused to break the food laws by eating the lavish meals provided for him when he was taken into exile. Should Esther have done the same? In doing so she would have had to admit that she was an Israelite and may have lost the opportunity to plead with the King. However, we can imagine that she often felt confused and unsure about how to behave.

Many of us are living, working and studying in places where the questions are just as pressing and confusing. How should we react when a friend who doesn't know Jesus decides to have an abortion? Do we tell them that they are wrong or should we support them as they go through with it? What about when you're asked to say that your boss is out of the office when he's there but doesn't want to answer the telephone call?

Paul had been through a bit of a hard time before writing this letter. He'd been laughed out of town in Athens and been forced out of Thessalonica. When he found out things were going well there again, he was understandably pleased . . .

Vintage Paul

1 thessalonians 1:4–7

4For we know, brothers loved by God, that
he has chosen you, 5because our gospel
came to you not simply with words, but
also with power, with the Holy Spirit and
with deep conviction. You know how we
lived among you for your sake. 6You
became imitators of us and of the Lord; in
spite of severe suffering, you welcomed the
message with the joy given by the Holy
Spirit. 7And so you became a model to all
the believers in Macedonia and Achaia.

This passage shows the key to Paul's technique. Where other 'salesmen' might settle for eloquently explaining their product in words, Paul takes it two stages further: not only did he live with them, showing them the gospel in his lifestyle, but he also encouraged them to get acquainted with the Holy Spirit and receive his deep conviction about the message of the cross.

Simply knowing the facts about Jesus isn't enough. And why should it be? After all, Jesus was massively into physical demonstration and spiritual revelation. If we're keen for our evangelism to be any good, we could learn a thing or two from Uncle Paul. We need an equal measure of each of these: words, works and wonders.

chew it over

Words, works and wonders: we find the ways to express, then let God impress.

Game over

1 thessalonians 4:11–12

11Make it your ambition to lead a quiet life,
to mind your own business and to work
with your hands, just as we told you, 12so
that your daily life may win the respect of
outsiders and so that you will not be
dependent on anybody.

These Thessalonians were caught up with the idea that Jesus Christ was about to return to earth. In fact, they were so serious about it that many of them had given up their day jobs, relying on others for financial support while they got on with far more 'spiritual' things. This belief that the apocalypse was just around the corner was ably assisted by the local Greek culture. It was a common belief there that manual labour was demeaning and that leisure was the prime ambition for all. Paul, thankfully, wades in and sorts it out: Christianity is not about dividing work from the spiritual stuff, nor is it about putting off our everyday duties until Jesus returns.

We could all do with hearing this. Too often we fall for the lie that we can only really serve God by working for the church in some way. We think that the people who are paid to be holy, who do the upfront church stuff full time are there because they are somehow more successful as Christians. But it's just not true. Some of us will be called in to church work, but the majority won't. Let's not lose sight of the fact that Christianity actually works out among the offices, schools and workshops.

chew it over

Getting a 'Christian' pay-cheque is not a sign of spiritual success.

2 THESSALONIANS

Like his recent letter to the church at Thessalonica, Paul writes with an aim: to encourage their growth and sort out a few misconceptions about Jesus' return. But not everything's the same . . .

Tough words

2 Thessalonians 1:5–10

[5]All this is evidence that God's judgment is right, and as a result you will be counted worthy of the kingdom of God, for which you are suffering. [6]God is just: He will pay back trouble to those who trouble you [7]and give relief to you who are troubled, and to us as well. This will happen when the Lord Jesus is revealed from heaven in blazing fire with his powerful angels. [8]He will punish those who do not know God and do not obey the gospel of our Lord Jesus. [9]They will be punished with everlasting destruction and shut out from the presence of the Lord and from the majesty of his power [10]on the day he comes to be glorified in his holy people and to be marvelled at among all those who have believed. This includes you, because you believed our testimony to you.

SEARCH

What a difference a few months can make. It's thought that Paul wrote this letter just six months after the first one, and the difference in tone is striking. Where 1 Thessalonians was warm and cosy this one is sharp and cool. Perhaps he's heard some bad news about the church – we just don't know – but whatever the reason for it, Paul's words send a shiver down my spine.

Paul knew about persecution – both giving and receiving – and so has something to say to the crew who appear to be going through it at the time. Just look at the words he uses: 'judgment . . . suffering . . . trouble . . . blazing fire . . . powerful angels . . . punish . . . everlasting destruction . . . shut out'. Too often we can forget that God is a God of vengeance: when his people are wronged, his love of justice and hatred of evil means that the wrongdoers will get their reward.

GO

We don't need to fight God's battles for him any more than we need to break his laws.

2 Thessalonians 3:6–10

6In the name of the Lord
Jesus Christ, we com-
mand you, brothers, to
keep away from every
brother who is idle and
does not live according
to the teaching you
received from us. 7For
you yourselves know
how you ought to follow
our example. We were
not idle when we were
with you, 8nor did we eat
anyone's food without
paying for it. On the
contrary, we worked
night and day, labouring
and toiling so that we
would not be a burden to
any of you. 9We did this,
not because we do not
have the right to such
help, but in order to
make ourselves a model
for you to follow. 10For
even when we were with
you, we gave you this
rule: "If a man will not
work, he shall not eat."

SEARCH

Here we return to the theme of tough love, as Paul marches in with a bit of 'advice' about unemployment. Or is it? 'If a man will not work, he shall not eat' sounds a little on the harsh side if you ask me – a million miles away from Jesus' message of radical generosity and collective responsibility. So what's the deal here? Has Paul had a bad day or is he just making a bid to be the first Christian Ultra-capitalist?

First up he's clearly talking about Christians ('brothers') who aren't working. This goes back to his earlier letter when he exposed the trend among the Thessalonians to give up work, sponge off others and take things easy. We have to assume that things hadn't sorted themselves out after that first letter and that Paul felt things were in need of a little further clarification.

If we dig a little below the surface, we see that Paul's words aren't quite as rigid and right wing as first thought. You see that bit about how he didn't 'eat anyone's food'? The phrase was a common Hebrew one meaning 'to make a living'. So Paul isn't saying that he never accepted hospitality from others, but that he didn't depend on others for his living.

Think about it for a minute: Paul, the pillar of the early Church, didn't look for funding from others. We know that before he wrote these letters he returned to his old profession as a tentmaker in order to raise a little cash. Do we consider some jobs to be more prestigious than others?

GO

Are we prepared to take a back seat if it's good for God's kingdom?

Like the early stories found in Genesis, the story of Job offers us much more if we put our feet up and allow it to speak to us on a deeper level than the basic plot. Dim the lights, put on something atmospheric and light a few joss sticks. Let me take you on a mind excursion . . .

Excuse me?

job 1:6–12

6One day the angels came to present themselves before the Lord, and Satan also came
with them. 7The Lord said to Satan, "Where
have you come from?"

Satan answered the Lord, "From roaming through the earth and going to and fro in it."

8Then the Lord said to Satan, "Have you considered my servant Job? There is no-one on earth like him; he is blameless and upright, a man who fears God and shuns evil."

9"Does Job fear God for nothing?" Satan
replied. 10"Have you not put a hedge around
him and his household and everything he has? You have blessed the work of his hands, so that his flocks and herds are spread throughout the land. 11But stretch out your hand and
strike everything he has, and he will surely curse you to your face."

12The Lord said to Satan, "Very well, then, everything he has is in your hands, but on the man himself do not lay a finger."

Then Satan went out from the presence of the Lord.

chew it over

Perhaps Job is you and me, the part of us that gets battered and bruised.

I mean, just how do you deal with something like this? What is Satan doing wandering around heaven like he owns the place, throwing down challenges to God? And what is God doing accepting them? Has the old man gone a bit soft in the head, or is the writer guilty of one visit to Amsterdam too many? It's just all a bit much for a good Christian to take in, don't you think?

Almost every culture has a Job story. From eastern religions to ancient Egyptian culture, the story of one person dealing with suffering as a god tests their faith is reasonably common. So what? Well, so this story picks up universal themes. Did it actually happen? Whether or not you think it did is to miss the point. We need to suspend our disbelief and go with the flow, exploring the dark night of Job's soul along with him, joining him on the search for answers.

In a way, Job is as much about you and me as the story of Adam and Eve. Just as those early gardeners tell us about our preciousness to God, so Job helps describe our perspective on God. The book explores some of the reactions that we may have to something that we all encounter – suffering.

Who was Job? Did he really live in Uz with his seven sons, three daughters, seven thousand sheep and all the rest? Perhaps we're thinking too literally.

True Faith

job 1:13–22

[13]One day when Job's sons and daughters were feasting
and drinking wine at the oldest brother's house, [14]a messenger came to Job and said, "The oxen were ploughing
and the donkeys were grazing nearby, [15]and the Sabeans
attacked and carried them off. They put the servants to the
sword, and I am the only one who has escaped to tell
you!"

[16]While he was still speaking, another messenger came
and said, "The fire of God fell from the sky and burned up
the sheep and the servants, and I am the only one who has
escaped to tell you!"

[17]While he was still speaking, another messenger came
and said, "The Chaldeans formed three raiding parties and
swept down on your camels and carried them off. They put
the servants to the sword, and I am the only one who has
escaped to tell you!"

[18]While he was still speaking, yet another messenger
came and said, "Your sons and daughters were feasting and
drinking wine at the oldest brother's house, [19]when suddenly a mighty wind swept in from the desert and struck the
four corners of the house. It collapsed on them and they
are dead, and I am the only one who has escaped to tell
you!"

[20]At this, Job got up and tore his robe and shaved his
head. Then he fell to the ground in worship [21]and said:

"Naked I came from my mother's womb,
  and naked I shall depart.
The Lord gave and the Lord has taken away;
  may the name of the Lord be praised."

[22]In all this, Job did not sin by charging God with wrongdoing.

chew it over

Will our words of praise still be there amidst the grief?

Job is hit by four body blows. The Arabs, the lightning, the Chaldeans and a tornado all wreak havoc and leave him stunned. What next? He shaves his head. The process of grief might change the way he looked, but the verses that follow show that his faith is still intact. His words are a truly beautiful submission to God. Why not read them over again a couple of times?

Preaching is the last thing on the man's mind, but there's little more that we can do after reading his words than go back and chew them over. They are another of those measuring sticks that God places in the Bible for us to hold up against our lives.

Are we living along the same lines: do our actions really show that we believe that material possessions count for nothing in the big scheme of things? Do we trust God enough to let go of the people we love most?

Advice? No thanks, I've just had some

job 11:13–19

13"Yet if you devote your heart to him
and stretch out your hands to him,
14if you put away the sin that is in your hand
and allow no evil to dwell in your tent,
15then you will lift up your face without shame;
you will stand firm and without fear.
16You will surely forget your trouble,
recalling it only as waters gone by.
17Life will be brighter than noonday,
and darkness will become like morning.
18You will be secure, because there is hope;
you will look about you and take your rest in safety.
19You will lie down, with no-one to make you afraid,
and many will court your favour."

Job's mates often get a hard time. OK, so they spend over thirty chapters chucking out the same advice – advice which, incidentally, is slightly off track – but at least they stay with him. Once they hear his news they take a trip to see him and sit with him in silence for seven days (see 2:11–13). Perhaps their gift of silence was worth more than their gift of words.

But enough of giving them an easy ride, let's stick the knife in. Their attempts at explaining the reason for Job's suffering all focus in on one issue: sin. Each of these three puts a different twist on the argument: Eliphaz reckons Job is suffering because he has sinned; Bildad assumes that Job is in denial, refusing to face up to hidden sin; Zophar – quoted here – goes one step further, suggesting that Job hasn't even got the half of what he deserves.

Could he be right? Well, it certainly seems plausible that God would want us to get rid of sin, but this whole idea about a life that's 'brighter than noonday' just doesn't add up. The way I see it God doesn't do a two-for-one deal with us: there's no Free Wealth and Popularity with Salvation. What's more, suffering doesn't only come with sin. Just look at Jesus – he suffered more than anyone, yet he remained pure to the very last. What are we telling ourselves that we're in this for? Don't start thinking that you're headed for a Job-style wave of personal tragedy, that would be to miss the point. Instead we need to stop and think: if we see suffering it doesn't mean that we should be getting ready with the harsh words of conviction.

chew it over

Are we telling people the wrong message at the wrong time?

A little better?

job 33:12–18

12"But I tell you, in this you are not right,
for God is greater than man.
13Why do you complain to him
that he answers none of man's words?
14For God does speak—now one way, now
another—
though man may not perceive it.
15In a dream, in a vision of the night,
when deep sleep falls on men
as they slumber in their beds,
16he may speak in their ears
and terrify them with warnings,
17to turn man from wrongdoing
and keep him from pride,
18to preserve his soul from the pit,
his life from perishing by the sword."

In comes Elihu, another friend but this time one with a mysterious past. Actually he doesn't have a mysterious past at all, although it seems to be the case that his sections were added at a later date as there's no mention of him either in the opening section or at the end. But let's not get too bothered about it, as Elihu's advice is a step up in quality from the three musketeers.

He seems to have a deeper understanding of the way of things, suggesting that God is a teacher, leading Job on to greater wisdom through his suffering. He also explains the reason for his thirty-chapter silence: he was allowing the older and wiser chaps to speak.

God is not the enemy, and Elihu warns Job about getting proud about his spiritual endurance. Like Joshua asking whose side the lone swordsman was on (Joshua 5:13), Job's belief that God could have taken sides is misguided: God is beyond our petty, squabbling ways.

Pride – whatever it is in – brings with it problems. Yeah, it makes us arrogant and unattractive, but it does something worse too: it turns our focus inwards, away from God and onto ourselves. Job was struggling to hold on to his identity, fearful that he would simply be defined by his sufferings. In viewing God as the enemy and in leaning towards self-congratulation, he threatened to turn away from God's face.

chew it over

We can trust God. Following, loving and trusting him does not mean that we lose our identity. Instead it's when we get to know our Maker that we truly get to know ourselves.

The answer

job 38:1–7

1Then the Lord answered Job out of the
storm. He said:

2"Who is this that darkens my counsel
with words without knowledge?
3Brace yourself like a man;
I will question you,
and you shall answer me.

4"Where were you when I laid the earth's
foundation?
Tell me, if you understand.
5Who marked off its dimensions? Surely
you know!
Who stretched a measuring line across it?
6On what were its footings set,
or who laid its cornerstone—
7while the morning stars sang together
and all the angels shouted for joy?"

And finally it's over. God's silence has been broken and the answers are coming. But if we were hoping for an ABC of why it all happened we're going to be disappointed. However, if we look closer, we'll also be surprised. 'Brace yourself like a man,' Job is told. What a weird thing to say. What's more, the original word used for 'man' does not imply a weak man – kind of as you'd expect for one standing in front of God – but a strong one, one ready to fight. Is God about to give him a good kicking?

God asks him questions, the sort none of us could answer. Job does no better than us, but standing face to face, hearing of all that God has done, recognising once again his place in the universe, Job bows down and worships (42:6). He is restored, and while the first three chums get a telling off, Job is held up as a righteous man.

But what's it all about? Was God angry, asking him to stand up like a man (twice)? God wants us face to face, to be in relationship with him.

chew it over

We have a problem? Take it to God. We're suffering? Tell him about it. He is not the enemy. Let's never forget it.

FEAR

From panic attacks to monsters under the bed, there seems to be plenty of fear about the place these days. Many of would rather not think about it, but when it comes to the Bible it seems as though God has something to say. *Emma Borlase*

Two sides of the coin

Proverbs 1:7, 14:26–7, 15:16

7The fear of the Lord
is the beginning of knowledge,
but fools despise wisdom and discipline.

26He who fears the Lord has a secure fortress,
and for his children it will be a refuge.

27The fear of the Lord
is a fountain of life,
turning a man from the snares of death.

16Better a little with the fear of the Lord
than great wealth with turmoil.

Unlike slugs, planes and getting stuck in a lift, fearing God opens up a whole new world of opportunities for us.

SEARCH

Most of us have a few things that we are afraid of, and it seems that many of those things will often get in the way of our relationship not only with God but with other people too. I know I'm scared of flying, and I've been on too many holidays when the last few days have been ruined by me getting wound up about going back on the plane. What about you? What things make you feel afraid or anxious? Fear about the future? Fear about other people's safety? About making wrong choices? Whatever it is, just spend a moment or two thinking about it.

We know that there were plenty of people in the Bible who were scared. Moses was afraid of the burning bush, Gideon was scared of his neighbours, the disciples were afraid of the storm, but these verses from Proverbs tell a different story. It seems that there is another type of fear to the type we share with Moses, Gideon and all the others: the Bible calls it 'fear of the Lord', and it's a different story altogether.

So what do these verses tell us? Fear of God is a very good thing, something to be treasured. It brings purity and wisdom, it helps us to worship God because we have a sense of how awesome and powerful he is, and it helps us not to sin.

The colour of fear

Exodus 20:20

[20]Moses said to the people, "Do not be afraid. God has come to test you, so that the fear of God will be with you to keep you from sinning."

SEARCH

We mentioned Moses in the last session, and it's funny to think about how things happened for him. In this section Moses has just returned from the top of Mount Sinai where God had given him the Ten Commandments. Explaining these new guides for living to the people Moses gives them this line about fear. Isn't it a bit odd, telling them not to be afraid because the fear of the Lord's coming to town? Weird stuff.

What we begin to see is that fear of God is very different from all other sorts of fear. It's not a crippling dread, the type that keeps us pinned under the duvet when the monsters are crawling under the bed. It's more of a reverence for who God is, his enormity, his power and his holiness. It's something that actually helps us, something that keeps us closer to God.

GO

Other sorts of fear just bring pain and confusion, but fear of God sets us free. I'll take that over a fear of flying any day.

Is it natural?

Matthew10:26–31

26“So do not be afraid of
them. There is nothing
concealed that will not
be disclosed, or hidden
that will not be made
known. 27What I tell you
in the dark, speak in the
daylight; what is whis-
pered in your ear, pro-
claim from the roofs.
28Do not be afraid of
those who kill the body
but cannot kill the soul.
Rather, be afraid of the
One who can destroy
both soul and body in
hell. 29Are not two spar-
rows sold for a penny?
Yet not one of them will
fall to the ground apart
from the will of your
Father. 30And even the
very hairs of your head
are all numbered. 31So
don’t be afraid; you are
worth more than many
sparrows.”

SEARCH

While getting the disciples warmed up for their first trip out without him, Jesus mentions fear too. It would be natural for the disciples to be afraid – after all, they were about to go out and ‘drive out evil spirits and heal every disease and sickness’ (10:1). But Jesus is clear: the only fear we should have is of God. In the same breath as reminding us that we should fear God because he has the power to destroy both our body and our soul, Jesus slips in something else that’s true: God loves us.

So this is all very well but how do we get to that point of fearing only God when there are still so many things around to be afraid of? Well, fear is a natural reaction to threat, and when we’re frightened our bodies produce adrenaline – a great little chemical that gets us ready to deal with a physical threat there and then. The problem is that these days we don’t usually do anything physical when we feel afraid, we’re not confronted with wild animals that we need to run away from. Instead we just get left with a racing pulse, sweaty palms and butterflies in the stomach.

This is where the problems come for many of us: fear of things that we cannot change. Often these fears are about things that might happen in the future. I’m generally OK when I’m frightened about something happening right now, I can get down to praying. But when I’m fearful about what might happen, I get distracted and distanced from God.

GO

Think about how much God cares about you. He is there for you today and will always be there.

Why pray when you can worry?

Luke 12:22–31

22 Then Jesus said to his disciples: "Therefore I tell you,
do not worry about your life,
what you will eat; or about
your body, what you will
wear. 23 Life is more than
food, and the body more
than clothes. 24 Consider the
ravens: They do not sow or
reap, they have no storeroom
or barn; yet God feeds them.
And how much more valu-
able you are than birds!
25 Who of you by worrying
can add a single hour to his
life? 26 Since you cannot do
this very little thing, why do
you worry about the rest?
27 "Consider how the lilies
grow. They do not labour or
spin. Yet I tell you, not even
Solomon in all his splendour
was dressed like one of these.
28 If that is how God clothes
the grass of the field, which is
here today, and tomorrow is
thrown into the fire, how
much more will he clothe
you, O you of little faith!
29 And do not set your heart
on what you will eat or drink;
do not worry about it. 30 For
the pagan world runs after
all such things, and your
Father knows that you need
them. 31 But seek his kingdom,
and these things will be given
to you as well."

SEARCH

Jesus gets to the heart of the matter here. The sort of worries he seems to be talking about are the ones about the future – even the immediate future. How many times have we sat through a worship time worrying about the state of our bank balance or the next crisis facing us on Monday morning? At times like that we find it hard to concentrate on meeting with God and the worry gets in the way.

But is Jesus telling us never to bother shopping, cooking or cleaning? Should we expect the things that we need to appear out of thin air? Of course not. I think he's encouraging us to live in the moment, to think about the problems we need to solve *when* we've got time to solve them, to enjoy the conversation with a friend rather than worrying about getting to the next appointment.

So, our aim is to try and keep concerned with what we are doing now, not with what might happen in the future. This probably means breaking a lot of habits and we are going to need God's help. Perhaps we need to think about why we have certain thought patterns – why we get worried about getting overwhelmed by work, why we worry about friendships going stale – as sometimes the roots are found back in something that happened to us a while ago.

Whatever it is, gaining a 'godly fear' and losing an 'ungodly fear' is going to take time and, especially, lots of time spent with God.

That means what?

1 John 4:18

18 There is no fear in love.
But perfect love drives
out fear, because fear has
to do with punishment.
The one who fears is not
made perfect in love.

SEARCH

So where next? We know that Jesus tells us not to worry, yet there are things that have happened to all of us that make us think life will be uncertain. But how do we move on?

Perhaps the answer has been here all along: a closer relationship with God. It might not make for a cosy experience because getting to know God means getting to know and revere all the aspects of his character, but knowing more about his incredible love for us can't be bad, can it? When we really know the truth about his holiness, righteousness and justice, we won't be paralysed either by complete terror or by being offhand about our relationship with God. Fear, love and hope will all be intertwined, and we will have a godly perspective on our very human fears and worries, because we'll have a sense of their place in eternity.

I know I forget about it all the time, often finding myself getting stressed about the things I cannot change instead of looking up to the only one with the real power to change things in our lives.

God's power to change might not mean nicer circumstances, but it will always mean helping us to learn how to trust in him more, whatever life throws at us.

Psalms

Sing-along-a-psalm

Have you ever heard a song being played on the radio and suddenly started singing along with it and been surprised (and embarrassed) by how many of the words you know? Words that we sing stay in our heads. The psalms are songs that have been around for centuries. Precisely thirty centuries. That's even longer than 'Twinkle Twinkle Little Star'. The reason why is not 'cos of the tune but for the words. These words help us express what we want to say to God. At the deepest level they connect us to our Maker.
Chris Russell

Psalm 103:1–2

[1]Praise the Lord, O my soul;
all my inmost being, praise his holy name.
[2]Praise the Lord, O my soul,
and forget not all his benefits—

We're going to sit under the Psalms for a few days to see what we can catch. So try Psalm 103 for starters.

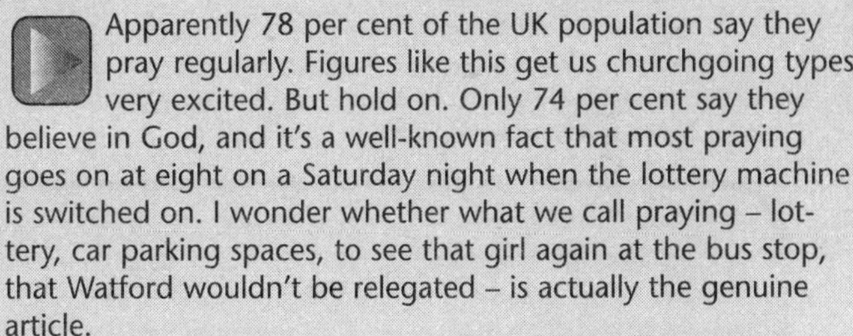

Apparently 78 per cent of the UK population say they pray regularly. Figures like this get us churchgoing types very excited. But hold on. Only 74 per cent say they believe in God, and it's a well-known fact that most praying goes on at eight on a Saturday night when the lottery machine is switched on. I wonder whether what we call praying – lottery, car parking spaces, to see that girl again at the bus stop, that Watford wouldn't be relegated – is actually the genuine article.

The more I go on the more I realise that I often don't have a scooby how to do this praying stuff. I can just about do the ones that ask God for help, but praying for others sometimes just seems like name-checking people before God. But when you read the Bible you find these wonderful inspiring praises, nation-changing prayers, God-inspired words which connect at a level far beyond anything I have ever got near. The aim of course isn't to be impressive prayers, but to communicate with God in a way that does justice to him, us and the world.

Here's some help. The psalms are ancient prayers, songs which are actually the most prayed prayers during the last 3000 years.

Can't be bothered?

Psalm 147:1–9

1 Praise the Lord.

How good it is to sing praises to our God,
how pleasant and fitting to praise him!

2 The Lord builds up Jerusalem;
he gathers the exiles of Israel.
3 He heals the broken-hearted
and binds up their wounds.

4 He determines the number of the stars
and calls them each by name.
5 Great is our Lord and mighty in power;
his understanding has no limit.
6 The Lord sustains the humble
but casts the wicked to the ground.

7 Sing to the Lord with thanksgiving;
make music to our God on the harp.
8 He covers the sky with clouds;
he supplies the earth with rain
and makes grass grow on the hills.
9 He provides food for the cattle
and for the young ravens when they call.

This prayer should keep you going for a couple of hours.

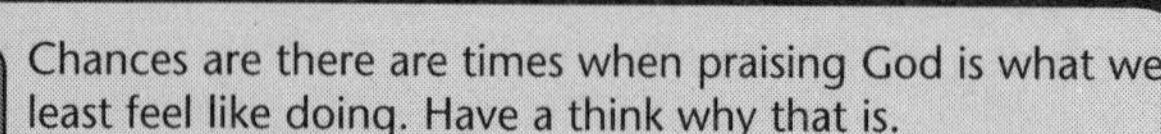

Chances are there are times when praising God is what we least feel like doing. Have a think why that is.

I bet what you thought about was when the shine seems to be a little dull on life – when God seems far away, when the demands of life seem overwhelming, when people around us are going through hard times and we feel helpless in the face of it all.

I remember someone once asking in a meeting what they should do because praying was really difficult. The speaker said, 'Pray.' But they protested, 'You don't understand, that's what I'm finding hardest to do.' The speaker insisted that 'When praying is hardest what you must do is pray.' This psalm is for those times.

In twenty verses (see the next page for the second half of the psalm) there are at least thirty-two reasons to praise God. You've got your cosmic incentives: 4, 8, 15, 16, 17, 18. Then you've got your ones about what he does for his people: 2, 3, 5, 14, 19, 20. So he does all this stuff in the universe, 'calling the stars by name' and still 'provides food for cattle'.

God's favourite

Psalm 147:10–11, 14–20

10His pleasure is not in the strength of the horse,
nor his delight in the legs of a man;
11the Lord delights in those who fear him,
who put their hope in his unfailing love.

14He grants peace to your borders
and satisfies you with the finest of wheat.

15He sends his command to the earth;
his word runs swiftly.
16He spreads the snow like wool
and scatters the frost like ashes.
17He hurls down hail like pebbles.
Who can withstand his icy blast?
18He sends his word and melts them;
he stirs up his breezes, and the waters flow.

19He has revealed his word to Jacob,
his laws and decrees to Israel.
20He has done this for no other nation;
they do not know his laws.

Praise the Lord.

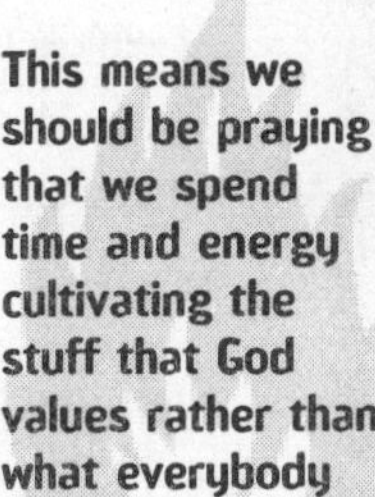

This means we should be praying that we spend time and energy cultivating the stuff that God values rather than what everybody else values.

So there's all this praising, all these things which state God's worth – have a look over it again and pick out today's favourite.

And in the middle of it all we are given an insight into what this extraordinary God loves: verses 10–11 talk about the fact that he doesn't get excited about what we've got (the stuff that we use to impress others, like the strength of your car engine, if you like). As well as not taking pleasure in possessions, he doesn't care what we look like: 'nor [is] his delight in the legs of a man' (what we spend most of our time worrying about). What does thrill him, however, is respect and hope. Such good news. The things that we all are encouraged to chase after to impress others don't move God. What he is pleased by is our love, devotion and awe.

David's prayer

Psalm 145:1–2, 8–13, 21

[1]I will exalt you, my God the King;
I will praise your name for ever and ever.
[2]Every day I will praise you
and extol your name for ever and ever.

[8]The Lord is gracious and compassionate,
slow to anger and rich in love.
[9]The Lord is good to all;
he has compassion on all he has made.
[10]All you have made will praise you, O Lord;
your saints will extol you.
[11]They will tell of the glory of your kingdom
and speak of your might,
[12]so that all men may know of your mighty acts
and the glorious splendour of your kingdom.
[13]Your kingdom is an everlasting kingdom,
and your dominion endures through all
generations.

The Lord is faithful to all his promises
and loving towards all he has made.

[21]My mouth will speak in praise of the Lord.
Let every creature praise his holy name
for ever and ever.

Which great things about God do you need to know about today? Praise them into reality.

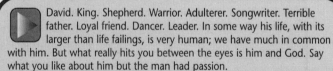

David. King. Shepherd. Warrior. Adulterer. Songwriter. Terrible father. Loyal friend. Dancer. Leader. In some way his life, with its larger than life failings, is very human; we have much in common with him. But what really hits you between the eyes is him and God. Say what you like about him but the man had passion.

Here his passion is ploughed into addressing God. And David was never so passionate as when he started to tell about him. Have a read of the psalm and see if you can find anything referring to particular events in David's life. There actually aren't any direct references. And this is a major lesson to us. David helps us to see, he gives us perspective beyond just the circumstances of our life. You don't just praise God because of what you have gone through, you praise him for who he is and what he does for the world.

So, breaking it down, praising David-style has its warm up (1–2; see also 3–7) where he says what he is going to do, followed by the action (8–13; see also 14–20). Have a go yourself and list every great thing you can about God.

Easy life?

Psalm 73:1–5, 7–11

[1]Surely God is good to Israel,
to those who are pure in heart.

[2]But as for me, my feet had almost slipped;
I had nearly lost my foothold.
[3]For I envied the arrogant
when I saw the prosperity of the wicked.

[4]They have no struggles;
their bodies are healthy and strong.
[5]They are free from the burdens common to man;
they are not plagued by human ills.
[7]From their callous hearts comes iniquity;
the evil conceits of their minds know no limits.
[8]They scoff, and speak with malice;
in their arrogance they threaten oppression.
[9]Their mouths lay claim to heaven,
and their tongues take possession of the earth.
[10]Therefore their people turn to them
and drink up waters in abundance.
[11]They say, "How can God know?
Does the Most High have knowledge?"

What we do need to be honest about is the draw that the world apart from God sometimes is, to all of us.

This psalm is one of Asaph's numbers. He was a great man with a big job. He was the worship leader of God's people, the one who stood at the front of the temple leading them all in praise. An upfront holy hero. The kind of people we are in awe of because they've got it all together. But what he is humble enough to teach us is how he nearly lost it all. Have a look how.

He's honest enough to say that he nearly lost it (2). Why did he find himself in this position? He took his eyes off the prize and had a look around (3). He lists what he saw around him (4–5, 7–11). Ever felt this? I've heard some people claim that holy people should just breeze through life with anything and everything they want. But we knows it's just . . . well let's just say it's complete and utter pap. Asaph looked around and saw those people who lived their life without any reference to God living the life of Riley.

Faith which is sold on the 'come-to-God-and-it'll-all-be-a-laugh' idea is a disgrace. You might get fullness of life, joy and gifts beyond telling but what you certainly can't do is measure it all in the same way as the world does.

Close to you

Psalm 73:13, 17–18, 21–6

13Surely in vain have I kept my heart pure;
in vain have I washed my hands in
innocence.

17till I entered the sanctuary of God;
then I understood their final destiny.

18Surely you place them on slippery ground;
you cast them down to ruin.

21When my heart was grieved
and my spirit embittered,
22I was senseless and ignorant;
I was a brute beast before you.
23Yet I am always with you;
you hold me by my right hand.
24You guide me with your counsel,
and afterwards you will take me into glory.
25Whom have I in heaven but you?
And earth has nothing I desire besides you.
26My flesh and my heart may fail,
but God is the strength of my heart
and my portion for ever.

This psalm helps us be honest about the draw of stuff around us. But it opens a window which sheds different light on it all and coaches us as to what we should do when it feels like our feet are slipping.

We rejoin Asaph when he thinks all his service and life in God has been a waste of time (13). But then a change happens and he realises he wasn't quite seeing it right. How did it happen? Because he had a warm fuzzy feeling from God? No. Because someone gave him a prophetic word? No. Because he got on with his duty to God and joined with people in praise (17)? Bingo. It was when he gathered with God's people that it changed. Then he got some God perspective. He saw how come-and-go such pleasures are (18–20). He realised what an ox he'd been (21–2), and God had been with him whatever he was doing (23–8). He sees it right and ends with no regrets; 'as for me, it is good to be near God'.

Timing

Psalm 24:1–7

1The earth is the Lord's, and everything in it,
the world, and all who live in it;
2for he founded it upon the seas
and established it upon the waters.

3Who may ascend the hill of the Lord?
Who may stand in his holy place?
4He who has clean hands and a pure heart,
who does not lift up his soul to an idol
or swear by what is false.
5He will receive blessing from the Lord
and vindication from God his Saviour.
6Such is the generation of those who seek him,
who seek your face, O God of Jacob. *Selah*

7Lift up your heads, O you gates;
be lifted up, you ancient doors,
that the King of glory may come in.

So often we pray the prayers calling God down from the mountain but rarely do we pray for discipline to ascend to him.

For all its benefits, our mobile phone, e-mail, online surfing-the-net culture does tend to make us want things now, now, now. It all feeds our expectation that things shouldn't take long. We are an impatient generation. And whilst that's not all bad, when we start to approach the things of faith in such a way we fall down. Whether it's healing, prayer, knowing God, wisdom, purity or whatever, the stuff of faith takes time. Nothing is instant when it comes to holiness.

Psalm 24 is a prayer for the journey. The first two verses tell us this is God's place. We have – like that wayward son in Jesus' story (Luke 15:11–32) – all run off, but in Jesus we have come home and are now journeying towards God's future.

To help out, here are some disciplines for the journey: we need clean hands, pure hearts, souls orientated only to the true God and truth-speaking mouths (4). To try to live like that takes a lifetime. It doesn't happen instantly. It happens as our journey with God progresses.

But that's how God works, choosing to show his face to a generation through his people (5).

Desert

Psalm 63:1–8

1O God, you are my God,
earnestly I seek you;
my soul thirsts for you,
my body longs for you,
in a dry and weary land
where there is no water.

2I have seen you in the sanctuary
and beheld your power and your glory.
3 your love is better than life,
my lips will glorify you.
4I will praise you as long as I live,
and in your name I will lift up my hands.
5My soul will be satisfied as with the richest of
foods;
with singing lips my mouth will praise you.

6On my bed I remember you;
I think of you through the watches of the
night.
7Because you are my help,
I sing in the shadow of your wings.
8My soul clings to you;
your right hand upholds me.

Whether you feel well watered or dry as a bone, times of desert will come. This psalm takes our roots down to the water table.

None of us like the desert. We all prefer the parties at the oasis, good food, good drink and endless fun. But life on the journey of faith takes us through deserts.

David was in such a place when he sang this one. He was actually in a desert. Sometimes everything outside – especially in the Church – tries to kid us everything is fine and hunky-dory on the inside, but all we are doing is hiding how dry we all are.

David knew he was dry and unable to do anything to quench his own thirst for God. But he makes some good moves, firstly by refusing to turn to anyone else for help (1). Accept no substitutes: it's God or nothing. There are lots of other offers posing as water, but they fail to satisfy in the long term and actually only wind up as poison. He goes over the past in a way that gives him hope for the future (2–5). Knowing about what God has done in the past gives us hope to feed off, a bit like a camel's hump. So what he does now is not just sit back – he remembers, he thinks, he sings and he clings (6).

Pure shores

Psalm 71:5–8, 10–13, 18

5 For you have been my hope, O Sovereign Lord,
my confidence since my youth.
6 From my birth I have relied on you;
you brought me forth from my mother's womb.
I will ever praise you.
7 I have become like a portent to many,
but you are my strong refuge.
8 My mouth is filled with your praise,
declaring your splendour all day long.

10 For my enemies speak against me;
those who wait to kill me conspire together.
11 They say, "God has forsaken him;
pursue him and seize him,
for no-one will rescue him."
12 Be not far from me, O God;
come quickly, O my God, to help me.
13 May my accusers perish in shame;
may those who want to harm me
be covered with scorn and disgrace.

18 Even when I am old and grey,
do not forsake me, O God,
till I declare your power to the next generation,
your might to all who are to come.

It's a prayer of hope, responsibility and faith whatever the weather.

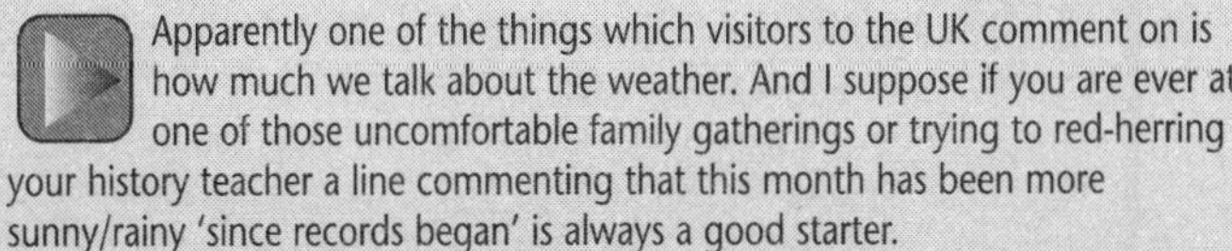

Apparently one of the things which visitors to the UK comment on is how much we talk about the weather. And I suppose if you are ever at one of those uncomfortable family gatherings or trying to red-herring your history teacher a line commenting that this month has been more sunny/rainy 'since records began' is always a good starter.

The weather forecast from the Bible seems to say 'changeable' more than anything else. Sun, rain, storms, cloudless skies, rain, dark clouds, torrents, heat waves, rain. It's all there. Living for the Son doesn't exclude the rain or any bad weather at all.

Psalm 71 is an all-weather psalm. Have a read. It tells of times past and times to come. Times of great warmth and fun (5–8) but times of real hardship and storminess (10–13). Through it all the hope and faith remain unshakeable.

But what is stunning is that at the middle of this prayer there is a plea not for an easy time, in fact not for anything for ourselves, but that we would take an active role in providing for those who come after us (18).

Protest singers

Psalm 137

1By the rivers of Babylon we sat and wept
when we remembered Zion.
2There on the poplars
we hung our harps,
3for there our captors asked us for songs,
our tormentors demanded songs of joy;
they said, "Sing us one of the songs of Zion!"

4How can we sing the songs of the Lord
while in a foreign land?
5If I forget you, O Jerusalem,
may my right hand forget [its skill].
6May my tongue cling to the roof of my mouth
if I do not remember you,
if I do not consider Jerusalem
my highest joy.

7Remember, O Lord, what the Edomites did
on the day Jerusalem fell.
"Tear it down," they cried,
"tear it down to its foundations!"

8O Daughter of Babylon, doomed to destruction,
happy is he who repays you
for what you have done to us—
9he who seizes your infants
and dashes them against the rocks.

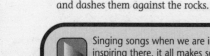

So how will you sing the Lord's song in the strange land?

Singing songs when we are in large gatherings can be easy. 'Cos it's inspiring there, it all makes so much sense and God is so obviously around. It's when we go out from the company of others that it's hard, especially when it feels like God's company is distant.

The people who sang this song had it harder than we ever will. They had been taken off as slaves from their land, God's land, away from God's own city Jerusalem, away from their favourite place on earth, the temple. This time was called the Exile – they were hundreds of miles away from home and seemingly away from God. It was a time of tears (1–2).

Their new owners wanted to hear some of the old tunes – the songs of the temple, the songs which celebrated God's presence. The question in verse 4 is the million dollar one: how do you sing the songs of God in a place where everyone lives their lives apart from him?

If ever there was a challenge for the Church now it is surely this: talking about, singing, praising, naming God in the middle of a culture and generation which seems alien to him. Oh yeah, it's easier to sing his songs in the cosiness of the Christian world. But it can't just stay there, because we don't just stay there.

We'll look at these two books together followed by 2 Timothy as they're all quite different from Paul's other letters. Practical and personal, they were written to two of his key players: Timothy, in charge of the church at Ephesus, and Titus, sorting things out in Crete.

You'll go far, my son

1 timothy 1:18–20

[18]Timothy, my son, I give you this instruction in keeping with the prophecies once
made about you, so that by following them
you may fight the good fight, [19]holding on
to faith and a good conscience. Some have
rejected these and so have shipwrecked
their faith. [20]Among them are Hymenaeus
and Alexander, whom I have handed over
to Satan to be taught not to blaspheme.

So here's the story: Paul's got some serious business to attend to, and in place to carry it out is Timothy. We know that Paul liked him ('Timothy, my son') and he was keen that he did well, as well as he could. You see, Timothy was a little on the shy side and Paul's letters to him are full of encouragement.

At this time he probably would have been in his late teens and like most of us Timothy probably felt out of his depth. He had been given the task of rooting out all the bad leaders from the church in Ephesus. We know that he'd been given the spiritual encouragement via an anointing at a ministry time with the leaders of the early Church. Yet he needs constant reassurance from Paul, reminding him to maintain his focus on the job in hand.

chew it over

Paul knew something special: gifting is a two-way street and it takes discipline on our part to help put into action the heavenly potential within us.

Something for the ladies?

1 timothy 2:9–15

9I also want women to dress modestly, with
decency and propriety, not with braided
hair or gold or pearls or expensive clothes,
10but with good deeds, appropriate for
women who profess to worship God.
11A woman should learn in quietness and
full submission. 12I do not permit a woman
to teach or to have authority over a man;
she must be silent. 13For Adam was formed
first, then Eve. 14And Adam was not the one
deceived; it was the woman who was
deceived and became a sinner. 15But women
will be saved through childbearing—if they
continue in faith, love and holiness with
propriety.

Ephesus was one tough cookie. It was one of the most important places in the Mediterranean section of the Roman Empire, and contained one of the seven wonders of the ancient world, the pagan temple to Diana. Paul had escaped a beating by a mob there and his instructions to Timothy – timid Timothy – are designed to solve a difficult problem.

So let's get it all out in the open, shall we? Do these instructions from Paul to Timothy apply to us today? Should our women be silent and steer clear of the pulpit? Here's why not.

The letter is specific. Paul wrote plenty of open letters to the Church and gave plenty of detail on specific church-leading techniques. In other places he commends women leaders and in 1 Corinthians 11:1–5 he seems pretty happy about women praying and prophesying as part of a public meeting. This letter was meant for Timothy to help him deal with a particularly difficult problem in a particularly difficult city.

Christianity is open to all. It is not sexist, racist or even ageist, and Paul knew it. He was so keen to do whatever he could to promote the gospel that he did whatever was necessary at the time and in the place. In Paul's book what mattered was gifting: once he knew what gifts God had given people he could easily find them a role.

chew it over

What about you? What gifts has God placed in you? Find out and then try to find a role that fits.

Who is your god?

1 timothy 6:3–10

3If anyone teaches false doctrines and does
not agree to the sound instruction of our
Lord Jesus Christ and to godly teaching, 4he
is conceited and understands nothing. He
has an unhealthy interest in controversies
and quarrels about words that result in
envy, strife, malicious talk, evil suspicions
5and constant friction between men of corrupt mind, who have been robbed of the
truth and who think that godliness is a
means to financial gain.
6But godliness with contentment is great
gain. 7For we brought nothing into the
world, and we can take nothing out of it.
8But if we have food and clothing, we will
be content with that. 9People who want to
get rich fall into temptation and a trap and
into many foolish and harmful desires that
plunge men into ruin and destruction. 10For
the love of money is a root of all kinds of
evil. Some people, eager for money, have
wandered from the faith and pierced themselves with many griefs.

A prime-time premium selection this, winding up with one of those top ten famous verses. There were some people in Ephesus who were using their position as spiritual leaders as a means of getting rich. Understandably Paul was not best pleased as this behaviour threatened to destabilise the church. Christianity was different from the mish-mash of pagan religions that ruled the show in Ephesus, and as Paul expands on the theme he sums up just what it is that makes the Christian faith so inspiringly different. Even today – especially today – his words cut to the core of our society. The love of money is all around us, leading to all sorts of trouble.

chew it over

The church at Ephesus faced the challenge of living in a different way to those around them. Are we up for it too?

Culture shock

1 timothy 4:4; titus 1:15–16

[4]For everything God created is good, and nothing is to be rejected if it is received with thanksgiving,

[15]To the pure, all things are pure, but to
those who are corrupted and do not
believe, nothing is pure. In fact, both their
minds and consciences are corrupted. [16]They
claim to know God, but by their actions
they deny him. They are detestable, disobedient and unfit for doing anything good.

These two go hand in hand and offer some fantastic insight into how we should live today. Surrounded by a thriving, varied and often 'sinful' culture, it would have been hard for both Timothy and Titus to find the right line to give to their congregation. Should they be told to lock themselves away and remain pure? What about getting out and embracing the culture – risky, yes, but how else were converts going to be made?

The solution was not only to find the balance between the shut-in and the all-out, but to give people a fresh, Christ-centred focus on life. For Christians who have been purified by Christ's death (in other words those who have asked for his forgiveness and who have decided to try and live by his rules in relationship with him), *everything is pure.* Get that? Everything. But there are limits to this 'everything': we have to be able to thank God for it. As Creator of the world God has left his fingerprints all over it: Paul suggests we look for them and enjoy what we find.

chew it over

God's side is the winning side: we have no need to be timid as we walk around his garden. Just look for his fingerprints.

Young man . . .

titus 2:6–8

6Similarly, encourage the young men to be self-controlled. 7In everything set them an example by doing what is good. In your teaching show integrity, seriousness 8and soundness of speech that cannot be condemned, so that those who oppose you may be ashamed because they have nothing bad to say about us.

Titus was a little tougher than Timothy, but it seems that they were both young. With the task of sorting out the church in Crete, Titus had plenty on his plate. He may well have felt out of his depth, but Paul's advice gets to the heart of the matter. Titus shouldn't just concentrate on sounding like a leader, he should live like one. Paul doesn't tell him to be the coolest, most radical or funniest of the young men around the church. Instead he tells Titus to measure his character against the ultimate ruler: that people might have nothing bad to say about him. That's some ambition. It might help to imagine this as a plumb line, a perfectly straight measure against which progress can be measured. Paul encourages Titus to keep measuring his character up against this ideal, aiming for the best.

chew it over

Fashion is nothing: character is everything. How do you measure up to Paul's challenge?

Command centre

titus 3:1–8

1Remind the people to be subject to rulers
and authorities, to be obedient, to be ready
to do whatever is good, 2to slander no-one,
to be peaceable and considerate, and to
show true humility towards all men.
3At one time we too were foolish, disobedient, deceived and enslaved by all kinds of
passions and pleasures. We lived in malice
and envy, being hated and hating one
another. 4But when the kindness and love of
God our Saviour appeared, 5he saved us,
not because of righteous things we had
done, but because of his mercy. He saved
us through the washing of rebirth and
renewal by the Holy Spirit, 6whom he
poured out on us generously through Jesus
Christ our Saviour, 7so that, having been
justified by his grace, we might become
heirs having the hope of eternal life. 8This is
a trustworthy saying. And I want you to
stress these things, so that those who have
trusted in God may be careful to devote
themselves to doing what is good. These
things are excellent and profitable for
everyone.

Now if I'd been given the job of sorting out a dodgy bunch of religious weirdos in a place like Crete I'd probably tell them to do nothing other than what I told them. Let them make up their own minds? You must be joking. Tell them to follow the instructions given by local pagan leaders? Not a chance. But Paul knows what he's doing. Not only is he showing that Christians are gracious and law-abiding, but he is also reinforcing Jesus' teaching about Christians being subjects of earth as well as subjects of heaven. This Christianity thing's not about separating ourselves from the rest, sticking our tongues out at the watching world. Christianity is about getting involved and it has something to say to the surrounding world – even if that happens to be pagan. All this doesn't mean that we should water down our faith, adding in a little of what we fancy from other sources. Throughout the Bible we find tons of relevant teaching on how we should live life this way: getting involved is precisely God's plan. After all, isn't that what he did?

chew it over

In encouraging the Cretans to obey and respect the local authorities, Paul's encouraging them to think for themselves, to work out how their faith interacts with life outside the church.

2 TIMOTHY

There's a change of tone in this letter. It was written after the other two, when Paul – that holy jailbird – was once again imprisoned. His spirits are low and he knows that he's getting towards the end of his life.

A lonely crowd

2 Timothy 2:3–7

3Endure hardship with us
like a good soldier of
Christ Jesus. 4No-one
serving as a soldier gets
involved in civilian
affairs—he wants to
please his commanding
officer. 5Similarly, if anyone competes as an ath-
lete, he does not receive
the victor's crown unless
he competes according to
the rules. 6The hardwork-
ing farmer should be the
first to receive a share of
the crops. 7Reflect on
what I am saying, for the
Lord will give you insight
into all this.

SEARCH

I don't know, maybe Paul is trying to encourage himself with some of this. We know that he went through plenty of hardship, but the tone in this passage suggests that he knows this challenge may be a little different.

Either way the words ring true as Paul encourages his young friend to think of himself as a soldier, athlete and farmer. I wonder what it meant to Timothy . . . I wonder what it means to you. To me the images are all bound up with ideas of isolation mixed with unity: the soldier as part of his army, the athlete as part of the team and the farmer as part of the family or community. As Christians we must take responsibility for our own actions, but never forget that we are part of a team, which, after all, has had some pretty decent players in it over the years.

GO

No one's going to live your Christian life for you, but there are plenty out there cheering you on.

One last thing

2 Timothy 4:1–6

[1]In the presence of God
and of Christ Jesus, who
will judge the living and
the dead, and in view of
his appearing and his
kingdom, I give you this
charge: [2]Preach the
Word; be prepared in
season and out of sea-
son; correct, rebuke and
encourage—with great
patience and careful
instruction. [3]For the time
will come when men will
not put up with sound
doctrine. Instead, to suit
their own desires, they
will gather around them
a great number of teach-
ers to say what their itch-
ing ears want to hear.
[4]They will turn their ears
away from the truth and
turn aside to myths. [5]But
you, keep your head in
all situations, endure
hardship, do the work of
an evangelist, discharge
all the duties of your
ministry.
[6]For I am already
being poured out like a
drink offering, and the
time has come for my
departure.

SEARCH

This makes me think of those dying moments of a desperate call from a pay phone. The pips are signalling that time is running out and it's a mad attempt to get all the instructions over in time. Forget the niceties, there's information to be passed on and Paul appears to be trying to get as much of it down on paper as possible. What we end up with is a brief formula for a successful Timothy, and in it Paul addresses his pupil's key points: keep on top of the false teachers, give a strong lead, keep in mind the way that things might change in the future, face hardship with your head turned towards the sky. Paul knew that his time was up, but he managed to keep his focus too. Without such guts and determination from members in the past, the church might look very different today.

GO

All this talk of hardship and tough times sounds like hard work. Why bother with it? Because the Church is worth fighting for.

The lighthouse

Sin is so hard to defend, yet – so unreasonably – we all try to shift the blame. Only we could be so dumb.

Living through a turbulent time in Israel's history, the prophet Isaiah had plenty to say: from delivering God's judgment to describing their redemption. His name means 'Yahweh is salvation', which was a good thing too as this was a key moment in Israel's history.

The first thirty-nine chapters of Isaiah concern themselves with the issue of Israel's sin and their need for judgment. It comes in all shapes and sizes, but early on we get this little gem. The writer knows it too, and plays around, drawing us in to what at first appears to be a regular love story, one with a lovely garden and plenty of fertility. Just the ticket for a Saturday afternoon.

But we're woken up with a large slap as it becomes clear that it's not just about some cosy love story. It's about Israel, and like David before Nathan, the Israelites would have found themselves arguing for their own guilt. What else could the man have done? Nothing at all, mate. Had he been a good farmer, preparing and generally doing all that he could? Absolutely. Was he right to be disappointed with such a poor crop? You bet.

But it doesn't just apply to Israel. What, after all, is our position here? Hasn't God done all he could? Hasn't his Son died for us? Yup. Didn't Jesus make it possible for us to gain eternal life? Too right. Didn't he promise the Holy Spirit to keep us close to God's presence? Yes indeedy. *So what are we doing with all this sin?*

Isaiah 5:1–7

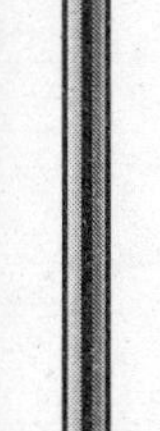

1 I will sing for the one I love
  a song about his vineyard:
My loved one had a vineyard
  on a fertile hillside.
2 He dug it up and cleared it of stones
  and planted it with the choicest vines.
He built a watchtower in it
  and cut out a winepress as well.
Then he looked for a crop of good grapes,
  but it yielded only bad fruit.

3 "Now you dwellers in Jerusalem and men of Judah,
  judge between me and my vineyard.
4 What more could have been done for my vineyard
  than I have done for it?
When I looked for good grapes,
  why did it yield only bad?
5 Now I will tell you
  what I am going to do to my vineyard:

I will take away its hedge,
  and it will be destroyed;
I will break down its wall,
  and it will be trampled.
6 I will make it a wasteland,
  neither pruned nor cultivated,
  and briers and thorns will grow there.
I will command the clouds not to rain on it."

7 The vineyard of the Lord Almighty
  is the house of Israel,
and the men of Judah
  are the garden of his delight.
And he looked for justice, but saw bloodshed;
  for righteousness, but heard cries of distress.

The comforter

Isaiah 42:5–7

5This is what God the Lord says—
he who created the heavens and stretched them out,
who spread out the earth and all that comes out of it,
who gives breath to its people,
and life to those who walk on it:
6"I, the Lord, have called you in righteousness;
I will take hold of your hand.
I will keep you and will make you
to be a covenant for the people
and a light for the Gentiles,
7to open eyes that are blind,
to free captives from prison
and to release from the dungeon those who sit in darkness."

It's not about keeping it small and cosy: God's message is for everyone. Are we sure that we're making it accessible?

We wake up on the other side of a disaster, as Isaiah writes of God's people living in exile at the hands of the Babylonians. Disaster has been avoided and the people finally realise something. They may be living in a foreign land, but they are still God's people, still chosen by him. Later someone would come and deliver them, come and offer rescue, but for now it's time to sit back and be amazed at God the comforter.

Taking their hand, the Lord will lead his people. Chapter after chapter is stuffed full with images of God leading his people, delivering them and once again stepping in to save. His presence will be right there with them and he will be 100 per cent in charge of all that goes on. An easy ride ahead? Of course not, but a good one, and one with the very best director in the hot seat.

But that's not all. They are to return not only to the safety of God but to that old covenant relationship. Remember the deal? They were to have no other gods than Yahweh. But there's a new twist, as this time they not only have to keep things up with God but take the message out to the rest of the nations, even to – gulp – their enemies. They were to be a powerful force for change, helping people out of moral and spiritual problems, bringing God's justice down wherever it was needed.

The teacher

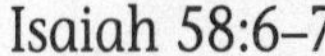

Isaiah 58:6–7

6"Is not this the kind of fasting I have
chosen:
to loose the chains of injustice
and untie the cords of the yoke,
to set the oppressed free
and break every yoke?
7Is it not to share your food with the
hungry
and to provide the poor wanderer
with shelter—
when you see the naked, to clothe him,
and not to turn away from your own
flesh and blood?"

Want to spot a true Christian? You shouldn't have to look further than their bank balance to see all the marks of a life lived for God.

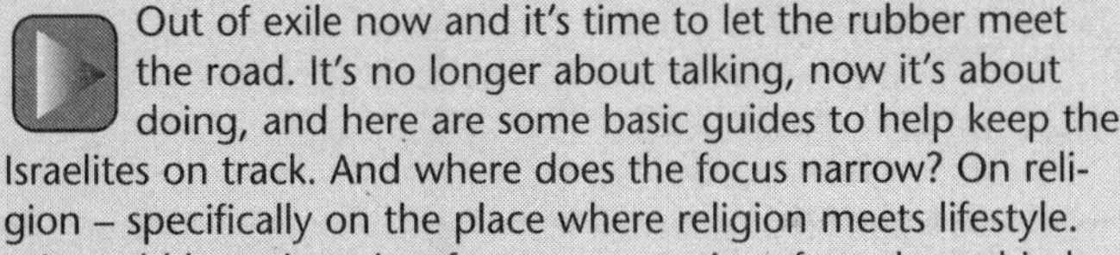

Out of exile now and it's time to let the rubber meet the road. It's no longer about talking, now it's about doing, and here are some basic guides to help keep the Israelites on track. And where does the focus narrow? On religion – specifically on the place where religion meets lifestyle.

It could be written just for us, as ever since formal worship has taken place and structure and sacrifice have been on the menu there has been a danger lurking somewhere in the shadows.

Let's be honest, all this stuff that surrounds Christianity about how lifestyle matters is a bit of a pain. Surely it would be so much simpler if all we had to do was wear a crystal, place a few mirrors above the right doors and wear nothing but natural fibres? If it was only about acquiring the right stuff or saying things in the right way, we'd all be laughing. But it's not. Oh dear.

Christianity cannot be separated from character. We cannot choose to be good at the ritual bits – good with communion or nice and loud when it comes to praying in public – and bad at the parts that involve our behaviour. In fact, it's not even as if our behaviour is just one little sub-section that makes up part of our faith. God says that the way we live – the way we treat people, the way we talk, the way we think, hope, fight and dream – are all important parts of our faith. They're not the added extras, they're at the core of everything we believe.

No turning back, that's the message from the unknown writer. Once we've signed up to God, things may be tough, but it's vital that we keep on keeping on.

A man for all seasons

hebrews 2:11–18

11Both the one who makes men holy and those who
are made holy are of the same family. So Jesus is
not ashamed to call them brothers. 12He says,

"I will declare your name to my brothers;
in the presence of the congregation I will
sing your praises."

13And again,

"I will put my trust in him."

And again he says,

"Here am I, and the children God has given me."

14Since the children have flesh and blood, he
too shared in their humanity so that by his death
he might destroy him who holds the power of
death—that is, the devil—15and free those who all
their lives were held in slavery by their fear of
death. 16For surely it is not angels he helps, but
Abraham's descendants. 17For this reason he had to
be made like his brothers in every way, in order
that he might become a merciful and faithful high
priest in service to God, and that he might make
atonement for the sins of the people. 18Because he
himself suffered when he was tempted, he is able
to help those who are being tempted.

Why did Jesus come down at all? Couldn't he have done it all – all the healing and the teaching – through people? It would have been so much easier, so much less messy to stay up there in heaven.

Yup. But who said God liked things being done the way we would consider 'easy'? By being both fully God and fully human, Jesus bridged the gap between an estranged people and a loving God. Thanks to him, we're part of the family.

The first quote used in this passage from Hebrews goes back to Psalm 22:22 – the most popular and often quoted psalm in the New Testament. In it the writer goes through a range of emotions that might make sense to us: first he's in anguish at the thought of God being distant. Then he talks about the attacks he's suffering from his enemy. Finally he realises that God saves him, and the poem is flush with a sense of triumph.

chew it over

Jesus went through the ultimate anguish and attack. He also came out on the other side with the ultimate triumph.

The new kid in town

hebrews 3:7–15

7So, as the Holy Spirit says:

"Today, if you hear his voice,
8 do not harden your hearts
as you did in the rebellion,
during the time of testing in the desert,
9where your fathers tested and tried me
and for forty years saw what I did.
10That is why I was angry with that generation,
and I said, 'Their hearts are always going
astray,
and they have not known my ways.'
11So I declared on oath in my anger,
'They shall never enter my rest.'"

12See to it, brothers, that none of you has a
sinful, unbelieving heart that turns away from
the living God. 13But encourage one another
daily, as long as it is called Today, so that
none of you may be hardened by sin's deceit-
fulness. 14We have come to share in Christ if
we hold firmly till the end the confidence we
had at first. 15As has just been said:

"Today, if you hear his voice,
do not harden your hearts
as you did in the rebellion."

This bit comes in the middle of an explanation of Jesus' connection to but superiority over Moses and, like the last passage, it takes a quote from a psalm. This time it's Psalm 95, and it explains how under Moses the Israelites were not, shall we say, at their best. They whinged, tested and refused to do as they were told. The result? God got mad.

But what's the point in bringing it up all over again? Wouldn't it be kinder to let it lie? Isn't there a use-by date on such embarrassing episodes?

But the writer has a point to make, much as the writer of the psalm did all those years ago. It's a warning against unbelief and disobedience – two things which certainly tripped the Israelites up.

chew it over

I wonder if we still need to hear the warning today?

Team talk

hebrews 5:11–13

[11]We have much to say about this, but it is hard to explain because you are slow to learn. [12]In fact, though by this time you ought to be teachers, you need someone to teach you the elementary truths of God's word all over again. You need milk, not solid food! [13]Anyone who lives on milk, being still an infant, is not acquainted with the teaching about righteousness.

Woah there! That's a bit harsh kicking off with that 'you are slow to learn' business. Isn't the Bible supposed to be nice? These people – the Hebrews – weren't exactly stupid: we know that they'd spent time and energy studying the Old Testament. Shouldn't they deserve a break?

The truth is that they had become lazy. Like the old times they'd been slipping back from the early promise they had shown, ending up like infants, dependent on others for the basics.

But wait. The writer goes on to deliver some meaty teaching of the sort which they may have struggled to take on board, but are we really sure that we are that much better? Are we sure that we've moved on leaps and bounds from our position of early promise?

chew it over

Here's the key: performance is relative. Don't match your spiritual progress against others: keep getting to know Jesus.

Not alone

hebrews 10:19

19Therefore, brothers, since we have confidence to enter the Most Holy Place by the
blood of Jesus,

Just think about these words for one minute. Close your eyes and repeat them. Chew them over good and proper.

It's all too easy to forget some of the most basic – yet important – facts about Christianity. Try this one on for size: Jesus has beaten a path for us to follow, one that leads to the very presence of God.

The way things used to be, the Jews had no chance of making it into the presence of God as no animal sacrifice was good enough. Enter Jesus and the whole story is changed: suddenly we can be forgiven and we can approach God.

chew it over

This is mind-blowing stuff: we can approach God . . . we can follow Jesus' path . . . we are not alone.

Fresh start

hebrews 10:1–4

1The law is only a shadow of the good
things that are coming—not the realities
themselves. For this reason it can never, by
the same sacrifices repeated endlessly year
after year, make perfect those who draw
near to worship. 2If it could, would they not
have stopped being offered? For the worshippers would have been cleansed once
for all, and would no longer have felt guilty
for their sins. 3But those sacrifices are an
annual reminder of sins, 4because it is
impossible for the blood of bulls and goats
to take away sins.

'The law is only a shadow . . . ' Steeped in religion and unsure how or whether to ditch old attachments to religious comings and goings, the audience get straightened out here by the writer. But why does he have to say it? If they know the law and they know Christ, why go over basics?

It seems that something has been pulling them back, getting in the way of their progress. The writer steps in and offers a solution. It's Jesus. His sacrifice has changed things, and there's no need to go through the old rituals any more. Surprised? There's no need to be: Jesus Christ is the most change-inspiring man on the team.

chew it over

Jesus' sacrifice gives us all the chance of a fresh start.

JEREMIAH

Jeremiah's probably one of those books that you've picked up, read a couple of chapters, then put it down again! Well, over the next couple of days we'll take a proper look at this book, see what's going on and think about what it tells us. *J. Foster*

Big deal

Jeremiah 1:5–10, 17–19

5"Before I formed you in the
womb I knew you,
before you were born I set you
apart;
I appointed you as a prophet
to the nations."

6"Ah, Sovereign Lord," I said, "I
do not know how to speak; I am
only a child."
7But the Lord said to me, "Do not
say, 'I am only a child.' You must
go to everyone I send you to and
say whatever I command you. 8Do
not be afraid of them, for I am with
you and will rescue you," declares
the Lord.
9Then the Lord reached out his
hand and touched my mouth and
said to me, "Now, I have put my
words in your mouth. 10See, today I
appoint you over nations and kingdoms to uproot and tear down, to
destroy and overthrow, to build and
to plant."
17"Get yourself ready! Stand up
and say to them whatever I command you. Do not be terrified by
them, or I will terrify you before
them. 18Today I have made you a
fortified city, an iron pillar and a
bronze wall to stand against the
whole land—against the kings of
Judah, its officials, its priests and
the people of the land. 19They will
fight against you but will not overcome you, for I am with you and
will rescue you," declares the Lord.

SEARCH

At this point Jeremiah is probably a young teenager, and here's God telling him that he is going to do huge things! Sounds great to start with, but then comes that bit about *everyone* opposing him, even the king. Add to this, Jeremiah hasn't got a clue about public speaking, and I reckon I'd be scared! God wants Jeremiah to tell God's chosen people that they're to be punished and sent out of the Promised Land into exile. How does God expect him to do that?

Simple, God doesn't expect him to do it by himself. God promises Jeremiah that he'll give him the ability and strength to do it, and he'll protect him when they make life hard for him (something that happens a lot). Now, you're probably not called to do the same stuff as Jeremiah, but that's not the point. God's looking for people who'll love and obey him. If you do that, like Jeremiah did, you'll encounter people who'll laugh at you and make life hard for you, but God's promises to Jeremiah are made to us too.

GO

Does the thought of being known as 'the Christian' at school/college/work scare you?

A real example

Jeremiah 13:1–8, 11

1 This is what the Lord said to
me: "Go and buy a linen belt
and put it round your waist,
but do not let it touch water."
2 So I bought a belt, as the
Lord directed, and put it
round my waist.
3 Then the word of the Lord
came to me a second time:
4 "Take the belt you bought
and are wearing round your
waist, and go now to Perath
and hide it there in a crevice
in the rocks." 5 So I went and
hid it at Perath, as the Lord
told me.
6 Many days later the Lord
said to me, "Go now to
Perath and get the belt I told
you to hide there." 7 So I went
to Perath and dug up the belt
and took it from the place
where I had hidden it, but
now it was ruined and completely useless.
8 Then the word of the Lord
came to me:
11 "For as a belt is bound
round a man's waist, so I
bound the whole house of
Israel and the whole house of
Judah to me,' declares the
Lord, 'to be my people for my
renown and praise and honour. But they have not listened.'"

SEARCH

This is not a happy message for the people to hear. God made a covenant (like a contract) with Moses saying that the Israelites would be special in God's eyes, all they had to do was worship him and live in a way that showed all the other nations what God was like. Did that happen? God doesn't seem to think so. The Israelites have completely disregarded this covenant and as a result are now useless to God for his plans for them.

God wants to change the world; he wants people to see who he is, he wants people to find him and all the amazing stuff he has for them. He wants to involve us in this as he involved the Israelites, but it means us being different to everyone else, to chase God instead of looking out for number one all the time. Israel and Judah had gone off to do their own thing and their relationship with God had become hollow. But God says that it's the heart that's the key.

Are you just going through the motions? Have you changed since you became a Christian?

Popular people

Jeremiah 38:2–6, 10

[2]"This is what the Lord says:
'Whoever stays in this city
will die by the sword,
famine or plague, but whoever goes over to the
Babylonians will live. He
will escape with his life; he
will live.' [3]And this is what
the Lord says: 'This city will
certainly be handed over to
the army of the king of
Babylon, who will capture
it.'"
[4]Then the officials said to
the king, "This man should
be put to death. He is dis-
couraging the soldiers who
are left in this city, as well
as all the people, by the
things he is saying to them.
This man is not seeking the
good of these people but
their ruin."
[5]"He is in your hands,"
King Zedekiah answered.
"The king can do nothing to
oppose you."
[6]So they took Jeremiah
and put him into the cistern
of Malkijah, the king's son,
which was in the courtyard
of the guard. They lowered
Jeremiah by ropes into the
cistern; it had no water in it,
only mud, and Jeremiah
sank down into the mud.
[10]Then the king com-
manded Ebed-Melech the
Cushite, "Take thirty men
from here with you and lift
Jeremiah the prophet out of
the cistern before he dies."

SEARCH

Jeremiah is going from bad to worse in the Mr Popularity charts. Here we find him in Jerusalem already under arrest, but he's still upsetting people with what he's saying (words which God has told him to say). So he gets lowered into what is effectively a big jug, and left to die in the mud in the bottom. How humiliating. How unfair.

Doing what God wants, even simply living as a Christian, will not make you Mr or Miss Popular. It will not make your life trouble free. Why not? 'Cos Christianity and popular don't share the same values. Even by saying that Christianity is the only true faith will see you getting a hard time for it. Plus when you do what God wants you to do, you will always have tough times; that's just the way it is. But here in Jeremiah we see God making good on the promises he made back at the beginning. He gives Jeremiah the strength to keep going, and the words he needs to say; he is still by Jeremiah's side and he continues to protect him.

GO

Are things tough for you at the moment? Are people getting at you? Is life just generally hard? Ask God for strength and help.

Life through a lens

Jeremiah 51:15–19

15"He made the earth by his power;
he founded the world by his wisdom
and stretched out the heavens by his understanding.
16When he thunders, the waters in the heavens roar;
he makes clouds rise from the ends of the earth.
He sends lightning with the rain
and brings out the wind from his storehouses.

17"Every man is senseless and without knowledge;
every goldsmith is shamed by his idols.
His images are a fraud;
they have no breath in them.
18They are worthless, the objects of mockery;
when their judgment comes, they will perish.
19He who is the Portion of Jacob is not like these,
for he is the Maker of all things,
including the tribe of his inheritance—
the Lord Almighty is his name.

SEARCH

Today's bit comes in a section in which Jeremiah is declaring God's judgment on all the nations (chapters 46–51). This gives us a fact about God that is so important and obvious that it is often missed. When people say to you, 'Don't worry, God is with you', do you sometimes think, 'Great, but how am I going to do this . . . ?' For a long time my picture of God was so small that it didn't really make a difference if God was with me or not. That picture of God is certainly not Jeremiah's picture! And here's the fact: God is the judge of the nations, he can raise them and destroy them. That means that he is massive! That means he is powerful and that he has authority over everything. That's the God whom we love and who loves us.

It's worth looking back to the promises from a couple of days ago; God doesn't expect us to go through life struggling by ourselves. He is with us, and he *will* give us *all* the strength and ability we need.

Do you feel that you're on your own in this or that situation? Does your picture of God match Jeremiah's? Ask God to show you more of what he's like.

Changing places

Jeremiah 33:7–11

[7]"'I will bring Judah and
Israel back from captivity
and will rebuild them as
they were before. [8]I will
cleanse them from all the
sin they have committed
against me and will forgive
all their sins of rebellion
against me. [9]Then this city
will bring me renown, joy,
praise and honour before all
nations on earth that hear
of all the good things I do
for it; and they will be in
awe and will tremble at the
abundant prosperity and
peace I provide for it.'
[10]"This is what the Lord
says: 'You say about this
place, "It is a desolate
waste, without men or animals." Yet in the towns of
Judah and the streets of
Jerusalem that are deserted,
inhabited by neither men
nor animals, there will be
heard once more [11]the
sounds of joy and gladness,
the voices of bride and
bridegroom, and the voices
of those who bring thank-
offerings to the house of the
Lord, saying,

"Give thanks to the Lord
Almighty,
for the Lord is good;
his love endures for ever."

For I will restore the fortunes
of the land as they were
before,' says the Lord."

SEARCH

Jeremiah's a bit more cheerful today! Despite all they've done, God's love for the Israelites is as strong as ever. Look at the words here; look again at the end of the chapter 13 reading. Then, God called them 'useless' for his plan, now he's offering them their part in the plan back. What's changed? They've turned back to God, and he's forgiven them. It's nothing they've done, it's all down to God.

That's how it works. God's got plans for us, but so often we just go off doing our own thing, still going through the motions of being a Christian, without our hearts being in it. But God sends a wake-up call to get our attention, then sorts our hearts out, forgives us, and gets us back into action again. It doesn't matter what you've done in the past, or where you've been; with God, loving him is all you need. That's what the book of Jeremiah tells us, and that's what Jesus Christ was all about – getting God's people back on track. So, are you going to trust in God's promises? Are you up for being involved in God's plans?

GO

Have you ever thought that you've really blown it this time? What do you think Jeremiah would have to say about that?

1 Peter

Holy hopes

From the pen of the most pumped-up disciple around: Peter gives us the inside story on how to follow Jesus.

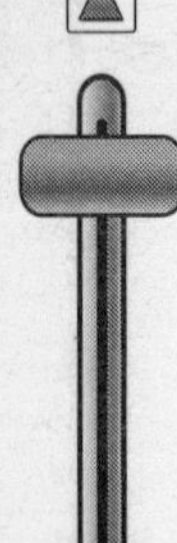

1 Peter 1:13–16

13 Therefore, prepare your minds for action;
be self-controlled; set your hope fully on the
grace to be given you when Jesus Christ is
revealed. 14 As obedient children, do not conform to the evil desires you had when you
lived in ignorance. 15 But just as he who
called you is holy, so be holy in all you do;
16 for it is written: "Be holy, because I am
holy."

It's not about how often you fall down, it's about which direction you're facing when you get up.

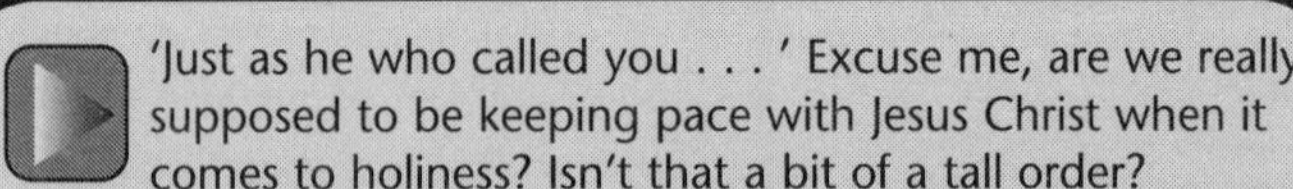

'Just as he who called you . . . ' Excuse me, are we really supposed to be keeping pace with Jesus Christ when it comes to holiness? Isn't that a bit of a tall order?

Well, yes. It's as tough a mountain as any human has climbed, and then some. Jesus – the Son of God – was without sin and therefore got to the top of the holiness league. If holiness is keeping away from sin, what chance have we got?

But let's remember Peter. Actually, let's be a little more specific and remember Peter's mistakes. On the night Jesus was arrested, apart from chopping off a servant's ear, all the man managed to do was lie three times about knowing Jesus.

So how could he write this? How could he have the guts? Because he knew about something very special: grace. He'd been forgiven for his sins and used his experience to push forward, to strive to steer clear of sin. Sure he stumbled again, but at least he never stopped trying.

No pain: no gain

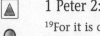

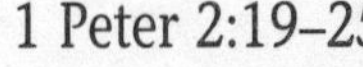

19 For it is commendable if a man bears up
under the pain of unjust suffering because
he is conscious of God. 20 But how is it to
your credit if you receive a beating for doing
wrong and endure it? But if you suffer for
doing good and you endure it, this is commendable before God. 21 To this you were
called, because Christ suffered for you, leaving you an example, that you should follow
in his steps.

22 "He committed no sin,
and no deceit was found in his mouth."

23 When they hurled their insults at him, he
did not retaliate; when he suffered, he made
no threats. Instead, he entrusted himself to
him who judges justly. 24 He himself bore our
sins in his body on the tree, so that we
might die to sins and live for righteousness;
by his wounds you have been healed. 25 For
you were like sheep going astray, but now
you have returned to the Shepherd and
Overseer of your souls.

Upside down: that's the way God likes it. With that in mind, it kind of makes sense that certain things act as a signal of godly living. What signs can you find in your life?

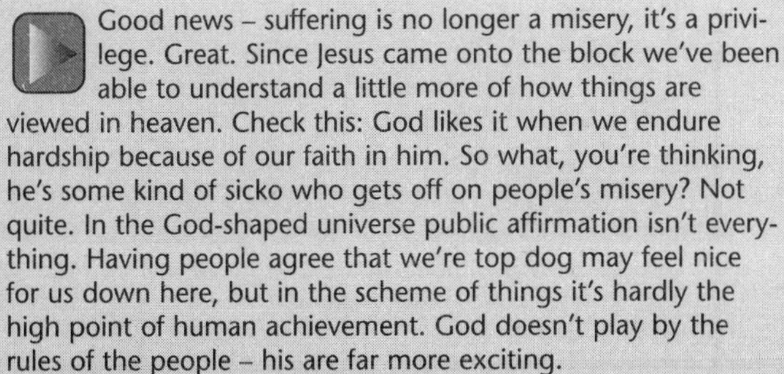

Good news – suffering is no longer a misery, it's a privilege. Great. Since Jesus came onto the block we've been able to understand a little more of how things are viewed in heaven. Check this: God likes it when we endure hardship because of our faith in him. So what, you're thinking, he's some kind of sicko who gets off on people's misery? Not quite. In the God-shaped universe public affirmation isn't everything. Having people agree that we're top dog may feel nice for us down here, but in the scheme of things it's hardly the high point of human achievement. God doesn't play by the rules of the people – his are far more exciting.

Men and women

1 Peter 3:1–7

1Wives, in the same way be submissive to your
husbands so that, if any of them do not
believe the word, they may be won over without words by the behaviour of their wives,
2when they see the purity and reverence of
your lives. 3Your beauty should not come from
outward adornment, such as braided hair and
the wearing of gold jewellery and fine clothes.
4Instead, it should be that of your inner self,
the unfading beauty of a gentle and quiet
spirit, which is of great worth in God's sight.
5For this is the way the holy women of the
past who put their hope in God used to make
themselves beautiful. They were submissive to
their own husbands, 6like Sarah, who obeyed
Abraham and called him her master. You are
her daughters if you do what is right and do
not give way to fear.
7Husbands, in the same way be considerate
as you live with your wives, and treat them
with respect as the weaker partner and as
heirs with you of the gracious gift of life, so
that nothing will hinder your prayers.

Relationships aren't about one person being in charge: they're about two people working together.

A well-known passage this, and one that frequently gets trotted out whenever we fancy talking about relationships. But there's a problem: it's called shortsightedness and too often we fall into the trap. Instead of taking the whole picture in, we select the odd snippet, using it to promote a distorted version of the truth. We end up telling people that women must submit while men have to love. It always sounds unfair on the women to me, and I'm sure it's not what Peter had in mind.

But do we really think that submission and love are separate? Can you really love someone without submitting to them? Can you really love them without putting their needs before your own? Or can submission really exist without love? Can we honestly submit without wanting the best for the other person? It's all about sacrifice: give and take as well as being able to put the other first.

The shepherd sorts out his flock here, giving them some handy hints about how to deal with that tricky filth they call False Teaching.

Not another list

2 peter 1:5–9

5For this very reason, make every effort to
add to your faith goodness; and to goodness, knowledge; 6and to knowledge, self-
control; and to self-control, perseverance;
and to perseverance, godliness; 7and to
godliness, brotherly kindness; and to brotherly kindness, love. 8For if you possess
these qualities in increasing measure, they
will keep you from being ineffective and
unproductive in your knowledge of our Lord
Jesus Christ. 9But if anyone does not have
them, he is short-sighted and blind, and has
forgotten that he has been cleansed from
his past sins.

I've got to admit it: I hate lists. They bug me and I usually avoid them. Why? Because they remind me of everything I haven't done and I end up feeling bad. This one's different. It's a call forward, a call for growth. You could spend years unpacking it and getting to the bottom, but you know what, he's got a point. Faith: it's not about knowledge but about believing. Goodness: looking for excellence in our deeds. Knowledge: in the face of false teachers, going for truth. Self-control: the result of true knowledge. Perseverance: a God-inspired gift if ever there was one. Godliness: reverence. Brotherly kindness: looking out for those in the faith. Love: sacrifice.

So what – we go through and get them into our lives, ticking them off systematically? Not quite. This list is about finding the meeting ground between 'spirituality' and practicality.

chew it over

Don't go for isolated excellence, leaving the rest up to others: go for the whole.

Mind the false teachers

2 peter 2:12

12 But these men blaspheme in matters they do not understand. They are like brute beasts, creatures of instinct, born only to be caught and destroyed, and like beasts they too will perish.

What's all this 'brute beasts' stuff? Whoever they are, they sound a bit weird, don't they? They are probably the Gnostics (more of them in 1 John), and let's just leave it that they were a bunch of people who valued knowledge above action, and believed that physical things were evil and that spiritual stuff was good.

Peter's clear about them: they may be brainy but their actions come from ignorance. They have failed to understand the finer points of Christianity, and Peter's attack shows just how rock hard he is.

Can we apply it to us today? Not if we're going to use it as an excuse to never again study the Bible: we're in a slightly different position than the Gnostics. But there is a message for us: are we prepared to look within ourselves and ask some searching questions?

chew it over

Are we really doing as well in our relationship with Jesus as we might have others believe?

The final countdown

2 peter 3:3–7

3First of all, you must understand that in
the last days scoffers will come, scoffing
and following their own evil desires. 4They
will say, "Where is this 'coming' he
promised? Ever since our fathers died,
everything goes on as it has since the
beginning of creation." 5But they deliberate-
ly forget that long ago by God's word the
heavens existed and the earth was formed
out of water and by water. 6By these waters
also the world of that time was deluged and
destroyed. 7By the same word the present
heavens and earth are reserved for fire,
being kept for the day of judgment and
destruction of ungodly men.

How things have changed. These days it seems like the only people who you find talking about the end of the world are the religious types. Back then – thirty years after Jesus' death and resurrection – it was the non-religious people who were bringing it up. They were pointing to the fact that life was still going on as normal as evidence to support their claim that Jesus was just a joker.

Peter's answer was simple: they'd missed the point. It's not about a ticking clock, not about predicting the precise date that God so happens to have pencilled in his diary. It's not about God sprinting back to earth as fast as he can either. God takes his time – *his* time – because he is still intervening and waiting for all to come back to him.

Instead of scaring people into the kingdom, shouldn't we try to be a little more godly? How about looking for ways to encourage divine interaction, getting people to hook up with God and his compassionate heart for the lost. After all, he's not some grumpy old bus conductor, only letting people on as fast as he can take their money. He's something else altogether.

chew it over

God's return has more to do with his heart than our calendar.

Daniel

Hi-Ho! Hi-Ho! it's off to work we go

Here's the story of another Old Testament chap whose relationship with God helped him through a testing time. There's more to it than lions and furnaces as Daniel lives his life out loud. *Neil Pearce*

Daniel 1:1–7

1 In the third year of the reign of Jehoiakim king of Judah,
Nebuchadnezzar king of Babylon came to Jerusalem and
besieged it. 2 And the Lord delivered Jehoiakim king of
Judah into his hand, along with some of the articles from
the temple of God. These he carried off to the temple of his
god in Babylonia and put in the treasure-house of his god.
3 Then the king ordered Ashpenaz, chief of his court officials, to bring in some of the Israelites from the royal family and the nobility—4 young men without any physical
defect, handsome, showing aptitude for every kind of
learning, well informed, quick to understand, and quali-
fied to serve in the king's palace. He was to teach them the
language and literature of the Babylonians. 5 The king
assigned them a daily amount of food and wine from the
king's table. They were to be trained for three years, and
after that they were to enter the king's service.
6 Among these were some from Judah: Daniel,
Hananiah, Mishael and Azariah. 7 The chief official gave
them new names: to Daniel, the name Belteshazzar; to
Hananiah, Shadrach; to Mishael, Meshach; and to
Azariah, Abednego.

What is your attitude towards learning things that you feel are completely irrelevant for the rest of your life? Is it possible that God is preparing you for future works of service?

Daniel and his mates appear as young men who have been forcibly removed from their homes and taken to another country to be trained in the language and literature of that culture. Now I don't know about you but doing English twice a week at school was enough to freak me out let alone being forced to do a degree in Ancient Babylonian Literature. The likely idea behind this was to have the Babylonian culture penetrate throughout the Israelite society, and what better way to do that than use some young handsome Israelites, train them up, give them powerful jobs and let them influence their own people?

Daniel and co. seem to take to the task of learning all this stuff very well and at the end of the day the king finds them to be ten times better than the rest. If I were Daniel I would not have been so willing but then I wouldn't have learnt the lingo that would give me the position to influence others. If you read the rest of Daniel you will find that he turns the tables: with the king ending up influenced by Daniel and his God.

Food, glorious food (or not!)

Daniel 1:8–16

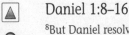

8But Daniel resolved not to defile himself with the
royal food and wine, and he asked the chief official for permission not to defile himself in this
way. 9Now God had caused the official to show
favour and sympathy to Daniel, 10but the official
told Daniel, "I am afraid of my lord the king,
who has assigned your food and drink. Why
should he see you looking worse than the other
young men of your age? The king would then
have my head because of you."
11Daniel then said to the guard whom the chief
official had appointed over Daniel, Hananiah,
Mishael and Azariah, 12"Please test your servants
for ten days: Give us nothing but vegetables to
eat and water to drink. 13Then compare our
appearance with that of the young men who eat
the royal food, and treat your servants in accordance with what you see." 14So he agreed to this
and tested them for ten days.
15At the end of the ten days they looked health-
ier and better nourished than any of the young
men who ate the royal food. 16So the guard took
away their choice food and the wine they were to
drink and gave them vegetables instead.

Where do you draw the line between your faith and the world? At what stage do you make no more compromises? Thankfully when you answer these questions you're probably not under threat of death if you don't conform.

God's favour continues to be upon Daniel as he puts the food of the king to the test. Daniel has been willing to compromise on some things but this is one area in which he will not budge. In eastern culture to share a meal as Daniel and his friends were asked to do with the king would be seen as a sign of friendship and it is at this point that Daniel makes his stand. He will do the job but won't be committed to friendship and complete integration into Babylonian society.

Daniel passes the test and the chief official orders that all the young men are fed vegetables, which I am sure made him very popular with the other lads! What Daniel asked the king's official to do could have resulted in the death of both of them, but Daniel had made such an impression and God's favour was on him so that the official agreed to his experiment.

All hot and bothered

Daniel 3:24–8

24Then King Nebuchadnezzar leaped to his feet in
amazement and asked his advisers, "Weren't there
three men that we tied up and threw into the fire?"
They replied, "Certainly, O king."
25He said, "Look! I see four men walking around
in the fire, unbound and unharmed, and the fourth
looks like a son of the gods."
26Nebuchadnezzar then approached the opening
of the blazing furnace and shouted, "Shadrach,
Meshach and Abednego, servants of the Most High
God, come out! Come here!"
So Shadrach, Meshach and Abednego came out
of the fire, 27and the satraps, prefects, governors
and royal advisers crowded around them. They saw
that the fire had not harmed their bodies, nor was a
hair of their heads singed; their robes were not
scorched, and there was no smell of fire on them.
28Then Nebuchadnezzar said, "Praise be to the
God of Shadrach, Meshach and Abednego, who has
sent his angel and rescued his servants! They trusted in him and defied the king's command and were
willing to give up their lives rather than serve or
worship any god except their own God."

Do you trust that God will help you in times of great need? How high is your faith level? Are you ready to put it all on the line to gain freedom in God?

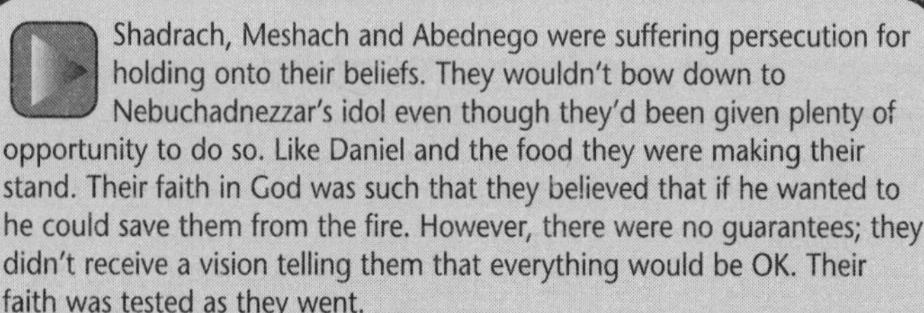

Shadrach, Meshach and Abednego were suffering persecution for holding onto their beliefs. They wouldn't bow down to Nebuchadnezzar's idol even though they'd been given plenty of opportunity to do so. Like Daniel and the food they were making their stand. Their faith in God was such that they believed that if he wanted to he could save them from the fire. However, there were no guarantees; they didn't receive a vision telling them that everything would be OK. Their faith was tested as they went.

We should expect God to perform miracles as we put our lives on the line for him but there is no guarantee that he will send an angel.

Nebuchadnezzar appears to be more impressed with the faithfulness of Shadrach, Meshach and Abednego than with the miracle itself and decides to set them free. They actually regained their freedom before Neb gave it to them. The three were not delivered *from* the fire, they were delivered *in* the fire. They were bound before being put into the furnace and were seen to be walking around with the angel.

True prayer

Daniel 9:4–11

4I prayed to the Lord my God and confessed:

"O Lord, the great and awesome God, who keeps
his covenant of love with all who love him and obey
his commands, 5we have sinned and done wrong.
We have been wicked and have rebelled; we have
turned away from your commands and laws. 6We
have not listened to your servants the prophets, who
spoke in your name to our kings, our princes and
our fathers, and to all the people of the land.
7"Lord, you are righteous, but this day we are covered with shame—the men of Judah and people of
Jerusalem and all Israel, both near and far, in all the
countries where you have scattered us because of our
unfaithfulness to you. 8O Lord, we and our kings,
our princes and our fathers are covered with shame
because we have sinned against you. 9The Lord our
God is merciful and forgiving, even though we have
rebelled against him; 10we have not obeyed the Lord
our God or kept the laws he gave us through his servants the prophets. 11All Israel has transgressed your
law and turned away, refusing to obey you.

"Therefore the curses and sworn judgments written in the Law of Moses, the servant of God, have been poured out on us, because we have sinned against you."

How does your prayer life stack up? Do you knock out a quick prayer when you get up and before you go to bed? Do you want to have a deeper relationship with God?

The really impressive thing about Daniel is his constant seeking after God; he doesn't appear to falter even for a moment. He is consistently found in prayer, but unlike my prayers his weren't always focused on the trivial things in life. My prayers are generally like, 'Sorry, God, for all the stuff I have done wrong, and by the way can you help me out with my overdraft?'

Daniel is in awe of God and is overwhelmed by his love. His prayers are detailed; he lists all the areas where he and his nation have fallen short of God's purposes for them. He even goes as far as confessing the sins of his own people which he feels responsible for as part of a community. He admits his shame and rebellion and asks for more of God's grace and mercy. What a lesson in how to go deeper with God.

Face down in the dirt

Daniel 10:8–15

8 So I was left alone, gazing at this great vision; I had
no strength left, my face turned deathly pale and I was
helpless. 9 Then I heard him speaking, and as I listened
to him, I fell into a deep sleep, my face to the ground.
10 A hand touched me and set me trembling on my
hands and knees. 11 He said, "Daniel, you who are
highly esteemed, consider carefully the words I am
about to speak to you, and stand up, for I have now
been sent to you." And when he said this to me, I stood
up trembling.
12 Then he continued, "Do not be afraid, Daniel.
Since the first day that you set your mind to gain
understanding and to humble yourself before your
God, your words were heard, and I have come in
response to them. 13 But the prince of the Persian kingdom resisted me twenty-one days. Then Michael, one of
the chief princes, came to help me, because I was
detained there with the king of Persia. 14 Now I have
come to explain to you what will happen to your people in the future, for the vision concerns a time yet to
come."
15 While he was saying this to me, I bowed with my
face towards the ground and was speechless.

Do you have an expectation that God may answer your prayers in a slightly more unusual way?

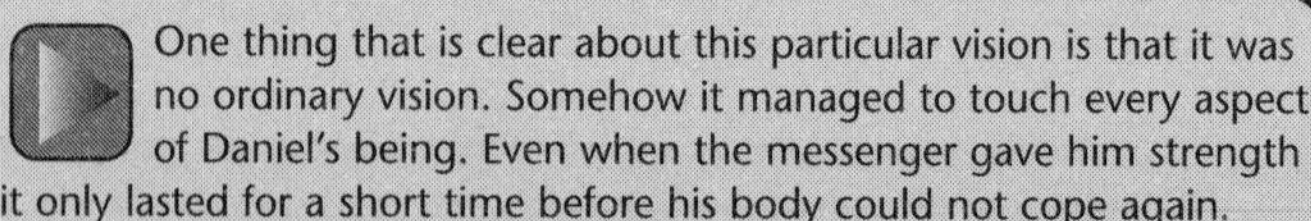

One thing that is clear about this particular vision is that it was no ordinary vision. Somehow it managed to touch every aspect of Daniel's being. Even when the messenger gave him strength it only lasted for a short time before his body could not cope again.

'Your words were heard' indicates that Daniel's prayer had been listened to and that this visitation is a direct result of Daniel's praying. Daniel's humility and faithfulness had been honoured by him receiving a messenger from God with an answer to his prayer. It might mean that a lot of us end up with our faces in the dirt, but wouldn't it be great if we all had prayers answered in that way?

The messenger didn't come straight away though. He was detained by problems in the heavenlies to such an extent that he needed help from Michael. Some people have written entire books about this verse trying to get a handle on what happens in the heavenlies and how we might influence it. Daniel doesn't appear interested and knows that his job is to deliver the message and to pray.

WORSHIP AND THE LEADER

Whether it's in the company of thousands or alone in your room, God is always worth praising. And if you're looking for clues how to do it, the Bible gives us all the guidance we need. *Matt Redman*

Perfect timing

Ecclesiastes 3:1–8

1 There is a time for everything,
and a season for every
activity under heaven:

2 a time to be born and a time
to die,
a time to plant and a time to
uproot,
3 a time to kill and a time to
heal,
a time to tear down and a
time to build,
4 a time to weep and a time to
laugh,
a time to mourn and a time to
dance,
5 a time to scatter stones and a
time to gather them,
a time to embrace and a time
to refrain,
6 a time to search and a time to
give up,
a time to keep and a time to
throw away,
7 a time to tear and a time to
mend,
a time to be silent and a time
to speak,
8 a time to love and a time to
hate,
a time for war and a time for
peace.

SEARCH

Right in the middle of all this heavier stuff come some fantastic poetic sections, oozing with wisdom and guidance for life. This bit is one of them. It's telling us that God works in seasons in our lives. We see it all around us with the weather – seasons come and go, and these verses are showing us it's the same in our lives.

There's a time to start something and a time to finish doing it. Maybe that's a ministry God's called you to, or a job in the future. When I was fifteen I got pretty into drama at school. I ended up with some good roles, and I loved it, thinking I may even like to do it for a living. At the same time I was starting to lead worship, and one day I felt God told me to choose between the two. I had a sneaking suspicion he'd rather I chose the worship thing so that's what I did. And it was a painful time – I'd loved drama – but now looking back I see God's wisdom all over that decision. It was just a season in my life. It taught me some good skills, and it even helped me regain some confidence I'd lost. But it was just a season in God's plan, and laying it aside also helped me concentrate on worship leading.

There's a time for everything in our lives and, as we seek God, he'll show us his wisdom and timing.

Just another meeting?

Ecclesiastes 5:1–7

1 Guard your steps when you go
to the house of God. Go near to
listen rather than to offer the
sacrifice of fools, who do not
know that they do wrong.

2 Do not be quick with your
mouth,
do not be hasty in your heart
to utter anything before God.
God is in heaven
and you are on earth,
so let your words be few.
3 As a dream comes when there
are many cares,
so the speech of a fool when
there are many words.

4 When you make a vow to
God, do not delay in fulfilling
it. He has no pleasure in fools;
fulfil your vow. 5 It is better not
to vow than to make a vow and
not fulfil it. 6 Do not let your
mouth lead you into sin. And
do not protest to the [temple]
messenger, "My vow was a mistake." Why should God be
angry at what you say and
destroy the work of your hands?
7 Much dreaming and many
words are meaningless.
Therefore stand in awe of God.

SEARCH

This is pretty strong stuff. We often hear about how God is calling us to come up close to him, but this passage is a great reminder that when we do so, we're approaching one who has no equal and is like no other.

There can be a danger of dashing in and out of church meetings like it's just some social club with a bit of singing in the middle. I've been going to church services for twenty years now, and sometimes I find myself forgetting what we've really come together to do . . . and I'm meant to be the worship leader! But, as verse 1 tells us, let's guard our steps when we go to the house of God. Let's think about what we're actually doing. The Bible tells us that it's a dreadful thing to fall into the hands of the living God (Hebrews 10:31). In other words, God is holy, and not to be messed around with. But, on the other hand, it's a wonderful thing to be beckoned into the arms of the living God. And that's what's happened to us. It's the mystery of all mysteries that the eternal, powerful God has called us to come close to him, to know him, but let's come realising who he really is.

My favourite part here says, 'God is in heaven, and you are on the earth, so let your words be few.' There's a time to let our hearts overflow to God with loads of words and songs and sounds. But there's also a time just to stand before him in awe, quietly enjoying the wonder of who he is.

I reckon we need a bit more of quiet contemplation in our worship.

Open heart

Psalm 51:1–6, 10–12

1Have mercy on me, O God,
according to your unfailing love;
according to your great compassion
blot out my transgressions.
2Wash away all my iniquity
and cleanse me from my sin.

3For I know my transgressions,
and my sin is always before me.
4Against you, you only, have I sinned
and done what is evil in your sight,
so that you are proved right when you speak
and justified when you judge.
5Surely I was sinful at birth,
sinful from the time my mother conceived me.
6Surely you desire truth in the inner parts;
you teach me wisdom in the inmost place.

10Create in me a pure heart, O God,
and renew a steadfast spirit within me.
11Do not cast me from your presence
or take your Holy Spirit from me.
12Restore to me the joy of your salvation
and grant me a willing spirit, to sustain me.

SEARCH

King David was known as 'Israel's singer of songs', or, in one translation of the Bible, 'the sweet psalmist of Israel'. In other words, he was a bit of a musical worship leader. But what strikes me even more about David is that he led worship with his life.

Just a couple of examples: one time, while still a shepherd he went out and fought for the honour of God's name with just a sling and some stones and a stick in his hand, against a Schwarzenegger of a man called Goliath. And he won. He led a whole nation in the worship of God that day. Another time, now as king, he danced like a lunatic (with hardly any clothes on!) as he celebrated the ark of God being brought back to the city. His wife was disgusted and despised him, but as David the unquenchable worshipper said, 'I will celebrate before the Lord, and I'll become even more undignified than this' (2 Samuel 6:22). What a worship leader, and again, I bet a whole nation took note.

Psalm 51, though, is one of David's most impressive acts of worship leading. But isn't this psalm all about David messing up? Yes. But check out what it says at the top of the psalm: 'For the director of music'. In other words, David committed this really personal confession of his hideous sin to public use. Isn't that amazing? When most people mess up (especially public figures) they want to sweep it under the carpet and hide it. David writes a song about it and wants it sung by the nation! Is he an idiot? No, he's a full-on worship leader.

GO

David's act of integrity has led millions of worshippers in times of confession, and hopefully just led you today.

The journey

1 Samuel 18:5–9

[5]Whatever Saul sent him
to do, David did it so suc-
cessfully that Saul gave
him a high rank in the
army. This pleased all the
people, and Saul's officers
as well.
[6]When the men were
returning home after
David had killed the
Philistine, the women
came out from all the
towns of Israel to meet
King Saul with singing
and dancing, with joyful
songs and with tam-
bourines and lutes. [7]As
they danced, they sang:

"Saul has slain his
thousands,
and David his tens of
thousands."

[8]Saul was very angry;
this refrain galled him.
"They have credited David
with tens of thousands,"
he thought, "but me with
only thousands. What
more can he get but the
kingdom?" [9]And from that
time on Saul kept a jeal-
ous eye on David.

SEARCH

The life of King David fascinates me. He was a shepherd boy, who one day would be made king. But the journey God takes him on for this to happen is not a quick or easy one. It's like God puts him through an intense training schedule to shape his heart, character and skills for where he's leading him.

This passage comes straight after David's amazing triumph over Goliath. In one day he goes from obscurity to fame – and the women are even singing songs about him (7). To top it all off, once living in uncomfortable fields he now gets moved to the palace. And more than that, God keeps adding to his victories (5). In other words David got heavily promoted really quickly. Perhaps if it was us we might be thinking, 'Right! Now it's time to be king . . . I'm in the palace, people love me more than Saul . . . That must be the next step in God's plan.' But it wasn't. The passage tells us of Saul's jealousy, and soon enough, David's out of the palace, on the run and being hunted down for his life. This goes on for years. And guess where he's living again? Back outdoors in caves and the like.

But why did God let this happen . . . Isn't it cruel? Not at all. It was all part of God's training schedule for him, preparing for the trust that lay ahead. And God will do that in our lives too. Sometimes we know he's called us to a certain thing, but we hardly ever know the timing. It can be so easy to try and make it happen, and to manipulate the situation. But just as David didn't do that, and God honoured him, he will honour us too if we play the game his way.

GO

The doors God opens no one can close, and the doors God closes no one can open.

Role model

Revelation 4:6–11

6Also before the throne there
was what looked like a sea of
glass, clear as crystal.
In the centre, around the
throne, were four living creatures, and they were covered
with eyes, in front and behind.
7The first living creature was
like a lion, the second was like
an ox, the third had a face like
a man, the fourth was like a
flying eagle. 8Each of the four
living creatures had six wings
and was covered with eyes all
around, even under his wings.
Day and night they never stop
saying:

"Holy, holy, holy
is the Lord God Almighty,
who was, and is, and is to
come."

9Whenever the living creatures
give glory, honour and thanks
to him who sits on the throne
and who lives for ever and ever,
10the twenty-four elders fall
down before him who sits on
the throne, and worship him
who lives for ever and ever.
They lay their crowns before
the throne and say:
11"You are worthy, our Lord
and God, to receive glory and
honour and power, for you created all things, and by your
will they were created and have
their being."

SEARCH

I love this chapter. As a worship leader, it's one of the passages I return to time and time again to get some insights on worship. A poet and hymn writer, Christina Rossetti, once said that in this part of the Bible, 'heaven is revealed to earth as the homeland of music.' More than that even, I think it also shows us what the best use of music is: the worship of God.

If you read right through chapters 4 and 5 you get a fantastic orchestration of praise building up. First there are four voices, with the living creatures speaking their praise. Then there are the twenty-four elders voicing God's worth. Then you get those two groups joining together (twenty-eight voices) singing a new song of worship. But then it gets *really* loud, with 'thousand upon thousand and ten thousand times ten thousand angels' singing to God (5:11). And it doesn't stop there; check out chapter 5 verse 13: 'Then I heard every creature in heaven and on earth and under the earth and on the sea and all that is in them *singing.*' That's one huge choir!

Perhaps even more amazing is that we too get to be part of this exciting stuff that's happening around God's throne. And that's a big encouragement to enter into worship. It doesn't matter if it's just you on your own, or if there are one thousand of you. It doesn't matter how good the band is or how hip the songs are. What matters is that, even here on the earth, we get to approach the heavenly throne of God.

GO

Every song, prayer and praise can touch the very heart of the Almighty.

James was a bit of a big cheese: he got namechecked by Paul, was the leader of the Council of Jerusalem and spoke with authority, wisdom and insight. Should be good then.

Death wish

james 1:13–15

13When tempted, no-one should say, "God is
tempting me." For God cannot be tempted
by evil, nor does he tempt anyone; 14but
each one is tempted when, by his own evil
desire, he is dragged away and enticed.
15Then, after desire has conceived, it gives
birth to sin; and sin, when it is full-grown,
gives birth to death.

James kicks off by looking at the three stages of temptation. First comes the desire, then the actual sin and finally, um, death. Perhaps a little study will clear this up . . .

Take Eve, for example. The snake triggers the desire to eat the apple. She then sins by shoving some of it down her gob. Finally death comes in the form of the ending of the unique relationship between her, Adam and God.

Or look at King David. There he was on the roof when he spies Bathsheba and gets the urge. Having her up to his room invited the sin and death was not far behind: not only for Uriah, but for the child born out of the affair and the grief David went through.

It feels funny talking about death, especially when we know that Jesus' sacrifice paid the debt of our sin on our behalf. Do we take it for granted? I know I do, and James's reminder does me good.

While God is gracious and forgiving, we should never underestimate the seriousness of sin. Perhaps that is why Jesus left us the hint, 'lead us not into temptation'.

chew it over

We need to ask God to help us resist temptation, as our defences alone are often not enough.

I'm all right, Jack

james 2:14–18

[14]What good is it, my brothers, if a man
claims to have faith but has no deeds? Can
such faith save him? [15]Suppose a brother or
sister is without clothes and daily food. [16]If
one of you says to him, "Go, I wish you
well; keep warm and well fed," but does
nothing about his physical needs, what
good is it? [17]In the same way, faith by itself,
if it is not accompanied by action, is dead.
[18]But someone will say, "You have faith; I
have deeds."

Show me your faith without deeds, and I will show you my faith by what I do.

Ah yes, the great division. Remember that bit of Paul's about the church being like a body made up of different parts (1 Corinthians 12:12–27)? Well, too often we take it a bit far, believing that it gives us licence to wade about in our own shallows while others concentrate on theirs. The Church is an unfortunate home to the attitude that goes something like this: leave the worship and praying to that lot over there, we'll stick to what we do best and help the poor. We've split actions from 'spirituality', and it's not only the denominations that are at fault: we do it as individuals too, letting ourselves off all manner of Christian duties.

We need to find the balance, and we also need to realise that some things just can't be separated. Like faith (we're not talking about the act of believing, but the act of following a vibrant relationship with Jesus) – it simply cannot be separated from action. It is impossible to have really got to know Jesus and stand by when injustice rears its ugly head. Christianity is all about action – both in the way we communicate with and relate to our heavenly Father and in the way we respond to his commands. It works the other way too: having the actions without the compassion misses the point; good deeds alone don't get you into heaven.

chew it over

Saying 'you have faith, I have action' makes no sense at all. Let's not bother keeping them apart.

Wisdom for the wise

james 3:13–18

13Who is wise and understanding among
you? Let him show it by his good life, by
deeds done in the humility that comes from
wisdom. 14But if you harbour bitter envy
and selfish ambition in your hearts, do not
boast about it or deny the truth. 15Such
"wisdom" does not come down from heaven
but is earthly, unspiritual, of the devil. 16For
where you have envy and selfish ambition,
there you find disorder and every evil practice.

17But the wisdom that comes from heaven
is first of all pure; then peace-loving, considerate, submissive, full of mercy and good
fruit, impartial and sincere. 18Peacemakers
who sow in peace raise a harvest of righteousness.

What? If you ask me wisdom is characterised by a totally different set of markers than the ones old Jimmy's come up with here. Let me see, there's the ability to keep cool in a crisis, the ability to take risks and win. A wise person has the strength to stand firm in the face of opposition as well as having a good degree and a decent suit. I've got a picture of one of them in my mind right now: they're rich, silver haired and wearing that healthy and tanned grin that makes you sick.

James has other ideas. Wisdom is pure, peace-loving, considerate, submissive . . . Sounds like an odd mix if you ask me. But thankfully I'm wrong. When it comes with the heavenly stamp of approval, wisdom is far removed from my more 'conventional' picture. This is good news, as according to James's markers, you can be wise without being well educated, wealthy, healthy, privileged or even respected.

chew it over

This is the kind of radical stuff that makes Christianity such a powerful force for change.

I beg your pardon?

james 4:4–12

4 You adulterous people, don't you know that
friendship with the world is hatred towards
God? Anyone who chooses to be a friend of
the world becomes an enemy of God. 5 Or do
you think Scripture says without reason that
the spirit he caused to live in us envies
intensely? 6 But he gives us more grace. That is
why Scripture says:

"God opposes the proud
 but gives grace to the humble."

7 Submit yourselves, then, to God. Resist the
devil, and he will flee from you. 8 Come near
to God and he will come near to you. Wash
your hands, you sinners, and purify your
hearts, you double-minded. 9 Grieve, mourn
and wail. Change your laughter to mourning
and your joy to gloom. 10 Humble yourselves
before the Lord, and he will lift you up.
11 Brothers, do not slander one another.
Anyone who speaks against his brother or
judges him speaks against the law and judges
it. When you judge the law, you are not keeping it, but sitting in judgment on it. 12 There is
only one Lawgiver and Judge, the one who is
able to save and destroy. But you—who are
you to judge your neighbour?

chew it over

So what have we got? Pursue God - live your life for his affirmation not the world's. Learn to serve.

Take it out of context and that verse about 'friendship with the world' being 'hatred towards God' could act as fuel for some pretty outrageous behaviour. It could also be kind of confusing; after all, aren't we supposed to be friends with people? How can James say that it's suddenly off limits?

The truth, thankfully, is out there in the surrounding verses. What does 'the world' mean? It can't mean creation, surely? It doesn't (phew). What James is actually referring to is the act of rebelling against God. So yes, we should love God and not rebel against him, but that doesn't mean we should be making ourselves a cosy little ghetto in which to hide away from the big bad world. James knows that Jesus' message was all about getting involved, both with God and with the world. Christianity in that sense is action based: submit, resist, come near, wash, purify . . . Look at all those commands for us to *do* something, each one helping us to have a full-on relationship with God. Then what, are we tip top and ready to rock? Are we allowed to get out and kick some pagan butt? No way, sonny, God's plan is different. Once we have truly submitted, washed, purified and all that, we will know our place: not to judge others – we should leave that to God.

Preach it, Jamie!

james 5:1–6

1Now listen, you rich people, weep and wail
because of the misery that is coming upon
you. 2Your wealth has rotted, and moths
have eaten your clothes. 3Your gold and silver are corroded. Their corrosion will testify
against you and eat your flesh like fire. You
have hoarded wealth in the last days. 4Look!
The wages you failed to pay the workmen
who mowed your fields are crying out
against you. The cries of the harvesters
have reached the ears of the Lord Almighty.
5You have lived on earth in luxury and self-
indulgence. You have fattened yourselves in
the day of slaughter. 6You have condemned
and murdered innocent men, who were not
opposing you.

Just who is this passage aimed at? Just those with a fat bank account? That's no good as a definition though, is it? In reality, we're all rich – or at least, there's always someone poorer than us around. No, comparing ourselves to others just won't do, so instead I've got a feeling that James is talking about something a little more specific. Don't get me wrong – I'm sure there are rich Christians who need to learn this lesson – but James appears to be talking to those who don't believe in God (see James 2:2 if you're keen). He seems to be warning them that their behaviour is 100 per cent at odds with the Christian way of life. But he gets even more specific: not only is he having a pop at those who flash their cash (that bit about clothes – a classic indicator of wealth in biblical times) and hoard their dosh (corrosion), but those who have failed to treat workers fairly. Whoever said God was only interested in the Church? Christianity is about as radical and relevant a faith as you can get.

chew it over

God loves a fair deal: bad employers had better watch out.

HOSEA

Knowing God as a person was important to Hosea, and through his book we follow his thoughts. The book is about more than Israel, and we come out the other side with a bag full of wisdom. But it's not all plain sailing, and at times it seems as though his relationship with his wife is teaching him about Israel, while at other times it feels as though Hosea understands more about his wife because of his understanding of Israel.

Outline

Hosea 1:2–3, 9–11

2 When the Lord began to
speak through Hosea, the
Lord said to him, "Go, take to
yourself an adulterous wife
and children of unfaithfulness, because the land is
guilty of the vilest adultery in
departing from the Lord." 3 So
he married Gomer daughter
of Diblaim, and she con-
ceived and bore him a son.
9 Then the Lord said, "Call
him Lo-Ammi, for you are
not my people, and I am not
your God.
10 "Yet the Israelites will be
like the sand on the seashore,
which cannot be measured or
counted. In the place where it
was said to them, 'You are
not my people', they will be
called 'sons of the living God'.
11 The people of Judah and
the people of Israel will be
reunited, and they will
appoint one leader and will
come up out of the land, for
great will be the day of
Jezreel."

SEARCH

Things kick off quickly as Hosea obeys God's commands. The plan is simple: God wants Hosea to marry the prostitute and give his children significant names so that the people of Israel will take notice. Nice plan.

The names given to his three children show just how serious the situation is. God's judgment is fully wound up and it looks as though the people are about to cop it, big time. God even threatens to break the covenant between him and his people when he says, 'you are not my people, and I am not your God' (9). Serious stuff, huh?

But God's character is so perfectly balanced, and in that perfection we see something wonderful accompanying the deserved judgment: undeserved mercy. Their hearts may have wandered, but God will still draw them back to himself. They may have pushed away from the covenant, but he cannot forget his promises to make their numbers grow.

GO

God's promises are for keeps. If only we could learn to take his commandments half as seriously we might not find Hosea's words so painful.

Break down

Hosea 2:2–5

2"Rebuke your mother, rebuke
her,
for she is not my wife,
and I am not her husband.
Let her remove the adulterous
look from her face
and the unfaithfulness from
between her breasts.
3Otherwise I will strip her naked
and make her as bare as on
the day she was born;
I will make her like a desert,
turn her into a parched land,
and slay her with thirst.
4I will not show my love to her
children,
because they are the children
of adultery.
5Their mother has been
unfaithful
and has conceived them in
disgrace.
She said, 'I will go after my
lovers,
who give me my food and my
water,
my wool and my linen, my oil
and my drink.'"

SEARCH

Hosea's wife, Gomer, returns to her old ways. As the emotion rides high, as we sense Hosea's pain, he moves the narration on from his own feelings about his wife to God's feelings about his unfaithful people.

We read about Israel becoming like a desert, but when they arrived in the Promised Land it was a place of great fertility. As the Israelites wandered away from God and soaked up other pagan influences, they took part in the Canaanite practice of sacrificing to Baal in return for fertile soil. God had provided something pure, something natural, that reflected his great powers as the Creator, and his people threw it back in his face. He offered them a fresh start, a new Eden, and what happened? They brought other gods in. Gomer had been with other men and God's people had turned to other gods. What was fertile and good became corrupt and abused.

We still have a talent for distorting the pure and the godly, from the earth on which we live to the talents within us, from the grace he gives us to the sacrifice of his Son.

Bring it back

Hosea 2:14, 3:1–5

14"Therefore I am now going
to allure her;
I will lead her into the
desert
and speak tenderly to her.

1The Lord said to me, "Go,
show your love to your wife
again, though she is loved by
another and is an adulteress.
Love her as the Lord loves the
Israelites, though they turn to
other gods and love the sacred
raisin cakes."
2So I bought her for fifteen
shekels of silver and about a
homer and a lethek of barley.
3Then I told her, "You are to
live with me for many days;
you must not be a prostitute or
be intimate with any man,
and I will live with you."
4For the Israelites will live
for many days without king or
prince, without sacrifice or
sacred stones, without ephod
or idol. 5Afterwards the
Israelites will return and seek
the Lord their God and David
their king. They will come
trembling to the Lord and to
his blessings in the last days.

SEARCH

And having listed the punishments that his unfaithful people deserve, God turns it around. It's strange to see that word 'therefore' – at first glance it simply does not make sense. I mean, if you've just detailed what someone deserves as punishment it hardly seems sensible to say, 'Therefore I'll let them off the hook.' Shouldn't it be something like: 'You ought to be thrown out for this *but* I'm going to draw you back'? Doesn't that make a bit more sense, for God to take Israel back in spite of what they deserve?

But our minds work on such a different level. When we talk about love it can only be a pale reflection of God's definition. Just look at the cross: could we ever have the love to go through with it ourselves? In the original Hebrew different words are used for love. There's *ahba*, which means affection for people and things, including sexual attraction. There's *rahamin*, which points to a sense of pity for someone helpless, as a parent loves a child. But there's something else: *hesed*, a type of love that involves choosing, that takes the strength, courage and determination to fulfil a relationship contract. When Hosea married Gomer it was from *ahba* and *rahamin* love. After this passage God tells him to bring her back: he is full of *hesed* love. And this is the love God had for his people, the ones with whom he'd made a contract, the ones who had his covenant-love. Why does he punish? Because he loves. Why does he bring back? Because he loves.

GO

What is the best love around? God's love; it holds both his judgment and his mercy.

The three holes

Hosea 4:1–3

1 Hear the word of the Lord,
you Israelites,
because the Lord has a
charge to bring
against you who live in the
land:
"There is no faithfulness, no
love,
no acknowledgment of God
in the land.
2 There is only cursing, lying
and murder, stealing and
adultery;
they break all bounds,
and bloodshed follows
bloodshed.
3 Because of this the land
mourns,
and all who live in it waste
away;
the beasts of the
field and the birds of the
air
and the fish of the sea are
dying."

SEARCH

But God's not into endless repetition of sinful cycles, and because he loves his people he offers an explanation of why they, like Gomer, wandered away. It's all pretty simple really: there are three key virtues that are missing from their lives. There is 'no faithfulness' in their daily lives. Some suggest that this points to the laws of the covenant, that the Israelites have given up on the right practice – we'll come back to that later. Others suggest something more interesting: that they lack honesty. Then there's a lack of love. It's not the sexual type we're talking about here, that's for sure. What they're missing is that good old *hesed* love, the sort that's full of kindness and strength. Hosea points out the final failing: no knowledge of God.

The people have turned away, watering down the passion for the truth and the desire to follow God's commands. They have become strangers and know nothing about who their Maker is, what he is like and how his heart beats. They've wandered and it's only through the dramatic example of Hosea that the message is loud enough for them to hear.

GO

Honesty, kindness, knowledge.
Do you need a top up?

It'll be OK

Hosea 6:1–3

1 "Come, let us return to the
Lord.
He has torn us to pieces
but he will heal us;
he has injured us
but he will bind up our
wounds.
2 After two days he will revive
us;
on the third day he will
restore us,
that we may live in his
presence.
3 Let us acknowledge the
Lord;
let us press on to
acknowledge him.
As surely as the sun rises,
he will appear;
he will come to us like the
winter rains,
like the spring rains that
water the earth."

SEARCH

And all they need to do is trust . . . right? According to the Israelites here, it all follows a nice little script. Perhaps these sentiments are what Hosea has picked up from the ground, words that he'd heard spoken out on the street. Wherever they came from, it's clear that Hosea doesn't think much of them.

First up there's no admission that they have done anything wrong. In fact it all looks as though they've been the victims of God's temper. 'Oh, he'll calm down after a couple of days, then we'll all be back to normal.' Back to normal is right, as there's still absolutely no sign of them knowing their God.

All that stuff about a third day resurrection just seems a bit too flippant, a bit too easy, don't you think? They were hoping for the best, but were they really prepared for the worst? 'God has torn us to pieces,' they said, but he *hadn't*, he had just said that he *would*. They expected blessing to follow sin as the sun follows the moon.

GO

The Israelites expected there to be no consequences at all to their actions. Not exactly a great model of repentance, is it?

The response

Hosea 6:4–6

4"What can I do with you,
    Ephraim?
  What can I do with you,
    Judah?
Your love is like the morning
    mist,
  like the early dew that
    disappears.
5Therefore I cut you in pieces
    with my prophets,
  I killed you with the words of
    my mouth;
  my judgments flashed like
    lightning upon you.
6For I desire mercy, not
    sacrifice,
  and acknowledgment of God
    rather than burnt offerings.

SEARCH

God responds to a half-hearted repentance by the Israelites. Their problems have already been listed – the lack of kindness, honesty and love – but we've just come across even more evidence that the Israelites needed some help. Their love is as permanent and strong as the morning mist, the stuff that hangs around for that hour or so when it's light but really too early to be out of bed.

It's all a matter of priorities, of what we think God sees as 'success'. The Israelites were putting on a good show, but slick services have never been God's ultimate aim for worship. It's about as far away from synchronised swimming as you can possibly get: forget the false smiles, the polished routines and the gala performance, it's about something far more important. God wants mercy (another word for *hesed*) over sacrifice; instead of the narrow focus on the perfect ritual God wants us to know him.

But is this leaning towards the unspeakable? Does God not want sacrifice, is he bored of worship? No way. Instead it's a matter of order: the heart – the love of God – doesn't come out of the sacrifice. If that was the case there would be no problem with the Israelites as they're clearly still burning the meats. It's supposed to be the other way around: pursue God, get to know him and discipline yourself to worship and sacrifice as an expression of that love.

GO

Jesus mentioned verse 6 twice (Matthew 9:13 and 12:7), sending a message out to the Pharisees: don't get smug and don't give your traditions higher importance than your relationships with God and other people.

Life in the grey

Hosea 9:1–6

1Do not rejoice, O Israel;
do not be jubilant like the other nations.
For you have been unfaithful to your God;
you love the wages of a prostitute
at every threshing-floor.
2Threshing-floors and winepresses will not feed the people;
the new wine will fail them.
3They will not remain in the Lord's land;
Ephraim will return to Egypt
and eat unclean food in Assyria.
4They will not pour out wine offerings to the Lord,
nor will their sacrifices please him.
Such sacrifices will be to them like the bread of mourners;
all who eat them will be unclean.
This food will be for themselves;
it will not come into the temple of the Lord.

5What will you do on the day of your appointed feasts,
on the festival days of the Lord?
6Even if they escape from destruction,
Egypt will gather them,
and Memphis will bury them.
Their treasures of silver will be taken over by briers,
and thorns will overrun their tents.

SEARCH

So living in the middle of a strange culture, one filled with many different beliefs and religions, is something that only we modern world people have to deal with, is it? Are we the first to face up to life in the grey, a world where difference of opinion makes big demands on our knowledge, love and respect for others? Take a look at this passage and you'll see we are not alone.

The Israelites have received the verdict. They are not to stay in the land but they are to be exiled in Assyria. The many generations of sinfulness have led them to this status of international refugees. How will they cope?

Good question. How would you cope? More to the point, how do you cope? What are the tensions that you live with? What are the restrictions? Israel were facing the threat of no more feasts, but as we've already seen their religious events were doing them little good. Would they take the lessons they had learnt on board and apply them in their new shared homeland?

What does it look like to be honest, kind and know God at the same time as being surrounded by differing beliefs? Can it be done?

Mercy

Hosea 14:1–3

1 Return, O Israel, to the
Lord your God.
Your sins have been your
downfall!
2 Take words with you
and return to the Lord.
Say to him:
"Forgive all our sins
and receive us graciously,
that we may offer the fruit
of our lips.
3 Assyria cannot save us;
we will not mount
war-horses.
We will never
again say 'Our gods'
to what our own hands
have made,
for in you the fatherless
find compassion."

SEARCH

And so we come to the end. Unlike their hurried words of 'Come, let us return (and get it over with)' of chapter 6, this time they have to own up to their sin by admitting it full on.

Remember all that stuff about them relying on sacrifices to gain them godly favour? Well, there's a twist in the tail as God asks for one more thing: a sacrifice. But this isn't any old lamb or goat, nothing that can be so easily bought. God wants something special: 'a broken spirit and a contrite heart'. You'll find the words back in Psalm 51:16–17, where David turns to God after his affair with Bathsheba.

Do we move forward with God or stay here? It's up to us. If we want more, if we've got things to confess and sin to get rid of, here's our model. Admit our fault.

Turn away from 'me' as the centre of our universe. Ask to be taken back. Put the sin behind us.

Luke Pt. III

Obeying the government

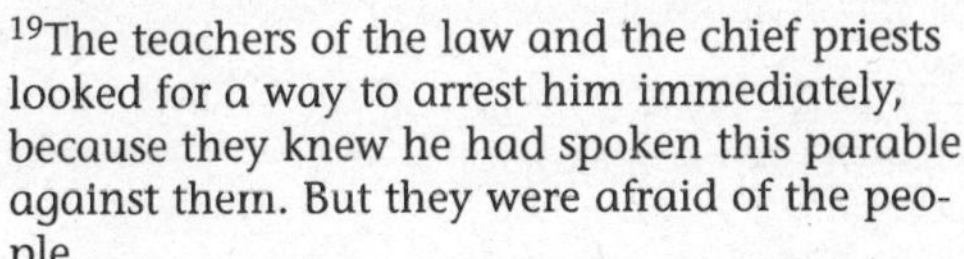

Take a deep breath. This is where things started to get really rough for our man in Jerusalem.

Matt Bird

Luke 20:19–26

19The teachers of the law and the chief priests
looked for a way to arrest him immediately,
because they knew he had spoken this parable
against them. But they were afraid of the people.
20Keeping a close watch on him, they sent
spies, who pretended to be honest. They hoped
to catch Jesus in something he said so that
they might hand him over to the power and
authority of the governor. 21So the spies ques-
tioned him: "Teacher, we know that you speak
and teach what is right, and that you do not
show partiality but teach the way of God in
accordance with the truth. 22Is it right for us to
pay taxes to Caesar or not?"
23He saw through their duplicity and said to
them, 24"Show me a denarius. Whose portrait
and inscription are on it?"
25"Caesar's," they replied.
He said to them, "Then give to Caesar what
is Caesar's, and to God what is God's."
26They were unable to trap him in what he
had said there in public. And astonished by
his answer, they became silent.

Pray for the governing authorities that God has put in place around the world that they might be filled with godliness.

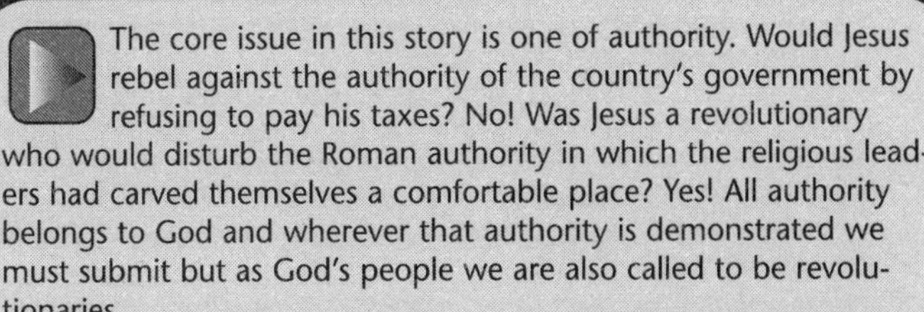

The core issue in this story is one of authority. Would Jesus rebel against the authority of the country's government by refusing to pay his taxes? No! Was Jesus a revolutionary who would disturb the Roman authority in which the religious leaders had carved themselves a comfortable place? Yes! All authority belongs to God and wherever that authority is demonstrated we must submit but as God's people we are also called to be revolutionaries.

In what countries around the world might you struggle to obey the government? What kind of revolution would you lead and how would you do it?

Prophecy

Luke 21:5–13

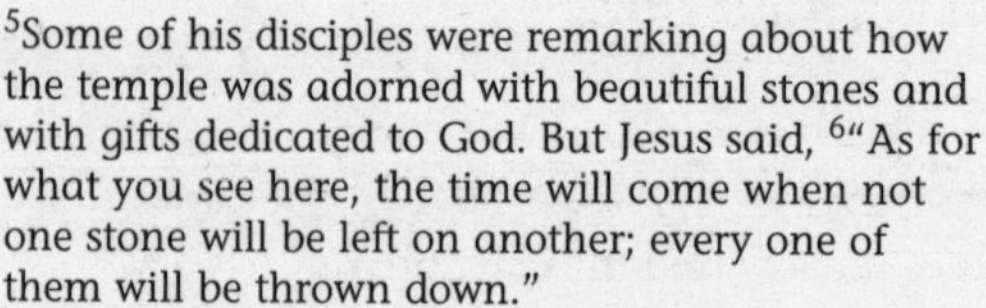

5 Some of his disciples were remarking about how
the temple was adorned with beautiful stones and
with gifts dedicated to God. But Jesus said, 6 "As for
what you see here, the time will come when not
one stone will be left on another; every one of
them will be thrown down."
7 "Teacher," they asked, "when will these things
happen? And what will be the sign that they are
about to take place?"
8 He replied: "Watch out that you are not
deceived. For many will come in my name, claiming, 'I am he,' and 'The time is near.' Do not follow
them. 9 When you hear of wars and revolutions, do
not be frightened. These things must happen first,
but the end will not come right away."
10 Then he said to them: "Nation will rise against
nation, and kingdom against kingdom. 11 There
will be great earthquakes, famines and pestilences
in various places, and fearful events and great
signs from heaven.
12 "But before all this, they will lay hands on you
and persecute you. They will deliver you to synagogues and prisons, and you will be brought before
kings and governors, and all on account of my
name. 13 This will result in your being witnesses to
them."

Pray for what you feel God wants to happen in the world.

The temple in Jerusalem had been destroyed in the sixth century BC by one of Israel's neighbours, and later rebuilt. So the temple at the time of Jesus is described as the second temple. Now here was Jesus in 30 AD-ish prophesying, 'As for what you see here not one stone will be left on another; every one of them will be thrown down' (6). No wonder his friendship with the religious leaders was going downhill fast – they'd worked hard to replace it once already and here was Jesus telling them to call the rubble-clearers back! He was right too: in 70 AD the second temple was plundered and flattened as Jesus had prophesied.

Prophecy is simply speaking God's message into the moment. It is not about magically predicting what is going to happen in the future. It's about getting people excited in God in the present because of what is on the horizon. Most of us don't start with massive prophecies – start by listening to God for the little things: the word of encouragement to a friend or support for someone upset. You will probably make one or two mistakes but allow God to develop the gift in you through practice and the guidance of others.

Prayer lifestyle

Luke 22:39–46

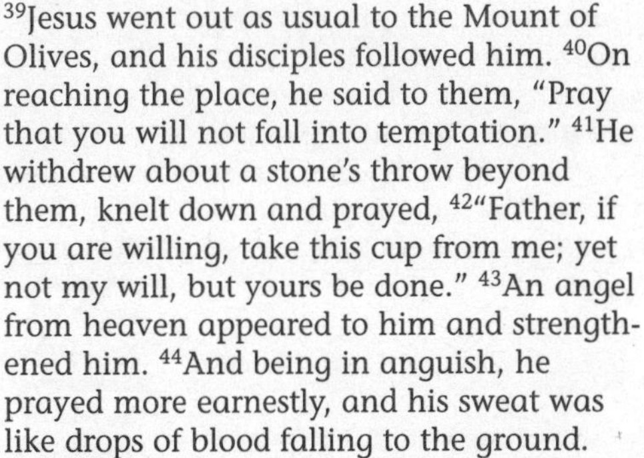

39Jesus went out as usual to the Mount of
Olives, and his disciples followed him. 40On
reaching the place, he said to them, "Pray
that you will not fall into temptation." 41He
withdrew about a stone's throw beyond
them, knelt down and prayed, 42"Father, if
you are willing, take this cup from me; yet
not my will, but yours be done." 43An angel
from heaven appeared to him and strengthened him. 44And being in anguish, he
prayed more earnestly, and his sweat was
like drops of blood falling to the ground.
45When he rose from prayer and went
back to the disciples, he found them asleep,
exhausted from sorrow. 46"Why are you
sleeping?" he asked them. "Get up and pray
so that you will not fall into temptation."

When do you normally pray? Try praying whilst you are doing the mundane today. If something unusual happens stop and find a quiet place to look to the Father.

The wave of public opinion against Jesus had grown to its height and he knew that his arrest, public trial and sentencing were imminent. So he took his disciples to a hill overlooking Jerusalem.

Jesus was a man of surprises and also a man of good habits. Perhaps one of the most obvious habits was that his life was one of prayer to his Father. In the mundane of everyday life and during unusual moments of pressure he made time to pray to his Father. In Luke we are occasionally told that Jesus went off to pray (5:16), but we are only told this because it was unusual for Jesus to 'go off'; he normally prayed wherever and in whatever he was doing. This is our model of a lifestyle of prayer to the Father both in the mundane and unusual moments.

Failing your mate

Luke 22:54–62

[54]Then seizing him, they led him away and
took him into the house of the high priest.
Peter followed at a distance. [55]But when
they had kindled a fire in the middle of the
courtyard and had sat down together, Peter
sat down with them. [56]A servant girl saw
him seated there in the firelight. She looked
closely at him and said, "This man was
with him."

[57]But he denied it. "Woman, I don't know
him," he said.

[58]A little later someone else saw him and
said, "You also are one of them."

"Man, I am not!" Peter replied.

[59]About an hour later another asserted,
"Certainly this fellow was with him, for he
is a Galilean."

[60]Peter replied, "Man, I don't know what
you're talking about!" Just as he was speaking, the cock crowed. [61]The Lord turned and
looked straight at Peter. Then Peter remembered the word the Lord had spoken to him:
"Before the cock crows today, you will disown me three times." [62]And he went outside
and wept bitterly.

What mistakes have you made this week? What have you learned through them about being a disciple of Jesus? Pray and ask God to make you someone who learns from their mistakes.

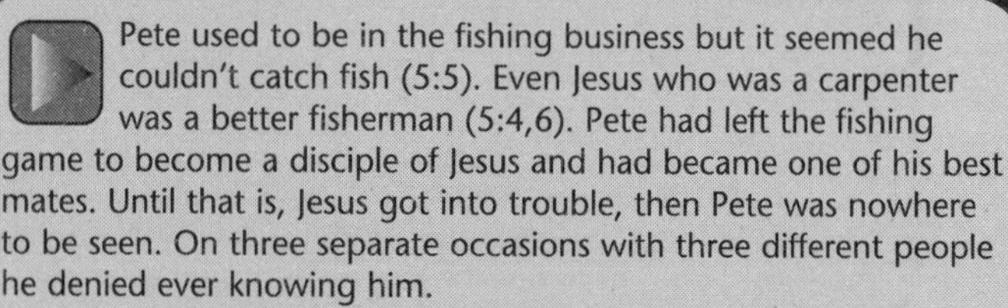

Pete used to be in the fishing business but it seemed he couldn't catch fish (5:5). Even Jesus who was a carpenter was a better fisherman (5:4,6). Pete had left the fishing game to become a disciple of Jesus and had became one of his best mates. Until that is, Jesus got into trouble, then Pete was nowhere to be seen. On three separate occasions with three different people he denied ever knowing him.

Pete was the epitome of a disciple. Disciple means 'learner', someone who isn't perfect but learns through mistakes. That was Pete. There wasn't another disciple that compared, and he always said the wrong thing, did the wrong thing or thought the wrong thing. I don't know about you but it encourages me that Jesus should choose someone like Pete to be his disciple and friend.

Jesus' forgiveness

Luke 23:39–43

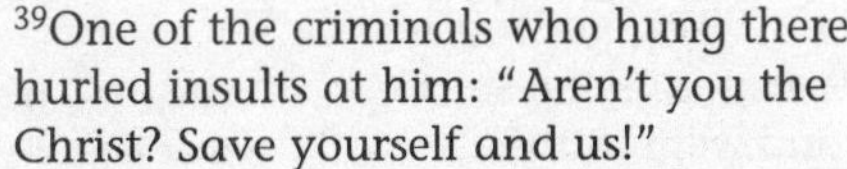

39One of the criminals who hung there
hurled insults at him: "Aren't you the
Christ? Save yourself and us!"
40But the other criminal rebuked him.
"Don't you fear God," he said, "since you
are under the same sentence? 41We are punished justly, for we are getting what our
deeds deserve. But this man has done nothing wrong."
42Then he said, "Jesus, remember me
when you come into your kingdom."
43Jesus answered him, "I tell you the
truth, today you will be with me in paradise."

Is there someone that you need to ask God to help you forgive? Is there a part of your life which you struggle to receive forgiveness from Jesus for? Is there something which you have done which you struggle to forgive yourself for?

Religious people might be quite offended that Jesus forgave a criminal. How would you react if Jesus forgave someone who stole your car or beat up your granny? The point of Jesus' forgiveness is that it is undeserved and given without condition. Now that's what I call good news!

Resurrection

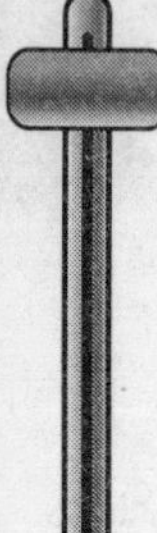

Luke 24:1–8

1On the first day of the week, very early in
the morning, the women took the spices
they had prepared and went to the
tomb.2They found the stone rolled away
from the tomb, 3but when they entered,
they did not find the body of the Lord Jesus.
4While they were wondering about this, suddenly two men in clothes that gleamed like
lightning stood beside them. 5In their fright
the women bowed down with their faces to
the ground, but the men said to them,
"Why do you look for the living among the
dead? 6He is not here; he has risen!
Remember how he told you, while he was
still with you in Galilee: 7'The Son of Man
must be delivered into the hands of sinful
men, be crucified and on the third day be
raised again.'" 8Then they remembered his
words.

What are the things that you might struggle to overcome today? What are your family and friends struggling to overcome? Pray and ask for Jesus' resurrection power to overcome.

What a remarkable miracle that a guy who was well and truly dead was alive again! This is one of the many unique marks of Christianity, that its leader is alive rather than dead like the founders of other religious belief systems. If he can overcome death then he can overcome anything.

The journey of life

Pray and ask God to give you the gift of faith to trust him even in the unknown.

Luke 24:13–35

13Now that same day two of them were going to a village called
Emmaus, about seven miles from Jerusalem. 14They were talking
with each other about everything that had happened. 15As they
talked and discussed these things with each other, Jesus himself
came up and walked along with them; 16but they were kept from recognising him.
17He asked them, "What are you discussing together as you walk along?"
They stood still, their faces downcast. 18One of them, named Cleopas, asked him,
"Are you only a visitor to Jerusalem and do not know the things that have happened
there in these days?"
19"What things?" he asked.
"About Jesus of Nazareth," they replied. "He was a prophet, powerful in word and
deed before God and all the people. 20The chief priests and our rulers handed him over
to be sentenced to death, and they crucified him; 21but we had hoped that he was the
one who was going to redeem Israel. And what is more, it is the third day since all this
took place. 22In addition, some of our women amazed us. They went to the tomb early
this morning 23but didn't find his body. They came and told us that they had seen a
vision of angels, who said he was alive. 24Then some of our companions went to the
tomb and found it just as the women had said, but him they did not see."
25He said to them, "How foolish you are, and how slow of heart to believe all that
the prophets have spoken! 26Did not the Christ have to suffer these things and then
enter his glory?" 27And beginning with Moses and all the Prophets, he explained to
them what was said in all the Scriptures concerning himself.
28As they approached the village to which they were going, Jesus acted as if he were
going further. 29But they urged him strongly, "Stay with us, for it is nearly evening; the
day is almost over." So he went in to stay with them.
30When he was at the table with them, he took bread, gave thanks, broke it and
began to give it to them. 31Then their eyes were opened and they recognised him, and
he disappeared from their sight. 32They asked each other, "Were not our hearts burning within us while he talked with us on the road and opened the Scriptures to us?"
33They got up and returned at once to Jerusalem. There they found the Eleven and
those with them, assembled together 34and saying, "It is true! The Lord has risen and
has appeared to Simon." 35Then the two told what had happened on the way, and
how Jesus was recognised by them when he broke the bread.

Life as a friend of Jesus is a journey. Journeys are full of times to stop and fill up, unplanned changes, unexpected delays, experiences of being lost, and questions of where we are going. The journey of life is exactly the same. Like those first disciples sometimes we fail to recognise Jesus alongside us on this journey.

What thoughts help you picture Jesus alongside you in the everyday humdrum of life? How do you respond to God when you don't know where you are going?

Divine empowerment

Luke 24:45–9

45Then he opened their minds so they could
understand the Scriptures. 46He told them,
"This is what is written: The Christ will suffer and rise from the dead on the third day,
47and repentance and forgiveness of sins
will be preached in his name to all nations,
beginning at Jerusalem. 48You are witnesses
of these things. 49I am going to send you
what my Father has promised; but stay in
the city until you have been clothed with
power from on high."

Find a place to pray and wait for God to empower you with the presence and power of the Holy Spirit to help you live this life for him.

The choice is to live with or without the power of God. How do you feel when you get a new set of clothes to wear? When we are clothed with power from on high by the Spirit of God, we are given a new confidence in God and ourselves. There is so much that we have read from the Bible about Jesus and have experienced in our lives. The big challenge to us as Christians is now to live the life in the power of the Holy Spirit.

If Amos was an actor, he'd be one of those struggling C-list types, appearing in TV movies and ads while the members of the A list – the Davids, Isaiahs, Moses and Abrahams – would be landing themselves meaty parts in Hollywood blockbusters. That's not to say that the man lacked talent, and God used him massively, giving him a message that is still ripe today.

Special treatment?

amos 2:9–11

9"I destroyed the Amorite before them,
though he was tall as the cedars
and strong as the oaks.
I destroyed his fruit above
and his roots below.

10"I brought you up out of Egypt,
and I led you for forty years in the desert
to give you the land of the Amorites.
11I also raised up prophets from among your sons
and Nazirites from among your young men.
Is this not true, people of Israel?"
declares the Lord.

Before we get stuck in, here's a brief overview of the book: Amos was a farmer, living a few miles south of Bethlehem. God gave him a vision of the future and told him to take his message to the northern kingdom. The people there were putting on a good show, doing some slick religious activities and failing to fool God. He saw their hearts and he saw the way that they oppressed the poor. First up Amos delivered a condemnation of all the nations who had sinned against both him and the Israelites. Perhaps it was real crowd-pleasing stuff, and it certainly makes for a nice build up to what comes next: Amos turned to his Israelite audience and pronounced God's judgment on them.

Amos' words pull no punches, and he refuses to allow the Israelites to get too cosy. In this passage he highlights Israel's privileged position in the eyes of God. Is Amos raising them up, allowing them off the hook? No way, as it's clear that God's privilege demands certain things in return. Israel's behaviour was not up to scratch – as we shall see over the next few sessions – and their history of special treatment, of being bailed out by God and warned by prophets, made God's judgment all the more severe.

Are we something special? Is God our personal Fix-It-Slave, the one we call on when it all goes wrong, only to shove him back in the drawer once things are rosy again?

chew it over

Face facts, we all could do with learning to take God more seriously. Ask him to help

Questions - part 1

amos 1:3–5, 2:10–13

3This is what the Lord says:

"For three sins of Damascus,
even for four, I will not turn back [my wrath].
Because she threshed Gilead
with sledges having iron teeth,
4I will send fire upon the house of Hazael
that will consume the fortresses of Ben-Hadad.
5I will break down the gate of Damascus;
I will destroy the king who is in the Valley of
Aven
and the one who holds the sceptre in Beth Eden.
The people of Aram will go into exile to Kir,"
says the Lord.

10"I brought you up out of Egypt,
and I led you for forty years in the desert
to give you the land of the Amorites.
11I also raised up prophets from among your sons
and Nazirites from among your young men.
this not true, people of Israel?"
declares the Lord.
12"But you made the Nazirites drink wine
and commanded the prophets not to prophesy.

13"Now then, I will crush you
as a cart crushes when loaded with grain."

chew it over

We cannot separate our actions from our faith. Whether it's how we treat people from Monday to Friday, the politics we sign up for or the attitudes we hold, how we treat others is how we treat God.

Amos gives us crystal clear insight into the nature of God, especially the issue of how he judges people. Want to know how he feels about crimes against humanity? Look at the first passage here. It relates to Syria, who – under Hazael (842–806 BC) – expanded his territory across the Jordan and into Israel using barbarous methods of torture. God may have held back in the past, refusing to act in haste, but after four major crimes, his judgment rolls on unstoppable.

What about judgment for God's people? Are the expectations on them higher than on others? Look at the second passage. Israel had been chosen, they were unique, but they confused privilege with the permission to sin. The result? 'Now then, I will crush you as a cart crushes when loaded with grain' (2:13).

Crimes against people are crimes against God. God, if you like, takes it personally. But can we hide behind his favour? Can we hope that our sins will get softer treatment? No way: God demands more from his people and his judgment on Israel showed just that.

Questions - part 2

amos 3:9–15

9Proclaim to the fortresses of Ashdod
and to the fortresses of Egypt:
"Assemble yourselves on the mountains of Samaria;
see the great unrest within her
and the oppression among her people."

10"They do not know how to do right," declares the Lord,
"who hoard plunder and loot in their fortresses."

11Therefore this is what the Sovereign Lord says:

"An enemy will overrun the land;
he will pull down your strongholds
and plunder your fortresses."

12This is what the Lord says:

"As a shepherd saves from the lion's mouth
only two leg bones or a piece of an ear,
so will the Israelites be saved,
those who sit in Samaria
on the edge of their beds
and in Damascus on their couches."

13"Hear this and testify against the house of Jacob,"
declares the Lord, the Lord God Almighty.

14"On the day I punish Israel for her sins,
I will destroy the altars of Bethel;
the horns of the altar will be cut off
and fall to the ground.
15I will tear down the winter house
along with the summer house;
the houses adorned with ivory will be destroyed
and the mansions will be demolished,"
declares the Lord.

chew it over

Money, faith, church . . . are these really signs that we are safe from God's judgment?

This passage comes towards the start of the charge against Israel. Amos tells the Israelites to confess to the Egyptians (metaphorically) about their true behaviour: they oppress their own, 'hoard plunder and loot in their fortresses' and have become so blunted by their wrong behaviour that they no longer 'know how to do right'.

What's the fate of Israel? At first glance this bit about bones being saved might seem optimistic – I mean, at least there will be something left – but it's nothing of the sort. If a shepherd brought back a few sheep bones after an attack from a wild animal he was covering himself. The bones were proof that the sheep had been entirely destroyed, that there was nothing left and that it hadn't simply wandered off. Doesn't look so good for Israel, does it?

Verse 14 mentions Israel's sins, and a quick reminder tells us that they are the 'oppressions' and 'hoards'. The crimes of war and corruption are sins.

There's a hint here that the Egyptians called to see Israel's sins would be shocked, that perhaps Israel was behaving worse than one of her heathen enemies. Amos goes further too, as the Israelites who will really suffer are those with winter and summer houses, the ones with beautifully decorated mansions. Those who have got rich from oppressing others will pay the price.

Priority

amos 5:21–5

21"I hate, I despise your religious feasts;
I cannot stand your assemblies.
22Even though you bring me burnt offerings
and grain offerings,
I will not accept them.
Though you bring choice fellowship
offerings,
I will have no regard for them.
23Away with the noise of your songs!
I will not listen to the music of your
harps.
24But let justice roll on like a river,
righteousness like a never-failing stream!

25"Did you bring me sacrifices and offerings
for forty years in the desert, O house of
Israel?"

As well as helping us understand more about God's judgment, Amos turns our attention to religion. It's clear that the Israelites had it all going on when it came to outward appearances, but beneath the surface things weren't so hot. Their religion was completely separated from God's laws, and Amos has pointed out that 'They trample on the heads of the poor as upon the dust of the ground and deny justice to the oppressed' (2:7). It didn't seem to help them live better lives (Israel's actions are described: 'Go to Bethel and sin; go to Gilgal and sin yet more. Bring your sacrifices every morning, your tithes every three years', 4:4), and it didn't bring about justice. This passage still turns the light on for us today, especially as we too can get carried away with the activities of worship and forget the heart behind it. Israel was far too busy getting the offerings looking right to remember to obey God. If they had been doing as they were told, justice would have been flowing, giving life to all around. Amos asks them about their ancestors' time in the desert: didn't they know how to be both obedient and 'religious' back then?

In these days when worship is 'cool', when so much is led from the stage and people are making money out of leading God's people, we face real dangers.

chew it over

Do we dare ignore the warnings that Amos passed on to the Israelites?

Hope?

amos 7:1–3, 9:11–15

1This is what the Sovereign Lord showed me: He was
preparing swarms of locusts after the king's share
had been harvested and just as the second crop was
coming up. 2When they had stripped the land clean, I
cried out, "Sovereign Lord, forgive! How can Jacob
survive? He is so small!"
3So the Lord relented.
"This will not happen," the Lord said.

11"In that day I will restore
David's fallen tent.
I will repair its broken places,
restore its ruins,
and build it as it used to be,
12so that they may possess the remnant of Edom
and all the nations that bear my name,"
declares the Lord,
who will do these things.

13"The days are coming," declares the Lord,

"when the reaper will be overtaken by the ploughman
and the planter by the one treading grapes.
New wine will drip from the mountains
and flow from all the hills.
14I will bring back my exiled people Israel;
they will rebuild the ruined cities and live in them.
They will plant vineyards and drink their wine;
they will make gardens and eat their fruit.
15I will plant Israel in their own land,
never again to be uprooted
from the land I have given them,"

says the Lord your God.

The final round of prophecies starts with something incredible: God tells Amos about a plan to unleash a plague of locusts. But this isn't just any plague: this one would wipe out all the land, and that means total destruction. But Amos prays; he pleads with God not to let it happen and amazingly God agrees. The verses that follow it show the pattern being repeated, this time with a threat of fire that destroys all life, which God again backs down from when Amos prays. God heard his prayers, and we can assume that he never wanted to destroy his creation. With this a little hope creeps in and Amos' prophecies carry on. Without the threat of destruction how will it all end for God's people?

Scoot forward to the last chapter (number 9) and we find our answer. In verses 7–10 we get back to the theme of judgment: the Israelites cannot just rely on their birth if they want to escape judgment. But there's something else: a hint that alongside God's judgment is the offer of salvation.

chew it over

Jesus came and drew a line in the sand. Do we accept Jesus as our Lord and as our Saviour or do we reject him? Judgment or mercy? Which way do we go?

1 JOHN

Gnosticism. No, it's not some kind of pasta and it's not the study of garden gnomes. It was something far more serious (although probably not quite as tasty or amusing). This religious movement threatened to dilute the Church throughout its first couple of centuries. Gnosticism may have been in its infancy, but 1 John is a book on a mission to sort things out.

Spring cleaning

1 John 2:26–7

26 I am writing these things to you about those who are trying to lead you astray. 27 As for you, the anointing you received from him remains in you, and you do not need anyone to teach you. But as his anointing teaches you about all things and as that anointing is real, not counterfeit—just as it has taught you, remain in him.

SEARCH

This open letter to believers everywhere confronted those who were trying to sell their own wacky brand of Christianity. Instead of relying on the teaching of the apostles, the Gnostics were suggesting that good little Christians needed to subscribe to their own 'higher knowledge' – something which only the Gnostics possessed. The problems really kicked in when it became clear that they were using this to justify all sorts of immoral acts, getting themselves into serious sin.

GO

The writer hits back with the truth that we all still need to hear today: take it back to Jesus, get stuck into his teaching as confirmed by the Holy Spirit.

The unbelievable truth?

1 John 3:1–3

1 How great is the love
the Father has lavished
on us, that we should be
called children of God!
And that is what we are!
The reason the world
does not know us is that
it did not know him.
2 Dear friends, now we
are children of God, and
what we will be has not
yet been made known.
But we know that when
he appears, we shall be
like him, for we shall see
him as he is. 3 Everyone
who has this hope in
him purifies himself, just
as he is pure.

SEARCH

Nice one, Johnny boy. If ever there was an underlining of the winning points of Christianity it's here. Following Jesus is separated from all other religions by one thing: a love lavished on us that allows us to be called the children of God.

If we assume that the writer was John the disciple (although there is some debate about the point) we can happily say that the writer knew about this amazing love. He'd been part of Jesus' inner circle, part of the core team along with James and Peter, and often referred to himself as 'the disciple whom Jesus loved'. He was in there, he'd made it. But did he see himself at the top of the pile with all the rest of us poor sinners fighting for scraps down below? Was he at the top of a league system, with him as crowned champion of Jesus' affection? No way.

Christianity is about equality and upside-down shifts of power: we are all children, we are all accepted. Nice.

Mystery

1 John 4:9–11

9This is how God showed
his love among us: He
sent his one and only
Son into the world that
we might live through
him. 10This is love: not
that we loved God, but
that he loved us and sent
his Son as an atoning
sacrifice for our sins.
11Dear friends, since
God so loved us, we also
ought to love one
another.

SEARCH

What does God look like? We're more used to seeing his work than his form. Our love (that's 'love' as in goodness, holiness and general godliness, not 'love' as in 'luuurve') has its own source in God's love, so when we see our love in action, we see the heart of God.

GO

What is love? The sacrificial, life-changing force that draws us to get involved.

Jude

What's wrong with a little sin?

It might be little, but it's beautifully formed. Jude gets straight into the action and no mistake.

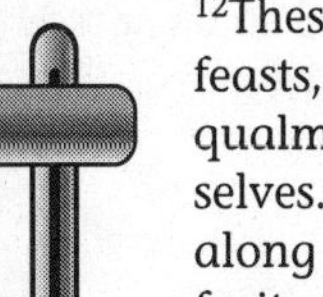

Jude 12–13

12These men are blemishes at your love
feasts, eating with you without the slightest
qualm—shepherds who feed only themselves. They are clouds without rain, blown
along by the wind; autumn trees, without
fruit and uprooted—twice dead. 13They are
wild waves of the sea, foaming up their
shame; wandering stars, for whom blackest
darkness has been reserved for ever.

Get back to basics. Live the Christian life.

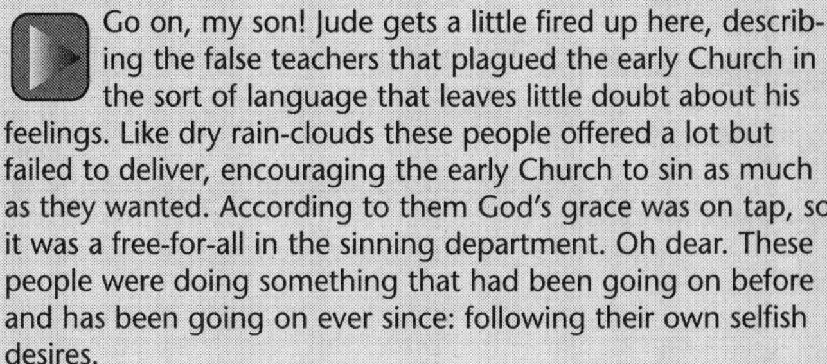

Go on, my son! Jude gets a little fired up here, describing the false teachers that plagued the early Church in the sort of language that leaves little doubt about his feelings. Like dry rain-clouds these people offered a lot but failed to deliver, encouraging the early Church to sin as much as they wanted. According to them God's grace was on tap, so it was a free-for-all in the sinning department. Oh dear. These people were doing something that had been going on before and has been going on ever since: following their own selfish desires.

If ever you wonder just how the early Church survived – not only from the external pressures (the Romans, Jews and so on), but the internal blind alleys and confusions – it was because of teaching like this. Straightforward and to the point, Jude is fully direct – Jesus saved our sins but it should never be taken for granted.

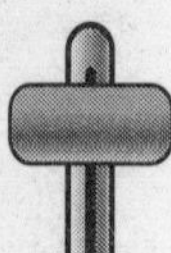

Jude 20–3

[20]But you, dear friends, build yourselves up
in your most holy faith and pray in the
Holy Spirit. [21]Keep yourselves in God's love
as you wait for the mercy of our Lord Jesus
Christ to bring you to eternal life.
[22]Be merciful to those who doubt; [23]snatch
others from the fire and save them; to others show mercy, mixed with fear—hating
even the clothing stained by corrupted flesh.

Sometimes we all need to be scared of the power of sin.

Here's a little more evidence of the careful pruning and fertilising carried out at crucial points in the early Church. Jude has it sussed, warning believers that it's up to them to look out for each other.

But he's sensible about things too. Perhaps he'd seen it before, but he knew that rescuing believers carried a risk. 'Show mercy, mixed with fear': fear of what? Fear of sin and getting caught up themselves. Too often we can get carried away with the knight in shining armour routine, drunk on our own potential and power. We imagine that we're invincible, that our relationship with God is rock solid and well able to cope with a few risks. For Jude this attitude can lead to faith being lost, an 'accident' which could easily be avoided. The solution? Wisdom: sin is sin and it spreads more easily than butter.

In pointing out about 'clothing stained by corrupted flesh' he may be going slightly over the top (after all, we don't really believe that sweaters have souls) but it makes a point: sin is serious. We should rescue those that have fallen but never underestimate sin's power to corrupt.

JONAH

Life is so much easier when things are black and white, don't you think? I mean, we're the good guys, right? And all we need to do is go and tell those baddies exactly where they're going wrong and everything will be sorted. OK? But then some stonking great fish comes along and messes everything up. Typical.

What's the score?

Jonah 1:1–2

1The word of the Lord came to Jonah son of Amittai: 2"Go to the great city of Nineveh and preach against it, because its wickedness has come up before me."

SEARCH

Here's the deal: Assyria was one of Israel's greatest and most powerful enemies. They were cruel, evil, in severe need of a good kicking. Israel had suffered at their hands, but in recent years had begun to get a little over-confident. God hated the foreigners and liked Israel, or so some people thought, but prophets such as Amos and Hosea warned them about these attitudes.

This book tells the story of one man's mission to deliver a prophecy to an enemy nation. It's odd that despite this only one verse contains his message to the people of Nineveh, especially as Nineveh was about 500 miles north-east of Jonah's homeland. Add to that the fact that the man went on a significant detour to reach Nineveh and you have to admit that it's kind of odd that so little attention should be paid to the message he delivered.

But excuse my ignorance, something's just clicked. What if the book isn't so much about the great sins of the Assyrians? What if it has more to do with Jonah himself? What if it's actually a book about how God's people relate to others?

Can you relate to Jonah's view of the Assyrians: so nasty and evil that the thought of spending time with them is enough to make you do a runner?

Is the view of the world as a frightening place really so helpful and godly?

Jonah and Jesus

Matthew 12:38–42

38Then some of the
Pharisees and teachers of
the law said to him,
"Teacher, we want to see a
miraculous sign from
you."
39He answered, "A
wicked and adulterous
generation asks for a
miraculous sign! But none
will be given it except the
sign of the prophet Jonah.
40For as Jonah was three
days and three nights in
the belly of a huge fish, so
the Son of Man will be
three days and three
nights in the heart of the
earth. 41The men of
Nineveh will stand up at
the judgment with this
generation and condemn
it; for they repented at the
preaching of Jonah, and
now one greater than
Jonah is here. 42The
Queen of the South will
rise at the judgment with
this generation and con-
demn it; for she came
from the ends of the earth
to listen to Solomon's wisdom, and now one greater
than Solomon is here."

SEARCH

Jesus was once asked for a miraculous sign to prove his identity. He told them about Jonah (also in Luke 11:29–32). Jesus and Jonah came from the same part of town – Nazareth was only one hour's walk away from Jonah's home at Gath-hepher – and Jonah is the only Old Testament prophet whom Jesus compares himself with. Perhaps Jesus grew up with the story louder than others in his mind. Perhaps the examples in Luke and Matthew weren't the first occasions on which he had chewed over the similarities.

So what is Jesus saying? The people wanted a sign, something flash and glitzy that would grab the attention and show others the truth. Would he give it? Not the way they wanted. Instead he turned their thoughts to Jonah, the man who was swallowed by the whale. But was that really his great sign?

Jesus' words help us find the answer. He tells them that the Israelites are hardly whiter than white, that just as the Ninevites needed correction so too do the Israelites. He goes on to talk about resurrection, but let's stick with this point here: the Israelites never entertained the possibility that they might be wrong, that Jesus might be coming to judge as well as to save them.

GO

What about us? Are we doing so well that we're immune from judgment? Are we too busy pointing out the specks to notice the plank in our own eyes?

Jonah's prayer

Jonah 2:4–10

4"I said, 'I have been banished
from your sight;
yet I will look again
towards your holy temple.'
5The engulfing waters
threatened me,
the deep surrounded me;
seaweed was wrapped around
my head.
6To the roots of the mountains
I sank down;
the earth beneath barred me
in for ever.
But you brought my life up
from the pit,
O Lord my God.

7"When my life was ebbing
away,
I remembered you, Lord,
and my prayer rose to you,
to your holy temple.

8"Those who cling to worthless
idols
forfeit the grace that could be
theirs.
9But I, with a song of
thanksgiving,
will sacrifice to you.
What I have vowed I will make
good.
Salvation comes from the
Lord."

10And the Lord commanded the fish,
and it vomited Jonah onto dry land.

SEARCH

Having refused to pray to his God on deck, Jonah now finds himself facing death. Not surprisingly he doesn't like it, and the experience is enough to see him turn back to God. Remember Jesus saying how he was greater than Jonah? It's all here. Jonah complains about being 'banished' from God's sight, Jesus cried, 'My God, my God, why have you forsaken me?' (Matthew 27:46). Where Jonah was facing death, Jesus actually died. Where Jonah escaped death, Jesus came back to life.

But there's more. See that line about 'Those who cling to worthless idols forfeit the grace'? He's talking about the Ninevites, and despite the fact that God is about to have mercy on his weaselly little soul, Jonah shows no compassion for the people he is being sent to help. Jesus, on the other hand, went through an agonising death *because of* his compassion. He truly was greater than Jonah could ever hope to be.

Even in the middle of our best prayers we still, like Jonah, have the capacity to forget all about some of God's commands. Pray and ask him to illuminate your own blind spots.

The preach

Jonah 3:4–7

4On the first day, Jonah
started into the city. He
proclaimed: "Forty more
days and Nineveh will be
overturned." 5The
Ninevites believed God.
They declared a fast, and
all of them, from the
greatest to the least, put
on sackcloth.
6When the news
reached the king of
Nineveh, he rose from
his throne, took off his
royal robes, covered him-
self with sackcloth and
sat down in the dust.
7Then he issued a procla-
mation in Nineveh:

"By the decree of the king and his nobles:

Do not let any man or beast, herd or flock, taste anything; do not let them eat or drink."

SEARCH

Hey, it worked! Nice one, Jonah, although something tells me that the credit isn't exactly all yours. From his attitude in the whale and the chat that comes in the next chapter we know that Jonah was in a bit of a mood with the Ninevites, and it seems that he wasn't exactly on top form in his preaching. The fact that he only includes one line makes the miracle even more amazing: God worked through even the smallest of openings. Whether there were other factors that influenced the Ninevites' quick turnaround we may never know, but it certainly leaves us with some decent conclusions: first, God wanted them saved. They may have been the enemies of his people but he wanted their hearts to turn to him. Second, God was prepared to do something amazing to get them. Whether or not there was a fish that swallowed Jonah, the point remains that he reckoned he was near death when God saved him. Finally, we know that God used someone who may not have been quite up to the job. Jonah didn't exactly jump at the task, and wouldn't another Amos or Hosea have been a little more compassionate? Probably, but God's grace to the Ninevites extended to his slightly moody servant.

Remember that bit about Jesus saying the 'sign of Jonah' was a miraculous sign to his generation? Do you think it still stands? Does God still want to show compassion to 'hostile nations'?

GO

Can he still use Jonahs like us? Ask God to show you your Nineveh.

The truth

Jonah 3:10–4:5

[10]When God saw what
they did and how they
turned from their evil
ways, he had compas-
sion and did not bring
upon them the destruc-
tion he had threatened.
[1]But Jonah was greatly
displeased and became
angry. [2]He prayed to the
Lord, "O Lord, is this not
what I said when I was
still at home? That is
why I was so quick to
flee to Tarshish. I knew
that you are a gracious
and compassionate God,
slow to anger and
abounding in love, a
God who relents from
sending calamity. [3]Now,
O Lord, take away my
life, for it is better for me
to die than to live."
[4]But the Lord replied,
"Have you any right to
be angry?"
[5]Jonah went out and
sat down at a place east
of the city. There he
made himself a shelter,
sat in its shade and waited to see what would
happen to the city.

SEARCH

And at last we find out the truth as Jonah admits why he ran away from God's task in the first place: jealousy, racial hatred, insecurity – call it what you like, Jonah simply couldn't stand the thought of God showing compassionate mercy to his enemies. His attitude should make us sad, as it leads him to throw God's miracle back in his face. Back in chapter 2 Jonah was rejoicing that God would save him. Now he wants to die. What a terrible state to be in.

Does he have any right to be angry? Of course not. God is not a trade secret, one only to be shared around the people we like. We cannot box him, and we should never try to limit him. He is the boss, the one whose mercy and compassion far outstrips our understanding. Let's steer clear of prejudice and cosy cliques.

But God's mercy is even more dramatic, and to prove it, while Jonah waits for the forty days to pass to see whether the Ninevites really will escape doom, God provides a vine to keep the sun away from his head. The vine perishes at the hands of a worm, and the next day the sun is fiercer than ever, aided by a scorching wind. Does Jonah have a right to be angry about the vine? Of course not. The cycles of nature are a sign of the power and immovability of God, and his last word points out Jonah's inability to rise above his own frustrations and God's own nature always to have mercy.

GO

There's more of Jonah in me than I'd like to admit, but that's no excuse for holding back on compassion.

Jesus' betrayal, death and resurrection were not just about him. There's something to learn for each one of us. *Matt Stuart*

Moon Palace

john 17:1–5

1After Jesus said this, he looked towards heaven and prayed:

"Father, the time has come. Glorify
your Son, that your Son may glorify
you. 2For you granted him authority
over all people that he might give eternal life to all those you have given
him. 3Now this is eternal life: that they
may know you, the only true God, and
Jesus Christ, whom you have sent. 4I
have brought you glory on earth by
completing the work you gave me to
do. 5And now, Father, glorify me in
your presence with the glory I had with
you before the world began."

'Doesn't the moon shine brightly, tonight?' said the man.

'No,' my friend said, as he walked away.

'It was a stupid question,' my friend said as he told me about this later. 'The moon doesn't shine at all. It's a reflection of the sun.'

That's what we are too. A reflection of the Son. If you want to be bigger, better and more popular than Jesus then you're in the wrong game. He's the best. The bee's knees. The business. And he deserves all the glory. Our job is to show him to people. To reflect him. To glorify him.

Now, I realise you probably don't think you want to be bigger than Jesus. But, do you live it? How often do you put yourself first when he should be number one? Ever walked away instead of telling someone what you believe? Thought so. Let's face it – we can all do better.

It strikes me that Jesus is actually our model for this too. Look at how he glorifies the Father. His whole life points to Father God; he lives to give him glory.

Let's try and live this thing. I mean really live it.

chew it over

As you do whatever you do today try asking yourself what Jesus would do in each situation. Make sure he gets the glory. Reflect the Son.

Moving on

john 18:1–3, 15–18

[1]When he had finished praying, Jesus left with
his disciples and crossed the Kidron Valley.
On the other side there was an olive grove,
and he and his disciples went into it.
[2]Now Judas, who betrayed him, knew the
place, because Jesus had often met there with
his disciples. [3]So Judas came to the grove,
guiding a detachment of soldiers and some
officials from the chief priests and Pharisees.
They were carrying torches, lanterns and
weapons.
[15]Simon Peter and another disciple were following Jesus. Because this disciple was known
to the high priest, he went with Jesus into the
high priest's courtyard, [16]but Peter had to wait
outside at the door. The other disciple, who
was known to the high priest, came back,
spoke to the girl on duty there and brought
Peter in.
[17]"You are not one of his disciples, are
you?" the girl at the door asked Peter.
He replied, "I am not."
[18]It was cold, and the servants and officials
stood round a fire they had made to keep
warm. Peter also was standing with them,
warming himself.

Betrayal is a nasty thing. It's even worse when it's a close friend that sticks the knife in. It's happened to me a couple of times and it hurts. A lot.

There are two people who let Jesus down in this story. Judas and Peter. Judas never really got what Jesus was all about. For a while he walked the walk and talked the talk, but when it came to the crunch, he didn't really love Jesus, so he bailed. Greed got the better of him. He took the money and ran. I reckon that hurt Jesus. It's worth making sure we know what Jesus is about and living like it matters. You can talk as much as you like but if you're not living it, it's worth diddly.

Let's move on to Peter. Peter loved Jesus. There's no doubt about that. He was Jesus' biggest fan. But he still stuffed it up and made out he didn't even know him. That hurt Jesus too. Probably more than what Judas did. But Peter still made it. When Jesus talks with Peter later on, he forgives him and they move on.

We need to hear this. If we love Jesus it doesn't matter what we've done or what we do, he'll forgive us and we can move on. There are no exceptions. So if you've got a problem with something you did that let Jesus down, say sorry, let him forgive you and move on.

chew it over

After all, what could be worse than cutting off some geezer's ear and then denying you've even met the bloke you did it for?

Truth

john 20:11-18

11 but Mary stood outside the tomb crying. As she
wept, she bent over to look into the tomb 12 and
saw two angels in white, seated where Jesus'
body had been, one at the head and the other at
the foot.
13 They asked her, "Woman, why are you crying?"
"They have taken my Lord away," she said,
"and I don't know where they have put him." 14 At
this, she turned round and saw Jesus standing
there, but she did not realise that it was Jesus.
15 "Woman," he said, "why are you crying?
Who is it you are looking for?"
Thinking he was the gardener, she said, "Sir, if
you have carried him away, tell me where you
have put him, and I will get him."
16 Jesus said to her, "Mary."
She turned towards him and cried out in
Aramaic, "Rabboni!" (which means Teacher).
17 Jesus said, "Do not hold on to me, for I have
not yet returned to the Father. Go instead to my
brothers and tell them, 'I am returning to my
Father and your Father, to my God and your
God.'"
18 Mary Magdalene went to the disciples with
the news: "I have seen the Lord!" And she told
them that he had said these things to her.

chew it over

You can count on Jesus, no matter what. Why don't you thank him for that, right now?

Oh dear. Mary's in a bit of a mess. One of her best friends, who also happens to be God, has just been betrayed and crucified, and now is in a tomb blocked by a four-ton stone. When she goes to visit the grave she discovers that the body's been nicked and that two dodgy-looking characters are hanging around the tomb. Imagine how you'd feel!

As she gets more and more upset she spots another man and asks him where Jesus might be. As soon as he says her name she sees that it's Jesus and falls into his arms.

Do you ever feel like Jesus has left you? That's what Mary felt like. He was dead. Normally that's pretty final. But somehow Jesus was there standing in front of her. He's there for you too. He's not dead. The grave couldn't hold him. He's there, calling your name, waiting to give you a hug.

Sometimes life gets pretty tough. There have been a couple of times when I've been at the end of myself. The whole thing has just been too much for me and I've needed help. Friends and family have often been there for me but one person is always there. Jesus never leaves me. He's always there.

Doubt

john 20:24–31

24Now Thomas (called Didymus), one of the
Twelve, was not with the disciples when Jesus
came. 25So the other disciples told him, "We
have seen the Lord!"
But he said to them, "Unless I see the nail
marks in his hands and put my finger where the
nails were, and put my hand into his side, I will
not believe it."
26A week later his disciples were in the house
again, and Thomas was with them. Though the
doors were locked, Jesus came and stood
among them and said, "Peace be with you!"
27Then he said to Thomas, "Put your finger here;
see my hands. Reach out your hand and put it
into my side. Stop doubting and believe."
28Thomas said to him, "My Lord and my
God!"
29Then Jesus told him, "Because you have
seen me, you have believed; blessed are those
who have not seen and yet have believed."
30Jesus did many other miraculous signs in
the presence of his disciples, which are not
recorded in this book. 31But these are written
that you may believe that Jesus is the Christ,
the Son of God, and that by believing you may
have life in his name.

I understand Thomas. I find faith quite hard work. I often have to see something before I'll believe it. So how can I believe in Jesus when I've never seen him? Easy, I have seen him!

I see Jesus all the time. I see the things that he does and the difference that he makes. I see the poor being provided for. I see the sick healed. I see children without any parents given love and a home. I see the unwanted and the unloved taken in and cared for. I think you get the picture.

I also see what life is like without Jesus. The world is full of people that have no hope, no purpose and no idea that they can know God. I want to see that change.

It's not wrong to want to see for sure that something is real, but we do need to hear what Jesus says here: 'Stop doubting and believe.' Some people spend a lot of time trying to find Jesus. They need to be 100 per cent sure before they'll believe. They never will be. All of us have doubts however long we've been following him. If we take the plunge and let Jesus run the show we'll soon see that he's for real and find it easier to believe.

chew it over

Maybe you just need to follow Jesus instead of following Thomas.

The Breakfast Club

john 21:7–14

[7]Then the disciple whom Jesus loved said to
Peter, "It is the Lord!" As soon as Simon Peter
heard him say, "It is the Lord," he wrapped
his outer garment around him (for he had
taken it off) and jumped into the water. [8]The
other disciples followed in the boat, towing
the net full of fish, for they were not far from
shore, about a hundred yards. [9]When they
landed, they saw a fire of burning coals there
with fish on it, and some bread.

[10]Jesus said to them, "Bring some of the fish
you have just caught."

[11]Simon Peter climbed aboard and dragged
the net ashore. It was full of large fish, 153,
but even with so many the net was not torn.
[12]Jesus said to them, "Come and have breakfast." None of the disciples dared ask him,
"Who are you?" They knew it was the Lord.
[13]Jesus came, took the bread and gave it to
them, and did the same with the fish. [14]This
was now the third time Jesus appeared to his
disciples after he was raised from the dead.

So a whole bunch of Jesus' mates are hanging around on the beach, feeling fed up, and having a good moan. Peter, in a bit of a huff, decides to go fishing. The others, not having a lot else to do, go with him. They're out in the boat all night and they catch nothing. Some fishermen!

In the morning this helpful bloke pops up on the shore and tries to give them a few hints. For some reason they follow his advice and the net comes back loaded. Now they sit up and take notice. It's funny how often we wait until something happens before we show an interest, isn't it?

Then one of the boys spots that the bloke on the shore is Jesus. Think about it. He's supposed to be dead. They saw him die on a cross and now he's giving them fishing lessons and tending a barbie. Despite their surprise they make for shore and pull the net onto the beach.

Imagine that you're Peter for a second. The last time you had a chance to chat with Jesus you messed it up big time and said three times that you'd never met him. Peter must have felt terrible. Guilty, shameful, and very uncomfortable. Feelings we can all relate to. And what does Jesus say? 'Come and have breakfast.'

After all that he'd been through, even though they'd let him down, he pushes past the barriers, forgives them and offers a fresh start.

chew it over

What does Jesus say to you today as you munch your cornflakes? No matter where you're at or how you feel, his words are the same: 'Come and have breakfast.'

Habakkuk

Pain

It's never going to be one of those trendy Old Testament names well-meaning Christian parents find to name their kids, and you'll need your index to find where it is in the Bible. But once you get there it's worth it. Habakkuk opens another valve of your heart, writing at one of the most tragic times in God's people's history. Who knows, perhaps you might want to name a son Habakkuk after all.

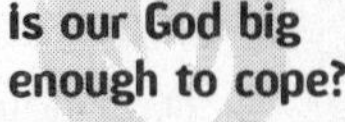

Is our God big enough to cope?

Habakkuk 1:2–4, 12–17

2How long, O Lord, must I call for help,
but you do not listen?
Or cry out to you, "Violence!"
but you do not save?
3Why do you make me look at injustice?
Why do you tolerate wrong?
Destruction and violence are before me;
there is strife, and conflict abounds.
4Therefore the law is paralysed,
and justice never prevails.
The wicked hem in the righteous,
so that justice is perverted.

12O Lord, are you not from everlasting?
My God, my Holy One, we will not die.
O Lord, you have appointed them to execute judgment;
O Rock, you have ordained them to punish.
13Your eyes are too pure to look on evil;
you cannot tolerate wrong.
Why then do you tolerate the treacherous?
Why are you silent while the wicked
swallow up those more righteous than themselves?
14You have made men like fish in the sea,
like sea creatures that have no ruler.
15The wicked foe pulls all of them up with hooks,
he catches them in his net,
he gathers them up in his drag-net;
and so he rejoices and is glad.
16Therefore he sacrifices to his net
and burns incense to his drag-net,
for by his net he lives in luxury
and enjoys the choicest food.
17Is he to keep on emptying his net,
destroying nations without mercy?

One of the few things we can be sure of in life is that we will suffer. In fact, as a generation we seem to suffer more, to break more easily than any other: self-harm, eating disorders, bullying, family break up, unhealthy addictions, the scars are there all around us. When faced with this stuff the temptation is to ask God just to wave a magic wand over it to make it all disappear, or at least to give a shot of heavenly anaesthetic to stop it from hurting quite so much.

Habakkuk teaches us. God's people are up against it – taken into slavery and exile. It hurts. And it's overwhelming, there seems no end to the pain. Chances are you've known times like that, or you know someone else that does. What do we do when that happens? Habakkuk teaches us that we should go to God and pour out our hurt hearts. We can do that with God because he listens and saves (2), he is the true God (12), he is good and merciful (13 and 17).

We might have been doing a bit of this already, involving God in our pain and calling out for his help. But are we willing to feel as much of the pain of this world as Habakkuk did?

Wait

Habakkuk 2:1–4

1 I will stand at my watch
and station myself on the ramparts;
I will look to see what he will say to me,
and what answer I am to give to this
complaint.

2 Then the Lord replied:

"Write down the revelation
and make it plain on tablets
so that a herald may run with it.
3 For the revelation awaits an appointed time;
it speaks of the end
and will not prove false.
Though it linger, wait for it;
it will certainly come and will not delay.

4 "See, he is puffed up;
his desires are not upright—
but the righteous will live by his faith—"

If someone were to describe our Christian lives would they use words like trust and faith?

Personally I think instant tea is going too far, but instant coffee is good. Instant soup doesn't do it for me, but there's nothing quite like instant mash.

All this instant stuff around us today is meant to help us have more time to live life. Trouble is, it means we don't value waiting nearly as much as we should. God takes his time over things, and we can see him doing it throughout the Bible. He's doing it here to Habakkuk.

Habakkuk commits himself to waiting in verse 1. He's going nowhere. There he is at the opening of the city walls standing, waiting, holding out for God. When God finally does answer him it seems he just tells him to wait a bit longer. As a Church we are so bad at this waiting thing. We so easily just give up or get frustrated and try and do God's work for him.

What kind of God have we got? Do we treat him as if he is at our service? Are there things which we are holding out for him on, long-term things?

Get real

Habakkuk 2:6, 8–9, 12, 14–15, 18–20

Get real and go for God instead.

[6]"Will not all of them taunt him with ridicule and scorn, saying,

"'Woe to him who piles up stolen goods
and makes himself wealthy by extortion!
How long must this go on?'
[8]Because you have plundered many nations,
the peoples who are left will plunder you.
For you have shed man's blood;
you have destroyed lands and cities and everyone in them.

[9]"Woe to him who builds his realm by unjust gain
to set his nest on high,
to escape the clutches of ruin!

[12]"Woe to him who builds a city with blood shed
and establishes a town by crime!

[14]For the earth will be filled with the knowledge of the glory of the Lord,
as the waters cover the sea.

[15]"Woe to him who gives drink to his neighbours,
pouring it from the wineskin till they are drunk,
so that he can gaze on their naked bodies.

[18]"Of what value is an idol, since a man has carved it?
Or an image that teaches lies?
For he who makes it trusts in his own creation;
he makes idols that cannot speak.

[19]Woe to him who says to wood, 'Come to life!'
Or to lifeless stone, 'Wake up!'
Can it give guidance?
It is covered with gold and silver;
there is no breath in it.
[20]But the Lord is in his holy temple;
let all the earth be silent before him."

Ouch! I mean, these verses aren't going to get into your top ten favourite passages.

But read a paper or watch the news and it should strike you how relevant they are and how little this world has changed: getting loaded, powerful and influential; abuse, violence and just living for pleasure. Can you see this stuff around you?

But naming and exposing these things is important because this is God's world. And he hasn't given up on it. Habakkuk isn't saying this stuff to gloat or do a *told you so* on them. Because God is who he is, this sin must be uncovered and will one day be judged. Yes, one day verse 14 will be true. God will remake this world and it will be full of his presence, his glory. The Bible never talks about God scrapping this world. This is the place he is intent on saving. That's why the warning is stark (18–20): stop chasing after what isn't God.

Habakkuk 3:1–5

1A prayer of Habakkuk the prophet. On *shi-
gionoth.*

2Lord, I have heard of your fame;
I stand in awe of your deeds, O Lord.
Renew them in our day,
in our time make them known;
in wrath remember mercy.

3God came from Teman,
the Holy One from Mount Paran.
Selah
His glory covered the heavens
and his praise filled the earth.
4His splendour was like the sunrise;
rays flashed from his hand,
where his power was hidden.
5Plague went before him;
pestilence followed his steps.

Standing on that foundation we can pray verse 2. Go on try it.

Habakkuk is on his knees. And the first thing he does is remember. And what he remembers isn't just what God has done for him in his lifetime, it's what he has done for all people.

Sometimes we can be so self-obsessed and focused on ourselves. Habakkuk is illustrating the godly theme that when we talk about what God has done for us we start with what he has done for the whole world. So Habakkuk is talking about the Exodus – that time when God plagued the Egyptians till they let his slave people go and then parted the sea so they could get away.

We've got more than that to go on – we've got the greatest story about liberation and freedom from slavery. It happened in a 33-year-old man's life, death and resurrection just under 2000 years ago.

If you want to list what God has done for you have a crack at trying to say everything that God did for you before you soiled your first nappy and you could probably keep going for the rest of the week.

New song

Habakkuk 3:16–19

16I heard and my heart pounded,
my lips quivered at the sound;
decay crept into my bones,
and my legs trembled.
Yet I will wait patiently for the day of calamity
to come on the nation invading us.
17Though the fig-tree does not bud
and there are no grapes on the vines,
though the olive crop fails
and the fields produce no food,
though there are no sheep in the pen
and no cattle in the stalls,
18yet I will rejoice in the Lord,
I will be joyful in God my Saviour.

19The Sovereign Lord is my strength;
he makes my feet like the feet of a deer,
he enables me to go on the heights.

For the director of music. On my stringed instruments.

Perhaps after reading Habakkuk we can sing some new tunes.

What's hard for you at the moment? What's tough about being a Christian? What are you longing for the Church?

Things aren't the way they should be. In the world. In the Church. In our lives. Sometimes the fault is ours, sometimes it's other people's, sometimes it's just the way it is. We need God and we long for his presence and action.

But if you have been a Christian for longer than five days you will know hard times and barren times in your life with God and the Church. So what do you do when that happens?

Habakkuk teaches us all: we wait and we hope (16). And we hope even when there seems to be no fruit, no signs of life, no glimmers of breakthrough.

Verse 18 is stunning and I wish it described my life. Looking at the state of the world, at the Church, at my life and still praising. How? Because of who God is and the hope that brings us about what will one day be.

And if we can do that then verse 19 will be true. Of all songs in the Church's history the songs sung by slaves are the most powerful. In the middle of pain, hardship and despair they sing honest songs of hope, heaven and joy. And they go to the heights.

Revelation

Scare story or God's story?

If you're looking for a film script to sell to Hollywood, this is it. The book of Revelation – or The Apocalypse as it's dramatically called by some versions – is surely the most controversial and misunderstood book in the Bible and the one most likely to give you nightmares. Written on the island of Patmos by a prisoner named John, it's part letter, part teaching, part vision for the future. But we're not looking into a crystal ball: we're looking into the Word of God.

Chris Russell

Revelation 1:4–8

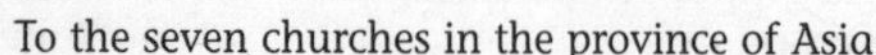

4 John,

To the seven churches in the province of Asia:

Grace and peace to you from him who is, and who was,
and who is to come, and from the seven spirits before his
throne, 5 and from Jesus Christ, who is the faithful witness,
the firstborn from the dead, and the ruler of the kings of
the earth.

Take time to recognise this Jesus.

To him who loves us and has freed us from our sins by
his blood, 6 and has made us to be a kingdom and priests to
serve his God and Father—to him be glory and power for
ever and ever! Amen.

7 Look, he is coming with the clouds,
  and every eye will see him,
even those who pierced him;
  and all the peoples of the earth will mourn because of
    him.
So shall it be! Amen.

8 "I am the Alpha and the Omega," says the Lord God,
"who is, and who was, and who is to come, the Almighty."

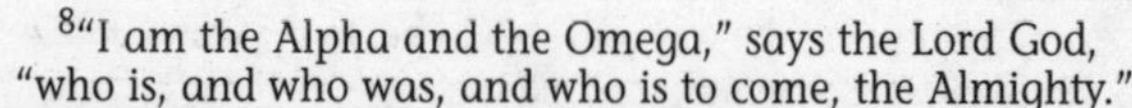

Perhaps it's just the fallout from the millennium but there are still lots of scare stories about how the world is going to end. Depending who you listen to it's either environmental tragedy (global warming, natural resources running out), scientific disaster (human cloning, genetic programming, technological wipe out, nuclear war or computers blowing us up) or a cosmic calamity (world wars in space, a collision with an asteroid). Theories abound, but Revelation isn't into theories. Neither is it about the end of the world at all. It's actually about the salvation of the world. And right at the centre of it all isn't a particular nation or disaster, not a way of thinking nor a set of factors which will spark it all off. At the centre of this world is a different, more real, more defining reality than anything we could bring on: God.

See how these verses describe him. John – who followed him around for three years, shared bread and wine with him, talked with him and woke up with him – introduces us to Jesus with no apologies or modesty. This is the one whom it all hangs on – not world events or technologies, but him: the beginning and the end. And even though John walked and talked with Jesus, when he sees him there is only one reaction: worship (see 1:17).

No fear

Revelation 1:10–18

10 On the Lord's Day I was in the Spirit, and I heard
behind me a loud voice like a trumpet, 11 which
said: "Write on a scroll what you see and send it to
the seven churches: to Ephesus, Smyrna,
Pergamum, Thyatira, Sardis, Philadelphia and
Laodicea."
12 I turned round to see the voice that was speaking to me. And when I turned I saw seven golden
lampstands, 13 and among the lampstands was
someone "like a son of man", dressed in a robe
reaching down to his feet and with a golden sash
round his chest. 14 His head and hair were white like
wool, as white as snow, and his eyes were like blazing fire. 15 His feet were like bronze glowing in a furnace, and his voice was like the sound of rushing
waters. 16 In his right hand he held seven stars, and
out of his mouth came a sharp double-edged sword.
His face was like the sun shining in all its bril-
liance.
17 When I saw him, I fell at his feet as though
dead. Then he placed his right hand on me and
said: "Do not be afraid. I am the First and the Last.
18 I am the Living One; I was dead, and behold I
am alive for ever and ever! And I hold the keys of
death and Hades."

Everything is tied up in Jesus. Pray that you'd see it. Pray for your mates who live their life away from him, that they'd see it too.

The other day I heard one speaker lament, 'When St Paul or St John used to preach they would cause a riot in the city and get thrown in prison. When I go to preach there's a tea party.' It is phenomenal just how much opposition the early Church got yet how chipper they remained.

This passage tells us how they kept on. John is in prison on the island of Patmos and he is writing with the intention of encouraging other Christians who are up against it. Encouragement. Who do you know who's having a hard time? Give them some. Verses 12–16 offer a vision of Jesus. John is on the edges of language: he is trying to describe the indescribable, the beauty of Jesus. Take time over it.

Although John falls down as dead he doesn't stay there. Look at what Jesus does to him in verse 17, putting his hand on his head and then speaking to his fears. Why does he not need to be afraid? How would this have spoken to his readers' fears? How does this speak to your fears?

Jesus is the one who has been through it, who is alive forever and who holds the keys.

The knower

Revelation 2:1–7

1"To the angel of the church in Ephesus write:

These are the words of him who holds the
seven stars in his right hand and walks among
the seven golden lampstands: 2I know your
deeds, your hard work and your perseverance. I
know that you cannot tolerate wicked men,
that you have tested those who claim to be
apostles but are not, and have found them
false. 3You have persevered and have endured
hardships for my name, and have not grown
weary.
4Yet I hold this against you: You have forsak-
en your first love. 5Remember the height from
which you have fallen! Repent and do the
things you did at first. If you do not repent, I
will come to you and remove your lampstand
from its place. 6But you have this in your
favour: You hate the practices of the
Nicolaitans, which I also hate.
7He who has an ear, let him hear what the
Spirit says to the churches. To him who overcomes, I will give the right to eat from the tree
of life, which is in the paradise of God."

So, in your heart of hearts, who do you love? What should you do next? Take a tip from verse 5.

This is the first of seven specific letters to churches in the first century. Some of it's hard to get – there seem to be lots of lampstands, stars and strange names – but there's stuff here which applies to every church that has ever churched. Now there's a start: God speaking to us as a group, as a collective. Did you ever notice how few of God's New Testament instructions are to individuals and how many are to groups? What do you think God would say to your fellowship or group if you gave him the chance?

The first thing that the Ephesians hear is that God knows (2–3). Nothing is ever hidden from him. Everyone else might be fooled but God never is. All you do – the secret things, good and bad – are seen by him. What's more, he knows what you are going through. How does that help you? Verse 4 suggests that as well as knowing what we're getting up to, God never lets us off the hook, sweeping it all under the carpet to keep the peace. The Ephesians needed to hear the truth: they'd been serving for all their worth, doing the 'religious' stuff well, but God doesn't want servants, he wants lovers. Just like a marriage partner he will settle for nothing less than passionate, all-out, fiery love.

Turn up the heat

Revelation 3:14–22

14"To the angel of the church in Laodicea write:

These are the words of the Amen, the faithful and
true witness, the ruler of God's creation. 15I know
your deeds, that you are neither cold nor hot. I wish
you were either one or the other! 16So, because you
are lukewarm—neither hot nor cold—I am about to
spit you out of my mouth. 17You say, 'I am rich; I
have acquired wealth and do not need a thing.' But
you do not realise that you are wretched, pitiful,
poor, blind and naked. 18I counsel you to buy from
me gold refined in the fire, so that you can become
rich; and white clothes to wear, so that you can cover
your shameful nakedness; and salve to put on your
eyes, so that you can see.

19Those whom I love I rebuke and discipline. So be
earnest, and repent. 20Here I am! I stand at the door
and knock. If anyone hears my voice and opens the
door, I will come in and eat with him, and he with
me.

21To him who overcomes, I will give the right to sit
with me on my throne, just as I overcame and sat
down with my Father on his throne. 22He who has
an ear, let him hear what the Spirit says to the
churches."

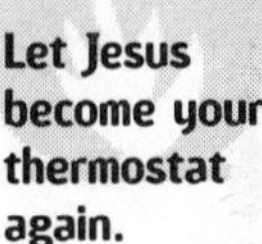

Let Jesus become your thermostat again.

Quick quiz: what's the difference between a thermometer and a thermostat? 'Cos at the beginning of this letter God acts like a thermometer which measures our temperature and at the end like a thermostat which regulates it.

The great thing about God is that he always tells us when things are wrong as soon as we will listen. If his thermometer measured your temperature, what would you be? Hot, cold, lukewarm? Lukewarm is the worst, a play-safe option. What makes us lukewarm? How do we get ourselves hotter? We can't. But that's good news rather than bad. Just as water can't heat itself we can't turn up the flames ourselves. We need help.

The trouble is that this Laodicea lot wouldn't even admit that anything was wrong. It is never a shameful thing to admit you need God, in fact much of the time it's the only possible reaction. Don't hide from God's correction (19), it's a sign of love.

So we need to come back to Jesus: he has all we need (17–18). In fact at the same time that we realise our need we'll probably hear a knocking sound. We don't need to go to him: he's already come to us. In fact, that's him knocking in verse 20. Go on then, let him in; let him show you how much you need him.

Worship

Revelation 4:1–8

1After this I looked, and there before me was a door standing open in heaven. And the voice I had first heard speaking to me like a trumpet said, "Come up here, and I will
show you what must take place after this." 2At once I was
in the Spirit, and there before me was a throne in heaven
with someone sitting on it. 3And the one who sat there had
the appearance of jasper and carnelian. A rainbow, resem-
bling an emerald, encircled the throne. 4Surrounding the
throne were twenty-four other thrones, and seated on them
were twenty-four elders. They were dressed in white and
had crowns of gold on their heads. 5From the throne came
flashes of lightning, rumblings and peals of thunder. Before
the throne, seven lamps were blazing. These are the seven
spirits of God. 6Also before the throne there was what
looked like a sea of glass, clear as crystal.
In the centre, around the throne, were four living creatures, and they were covered with eyes, in front and
behind. 7The first living creature was like a lion, the second
was like an ox, the third had a face like a man, the fourth
was like a flying eagle. 8Each of the four living creatures
had six wings and was covered with eyes all around, even
under his wings. Day and night they never stop saying:

"Holy, holy, holy
is the Lord God Almighty,
who was, and is, and is to come."

Why not take some time to join in the worship of heaven? Use some of the words and pictures from this chapter.

To paraphrase a wise old bird from the last century, 'When people stop worshipping God they don't worship nothing, they will worship anything.' Mmmm, good one, and don't we see it all around us: people worshipping pleasure, sex, fame, cash, stuff? But, not making excuses or anything, I wonder if the way we Christians have done worship hasn't actually been the best model. Because of our limitations, we've made the options for worshipping something other than God quite a bit more attractive than they actually are.

One of the stunning things about these visions is the vibrancy of the language used to describe the worship. Here are pictures of heaven – not a cloud or a cupid in sight – just delighted, consuming praise of Jesus. And if you think that sounds boring that's probably just another example of how our worship here on earth is just a pale reflection of how it's done in heaven.

Look at these songs which we overhear them singing: what does it say about the one who is worthy? What picture does it paint of the worship of heaven? Who's doing it?

One of the things the Holy Spirit does is to give us a glimpse of the worship of heaven and to help us get involved.

The Lamb who has been slain

Revelation 5:6, 12

6Then I saw a Lamb, looking as if it had
been slain, standing in the centre of the
throne, encircled by the four living creatures
and the elders. He had seven horns and
seven eyes, which are the seven spirits of
God sent out into all the earth.
12In a loud voice they sang:

"Worthy is the Lamb, who was slain,
to receive power and wealth and wisdom
and strength
and honour and glory and praise!"

it means in heaven there is one who shows the marks of suffering which tell us how much he loves us.

Sometimes, even when we're doing it with the best motives, we can be guilty of glossing over the sufferings of the world. When people have been through huge pain, often we wind up telling them how heaven is the place where they will be free from all that hurts them. And it's true – as we will see in a couple of pages – but one of the really strange pictures which Revelation gives us is of the Lamb, who looked 'as if it had been slain'.

The only human-made things in heaven are the wounds of Jesus. The risen Jesus has the wounds of the nails of the cross on his body. While his body is transformed and made new, it still has the marks of suffering that indicate our salvation.

Why might this be important? Well, it ties in with the Bible's idea of redemption. Broken things aren't thrown away and replaced with new, improved models formed from scratch. God takes the ugly, painful stuff and brings something new and transformed out of it.

This means that the suffering that people go through here is recognised by God. It means the stuff of this life is the stuff he redeems.

Multitudes

Revelation 7:9–17

9After this I looked and there before me was a great multitude that no-one could
count, from every nation, tribe, people and language, standing before the throne and
in front of the Lamb. They were wearing white robes and were holding palm branches in their hands. 10And they cried out in a loud voice:

"Salvation belongs to our God,
who sits on the throne,
and to the Lamb."

11All the angels were standing round the throne and
around the elders and the four living creatures. They fell down
on their faces before the throne and worshipped God, 12saying:

"Amen!
Praise and glory
and wisdom and thanks and honour
and power and strength
be to our God for ever and ever.
Amen!"

13Then one of the elders asked me, "These in white robes— who are they, and
where did they come from?"
14I answered, "Sir, you know."
And he said, "These are they who have come out of the great tribulation; they
have washed their robes and made them white in the blood of the Lamb. 15Therefore,

"they are before the throne of God
and serve him day and night in his temple;
and he who sits on the throne will spread his tent over them.
16Never again will they hunger;
never again will they thirst.
The sun will not beat upon them,
nor any scorching heat.
17For the Lamb at the centre of the throne will be their shepherd;
he will lead them to springs of living water.
And God will wipe away every tear from their eyes."

Is your God big enough to save the whole world? Let it excite you and get you praying.

Think of a number between 1000 and 9999. Double it. Double it again. And again. And again and again and again. Nope, still not big enough.

List as many nations in the world as you can. Let's be kind and assume you missed at least 100. Still not enough.

Our new kettle arrived with the instructions printed in eighteen different languages. In some African countries over 120 different languages are spoken. That's lots of instructions, but it still wouldn't be enough. The numbers we're talking about here are so big that they're way longer than telephone numbers, even international ones.

This vision of heaven is packed full of people, more people than you could ever count. All of them are different: different backgrounds, experiences and pains. But they are all united in Jesus.

This stuff blows me away. Why are so many of our pictures and images of heaven so boring and lacking in life? Revelation offers us huge images, and what's sure is that God is intent on saving many, many, many, many people. Can you get your head round this? Are you expecting to see so many in heaven?

Prayer

Revelation 8:1–5

1When he opened the seventh seal, there
was silence in heaven for about half an
hour.
2And I saw the seven angels who stand
before God, and to them were given seven
trumpets.
3Another angel, who had a golden censer,
came and stood at the altar. He was given
much incense to offer, with the prayers of
all the saints, on the golden altar before the
throne. 4The smoke of the incense, together
with the prayers of the saints, went up
before God from the angel's hand. 5Then
the angel took the censer, filled it with fire
from the altar, and hurled it on the earth;
and there came peals of thunder, rumblings, flashes of lightning and an earthquake.

So think, then pray.

I used to work for this guy who had an incredible gift. You would be chatting to him and he made it look as if he wasn't paying the slightest bit of attention to what you were saying. And he wasn't.

There is nothing more frustrating than talking to someone who you don't think is listening. And that's what's hard about praying, because we trust God is listening but it's not like we can ask him to repeat back to us what we've just said to check, is it?

But here come these fantastic five verses. Read them through.

The prayers of the saints are represented in terms of incense. Why? 'Cos it goes up. It might feel like your prayers are stopping at the ceiling but these verses tell us they get all the way to heaven. And that's where verse 1 comes in. I love that 'about': it's as if John just lost count of the minutes. This silence is tied in with the prayers: as we pray all heaven listens in silence. Heaven takes us so seriously that they listen in quietness to what we say and ask. Makes you think about what you pray.

Revelation 21:1–6

[1]Then I saw a new heaven and a new earth, for the
first heaven and the first earth had passed away,
and there was no longer any sea. [2]I saw the Holy
City, the new Jerusalem, coming down out of heav-
en from God, prepared as a bride beautifully dressed
for her husband. [3]And I heard a loud voice from the
throne saying, "Now the dwelling of God is with
men, and he will live with them. They will be his
people, and God himself will be with them and be
their God. [4]He will wipe every tear from their eyes.
There will be no more death or mourning or crying
or pain, for the old order of things has passed
away."

[5]He who was seated on the throne said, "I am
making everything new!" Then he said, "Write this
down, for these words are trustworthy and true."

[6]He said to me: "It is done. I am the Alpha and
the Omega, the Beginning and the End. To him who
is thirsty I will give to drink without cost from the
spring of the water of life."

What a hope: free, certain, real, full of life, healing and joy. Imagine it. Dream it. Stake your life on it. How does this make a difference to how you live?

I reckon this passage does for our thinking about the future what Christopher Columbus did for world travel. You know, before CC set off most people thought the world was flat – then, when he didn't drop off the end of the horizon but came back with goodies he'd nicked from the Caribbean, everything had to change. After this chapter everything has got to change. We have to look again at what we think is going to happen in God's future.

You see, there's all this talk of going to heaven when you die. But, frankly, that isn't really right. You see heaven is only the place the saved wait in – a departure lounge if you like, with lots to do and better views than most. But the place we are intended for is mentioned in verse 1: the new heaven and new earth. This earth. Not chucked away, got rid of, blown up or dumped. He remakes it, he redeems it, he transforms it into the place of his glory. The terrorists try to blow the world to pieces, but it's God who puts it back together. This means our action on this planet is never in vain.

And it's not only the planet that he puts back together: we get a remix too as he makes us ourselves new (3–6). What a vision.

Arrival

Revelation 22:16–21

16"I, Jesus, have sent my angel to give you this
testimony for the churches. I am the Root and
the Offspring of David, and the bright Morning
Star."

17The Spirit and the bride say, "Come!" And let
him who hears say, "Come!" Whoever is thirsty,
let him come; and whoever wishes, let him take
the free gift of the water of life.

18I warn everyone who hears the words of the
prophecy of this book: If anyone adds anything
to them, God will add to him the plagues
described in this book. 19And if anyone takes
words away from this book of prophecy, God will
take away from him his share in the tree of life
and in the holy city, which are described in this
book.

20He who testifies to these things says, "Yes, I
am coming soon."

Amen. Come, Lord Jesus.

21The grace of the Lord Jesus be with God's
people. Amen.

They couldn't wait. After reading Revelation I can't wait either. It's time to pray.

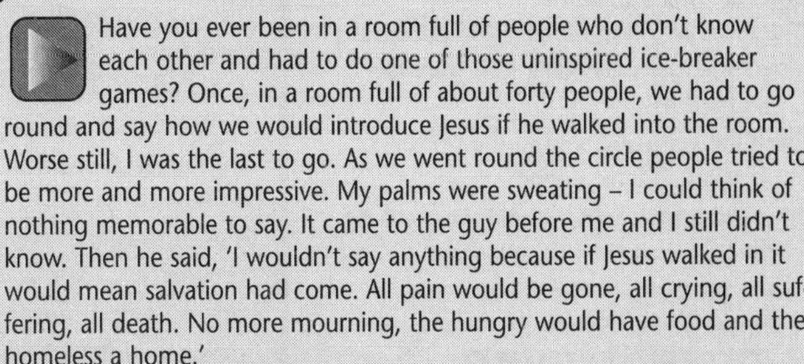

Have you ever been in a room full of people who don't know each other and had to do one of those uninspired ice-breaker games? Once, in a room full of about forty people, we had to go round and say how we would introduce Jesus if he walked into the room. Worse still, I was the last to go. As we went round the circle people tried to be more and more impressive. My palms were sweating – I could think of nothing memorable to say. It came to the guy before me and I still didn't know. Then he said, 'I wouldn't say anything because if Jesus walked in it would mean salvation had come. All pain would be gone, all crying, all suffering, all death. No more mourning, the hungry would have food and the homeless a home.'

That was it. We all stopped and imagined. For a split second we tasted it. Then someone started to sing. The vision of Revelation is that Jesus will come and when he does all will be well. Well like it has never been before, and well like it will always be after. And so in these last verses you have one prayer repeated three times: 'Come, come, come, Lord Jesus.' It was a prayer they prayed regularly in the first years of the Church.

Here is the question at the heart of Christianity. You see, Jesus' death on the cross put a marker in history, and it remains to this day the most significant point in the human story. Thanks to his sacrifice, we now have salvation. But why did it have to be that way? Join this little wander through the Bible's backstreets, at the end of which hopefully things will become clear.

Sin and separation

genesis 3:8–13

8Then the man and his wife heard the sound of
the Lord God as he was walking in the garden
in the cool of the day, and they hid from the
Lord God among the trees of the garden. 9But
the Lord God called to the man, "Where are
you?"
10He answered, "I heard you in the garden,
and I was afraid because I was naked; so I hid."
11And he said, "Who told you that you were
naked? Have you eaten from the tree from
which I commanded you not to eat?"
12The man said, "The woman you put here
with me—she gave me some fruit from the
tree, and I ate it."
13Then the Lord God said to the woman,
"What is this you have done?"
The woman said, "The serpent deceived me,
and I ate."

chew it over

What is sin? What does it do to you and your relationship with God? What do you think God would be like if he said sin and evil just didn't matter?

Here we find the first – but not the last – of the Bible's depictions of sin. Eve eats an apple. Big deal. But God told her not to. Fair enough. But there's something else, something that the serpent does, something that he achieves that will help us on our way.

It needn't have been an apple – the fruit itself is symbolic – and I think we can assume that the serpent wasn't merely interested in passing on a tip to his fellow garden-dwellers to help them have a more pleasant stay. No, the serpent wanted to bring a separation between human beings and God. And it worked, nearly. You get that bit about God strolling about the garden, quite likely that he'd bump into Adam and Eve? That all stopped after this incident, as the two young pups were no longer allowed to be within strolling distance. You see, God cannot have sin around. It's not that he doesn't like it, not that it makes him itchy and uncomfortable. He *cannot* have it around, and sin cannot be around him.

Passover

exodus 12:3, 5–8, 10–13

3“Tell the whole community of Israel that on the
tenth day of this month each man is to take a lamb
for his family, one for each household.
5The animals you choose must be year-old males
without defect, and you may take them from the
sheep or the goats. 6Take care of them until the
fourteenth day of the month, when all the people of
the community of Israel must slaughter them at twilight. 7Then they are to take some of the blood and
put it on the sides and tops of the door-frames of
the houses where they eat the lambs. 8That same
night they are to eat the meat roasted over the fire,
along with bitter herbs, and bread made without
yeast.
10“Do not leave any of it till morning; if some is
left till morning, you must burn it. 11This is how you
are to eat it: with your cloak tucked into your belt,
your sandals on your feet and your staff in your
hand. Eat it in haste; it is the Lord's Passover.
12“On that same night I will pass through Egypt
and strike down every firstborn—both men and animals—and I will bring judgment on all the gods of
Egypt. I am the Lord. 13The blood will be a sign for
you on the houses where you are; and when I see
the blood, I will pass over you. No destructive
plague will touch you when I strike Egypt.”

This passage comes on the eve of the Israelites' miraculous escape from the hands of the Egyptians – you know, the one with Moses, the parting of the Red Sea and all that. So here we are as God prepares to send his judgment down on the people who have enslaved and oppressed his own. To say that it's scary stuff is a bit of an understatement: this is a matter of life and death and if the instructions are not carried out to the letter then death will come to the first-born of the house.

These instructions are full of meaning, like the fact that the lamb or kid was to be a year-old male – much more expensive than a female – which was perfect. The blood loss that caused its death was to be a token of the sacrifice, one that God would recognise. The way that it was to be completely consumed showed that the whole animal was to be considered part of the sacrifice.

So what do we have? God's judgment was due on a whole bunch of people who had done wrong. For others – for his own people – these instructions were the way to avoid that judgment. Only something that was costly could pay the price, and what's more, only someone who obeyed his instructions would know how to prepare themselves. Oh, and one last thing, God told them to remember this Passover every year from then on. That's how significant it was.

chew it over

The pattern formed here, with God saving his people from his judgment.

Paying the price

leviticus 4:27–35

27"'If a member of the community sins unintentional-
ly and does what is forbidden in any of the Lord's
commands, he is guilty. 28When he is made aware of
the sin he committed, he must bring as his offering
for the sin he committed a female goat without
defect. 29He is to lay his hand on the head of the
sin offering and slaughter it at the place of the burnt
offering. 30Then the priest is to take some of the
blood with his finger and put it on the horns of the
altar of burnt offering and pour out the rest of the
blood at the base of the altar. 31He shall remove all
the fat, just as the fat is removed from the fellowship offering, and the priest shall burn it on the
altar as an aroma pleasing to the Lord. In this way
the priest will make atonement for him, and he will
be forgiven.
32"'If he brings a lamb as his sin offering, he is to
bring a female without defect. 33He is to lay his
hand on its head and slaughter it for a sin offering
at the place where the burnt offering is slaughtered.
34Then the priest shall take some of the blood of the
sin offering with his finger and put it on the horns
of the altar of burnt offering and pour out the rest
of the blood at the base of the altar. 35He shall
remove all the fat, just as the fat is removed from
the lamb of the fellowship offering, and the priest
shall burn it on the altar on top of the offerings
made to the Lord by fire. In this way the priest will
make atonement for him for the sin he has committed, and he will be forgiven.'"

Here's Moses establishing a few ground rules to help everyone get along. This is not some divinely-inspired ego trip, nor is it Moses coming out as a pure control freak. This is God's way of caring for his people. He has given them guidelines about how to behave well, but now he details how they should act when their behaviour is less than ideal.

Sin – whether intentional or not – needs to be paid for. Back in those days the currency was sacrificial offerings, and there were a whole load of them to choose from. The burnt, grain and fellowship offerings were optional, but the sin and guilt offerings had to be done and there was simply no getting away from it. But why? God was after the hearts of his people, and this complex set of rituals was designed with one purpose in mind: to remind them of all that he had done for them.

chew it over

In making sacrifices expensive he was yet again sending a clear message: sin does not go without consequences and it demands payment.

Jesus takes our place

Isaiah 53:1–9

1 Who has believed our message
and to whom has the arm of the Lord been revealed?
2 He grew up before him like a tender shoot,
and like a root out of dry ground.
He had no beauty or majesty to attract us to him,
nothing in his appearance that we should desire him.
3 He was despised and rejected by men,
a man of sorrows, and familiar with suffering.
Like one from whom men hide their faces
he was despised, and we esteemed him not.

4 Surely he took up our infirmities
and carried our sorrows,
yet we considered him stricken by God,
smitten by him, and afflicted.
5 But he was pierced for our transgressions,
he was crushed for our iniquities;
the punishment that brought us peace was upon him,
and by his wounds we are healed.
6 We all, like sheep, have gone astray,
each of us has turned to his own way;
and the Lord has laid on him
the iniquity of us all.

7 He was oppressed and afflicted,
yet he did not open his mouth;
he was led like a lamb to the slaughter,
and as a sheep before her shearers is silent,
so he did not open his mouth.
8 By oppression and judgment he was taken away.
And who can speak of his descendants?
For he was cut off from the land of the living;
for the transgression of my people he was stricken.
9 He was assigned a grave with the wicked,
and with the rich in his death,
though he had done no violence,
nor was any deceit in his mouth.

This whole chapter is a key player in the Bible. Bits get quoted in the New Testament in John, Matthew and Romans, to name but three, and it presents us with the clearest explanation of sin and atonement. But before we jump too far too soon, let's talk basics. Isaiah's poem is at the heart of his book and it points to the life of Jesus and to the salvation of his people. It was intended to be relevant to Isaiah's contemporaries, yet the truths echo across the centuries.

So what's the deal with this Messiah? First, it's clear that he comes not because he's bored or lonely, but because we need him: he comes for 'our infirmities . . . our sorrows'. It's foolish for us to think that he deserved what happened: he wasn't 'stricken by God'. The truth is harder for us to bear, but we must take it in: 'he was crushed for our iniquities'. It was our sin, our wrongdoing, our wanderings away from God's laws that he paid for. We accumulated the bill and he was the one that paid. What's more, that payment bought something very special: peace, healing, salvation.

But there's more to say, and Isaiah puts it brilliantly. We're all guilty, we all 'like sheep have gone astray', and we all are in debt to God. This whole chapter has so much to say. Read it through slowly.

chew it over

It's impossible to deny the links between our sin and Jesus' suffering, between his sacrifice and our salvation.

No longer God's enemies

romans 5:6–11

6You see, at just the right time, when we
were still powerless, Christ died for the
ungodly. 7Very rarely will anyone die for a
righteous man, though for a good man
someone might possibly dare to die. 8But
God demonstrates his own love for us in
this: While we were still sinners, Christ died
for us.
9Since we have now been justified by his
blood, how much more shall we be saved
from God's wrath through him! 10For if,
when we were God's enemies, we were
reconciled to him through the death of his
Son, how much more, having been reconciled, shall we be saved through his life!
11Not only is this so, but we also rejoice in
God through our Lord Jesus Christ, through
whom we have now received reconciliation.

Can you see the links and parallels between this passage and Isaiah 53? It's all there; we are all sinners, Jesus died for us, his blood paid the price, bringing us back out of exile and home to God.

It is through not only Jesus' death (6–8) but his resurrection (9–11) that we can now stand before God, secure that the debt has been paid, that the guilt and sin have been dealt with.

But what's all this stuff about us being God's enemies? Surely that can't be right? Well, it is. Unbelief is hostility, choosing to reject God places us opposite him. But Jesus' actions were so loving, his arms so strong to hold around his wayward children that he made the first move. While we were against him, his death put things right. Remember all that stuff in Leviticus about the ways to pay for sin, about how sin demanded some form of exchange in order to be wiped out? Verse 11 here makes it clear: Jesus has bought us back, has made the ultimate exchange and prepared the way for us to approach God.

chew it over

Jesus' death was enough to sort out our relationship with God.

Part of the plan

matthew 26:47–50

47While he was still speaking, Judas, one of
the Twelve, arrived. With him was a large
crowd armed with swords and clubs, sent
from the chief priests and the elders of the
people. 48Now the betrayer had arranged a
signal with them: "The one I kiss is the man;
arrest him." 49Going at once to Jesus, Judas
said, "Greetings, Rabbi!" and kissed him.
50Jesus replied, "Friend, do what you
came for."

Then the men stepped forward, seized Jesus and arrested him.

But all this talk about Jesus' death being a symbolic act might threaten to take us away from an important fact. Yes, Jesus died to give us life, he died to pay the price, but there were other reasons too. Jesus was betrayed by his friend Judas. He had enemies in high places. He was a victim of complex politics. He was let down by the crowd. Why did Jesus die? Because he was a man, and this world stained by sin has a habit of throwing bad things at us. Jesus died because, well, tragedy happens.

But does this mean it was all a mistake? Was Jesus unlucky? Could he just as easily have eased out the rest of his days sipping wine by the sea? Of course not: Jesus was always going to die. It was part of God's plan, part of the route towards our salvation. In choosing to come to earth, Jesus chose the ending on the cross. And that is where the power comes: as a willing, living, perfect sacrifice Jesus' death was worth more than all the year-old lambs that would ever exist.

chew it over

Why did Jesus have to die? We may have worked out a little of the mathematics, but perhaps until we see God, until we sense the full power of his love and holiness, we may never really understand.

Contributors

Chris Russell: Preacher, writer and golfer, Chris is now vicar of St Lawrence's, Reading, where he and Mrs Russell are setting up something special . . .

J. Foster: Student at London Bible College and ardent Watford FC supporter. Such faith.

Pete Greig: Based in Chichester where he works for Revelation and heads up the 24/7 project.

Emma Borlase: Counsellor, member of Soul Survivor and superb wife.

Colin Brookes: Freshly moved to Cambridge where he's training to become a vicar.

Greg Valerio: Heads up CRED, an organisation that aims to increase awareness and understanding on issues such as homelessness, global poverty and consumer action.

Matt Redman: Worship leader, lives in Watford where he helps run the Soul Survivor Watford church.

Mike Pilavachi: Heads up the Soul Survivor ministries and threatens to move to South Africa if the weather doesn't improve.

Matt Bird: Director of Joshua Generation, author, speaker and management consultant.

Matt Stuart: Trainee director of Joshua Generation which works to equip young people to fulfil all their future potential.

Neil Pearce: Neil works for Soul Survivor and studied at London Bible College.